NINE DIVISIONS IN CHAMPAGNE

The British and Americans in the Second Battle of the Marne

An account of the nine British and nine American divisions which fought under French command in the BATTLE OF THE AISNE and in the SECOND BATTLE OF THE MARNE 1918

Patrick Takle

Pen & Sword
MILITARY

First published in Great Britain in 2015 by
Pen & Sword Military
An imprint of
Pen & Sword Books Ltd
47 Church Street
Barnsley
South Yorkshire
S70 2AS

Copyright © Patrick Takle

ISBN 978 1 47383 422 4

The right of Patrick Takle to be identified as Author of this work has been asserted by him in accordance with the Copyright, Designs and Patents Act 1988.

A CIP catalogue record for this book is
available from the British Library

All rights reserved. No part of this book may be reproduced or transmitted in any form or by any means, electronic or mechanical including photocopying, recording or by any information storage and retrieval system, without permission from the Publisher in writing.

Typeset in Palatino by
Replika Press Pvt Ltd, India
Printed and bound in England
By CPI Group (UK) Ltd, Croydon, CR0 4YY

Pen & Sword Books Ltd incorporates the Imprints of Pen & Sword Aviation, Pen & Sword Family History, Pen & Sword Maritime, Pen & Sword Military, Pen & Sword Discovery, Pen & Sword Politics, Pen & Sword Atlas, Pen & Sword Archaeology, Wharncliffe Local History, Wharncliffe True Crime, Wharncliffe Transport, Pen & Sword Select, Pen & Sword Military Classics, Leo Cooper, The Praetorian Press, Claymore Press, Remember When, Seaforth Publishing and Frontline Publishing

For a complete list of Pen & Sword titles please contact
PEN & SWORD BOOKS LIMITED
47 Church Street, Barnsley, South Yorkshire, S70 2AS, England
E-mail: enquiries@pen-and-sword.co.uk
Website: www.pen-and-sword.co.uk

Dedication

Before Action

By all the glories of the day
And the cool evening's benison,
By that last sunset touch that lay
Upon the hills when day was done,
By beauty lavishly outpoured
And blessings carelessly received,
By all the days that I have lived
Make me a soldier, O Lord.

By all of man's hopes and fears,
And all the wonders poets sing,
The laughter of unclouded years,
And every sad and lovely thing:
By the romantic ages stored
With high endeavour that was his,
By all his mad catastrophes
Make me a man, O Lord.

I, that on my familiar hill
Saw with uncomprehending eyes
A hundred of Thy sunsets spill
Their fresh and sanguine sacrifice,
Ere the sun swings his noonday sword
Must say goodbye to all of this:
By all delights that I shall miss,
Help me to die, O Lord.

Lieutenant W. N. Hodgson MC.

Noel Hodgson published this poem just two days before he was killed on 1 July 1916, as were some 20,000 other British soldiers in the first day of the Battle of the Somme. Lieutenant Hodgson, aged just 23, was the Bombing Officer of the 9th Battalion Devonshire Regiment.

His body was buried together with some 160 other men of the Devonshire Regiment in the trenches they had occupied before the attack. An inscription was carved on the cross which marked their battle graves: 'The Devonshires held this trench, the Devonshires hold it still.'

Their undisturbed graves are now included within Devonshire Cemetery near Mansell Copse, Mametz, close to Albert, France.

Contents

Acknowledgements	ix
Maps	xi
Preface	xvii
Chronology of Main Events in the final year of the War	xxii
Introduction	1
The German Spring Offensives of 1918	8
The formation of IX Corps and the training of Generals	35
The destruction of IX Corps on the Chemin des Dames	54
The Foch Offensive and the arrival of the Americans	83
XXII Corps with 51st and 62nd Divisions joins French Fifth Army in the Ardre Valley	125
The 51st (Highland) and 62nd (West Riding) Divisions fight their way up the Ardre Valley	150
The 15th (Scottish) Division joins XX Corps in Tenth Army	202
The New 34th Division joins XXX Corps in Tenth Army	222
The British contribution to Victory in the Champagne and its impact on eventual Allied Victory	241
Tributes to the British Units which fought in the Champagne Battles of 1918	265
Address by General Mangin to the American Army	272
British Units which fought in the Champagne Battles	273
Total Casualties of the Nine British Divisions in the Champagne Campaigns	282

American Cemeteries and Memorials in the Champagne 284

British Cemeteries and Memorials in the Champagne 286

The Italian Military Cemetery at Chaumuzy 290

French Memorials to the Second Battle of the Marne 291

Bibliography 295

Acknowledgements

Remarkably little attention has been given, over the years, to the two notable British campaigns in the Champagne Region under French Command. I am grateful principally to Dr. Anthony Clayton, formerly lecturer at the Royal Military Academy Sandhurst, who brought this deficit to my attention and furthermore provided constant support and advice during the writing of this book. My thanks are also due to:

Mr. Andrew Orgill, librarian of the Royal Military Academy Sandhurst Library, for his constant interest and help as well as access to the many rare regimental and divisional histories in this magnificent library.

The Library and staff of the Imperial War Museum at South Lambert, London, for access, once again, to its outstanding collection of German Regimental Histories.

The Museum of the Devon and Dorset Regiments at the Keep, Dorchester for permission to use the photograph of the Devon's Camp Flag and its Croix de Guerre.

Bill MacKay of Berkley California for permission to quote from the diaries of his grandfather Robert Lindsay Mackay (1896-1981), OBE, MC, MB, CHB, MD, DPH.

The George C. Marshall Foundation on the campus of the Virginian Military Institute at Lexington, Virginia; for the opportunity to visit this magnificent facility and memorial to the life of General Marshall. Thanks are due particularly to Paul B. Barron the Director of Library and Archives and Jeffrey Kozak the Assistant Librarian and Archivist, who were both unfailingly helpful in providing direction and assistance.

Mr Geoffrey Arnio, Superintendent of the American Military Cemetery at Fère-en-Tardenois, for his kind help in understanding the impact of the American troops on the Second Battle of the Marne.

I am also particularly indebted to Richard Doherty for his careful reading of my script and many knowledgeable suggestions and to the support of the whole production team at Pen & Sword and the encouragement of their redoubtable editor Brigadier Henry Wilson.

Maps

xii *Nine Divisions in Champagne*

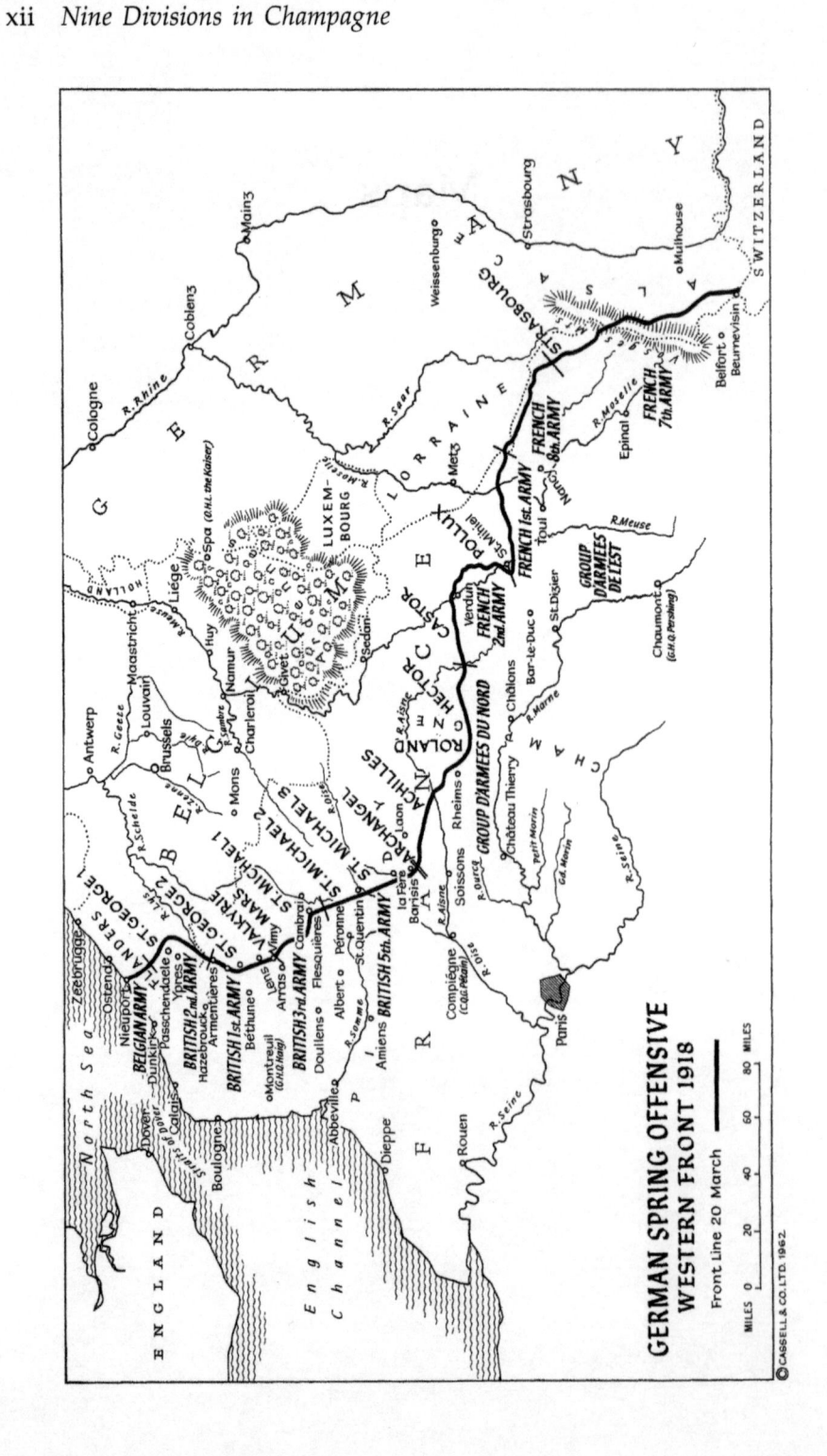

Maps xiii

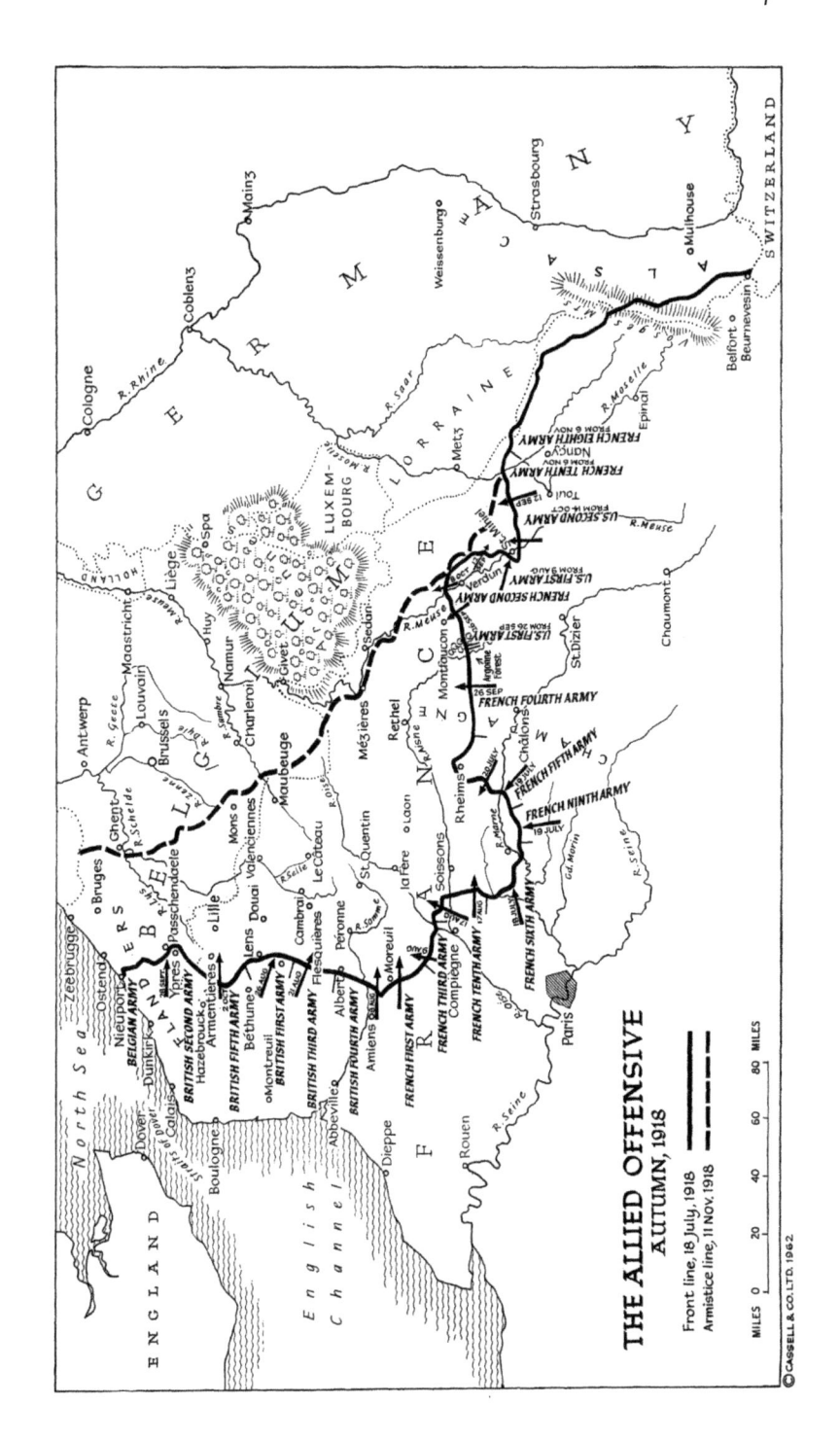

xiv *Nine Divisions in Champagne*

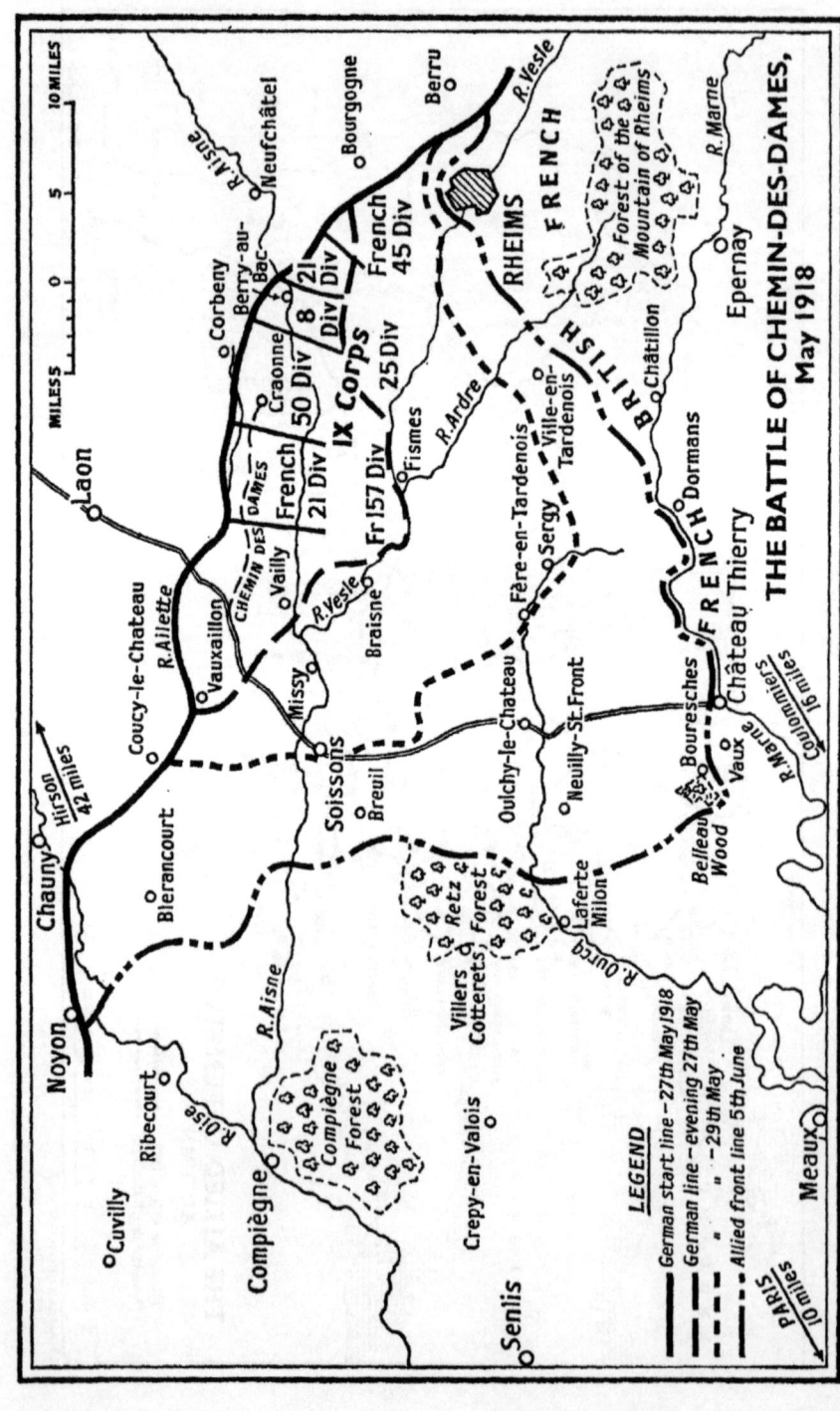

THE BATTLE OF CHEMIN-DES-DAMES, May 1918

Maps xv

xvi *Nine Divisions in Champagne*

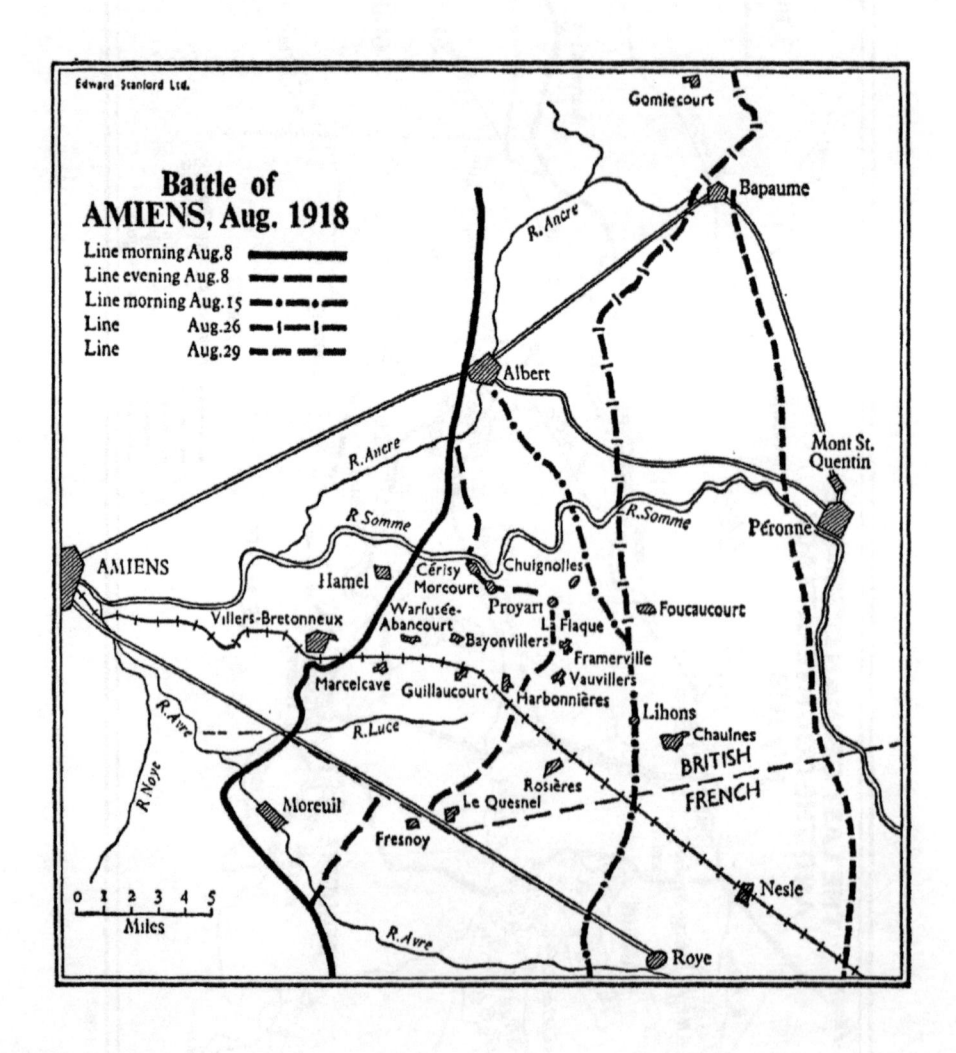

Preface

In a previous book I wrote about the limited but significant engagement at the tiny village of Néry, near Compiègne, on 1 September 1914. This short engagement occurred during the opening days of the First World War, when the steadfast defence by a small group of British cavalrymen and gunners stopped and dispersed the German 4th Cavalry Division, as it was undertaking a bold foray to threaten Paris. The plucky British defence had a significant impact on the route taken by the huge German First Army, and made possible a surprise attack by the French Sixth Army on the flank of General von Kluck's First Army, thereby beginning the rolling-back of the German advance, in what became known as the First Battle of the Marne. At that time the Expeditionary Force (which was soon renamed the British Expeditionary Force (BEF)) of just five divisions, was retreating through the area near Compiègne and Soissons. Later, in October, after a short period attacking the Germans unsuccessfully in their entrenched positions on the Chemin des Dames feature, the BEF redeployed north to the soggy fields of Picardy and Flanders. There it slogged it out with the Germans over four desperate long years of attack, defence and counter-attack. During these desperate battles it sustained two and half million casualties, of whom 565,000 British and Empire soldiers were killed (another 392,000 British servicemen died at sea or in other theatres), until it finally defeated the Germans and drove them out of France.

During those four bitterly-fought years the British Army remained sandwiched between the remnants of the Belgian Army holding the flooded coastal stretch, and the armies of France, whose lines extended all the way to the Swiss border. Occupying trenches in the wet mud of Flanders and Picardy, it stuck grimly to its formidable task of expanding its forces and learning how to deal with the consummate soldiers who made up the German Army, as well as sending troops to fight in many other theatres. Large British contingents were sent to the Italian Front, Gallipoli, Thessalonica, and particularly to Egypt and Palestine. However, it is less well-known that in May and July of 1918, two British corps, comprising some nine divisions, found themselves fighting in the Champagne region alongside French and Allied units. While it was never part of any deliberate Allied plan to use British troops in this way, their presence nevertheless resulted in the British making a significant contribution, at a critical time, to the French Army's struggle with the Germans in the verdant rolling hills and valleys of the Champagne region.

In early May 1918, as the result of personal agreements between Haig and Foch, IX Corps had been sent to rest and recover in a quiet part of the French front. However, in the ensuing surprise German attack (BLÜCHER), its five divisions suffered devastating losses. Battalions, brigades and even divisions ceased to exist, as formations wilted under the overwhelming weight of enemy firepower and numbers. Even the divisional artillery batteries were swamped and lost most of their guns. Total casualties amounted to almost 29,000 men (including seven brigadier generals). After two days of bombardment and retreat, only composite units were left to continue fighting to hold back the grey avalanche of enemy troops. Nevertheless, despite suffering the chaos of retreat, these composite units managed to continue to resist gamely and eventually were able to establish a joint defence line with French divisions, on the Montagne de Bligny, just south-west of Reims. Although initially driven off that hill, a last courageous assault on the Montagne by the tattered remnants of three British battalions carried the hill. Against all odds this successful assault brought a final halt to the German advance, and thereby entered into the annals of British military history.

Barely a month later, Haig again agreed reluctantly to send XXII Corps to the same Champagne region to aid the French defence against anticipated ferocious German offensives around Reims. However, Reims was not taken and at the last moment its orders were changed, and it was sent to bolster the French Fifth and Tenth Armies, who were counter-attacking the German attempt to seal off the Reims basin. The four divisions of XXII Corps hurried forward to be thrown into the raging Second Battle of the Marne without time for reconnaissance, or even for registering their artillery. As a result each of its divisions paid a heavy price in blood for their courageous advances against German artillery and machine-gun nests, particularly on their first day of combat. Initially the four divisions sustained very heavy casualties, as the infantry adapted to advancing in the close wooded country, but eventually learned how to defeat the German machine guns using firepower and stealth.

Eventually the two divisions, which had fought their way up the Ardre Valley, found themselves positioned below the Montagne de Bligny, which once again needed to be assaulted by gallant understrength battalions. On the other side of the German salient, south-west of Soissons, two other British divisions found themselves serving separately under direct French command as the second wave of a major counter-attack to recover the Aisne Salient. They relieved the first wave of French and American troops, and then successfully battled alongside their Allies to push the German invaders out of their strongpoints and back over the ground the Germans had so recently occupied. The four British divisions eventually triumphed, but suffered over 13,000 casualties as they added gloriously to their reputation for courage and tenacity in adversity.

The French general, Henri Berthelot, who commanded Fifth Army, was able to witness and appreciate the efforts of the British soldiers, and the contribution they had made to bolster the French attacks at a critical moment. He not only initiated the award of the Croix de Guerre to some of the battalions, but took the trouble to come to England after the war to present the award to the survivors in moving ceremonies. Sadly unbeknownst to most British people, these four British divisions had fought courageously under French command, thereby helping to ensure Allied victory in the Second Battle of the Marne. This great multi-national battle demonstrated the renewed determination of the Allies to defeat their enemies, and was the clear turning point of the war in 1918. It made possible the ensuing sequence of ever more vigorous attacks by the renascent Allies, leading to the rapid defeat of the German Army.

1918 had started so badly for the Allies, as their weaknesses were exposed by the series of surprise German attacks, which began in March. These attacks were so well planned and so heavy that they came close to causing overwhelming routs, right up until 17 July. Then, literally overnight, the course of history was changed. Early the following morning Foch was able to launch the first of a series of widely spread counter-attacks, which overwhelmed the German ability to resist and it was their turn to suffer a swift succession of battlefield defeats.

The counter-attack by four French Armies, launched on 18 July, was pressed forward in two waves. The first surprise attack was spearheaded by two hefty American divisions and totally shocked and defeated the German defenders. The second wave was more deliberate and used scarce, but quickly gathered American, French and British reserves. By 2 August, the ancient city of Soissons was liberated, and the Germans were pressed back to the Vesle river. The course of history was changed irrevocably as the previously triumphant German troops were forced to retreat and eventually evacuate the entire Marne salient.

Throughout the spring of 1918 the Germans had looked invincible. Only in retrospect was it possible to recognize the increasing weakness of the German situation. Each month from March to July, Ludendorff had launched five devastating attacks against the Allies. However, due to the need to assemble heavy support artillery and crack reserves to ensure success in each new attack area, Ludendorff had been limited to consecutive attacks. Foch, on the other hand, once having secured the strategic initiative on 18 July, was able to deploy his separate Allied armies to attack the Germans virtually simultaneously at different points all along their front. These co-ordinated and well-prepared attacks by the Allies rarely achieved a dramatic break-through but they overcame the German forward defences and defeated their counter-attacks. This kept the Germans off balance and gradually forced them to withdraw to their prepared defence lines. These fortified lines were considered impregnable by the Germans, who hoped that they would allow them a respite to rebuild their strength. However, the Allies kept up the pressure, and by September they began dramatically breaking through the deep well-prepared defences of the Hindenburg Line, leaving the Germans with little alternative but to retreat, and then to request an armistice.

Although this history focuses on the detailed battles of the four British divisions of XXII Corps it would be unfair to ignore the courage and commitment of the French Army, which provided the bulk of the troops, or more particularly the effect of the entry into the battle of the fresh divisions of the United States Army. The Second Battle of the Marne was the first major battle involving large contingents of Americans which, by a coincidence of history, included nine of their huge fresh divisions, and this account also covers part of their story and highlights the decisive contribution they made to this epic battle.

The Second Battle of the Marne resulted in an astounding and dramatic victory for the Allies. On 17 July the Germans had paused in their abortive attempts to encircle Reims, but remained confident of resuming the offensive as their earlier attacks had seemed to demonstrate so clearly the war-winning strength and ability of the German Army. They had no inkling of the Allied forces secretly gathered around their salient, and they were profoundly shocked to be attacked so fiercely the next morning. Thus the combined attacks by four French Armies on 18 July not only brought an end to the run of German successes, it also marked the passing of the strategic initiative to the Allies. Under the visionary leadership of General Foch, the French, American, British and Italian divisions in those armies showed just how quickly they could retake the territory occupied by the Germans, and inflict defeat on a German Army that, until then, had believed itself on the cusp of final victory.

Victory did not come because of an infusion of unlimited numbers of men. The Allied formations rarely had a surplus of manpower as they advanced against a frightful network of German machine guns, manned by a stubborn and determined enemy. However, they showed that even these terrible obstacles could be overcome by brave, well-motivated troops, properly supported by artillery, tanks and aircraft. The Allied infantry demonstrated repeatedly not only their ability to outflank and destroy myriads of interlocking machine guns when conditions were favourable, but also their ability to attack without support, against great odds, to achieve their objectives.

Today it is hard to imagine that some 100,000 British soldiers could take part in two ten-day battles, in a foreign land in which they distinguished themselves and thereby suffered 43,000 casualties (of whom 6,000 were left dead), with very few reports reaching their families at home. Sadly, while their sacrifice helped to change the course of the war, very few in Britain knew anything of their exploits.

Fittingly, while this account focuses on the role of British soldiers within this great turning-point battle, it also seeks to explain just how this signal victory came as a result of united Allied action and, particularly, the entry into battle of large numbers of fresh untried American troops. At the same time it pays tribute to all the soldiers of the Allied nations who sacrificed themselves in the effort to defend freedom and vanquish the invading German Army. The Second Battle of the Marne stands out as the first of the series of Allied victories, which, following four years of inconclusive bloody struggle, undermined the German Army's ability to defend its conquests, and within little more than three months, finally brought peace.

Chronology of Main Events in the final year of the War

11 November 1917. Fateful meeting of the German High Command (OHL) at Mons, in occupied Belgium. How could the Germans exploit their victory over the Russians to achieve a decision in the West? Ludendorff obtains support for his prime intention to destroy the British Army in Flanders using troops switched from the Eastern Front.

21 March–5 April 1918. **Operation MICHAEL**. First, heaviest, and most successful German surprise attack against the British in the thinly-held Somme area. Three German Armies, with seventy-two divisions available, drive the British back some twenty-five miles on a fifty-mile front. 72,000 British prisoners are captured, out of a total Allied loss of 255,000 but the Germans suffer some 239,000 casualties, and fail to capture the key towns of Arras and Amiens.

9 April–29 April 1918. **Operation GEORGETTE**. Second smaller attack by just two German armies in the Lys valley area aims to capture strategically important features and weaken the British, prior to a third attack against the Channel ports. It includes an unsuccessful diversionary attack using tanks on Villers-Bretonneux in the Somme area on 24 April. An advance of some five miles is made around Armentières, but fails to secure its main objectives. Casualties for both sides estimated at around 110,000.

27 May–6 June 1918. **Operation BLÜCHER-YORCK**. Third German attack against the weakly-held French and British lines on the Chemin des Dames. It dramatically crashes through to the rivers Aisne and Vesle, then sweeps on to the River Marne, and establishes the huge Marne salient. Initially extremely successful, it causes panic in Paris, but the attack is held around Reims by French reserves and the remnants of five British divisions. At Château-Thierry the American 3rd Division halts the German expansion to the west. German victory creates a triangular salient some twenty-five miles deep, just fifty miles to the east of Paris; but the new salient lacks real strategic benefit,

and although the Allies suffer 127,000 casualties, German losses are estimated at 130,000.

28 May 1918. **Cantigny.** The first independent attack by the 28th Infantry Regiment of the American 1st Division successfully captures and then defends the small salient at Cantigny, near Montdidier.

1–26 June 1918. **Belleau Wood.** The stubborn defence of Château-Thierry leads into aggressive action by the American 2nd (including 4 Marine Brigade) and 3rd Divisions to clear Bouresches, Belleau Wood and Vaux at a high cost in casualties.

9–14 June 1918. **Operation GNEISENAU.** Fourth major attack by twenty-one divisions in the Matz valley against the French Third Army in a bid to widen the Marne salient. It has only limited success and is quickly contained by General Mangin and French reserves.

15–17 July 1918. **Operation FRIEDENSTURM**. The fifth and final German 'Peace Offensive' against the French in Champagne. The offensive is thirty-five miles wide and designed to envelop and capture Reims, threaten Paris, and thereby bring the French to the negotiating table. However, the French crush the offensive east of Reims. Although a significant second pocket is established south of the Marne, this western offensive is also contained within three days. The American 3rd Division again blunts the attack toward Château-Thierry and earns the nickname 'Rock of the Marne'.

18 July–7 August 1918. **The Second Battle of the Marne**. Foch launches four French armies in a surprise counter-attack against the Germans holding the Aisne and Marne salients. Mangin's Tenth Army, which was concealed in the forest of Villers-Cotterêts, is particularly successful. In the following three weeks the Germans are forced to withdraw from most of the territory they have so recently occupied at the cost of a further 160,000 casualties, including 25,000 prisoners. Nine American and four British divisions contribute significantly to this victory, which snatches the strategic initiative from the Germans and leads inexorably to their collapse.

8–13 August 1918. The British Fourth Army (including the Australian and Canadian Corps) and the French First Army attack at Amiens and drive the Germans back six miles. Six divisions are broken and the Germans suffer 24,000 killed and wounded, as the Allies capture 50,000 prisoners and 500 guns. Ludendorff calls 8 August the 'Black Day' for the German Army as frontline morale collapses. **The Battle of Amiens** launches the **Hundred Days** of Allied victories, which end the war.

18 August–16 September 1918. General Mangin's Tenth Army launches the **Oise-Aisne offensive** north-west of Soissons, and forces the German Army to pull back across the Vesle river to the river Aisne. The American 32nd Division takes Juvigny and its units are awarded the Croix de Guerre.

21 August–2 September 1918. **The Second Battle of the Somme**. The British Third Army (with the US II Corps) attacks Albert and drives the German Army back to the Hindenburg Line. The British First Army joins the attack. The Canadian Corps takes the Canal du Nord Line and the New Zealand Division captures Bapaume while the Australians capture Péronne. On 28 August, the northern British Second Army, including the American 27th Division, re-takes part of the **Ypres salient**.

12–14 September 1918. The new US First Army attacks and quickly occupies the **St Mihiel Salient**, which has been held by the Germans since September 1914.

18 September 1918. The British Fourth Army captures **Épehy** just in front of the Hindenburg Line, including 11,750 prisoners and 100 guns.

26 September 1918. The US First Army and the French Fourth Army launch the **Meuse-Argonne Offensive**. Twenty-two American divisions are involved in the attack, which later includes the US Second Army. Despite stubborn German resistance and difficult terrain, supply, and weather conditions, Sedan, close to the Belgian border, is eventually reached just before the Armistice.

28 September 1918. The British Third Army (including Australian and American divisions) breaks through the deep German defences of the **Hindenburg Line** at St Quentin and Bellenglise.

October 1918. Lille is liberated. Germany requests meetings with the Allies to agree terms for an armistice. German representatives meet Marshal Foch in the Forest of Rethondes.

11 November 1918. **Armistice** agreed between Germany and the Allied Powers.

Introduction

Almost ignored in the centre of the ancient city of Soissons, on the edge of the Champagne district of France, is a huge stone memorial which records the names of 3,987 officers and men from the two British corps and nine divisions who were killed fighting in the area in 1918, and have no known graves. Nestling in the rolling hills of the Champagne countryside to the south and east of Soissons, are numerous small British cemeteries, whose neat white headstones nestling in flowers bear further witness to the sacrifice of British lives during the First World War, particularly in its final year. However, Soissons is far from the sodden muddy fields of Flanders and Picardy, where most of the British casualties of the Great War are buried; yet the memorial stands in silent tribute to the heavy sacrifice by the nine British divisions who were present in this area from May to August 1918 and who suffered such severe casualties.

While there are numerous accounts of the Second Battle of the Marne and the courage displayed by hundreds of thousands of French and American troops in this battle; few accounts have focused on the significant role played by British forces in Champagne. As a result, the events which led to these divisions being present in the Champagne area of France are not well known, nor are the reasons for the sacrifice of so many British lives far from most of their comrades. This book attempts to redress the lack of awareness of the harsh conditions and losses faced by the men of those nine divisions who, within the space of two months, experienced waging a stubborn defence against overwhelming attacks and then achieved an obstinate victory over an enemy driven to retreat. In so doing the nine divisions suffered a total of more than 43,000 casualties (of whom 6,000 were killed), and the story of their courage in adversity and victory well deserves its niche in military history.

By early 1918 all the main protagonists in the war were utterly exhausted and drained in a struggle which had cost millions of casualties, and which no one seemed able to win. Only the Americans, with their promise of a million new soldiers by 1918 and three million by 1919, offered the prospect of fresh war-winning troops. However, the Germans, following their defeat of the Russians in 1917, saw an opportunity to switch at least a million soldiers to their Western Front. There they hoped to snatch a decisive victory early in 1918, before the newly-arriving Americans could provide sufficient trained troops to ensure their clear victory was impossible. Thus, in March 1918, Ludendorff launched the first of a series of major offensives which were intended to exploit the German's temporary numerical superiority as well as their development of new tactics and weapons to force a decisive breakthrough.

The initial German attacks in the British Somme and Flanders sectors were extremely successful. The attacks opened with a devastating and relatively short, but accurate, artillery bombardment, particularly using gas shells. This was coupled with new infantry 'storm' tactics which overwhelmed the British. The first attack drove a deep bulge into the southern part of the British line, which they had recently taken over from the French. Two more attacks in the north near Ypres and in the south against the French in the Aisne area, west of Reims, were also successful and resulted in the occupation of huge swathes of territory. The Germans were convinced that final victory lay within their grasp. Ironically the Aisne attack against the weak French defences on the Chemin des Dames, had struck the unfortunate British IX Corps, which had been sent during May to the 'quiet' Champagne sector of the French front to recover from the earlier battles.

The four divisions of IX Corps had already suffered grievously in the first two German attacks, and its recuperating units were almost totally destroyed by the fierce German assault which began on 27 May, and advanced rapidly to the River Marne. The British 19th Division was then brought up quickly to the area of the Ardre valley, and alongside the survivors of IX Corps and French divisions, it helped to stem the German advance on the western hills of Reims. On 6 June a final infantry counter-attack on Mont Bligny drove the Germans from the trenches on its summit and halted their advance. Further German attacks in the west of the salient at Château-Thierry, Bouresches and Belleau Wood aimed to break through to Paris. However, these dangerous attacks were contained by the stubborn gallantry of American (particularly the American 2nd and 3rd Divisions) and French formations, which were hurriedly rushed to the area. The third attack did partially achieve one of its aims in that it attracted some of the French reserves to the Aisne area, but not in the numbers desired by Ludendorff. Moreover, this desirable outcome was outweighed by the need for Crown Prince Rupprecht's army group to send some of its precious reserves to the Aisne area to support the expansion of the burgeoning salient.

Despite all the efforts and hopes of the Germans, the Allies (including the advance guard of the American Army) took their beating but remained united. The French and British Armies suffered and were pressed back, but they were not split apart. Nor were the Germans able to achieve a war-winning breakthrough to either the Channel ports or Paris. On the contrary, the Allies recovered and, recognizing their peril, agreed to co-operate more closely under General Ferdinand Foch, who was appointed overall Allied Supreme Commander. As a result, the Allies began to co-ordinate their plans to provide reserves to meet attacks in their respective sectors and for major counter-attacks to recover the lost areas.

Using concentrated artillery firepower to prepare the way for overwhelming infantry attacks, Ludendorff launched his fifth and most dangerous attack (FRIEDENSTURM) on 15 July with the intention of capturing Reims and the River Marne from Château-Thierry to Châlons. To the east of Reims, the attack by two armies was halted on the first day in front of the main French defence line, with very heavy German casualties. However, the attack by the German Seventh Army, holding the river Marne, west of Reims, made considerably better progress. Six divisions managed to cross the Marne, and were able to carve out a new threatening salient south of the Marne centred on Dormans. Initial German success caused civilian panic in Paris. However, a stubborn defence by American and French divisions inflicted heavy German casualties and limited their advance, particularly around Château-Thierry. On the high forested hills west of Reims, the heavy attacks by Schmettow's and Borne's corps gained some five to ten kilometres in difficult defensive country, but were eventually halted by the French and Italian divisions of the Italian II Corps.

It was intended that FRIEDENSTURM should be closely followed by the sixth major attack in Flanders code-named HAGEN. However, the limited successes of the fifth attack marked the high-water mark of German victories. Within two days this great assault was halted on every front and the Germans began planning withdrawal from their difficult salient south of the river Marne, which had been established with such bloody sacrifice. Defiantly, Ludendorff ordered a new assault plan to be prepared for a fresh attack eastwards along both banks of the Marne to surround Épernay. However, the following day, the strategic initiative was snatched by the French. They counter-attacked using French reserves, secretly amassed for this eventuality, supported by hastily gathered American divisions. It was now the turn of the Germans to be surprised and forced to retreat. Although they defended skilfully and stubbornly, the Germans faced Allies who were courageous and just as skilful, and who had the benefit of possessing the strategic initiative to impose their will on the battlefield. Thus the Germans were forced to postpone the plans for their sixth great attack in Flanders against the British. Within the following three months, the German Army had suffered a multitude of defeats, which reversed most of the territorial gains of the previous four years, and forced its representatives to petition for an Armistice.

Significantly, the Second Battle of the Marne commenced as soon as the fifth and final German offensive, to envelop Reims and Château-Thierry, had been contained. Early on the morning of 18 July Foch launched four French Armies in a great surprise counter-attack against three sides of the Aisne salient. In particular, he had given command of his strongest force, the Tenth Army, to the fiery General Mangin. Mangin deployed over 200 tanks and some sixty air squadrons to support his seventeen attacking divisions, which were spearheaded by the American 1st and 2nd Divisions. Mangin achieved total surprise, as, without any preliminary bombardment, his tanks and infantry debouched from the forest of Villers-Cotterêts, and within hours, destroyed six German divisions.

As evidence of the new spirit of co-operation, four divisions were rushed south from the British sector to add weight to the French attacks. Although organised as XXII Corps under Lieutenant General Sir Alexander Godley, the divisions were divided into two separate groups fighting on either flank of the Aisne salient. The two divisions in the west of the Aisne salient were separated and placed under direct French corps command. There they relieved the French and American divisions, which had so successfully driven in the vulnerable western flank of the huge Aisne salient, and launched their own attacks.

In the east of the Aisne salient, where the high valley of the river Ardre flows through the Montagne de Reims, the 51st (Highland) and 62nd (Yorkshire) Divisions attacked alongside each other on 20 July, not far from the area where the convalescing British IX Corps had been overwhelmed by the German onslaught just two months earlier. The XXII Corps attack reflected the multi-national character of the Allies. Scottish and Yorkshire troops advanced through an Italian corps, and were sandwiched between French, Senegalese and Algerian troops. In support were Australian and New Zealand cavalry and cyclists, as well as French, Italian and British artillery.

The two small British divisions had already experienced tough conditions and heavy losses during the German spring attacks which had fallen on the British sector. Then at short notice they had been moved by rail and bus, followed by three days of marching to arrive at their start lines in the Champagne region. On the morning of the 20th the whole of the French Fifth and Sixth Armies attacked along the southern front of the German salient. In fact the Germans south of the Marne had already vacated their salient during the night of the 19th while they had actually strengthened their defences on the shoulders of the salient. On the Ardre front the British faced some six German divisions, which, resisting with great tenacity, stubbornly defended the small stone villages in the high woods and valleys.

Nevertheless, the British troops stormed forward doggedly through thick brushwood against an obstinate defence which linked mutually-supporting machine-gun nests. Casualties were heavy and progress slow for the Highlanders thrusting through the thick undergrowth of the Bois de Courton. It took three days before the Yorkshire infantry and New Zealand cyclists could finally advance one mile, and mount a successful attack on the key village of Marfaux. These hard-won successes forced the Germans to abandon their forward defence positions, and pull back almost three miles to a new defence line. On 28 July, the Highlanders captured the village of Chaumuzy and then, with desperate bravery, the 8th West Yorkshires (Leeds Rifles) took the heights of Bligny at the point of the bayonet from its ensconced German defenders; thereby unlocking the second German defence line.

Over on the western side of the Aisne Salient, the 15th (Scottish) and 34th (Tyneside) Divisions arrived on 21 and 22 July and were incorporated into different French corps to bolster their attacks. The 15th Division joined XX Corps and relieved the American 1st Division, but kept the support of the American guns for its first attack near Berzy-le-Sec. Then, on 28 July, it attacked and took Buzancy. Although the Scots achieved their objective in desperately bloody fighting, they were eventually driven back in the evening by an overwhelming German counter-attack. The 15th (Scottish) then exchanged places with the French 87th Division on its right for a new attack, which was launched against the Hartennes Forest on 1 August. Once again, after tremendous losses, and suffering from the German use of gas, they stormed forward and advanced some three miles to the Crise river on 2 August, and 9th Gordons took Villeblain. So fierce was the fighting that five of the ten battalion commanders were either killed or wounded.

A little farther south 34th Division joined the French XXX Corps. The division had just been entirely reformed with infantry who were new to France, but were actually veteran Territorial Force soldiers, who had already campaigned for years in the Middle East. They too had spent three tiring days getting to the front by train, bus and foot. Launched early on the 23rd, without opportunity for any reconnaissance, against strong German artillery and machine-gun defences, they paid a heavy price. Again on the 25th and the 27th, the division advanced alongside French divisions, with the objective of capturing the important road from Soissons to Château-Thierry and the heights of Rozoy. Finally on 1 and 2 August they took Beugneux and Rozoy, which were the key to the German western defences, and the French Army was able to liberate the great rail centre of Soissons. Yet again five lieutenant colonels were killed.

After just ten days of exhausting combat the four divisions returned to their original British formations in Picardy and Flanders. During their detachment to the French they had played an important role in driving back the Germans from their recent conquests but had suffered very heavy casualties. Each division had lost close to 4,000 officers and men, killed, wounded or missing. The Second Battle of the Marne is justly considered to be a great Franco-American victory, as it featured significant participation by nine American divisions, many in combat for the first time, alongside almost thirty French divisions. However the bravery, dash and courage of the four small British divisions made an immense impression on the French at the time. Their commitment and ready sacrifice is still marked by the many small poignant British cemeteries located close to the decisive actions as well as by the huge memorial in Soissons to the unidentified dead. General Berthelot recorded in a special order that the two British divisions fighting in the Ardre valley had fought against superior German numbers and captured twenty-one officers and 1,300 soldiers together with forty cannon and 140 machine guns. Furthermore, the Black Watch and the West Yorkshire Regiment were each awarded the Croix de Guerre, and 'Tardenois' as a battle honour.

The men could take pride in the fact that during their ten days of campaigning alongside the French, the four divisions of XXII Corp had helped to recover part of the territorial losses suffered by the French XI Corps and the British IX Corps. They had played a significant role in pushing the Germans out of key defence positions in the Ardre valley and the area south of Soissons, which contributed to the withdrawal of the whole German line. Thus the costly conquests achieved by the Germans during their third and fifth offensives, proved vulnerable and of short duration. As a result the German line fell back swiftly to the river Vesle and within three months was driven back to the borders of France.

The First Battle of the Marne had prevented an almost assured German victory in 1914. The Second Battle of the Marne in 1918 demonstrated that the Germans, even with superior numbers in the attack areas, supported by tremendous firepower and new weapons and tactics, could not totally overwhelm the Allies. Most significantly it marked their inability to retain the strategic initiative, without which the Germans could not hope to achieve victory. It also highlighted the growing capability, determination and unity of the multinational Allies, who, strengthened by the arrival of dozens of newly-formed American divisions, were finally able to defeat the German invaders.

The German Spring Offensives of 1918

After more than three years of murderous trench warfare both groups of the main protagonists – Germans, Austro-Hungarians, Bulgarians and Turks on one side and the French, Italian, Russian and British on the other – were exhausted. Nevertheless, it appeared to many that, by the latter half of 1917, the Germans had come very close to achieving final victory. The slaughter of thousands of soldiers at Verdun and in the bloody Nivelle spring offensives of 1917 had so weakened the French Army that it had been forced onto the defensive, under the more realistic leadership of General Philippe Pétain. The British, despite their unrivalled command of the sea, had been unable to use this advantage to outflank the Germans in a meaningful way, and had frittered away much of their strength at the end of 1917 in the wet marshes and flooded shell-holes of Passchendaele. Moreover, they faced a continuing threat from German submarine warfare. The Italians had also suffered from unimaginative leaders such as Cadorno, who had exhausted their manpower in repetitive attacks along the Isonzo. After its defeat at Caporetto on 24 October 1917, the Italian Army had required bolstering by hastily despatched French and British divisions, just to stay in the war. The Russians had already succumbed to the destructive effect of three years of war, and had withdrawn and signed a separate peace treaty with the Germans. This left the Germans in possession of much of eastern Europe, including the important food-producing region of the Ukraine. Most importantly, peace in the East offered Germany the prospect of transferring a decisive numbers of its divisions to the Western Front.

The Germans needed to act swiftly if they were to take advantage of their temporary numerical advantage. The defeat of the Italians had obliged the British and French to send eleven divisions to support them, and thus weakened them at precisely the moment when they faced a new threat from a strengthened and resurgent German Army. As each of the Allies fell back in the face of heavy German attacks they were driven to sink their differences by the desperation of their situation, and attempted to develop a more co-ordinated response to the Germans. A Supreme Allied War Council had been established in November 1917, and its military representatives met at Versailles. Although the United States had declared war on Germany on 6 April 1917, its ability to contribute armed forces was initially minute. Woodrow Wilson had sent General Bliss (the American Chief of Staff) to join the Council as both his personal and military representative, but both knew that, while the American ability to contribute forces to the Allied cause was full of promise, it was likely to remain extremely limited. This was not lost on Ludendorff, who had estimated that the United States would need from one to two years before its inexperienced troops could be committed to battle. In any event, the German Navy had promised him that they would use their submarines to sink every troopship crossing the Atlantic.

For their part the Germans wanted to use their victories in 1917 to defeat the Allies decisively before the anticipated arrival of huge American forces and the weakening political and economic situations of Austro-Hungary, Bulgaria, and Turkey, swung the balance of advantage back to the Allies. The Allies feared particularly that the Germans would be able to transfer at least 1,500,000 trained soldiers from the Eastern Front. However, the Germans dissipated much of their strength by garrisoning the Ukraine and other areas, which kept some fifty divisions in the East. According to Ludendorff, they were only able to move forty divisions (considerably less than 1,000,000 trained men) to reinforce their western armies (although most western estimates were higher). Nevertheless, it was a very optimistic German High Command (the *Oberste Heeresleitung* (*OHL*), run by Ludendorff) which gathered at Mons in Belgium on 11 November 1917 to plan how to use these additional experienced forces to gain the strategic initiative and achieve a decisive victory.

The Germans considered that the French Army had been weakened and was very vulnerable to a threat to Paris. However, it was fighting to defend its homeland and it was thought to be cleverer and tactically superior to the British, who were considered slower and more deliberate, both in attack and defence. Nevertheless, the Germans feared that the British would recommence their heavy attacks in the spring of 1918, which would inflict further heavy losses on them, just as the autumn attacks at Ypres had done. In order to pre-empt Allied attacks, the staff officers in the respective German armies had developed alternative attack plans for each part of the front where a decisive breakthrough was thought possible. These comprehensive attack plans were gathered and presented to the First Quartermaster General, Erich Ludendorff. General Ludendorff was nominally only the assistant to the Kaiser's Chief of Staff, Field Marshal Paul von Hindenburg, but he actually dominated domestic policy and events and, with all the main political and military decisions in his hands, operated as virtual dictator of Germany.

Some staff officers favoured an attack on the French around Verdun, but Ludendorff was determined to defeat the British first. His favourite plan was GEORGE I, which envisaged a major attack in Flanders breaking through to the nearby Channel ports. However, after touring the front, he decided that the ground in Flanders would still be too wet in March for large-scale exploitation and opted for Operation MICHAEL, to precede the intended 'break-through' attack in Flanders. MICHAEL was to be launched by three German armies just a little farther south in the Picardy region against the St Quentin-Arras area. This covered the section of the front on the right wing of the British zone. There the British Third Army with fourteen divisions joined its Fifth Army, which had just taken over an additional twenty-five-mile section of the front. This was a poorly fortified section of the front, formerly held by the French, and resulted from a decision by Lloyd George to relieve the weakened French Army of part of its responsibilities. As a result, General Gough's British Fifth Army practically seemed to invite attack, as it had just twelve divisions to defend this much longer and far less well fortified front of some forty-four miles. Thus it appeared to be particularly vulnerable, but Ludendorff's prime aim was to penetrate the centre of the British Third Army and roll it up towards the coast.

In eastern Europe the Germans had been able to break through the Russian lines and use the open terrain beyond to their advantage. However, in the west, they had been largely forced onto the defensive since the First Battle of the Marne, and had spent more than three years perfecting their defence capabilities. Initially the Germans had suffered greatly from the British and French artillery fire during the Somme and Verdun campaigns. However, under Ludendorff's leadership, they had, from 1916, developed a 'flexible' defence, which emphasized retaining their conquests in France and Belgium while preserving lives by reducing the number of troops in the actual front line. Behind the front line they had methodically excavated very deep trenches equipped with even deeper reinforced accommodation bunkers. Three and even five lines of double trenches were excavated, with up to 2,000 metres between them. These were shielded by deep aprons of barbed wire designed to channel attackers into killing zones overlooked by solid concrete MEBUS bunkers (pillboxes) containing resolute machine-gun teams.

It was anticipated that the thinly-manned front line would be lost to Allied artillery-supported infantry attacks. However, the second and third lines also contained well-protected counter-attack forces, often sited in rear slope locations and thus beyond Allied field artillery observation. Their role was to mount immediate counter-attacks to retake the ground which had been lost before the attackers could consolidate. This tactical placing of reserve troops and artillery emphasized the ability to mount speedy counter-attacks against any Allied breakthroughs. Although effective, this strategy of manpower conservation and rapid response was essentially defensive, and left the strategic initiative in the hands of the Allies. Therefore any plans to switch to the offensive required the restoration of the offensive spirit and the development of new attack skills.

Accordingly, during the winter of 1917 divisions were re-trained to embrace attack and infiltration tactics contained in a new training manual *The Offensive Battle in Position Warfare*. The aim was to restore the ability to break though the enemy defences and conduct manoeuvre warfare. These new tactics, which had been further developed under General von Hutier, had been successfully tested against the Russians at Riga and against the Italians at Caporetto. It also incorporated the successful lessons of the German counter-attack at Cambrai against the British in November 1917. It featured the employment of special *Stoss* or assault troops, which were units withdrawn from the front and given training in flexible assault tactics. Supported by an intense and focused, but relatively brief, artillery barrage, special assault infantry were trained to move forward in small fighting squads grouped around the mobile firepower provided by light machine guns, trench mortars and flamethrowers. In addition, they were usually accompanied by mobile support artillery and combat engineers to assist them over obstacles. The *Stoss* troops were trained to keep pushing forward, employing 'infiltration tactics', finding soft spots in the enemy's defences (some of which had been created by the artillery barrage) and avoiding well-defended strongpoints. These tougher defensive positions were left for the follow-on infantry and artillery to deal with.

The second offensive element developed by the Germans was the grouping of formidable quantities of artillery pieces into a fire-plan with which to hammer the defence virtually senseless. This fire-plan, called a *Feuerwaltze* (Rolling Fire), had been perfected by Hutier's artillery advisor, Colonel Georg Bruchmüller. Bruchmüller's talent lay in grouping and aligning substantial numbers of heavy guns, mortars and gas projectors in order to surprise and suppress enemy defence lines by an overwhelming avalanche of fire and gas shells, without first alerting the enemy by protracted registering of the guns.

Bruchmüller's targeting focused on paralyzing the defence throughout its depth by switching fire to destroy key features such as enemy headquarters, communications and artillery positions, and then culminating in a destructive firestorm on the frontline enemy trenches. The enemy's counter-battery capability was targeted particularly by Bruchmüller's own long-range artillery. His fire-plan emphasized the predominant use of gas shells, which incapacitated or at least reduced the efficiency of enemy troops (who were forced to wear clumsy gas masks), and did not damage the terrain in the same way as high explosives. The artillery plan then included a timetabled creeping barrage that moved just ahead of the assault troops. To maintain secrecy, most guns were concealed and were carefully registered, from the map, under central control. Ideally, the artillery fire-plan and the specialized infantry were to be brought together to a decisive area of the front in the greatest secrecy in order to achieve tactical and strategic surprise. Thus many of the assault infantry divisions and supporting artillery batteries were kept well away from the attack zone until the very last moment, in many cases only being brought forward on the very night of the attack.

For all the battles of the spring offensive the Germans enjoyed an overall and local superiority in numbers of men and guns. By the spring of 1918 the Germans had massed some 191 divisions on the Western Front, to pit against ninety-nine French and sixty-three British divisions. Four brand-new American divisions (the 1st, 2nd, 26th and 42nd) had arrived in France by the end of 1917, but they were still in training and were not expected to affect events for many months. As Ludendorff presciently foresaw, 'We must strike at the earliest moment before the Americans can throw strong forces into the scale. We must beat the British.' For this first and greatest attack, scheduled for launch on 21 March, Ludendorff assembled seventy-six divisions (of which fifty-six were designated *Stoss*), massed in three powerful armies, General von Hutier's Eighteenth Army, von der Marwitz's Second Army, and von Below's Seventeenth Army. In addition, almost two-thirds of all available artillery on the Western Front, totalling some 6,473 guns and 3,534 mortars, had also been secretly assembled. Under the direct control of Colonel Bruchmüller, they were to concentrate their fire on just twenty-six defending divisions..

At 4.40am on the damp misty morning of 21 March 1918, 10,000 guns, howitzers and mortars, opened up along forty-four miles (seventy kilometres) of the British front lines and, within five hours, fired off more than 3,000,000 shells. Five hours later the German assault troops began to move forward under a covering barrage. The morning mist had been thickened by smoke and gas, making it very difficult for any surviving defenders to see their targets. In addition, the Germans had some 1,000 aircraft available as well as hundreds of observation balloons spotting targets for their artillery.

Everywhere the German infantry outnumbered the British three to one, but in the south around St Quentin the thinly-spread British Fifth Army defenders were struck particularly heavily. They had only recently moved into the area and they had not had sufficient time to perfect their defences. As a result, despite desperate fighting, the British battle zone was quickly penetrated. Farther north, General Byng's Third Army occupied better prepared defences, and was helped by a clearing of the fog. Therefore, although von Hutier's Eighteenth Army made considerable progress south of the River Somme, the Second and Seventeenth Armies were held by a stubborn Third Army defence and made little progress towards the key city of Arras, which was Ludendorff's prime strategic target.

Ludendorff tried to restrain his successful left wing, but nevertheless the Eighteenth Army continued advancing as the remnants of General Gough's Fifth Army fell back. Within six days there was a deep bulge in the British front almost fifty miles long and twenty-five miles deep. However, although the desperately tired German attackers finally reached Montdidier and Villers-Bretonneux, the British and French defenders struggled and fought back hard to prevent their front from splitting. General Gough was replaced on 27 March by General Rawlinson, who renamed the Fifth Army as Fourth Army, and attempted to restore British morale.

Despite the huge loss of territory, the Allied front had not split and, in desperation, Ludendorff launched Operation MARS. This subsidiary attack, on 28 March, was supposed to finally crack open the British defences. Preceded by the usual heavy artillery barrage, eight assault divisions, supported by four reserve divisions (a force ratio of 3:1), struck part of the Third Army defending Arras and Amiens and the junction of the British Third and First Armies. However, there was no fog and no surprise to help the Germans overcome the four tough defending British divisions, which included the 15th (Scottish). Although depleted, they had learned to thin out their forward positions to reduce casualties, and they managed to smother this attack, which was abandoned by the Germans on the first day. The British and French defence hardened with each attack, and finally, on 5 April, the Germans closed down their attempt to break through in Picardy.

Operation MICHAEL had achieved an eye-watering success for the Germans. It had demonstrated the value of their new tactics and administered a drubbing to the British. Superficially, Ludendorff's strategy had appeared successful, but he had actually squandered the opportunity given him by possession of the strategic initiative. He had allowed the Eighteenth Army to expand its conquests across a devastated wasteland instead of focusing on capturing strategic targets. The British, despite being forced into an ignominious retreat had, in reality, fought extremely well to survive such a powerful and overwhelming attack, and they had been bolstered by French reserves. More than 1,200 square miles of Allied territory (3,100 square kilometres) had been lost with over 255,000 casualties, of whom some 72,000 were prisoners.

This German success hid the realization that the gains had actually created enormous problems for them. They had moved forward from their heavily fortified lines and now occupied a deep salient, with a much longer and vulnerable front to protect. They had also suffered almost as many casualties as the Allies (estimated at some 239,000), particularly amongst their best assault troops, who were irreplaceable. The huge territory they now occupied was a war-torn wasteland of little military value which the Germans themselves had laid waste as they retreated to their Hindenburg Line the previous year. A decisive breakthrough somewhere else was still needed.

Thwarted by the lack of strategic success in Picardy, Ludendorff reverted to his original plan, which was an attack in the area farther north, towards the English Channel ports. Originally it had been planned to launch this attack just two weeks after the start of MICHAEL. However, the Somme attack had been allowed to absorb more troops than anticipated, and it took far too much time to move troops, guns and supplies to the new area while trying to maintain total secrecy. For their part, the Allies were anticipating another attack, but thought it would probably come in the French zone, perhaps aimed at Paris. Therefore Ludendorff managed to surprise them once again, by striking in the Lys valley in Flanders.

In view of the heavy casualties they had already suffered among their best troops, the Germans only had eleven fresh divisions available to add to those already in position in the area. Thus they opted for a reduced version of the original GEORGE I and GEORGE II plans, renamed appropriately Operation GEORGETTE, which encompassed an attack front of just twelve miles (nineteen kilometres). GEORGETTE aimed at the capture of the vital terrain of the Mont Kemmel ridge, which overlooked the Flanders plain, and the transport centre of Hazebrouck, and was launched within barely five days of halting the MICHAEL offensive. Two German armies, the Fourth and Sixth, attacked with twenty-six divisions on either side of Armentières (a further fourteen were brought in later). Some of these were divisions which had been moved from the Somme area fighting, and this mirrored the British action of transferring north to the Lys area some of their badly-mauled divisions to rest.

Once again, on the damp foggy morning of 9 April, thousands of guns and mortars, directed by Colonel Bruchmüller, opened up with high explosive and mustard gas shells on the British lines. Actually, the spearhead of the main attack by nine German divisions towards Armentières struck a weakened Portuguese division, which was soon overwhelmed. However, the British brought up reserves, and a stubborn defence by the 55th (West Lancashire) Division soon closed the breach. The GEORGETTE attack is sometimes called the Fourth Battle of Ypres, as the town of Ypres was a major objective of the German assault. Although the British were forced to give ground against these violent attacks their competent artillery prevented the German infantry from exploiting their success, and they were unable to make any real progress after 18 April.

As before, Ludendorff attempted to pull the British defence off balance by a diversionary attack, this time farther south. On 24 April two German divisions struck in the area close to the River Somme, at Villers-Bretonneux. This attack included the use of thirteen of the new huge German monster tanks (the A7V) and, when met by a few British tanks, featured the first-ever tank-on-tank battle. Initially the Germans broke through the British 8th Division and took the village of Villers-Bretonneux, and thereby threatened Amiens. However, that night and the following day, they were counter-attacked by two Australian brigades and the remnants of 8th Division. The exuberant Australians drove the Germans from the town, thereby ending German ambitions on the Somme. This action by the Australian soldiers passed into legend for the Australian nation, which continues to celebrate its notable feat of arms at Villers-Bretonneux on Anzac Day (25 April) each year. Anzac Day was originally named after the first landings at Gallipoli in 1915.

While the Scherpenberg hill near Mount Kemmel was lost as the Germans achieved a five-mile deep penetration no other significant towns or vital ground were captured by the German attack in the Lys valley. Eventually, on 29 April, Ludendorff called off the Lys attack. Both sides had probably suffered an almost equal number of casualties (about 110,000), but the Allies had been drawn even closer together by the realization of their common danger, and the recognition of the need to provide reserves for each other's fronts. The French had sent eighteen divisions to the Flanders area, and had involved some thirty-four divisions in the great Battle of Picardy. The British prime minister, David Lloyd George, had also been obliged to allow substantial British reinforcements to move from England to join the fighting. Perhaps most critically for the Allies they had finally agreed to accept the trenchant General Foch as the overall Allied commander.

Ludendorff remained convinced that the Flanders front, lying within a day's march from the Channel ports, offered the Germans the very best opportunity to break through the British lines. He therefore gradually gathered additional reserves and positioned them close to that front ready for his next planned attack on the British army, code-named Operation HAGEN. However, the GEORGETTE experience had also shown that the British and French reserves were still too strong in this area. Therefore his third attack was aimed at persuading the Allied commanders to move some of the British and French reserves farther south, by threatening Paris, and thus hopefully denuding the Flanders area of troop reserves.

Early on the morning of 27 May the Germans launched their third great attack, Operation BLÜCHER-YORCK, which struck the French and British positions astride the Chemin des Dames. (The original operation was named BLÜCHER but, as it was extended to the west it incorporated the YORCK operation). This important stretch of the French front was defined by a narrow historical road called the

Chemin des Dames. It ran for some thirty kilometres along the high ridge between the valleys of the rivers Aisne and Ailette. The attack, delivered by seventeen divisions supported by eight divisions in the second echelon, achieved complete strategic surprise. Despite some warnings, the French (particularly the local Sixth Army commander, General Denis Duchêne) refused to believe that the next German attack would be launched in this area. Already, the British troops had recognized the warning signs from their experience of the previous attacks in Picardy and Flanders and had sounded the alarm. However, their commanders had been compelled by Duchêne to place far too many of their troops and artillery in the forward zone where they were particularly vulnerable to German shelling and gassing.

The huge well-planned artillery onslaught by almost 5,000 guns and mortars, another Bruchmüller *Feuerwaltze,* which switched rapidly between key targets to the full depth of the defence, achieved its anticipated effect. The rain of shells rapidly destroyed command posts, communications, artillery positions, and finally the overcrowded frontline trenches, completely shattering all hopes of maintaining a coherent defence.

The area behind the Chemin des Dames front was bisected by river lines flowing east to west and was deeply folded with steep valleys and narrow ridges. It should have been easy to defend, given time and adequate artillery but the control of bridge demolitions was poor, and the Germans found it easy to bypass the short-lived attempts at establishing improvised defence lines. As a result, the German advance was far more successful than they could ever have hoped for and the German infantry pressed triumphantly forward across the Aisne and Vesle rivers, gaining some twenty miles in twenty-four hours, and capturing the ancient royal city of Soissons. Eventually the tip of the new German salient was halted at the river Marne, and particularly at Château-Thierry, by rapidly-mobilized French and American reserves. Importantly, the stubborn defence on the Montagne de Reims by British and French troops hindered further progress towards capturing Reims and exploitation of the Aisne salient. A German battalion established a token bridgehead on the southern bank of the Marne at Jaulgonne, but was soon wiped out by a Franco-American force.

The possession of the triangular Aisne salient was initially immensely advantageous for the Germans. What had been intended as a diversionary attack to the River Vesle by just seventeen divisions had succeeded beyond all expectations, and brought the leading German troops to within forty miles (sixty-four kilometres) of Paris. The threat to Paris had been made even more unambiguous by the surprise bombardment from the 'Paris gun'. This had been moved secretly from Crépy to a new site at Beaumont, east of la Fére, and it began a fresh bombardment of Paris to coincide with the start of the attack. Naturally, the renewal of shelling from this carefully concealed 'terror weapon' shocked civilian morale in Paris. The frequency and targeting of its shells was completely unpredictable, causing widespread panic among the civilian population, and many French politicians blamed General Pétain for the disaster (Duchêne was his nominee). Moreover, the military catastrophe was amplified by the Germans overrunning the batteries of heavy large-calibre guns, which had been brought up to the Vailly area, just east of Soissons. They had been positioned there in order to seek out and destroy the 'Paris gun' in its previous location in the Laon corner. Not only were these important counter-batteries overrun, but, by advancing to the River Marne, the Germans were eventually able to relocate their gun to a new site in the Tardenois area, from where they could more easily threaten the citizens of Paris.

The rapid victory highlighted French weaknesses and dealt a serious blow to French prestige as it proved that the Germans were just as capable of succeeding against them as they had already demonstrated against the British. In the ensuing panic Pétain pulled his reserves back from the north and east to cover the approaches to Paris. But it was feared that even this would not be enough to stop the next German attack, and the training of the American 2nd and 3rd Divisions at Chaumont was interrupted to throw them into the line at Château-Thierry (the 1st Division was already fully involved at Cantigny). The promise of fresh American manpower provided the only hope at that crucial time, but the new American troops were initially an unknown quantity. Nevertheless, faced with this crisis, the Allies then prevailed upon the Americans to commit to using every available ship to send 250,000 troops, whether fully-trained or not, in both June and July.

Facing these multiple German threats it was still difficult for the Allied commanders to sink their differences. While Haig was convinced that he needed all his reserves to resist a new offensive in Flanders, where the preparations for Operation HAGEN were becoming apparent, Pétain maintained that he needed every reserve to resist a further drive on Paris, where the preparations for Operation GNEISENAU were also becoming obvious. Foch held the new post of Supreme Commander but he had limited powers of command. Moreover, in line with his philosophy of attack to destabilize the enemy, Foch was also trying to build a reserve force for a strategic counter-attack. On 31 May Pétain warned that he had used thirty-seven divisions in the Aisne defence, of which seventeen, including the five British divisions of IX Corps, were completely worn out. He therefore requested Foch to move the five American divisions, which were under training in the British sector (4th, 28th, 35th, 77th and 82nd) to the French sector, where they could hold quiet sections of the line, thus relieving French troops to be used elsewhere; some American divisions were so large that they could hold complete French corps sectors. Haig was perplexed as he had anticipated being able to use the Americans he had trained in his future battles, but in the crisis had no alternative but to agree to their rapid redeployment to the French Sector.

Although the occupation of Soissons had secured an important railway centre for the Germans it had limited value without the complementary rail centre lying to the east at Reims, and it was still vulnerable to French heavy artillery. Furthermore, without possession of Reims, the Germans were limited to only two viable north-south roads, and the top of the new triangular salient around Soissons could easily be converted into a trap. Although Ludendorff had cautioned against extending the attack southward beyond the River Vesle he was only too aware that von Kluck's victorious First Army had actually marched far south of the River Marne in September 1914, and now, after four years of struggle, the river once again beckoned. Therefore, despite his misgivings, Ludendorff agreed to transfer seven of his precious HAGEN reserve divisions to support the attack, and placed as positive a gloss on this exceptional advance as possible: 'The chances for a successful execution of an attack in Flanders against the English, planned as the principal issue of the whole undertaking, had been essentially enhanced.'

In fact precisely the opposite was true. The conquest and occupation of the Aisne salient had been a highly successful military operation, but it absorbed many more troops than originally planned. This exacerbated the salient's poor communications, which severely hindered resupply, and made it a poor platform for further attacks. The perverse outcome for the Germans was that, in order to garrison yet another salient, far more of their own precious reserves were drawn away from the projected mighty HAGEN attack.

Nevertheless, Ludendorff could feel tremendously satisfied. In barely three months the German Army had been able to drive three huge salients into the main Allied fronts. This succession of quick victories had left the Allies in disarray and seemed to demonstrate that the Germans had uncovered the key to success, and thus were on the verge of final victory. Despite the fact that these three successes had not resulted in the capture of any strategically important cities or terrain, they seemed to portend that not just Russia and Italy, but also France and Britain were tottering on the edge of defeat. It was less immediately obvious that these victories had cost the Germans more than 15 per cent of their army in casualties, and many of these casualties were among their very best soldiers and officers. Moreover, Ludendorff was diverted from his original plan of defeating the British army early in 1918 in Flanders, and to consider how he might link up these salients. He was also tempted to secure an unexpected strategic advantage from these victories by exploiting his advanced positions around Reims to conquer that important city.

At the bottom of the new salient around Château-Thierry the German advance had been held up by the appearance of French reserves and, significantly, the arrival of the first inexperienced American troops from the newly arrived 2nd and 3rd Divisions. Although the third German attack is usually recorded as lasting from 27 May to 6 June, the fighting in the area west of Château-Thierry continued at full tempo almost until the end of June. Here the troops of the German Conta Corps, including the elite 10th Division, together with elements of four other divisions, continued to press westward along the Ourcq valley towards Paris. Initially this area was defended by a French division, but on the evening of 3 June it was relieved by the arrival of the American 2nd Division, comprising 3 Infantry Brigade and 4 US Marine Brigade. Three Infantry Brigade was split as the 23rd Infantry Regiment took up the ground on the left in front of Bussiares, and the 9th Infantry Regiment occupied the right flank. In the centre of the line, just in front of Belleau Wood, lay the Marine brigade, with its 5th and 6th Marine Regiments, defending Lucy-le-Bocage. The Americans quickly dug defence positions (although the marines refused to dig a second defence line as they stated they had no intention of retreating).

The first heavy German attack came on 5 June and, after it was repelled by the 6th Marine Regiment, the Americans then launched their own attack on 6 June against Hill 142. Later that evening, the marines launched a particularly bloody assault against the village of Bouresches, which cost them more than 1,000 men killed and wounded. This brave attack highlighted the heavy cost to infantry of attacking without proper reconnaissance and artillery support, bunched together in serried lines through corn fields against a concealed enemy sitting behind well-emplaced machine guns. This experience was to be repeated by the two British divisions in their initial attacks in the Ardre valley, where they suffered some 3,000 casualties on 20 July, and again by the new US First Army when it attacked in the Argonne Forest in late September. Eventually the marines were supported by their own 2nd Engineer Regiment and the 7th Infantry Regiment from the American 3rd Division. Bloody attack succeeded bloody counter-attack in the woods, until the French brought up significant numbers of heavy artillery to pulverize the German positions in Belleau Wood. Finally, on the morning of 26 June, after a night attack by the marines, they could announce that the Germans had finally been driven from Belleau Wood.

Belleau Wood was by far the most significant battle fought by the American forces up to this point, and established their fighting reputation and courage, most particularly that of the US marines. The American reporter Floyd Gibbons, who was with 4 Marine Brigade, was wounded in the battle and, as a result, his eyewitness accounts got through the censor, thus publicizing the bravery of the marines. It was certainly a brave, but not well-judged action, as the marines had attacked without making a reconnaissance, and seemed unaware that the Germans had rapidly converted the wood into a defensive bastion.

On 1 July the clearing of Belleau Wood was followed up by a textbook attack put in by 3 Infantry Brigade. Following a well-planned artillery barrage, it cleared the eighty-two stone houses of the village of Vaux (this is very close to what is now the site of the impressive American Monument on Hill 204). Altogether, the 2nd Division had suffered very severely in a month of fighting against elements of five German divisions, with losses totalling some 9,777 casualties, including 1,811 killed. However, its brutal baptism of fire had halted the westward drive of the Germans towards Paris. Despite these losses the division had inflicted at least as many casualties on the Germans, with over 1,600 prisoners captured. Just two weeks later the barely recovered 2nd Division was ordered to move north rapidly to join Mangin's counter-offensive to retake Soissons.

Belleau Wood is now the site of the large Aisne-Marne Military Cemetery containing a memorial chapel and 2,289 graves. The woods contain many relics of the fighting and remain an evocative memorial to the many Americans (particularly marines) killed in the River Marne and Aisne area in the First World War. Each year this epic sacrifice is commemorated in a huge Franco-American ceremony at the cemetery (usually around the last Sunday in May). Some 8,625 German dead are buried in their neighbouring cemetery.

Whilst the fighting in the Belleau Wood area continued the Germans launched the fourth of their offensives, at just after midnight on 9 June. It was an opportunistic and ambitious two-pronged attack intended to round out the Somme and Aisne salients. Von Hutier's Eighteenth Army attacked south from the Noyon area, where it struck the French Third Army, while part of von Boehn's Seventh Army attacked west from Soissons.

This fourth attack named Operation GNEISENAU highlighted the threat to Paris but the immediate target was the city of Compiègne. However, the assaults had been poorly prepared with just too few troops available (there were only twenty-seven in-situ divisions) to overcome a French defence which was forewarned and growing more competent. Nevertheless, although the French thinned out and retreated as a planned element of their flexible defence, three of their divisions were destroyed by the violence of the initial Bruchmüller artillery bombardment. The centre German divisions broke through the French forward defences and quickly advanced seven miles as far as the Oise and the Aronde valleys, but then the French defence hardened. In the east, the Seventh Army advance was also held in fierce fighting at Ambleny.

General Mangin, who had been recalled from disgrace by General Foch, was given command of a counter-attack corps of seven divisions and 150 tanks, which struck the Germans from Compiègne on 11 June. Mangin's counter-attack, in what the French called the Battle of the Matz, completely halted the German advance. Although Mangin was unable to make much headway and suffered heavy tank losses, his attack demonstrated the potency of a surprise counter-attack and his forces took back the Aronde valley.

At a cost of some 30,000 casualties, the Germans had managed to advance some nine miles (fourteen kilometres) along a twenty-three mile (thirty-seven kilometres) front. This was a substantial advance but critically GNEISENAU had failed to capture the important city of Compiègne, or link up the two salients and the Germans had little option but to downplay the importance of this offensive. Significantly, General Humbert's Third Army had stopped the enemy offensive without external support, and Charles Mangin (nicknamed 'Butcher' Mangin) had once again proved his abilities as a ruthless counter-attack general. Mangin would tolerate no delays, and his counter-attack force had only begun to assemble on the evening of the 10th. Foch rewarded him with promotion to command of his key battle reserve, the French Tenth Army. To add to the German army's difficulties, their troops began to suffer from the worldwide influenza epidemic, as indeed did the Allies, known as the Spanish Flu.

GNEISENAU was an opportunistic attack which demonstrated fully the ability of the German army to mount a substantial operation at short notice and startle the French civilian population. However, there was barely sufficient time to move all the heavy artillery to support the offensive, and too many movements during daylight betrayed the coming offensive to the French. GNEISENAU also illustrated the limits to the German army's strength as well as Ludendorff's lack of strategic focus. Having agreed to expand BLÜCHER-YORCK, Ludendorff might have been better served by taking advantage of French difficulties and allowing Seventh Army to outflank Reims from the south, which might well have been achieved with considerably fewer losses to the Germans. However, the failure to overcome the British and French defenders on the Montagne de Reims in early June left the Germans without a good jumping-off point, and Ludendorff was tempted to switch his main effort farther east.

More importantly, if the Germans had not been absorbed by their own planning for the forthcoming attacks in Flanders and Champagne they might have paid more attention to analyzing how quickly the French army had reacted to the shock of the GNEISENAU attack. In a foretaste of what was to follow on 18 July, the French army had clearly demonstrated its remarkable powers of recovery. On the third day of the battle, just as the exhausted German infantry ran out of steam, Mangin had mounted a sharp counter-offensive, deploying rapidly assembling reserves and tanks, which brought the German offensive to a shuddering halt.

Meanwhile, Ludendorff had ignored these portents and turned with full energy to concentrate on an even more important plan to envelop the key northern city of Reims. For this, three German armies spent more than five weeks carefully preparing an attack which they considered so important that they called it FRIEDENSTURM, the *Peace Offensive*. This attack was designed to capture Reims and inflict such a severe blow on the French that they would be forced to discuss a peace treaty. In addition, it was hoped that it would, at the very least, pull substantial reserves from the north, which would then allow Ludendorff, within two weeks, to launch his great HAGEN attack against the British in Flanders. However, the long build-up of the two wings of the attack, Operation REIMS in the east and Operation MARNE DEFENCE in the south, allowed rumours of the planned offensives to leak out. As a result, the French prepared their own special welcome and counter-attack from the forest of Villers-Cotterêts.

FRIEDENSTURM was clearly intended to be a great pivotal battle for the Germans, who, deploying three thoroughly-prepared armies, were convinced of its certain success. However, it was destined to be more than overshadowed by the French response, which was to enter history as the Second Battle of the Marne and become the turning point battle which marked the demise of the German offensive capability. Altogether some 500,000 German troops in fifty-two divisions were gathered to attack along sixty miles (ninety kilometres) of fronts on the eastern side of Reims and along the River Marne. Against them were arrayed some 100,000 French defenders, who were expected to be overwhelmed by the assault. General Bruno von Mudra, commanding First Army attacking immediately east of Reims, anticipated reaching the Marne within one day. On his left, General Karl von Einem was attacking with his Third Army due south, towards Châlons, lying farther south along the Marne. Their operation, in which twenty-two divisions actually attacked, was the major wing of the two-pronged assault, which was expected to isolate and capture Reims. They were fully supported by Bruchmüller's artillery, and both these veteran generals, who had first fought in the Franco-Prussian War, were confident of victory. However, the long preparation time gave the French ample warning and abundant time to prepare their own flexible defence, specifically tailored to defeat the pattern of German attacks.

On the front line running east from Reims, the well-prepared divisions of von Mudra and von Einem were faced by the French Fourth Army commanded by the bearded one-armed General Henri Gouraud. To counter their 300,000 troops, Gouraud had just 40,000 defenders. However, he had, somewhat reluctantly, fully implemented Pétain's new defence directive, which involved the drastic thinning out of his forward defence line. Grudgingly Gouraud had agreed to accept a certain loss of the sacred territory of France by concentrating his main defence effort in his intermediate and second lines. There he had stationed the bulk of his infantry, which included the American 42nd (Rainbow) Division, and masses of artillery. As a result most of his artillery and infantry were placed well out of range of the German guns and thus avoided destruction in the devastating Bruchmüller barrages. In addition, the French had copious aircraft in support including forty-two squadrons of their own, as well as nine squadrons of the British Royal Air Force.

Cunningly, Gouraud had prepared his elastic defence with great thoroughness to act as a trap to destroy the German storm troops. Unbeknown to the Germans, the majority of French troops were pulled back some three kilometres from the front line of trenches to a new deep main battle line along the Roman road. The frontline trenches were largely abandoned, apart from a number of strongpoints intended to delay the enemy advance and inflict casualties, which thus became known as the 'Sacrificial Line'. The volunteers ensconced in these sacrificial redoubts were not expected to survive but were intended to act as obstacles to a swift advance and to shoot the infiltrating columns of Germans from behind as they flowed around them. Consequently, most of Bruchmüller's three-hour-long deluge of HE and gas shells fell on largely vacant forward trenches.

At 5.00am a covering barrage moved ahead of the advancing storm troops who naturally found it easy to capture the smashed front trenches as they were essentially devoid of defenders. However, after struggling forward for several kilometres through the gas-soaked shell-torn terrain, the exhausted attackers then came under heavy fire from the unharmed waiting defenders of the second and third French trench lines who were handsomely supported by copious batteries of artillery firing 'curtain barrages' which turned the open chalk terrain into a 'killing zone' for the German attackers. The Allied artillery bombarded the German infantry not only in front of their second position, but right back to the trenches of the French first position. Thus the foremost stormtroopers were cut down in swathes and the follow-on forces were jammed into the same 'killing-zone'. Although they doggedly persisted with their attacks, the waves of German assault troops were caught in the barren terrain by a hail of well-directed HE, gas and shrapnel shells, and by 9.00am on the 15th it was abundantly clear that this great attack by two German armies had ground to a complete halt. In three crucial hours, Gouraud's tiny army had inflicted a stinging defeat on a well-planned attack by twenty-two German divisions supported by the usual shattering Bruchmüller bombardment. Gouraud had proved that a strong well-organized defence in depth could overcome the offensive, no matter how powerful, and thereby laid the foundation for the successful counter-attack three days later. The failed offensive east of Reims was estimated to have cost the Germans at least 40,000 casualties, against just 5,000 French.

The first-hand account by Captain Rudolf Binding vividly conveys the disillusionment of the Germans. Binding was an experienced German officer who had managed to survive four years of the war. In July 1918 he was assigned to act as liaison officer to the easternmost attack division. Prior to the battle he observed the thorough preparations on the plain extending east of Reims, and expressed guarded optimism in his private journal. However, on the 15th he was able to witness, at first hand, the bitter defeat of the immensely strong assault mounted by thousands of guns and hundreds of thousands of German soldiers. On 16 July he wrote:

> I have just lived through the most disheartening day of the War. ... The wilderness of chalk is not very big. ... Into this the French deliberately lured us. Our guns bombarded empty trenches; our gas shells gassed empty enemy artillery positions; ... We did not see a single dead Frenchman, let alone a captured gun or machine-gun, and we had suffered heavy losses.

On the 19th he wrote, 'Since our experiences of July 16th I know we are finished.' By the 25th his division had been moved to the west of Reims, where the military chaos continued in the aftermath of the withdrawal from the River Marne and Binding could only lament, 'Today everything seems to be at a standstill. .... The American Army is there – a million strong. That is too much.'

On the other side of Reims, von Boehn's huge Seventh Army, occupying the Aisne salient, had been reinforced and re-organized to achieve success. The three corps in the north-west (commonly named after their commanders, the Generals Francois, Staabs and Watter) had been split off and reformed under a new Ninth Army Headquarters, newly arrived from Romania, so that von Boehn would not have to concern himself about the defence of the 'Soissons Corner'.

The two corps facing directly west (Winckler's and Schoeller's), stationed on either side of the River Ourcq, were to remain on the defensive. Their effective strength was supposed to be made up to 750 men per battalion (from about 450, of which only 250 were combat troops) so they could protect the rear and right flank of Seventh Army. However, given that Ludendorff was already scraping the bottom of the manpower barrel, it is doubtful if enough men were found to achieve a full reinforcement of this quiet sector.

The three corps facing directly south (commanded by the Generals Kathen, Wichura and Conta), were to undertake the difficult crossing of the River Marne and then drive east. Finally Seventh Army had taken over Borne's corps from First Army, so that its two eastern corps (commanded by Schmettow and Borne) could drive south-east down the Montagne de Reims to the river, and then east along the north side of the River Marne to Épernay. To complete the encirclement of Reims, Seventh Army still commanded seven powerful corps, but its tasks had been reduced and focused on the south-east of the salient, where it had trained its troops for weeks to mount a major river assault along almost twenty miles (thirty kilometres) of the River Marne.

The major aim of Operation FRIEDENSTURM was to capture Reims and only incidentally to threaten Paris, but the Germans once again deployed the weapon targeted specifically at Parisian's morale, the 'Paris gun'. Three of these huge 210mm weapons had originally been fired against Paris on 21 March 1918 from the Crépy site in the 'Laon Corner'. The Crépy site lay at the maximum range from Paris of eighty miles (128 kilometres), and the guns suffered from heavy wearing of their barrels. The Germans had then moved them to the new site at Beaumont, west of la Fére, where they had supported the BLÜCHER-YORCK offensives by firing from 27 May to 11 June, but they had remained silent since then. The French had frantically used every possible means to try to locate the exact position of these guns, establishing teams of observers equipped with line of sight and sound-ranging equipment, and hundreds of aircraft had flown missions unceasingly to discover the guns, but without success. Actually, one gun had blown up and the crew of another had been hit by French fire at Crépy, which had caused the Germans to seek a new safer firing position for the remaining third gun.

The surviving 200-tonne monster gun had been re-bored to a 232mm (9.13-inch) calibre. Possession of the Aisne salient now allowed the Germans to bring this terror weapon to within a much more comfortable range of just fifty-seven miles (ninety-two kilometres) from Paris. Significantly, the shorter range also allowed them to reduce the required powder pressure to 42,000 pounds from 58,000 pounds, thereby reducing appreciably the barrel wear. The gun and its ammunition were so heavy that they could only be transported by rail, so a new branch line had been constructed to bring it, in great secrecy, to a superbly camouflaged site in the Bois de Bruyéres, west of Fère-en-Tardenois. A new batch of ammunition had also been specially prepared for the re-bored weapon, which the Germans confidently expected would allow them to fire at least 200 shells from the new location before the barrel would need another re-bore. Due to the anticipated wear on the barrel, each shell was made fractionally larger than the previous one, and the numbered shells had to be fired in strict sequence.

The Germans took enormous pains to protect and camouflage the location of their formidable long-range gun, whose shells rose some twenty-five miles (forty kilometres) into the sky. Its barrel was so long (ninety-two feet or twenty-eight metres) that it required a supporting frame, and always fired at a fixed angle of 45 degrees, range being altered by changing the size of the charge. Numerous anti-aircraft batteries were set up around the site, although care was taken never to fire the 'Paris gun' when enemy aircraft were operating overhead, and a decoy 11-inch gun, also on a railway carriage was installed nearby. In addition, to further confuse the French, a second almost identical site for a 15-inch naval gun mounted on a train carriage, a Max battery, was established in the nearby Bois de Châtelet.

The huge city of Paris was a temptingly large target which lay at the centre of France's vital rail network, as well as the location for many of the most important munitions factories, crucial to the continued prosecution of the war. The long-range shelling was intended to make more than a symbolic attack on the morale of Parisians; it struck at the seat of the enemy's government. Quite intentionally, the relocation to the Bois de Bruyéres was intended to make it easier for the Germans to strike Paris more frequently, and to cause panic in the population.

As on the eastern side of Reims, the attack by Seventh Army was pre-empted by the Allied counter-preparation fire, which opened up just before 1.00am. The French shelling fell on the massed infantry waiting for the signal to attack close to the River Marne, and on Bruchmüller's artillery itself, whose rate of fire suffered somewhat, not only from direct hits, but also from the gunners being gassed. Much of the swift-flowing River Marne lay in a steep valley and was in places almost 200 feet (sixty metres) wide. There was a lack of cover down to the river on the north side of the Marne, with a steep climb up on the south side. The attack by the German infantry carrying temporary bridges and boats was scheduled to start at 4.50am behind a rolling barrage. However, the outnumbered but forewarned Allies were waiting to ambush the Marne river crossing. Many of the massed enemy troops were caught by the Allied artillery shelling, and then the accurate small-arms fire, particularly of the Americans.

Nevertheless, enough of the boats and temporary pontoon bridges survived for the German infantry to force the crossing, but they suffered very heavy casualties. Elements of ten divisions in the three corps eventually managed to establish a bridgehead on the south bank, which was centred on the village of Dormans and extended for some ten miles, but it was barely four miles deep at its greatest penetration. In the south-west, the 36th and 10th Divisions had suffered very heavy losses. The 6th Regiment of Grenadiers was reduced to about 150 men, with the result that the whole 10th Division had to be withdrawn back across the Marne on the evening of the 15th. It had been hoped that 10th Division would complete the occupation of the city of Château-Thierry. However, the American 3rd Division was still on station. The stubborn defence of its 38th and 30th Infantry Regiments held the Germans, but suffered 50 per cent casualties as they defended the Surmelin valley, and also justifiably earned the nickname 'The Rock of the Marne'. The German 36th Division had also suffered very heavy casualties in all three of its regiments, but continued to hold the right flank of the German salient.

The launching of the FRIEDENSTURM offensive certainly did cause immediate panic in Paris, which was exacerbated by shelling from the 'Paris gun' from its new site in the Bois de Bruyéres. However, a heavy Allied presence in the air over the sector prevented the firing of the gun until 1.54pm and then only ten shells could be fired on 15 July. The following day there was even more air activity and just four shells were fired. On the 17th aircraft were overhead almost the whole day, and no firing was possible at all. By the 18th the Allied counter-attack had begun, and this quickly threatened to sever the battery's only exit point, the railway line running through the junction at Soissons. It was left with little option but to pack up its equipment and vacate the site as quickly as possible. The battery was fortunate to be able to get most of the vital equipment out on the railway line before it was closed by enemy fire, and it returned to the Beaumont site where it was set up again by 5 August. The Allies came upon the main firing position on 28 July, as well as the one in the Bois de

Châtelet site, where the hurried departure had left a huge revolving metal base-plate in situ.

While the shelling by the 'Paris gun' undoubtedly increased the short-term panic in Paris the whole expensive and difficult installation of the giant gun in the Bois de Bruyéres had resulted in just fourteen shells being fired. Altogether the three Krupp-made 'Paris guns fired only 367 shells during their existence, and caused fewer than 1,000 civilian casualties (of whom some 250 were killed). The shelling undoubtedly contributed to the sense of gloom, defeat and panic which gripped Paris for more than two months until this was relieved by victory in the Second Battle of the Marne. Ludendorff, like Adolf Hitler decades later, hoped that the use of a 'terror weapon' would achieve political results. Clearly, the 'Paris gun' failed totally to achieve the results anticipated and produced a very poor return for such a huge engineering effort. Indeed, it proved just as ineffective as the three-week long Prussian bombardment of Paris during January 1871, when 12,000 shells killed and wounded just 375 Parisians. However, the long-range artillery bombardment was completely unpredictable, and was probably more frightening than the seventeen air raids against Paris by the German Air Service during 1918, which dropped 615 bombs and caused some 842 casualties.

The heavy casualties inflicted on the Seventh Army troops south of the Marne, as well as the stubborn French-American defence and their fierce counter-attacks, soon made the Germans realize that they were not going to be able to exploit their initial success and maintain their threatening posture south of the Marne. Moreover, their makeshift pontoon bridges suffered continually from heavy Allied air and artillery attacks, which made resupply very difficult. Nevertheless, Ludendorff was reluctant to admit the failure of the great victory that he had promised, and he ordered that the attacks should be continued on the 16th, concentrating on encircling Reims. Third Army had been so badly damaged that it was no longer in a fit condition to attack. However, First Army was once again ordered to commence its attack east of Reims early in the morning of the 16th, but it again failed to make any progress. In the Montagne de Reims area, south-west of Reims, where the two corps of Schmettow and Borne had experienced some success against the Italian II Corps, they were again ordered to attack with the objective of reaching the northern bank of the River Marne.

Despite some limited advances, all these attacks soon began to run out of steam during the morning as fresh French reserves arrived. Finally, at midday on the 16th, a disappointed Ludendorff reluctantly ordered most of the troops to adopt defensive positions. Determined to salvage something positive from his abortive attacks by continuing to threaten a further advance to the Marne, Ludendorff ordered Schmettow's and Borne's troops to continue attacking on the 17th.

Meanwhile French counter-attacks were mounted against the German positions on the 16th and 17th, particularly south of the Marne. East of Reims, Gouraud's forces were actually already able to retake most of their first position on the evening of the 16th. Only in the difficult terrain of the Montagne de Reims were some limited German attacks successful on the 17th, but they were soon halted and counter-attacked. Ludendorff had already ordered that the designated artillery batteries, aircraft and infantry divisions should be despatched for use in Operation HAGEN, which had provisionally been scheduled to start on 20 July. He himself travelled on the 17th to his new headquarters at Tournai, close to Lille, which he planned to use to command the forthcoming battle. In the meantime, a further attack by fresh divisions was planned to drive up the Ardre valley. Ludendorff clung to the hope that by narrowing the focus of the battle to an advance in the Montagne de Reims area he could still capture Épernay and Châlons, thereby finally completing the encirclement of Reims. In any event, unbeknown to Ludendorff, these ambitions were soon to be curtailed by the arrival of the British XXII Corps and fresh French reserves.

Even more dramatically, Ludendorff was to be smartly up-staged by Foch, who launched his own great attack on 18 July, thereby snatching the strategic initiative from him and threatening the whole of the Aisne salient. Actually on the morning of 18 July, Ludendorff was holding a planning conference at Tournai. He had just delivered his opinion, backed up by logical intelligence estimates, that the French were in a weak state and could not possibly launch a new attack, when the news arrived of Mangin's surprise offensive. The astonishing news was that thirteen French and three American divisions, supported by 400 tanks, had launched major attacks which had broken open the German front on the whole western side of the Aisne salient.

Actually General Mangin had been making small-scale attacks in this area for weeks. These limited attacks were designed to keep the Germans off balance and gain advantageous jumping-off points for his forces, without alerting the Germans to their growing danger. As a result the unsuspecting Germans anticipated that small French counter-attacks would continue along a German front line that had actually become compressed. Meanwhile, OHL and Seventh Army had been focusing on the battles around Reims and simply did not expect to be attacked so fiercely on their vulnerable western flank.

An astounded Ludendorff was physically shocked as he realized immediately that this successful attack on his flank threatened not only the precarious German positions south of the Marne, but also his whole strategy. He later admitted that he finished his remarks in a state of great nervousness. That afternoon Ludendorff returned to the OHL headquarters at Avesnes where he had to explain the sharp reversal in fortune to Hindenburg and, more painfully, to the mortified Kaiser. Initially he would deny that he had been surprised by Foch, as he focused on extracting Seventh Army from its trap south of the Marne. However, it soon became clear that not only had the sequence of shattering German attacks against the Allies been brought to a premature end, but the strategic situation had completely changed.

The efficient German staff officers at Ninth Army and OHL quickly despatched reserves to block the French attacks; but, reinforced by the fresh British and American divisions, four French armies continued pressing forward around the German salient, and threatening to cut the main German supply route through Soissons.

At one stroke Ludendorff's strategy was in tatters. He had planned to reach the zenith of his strategic threats by dealing two mighty body blows to the Allies during the month of July. His FRIEDENSTURM attacks should have paralyzed the French, and drawn all their reserves to the Marne area. Had FRIEDENSTURM succeeded, the Germans would have dramatically encircled Reims and seized the entire length of the River Marne from Château Thierry to Châlons. Days later, his great HAGEN attack was intended to break through the weakened British lines to the Channel ports, depriving the British Army of its bases and supplies, leaving it with little alternative to surrender. Instead of being able to savour these great culminating victories, Ludendorff found himself in danger of being encircled on the Marne, and humiliatingly forced to dance to Foch's tune as he had to send his battle reserves scurrying to the threatened fronts. Faced with the undeniable failure of both arms of the FRIEDENSTURM attack, Ludendorff finally agreed to withdraw the beleaguered Seventh Army divisions back across the Marne.

Ludendorff had exhibited enormous self-discipline and tactical genius by withdrawing the German Army to the fortified Hindenburg Line in early 1917. This had protected and economized on his forces, but left the initiative with the enemy. As a result the German Army was forced to defend itself against extremely costly French and British attacks in 1917. Leaving these secure fortified defences in 1918 to engage the Allies in the open and regain the initiative was a huge gamble, which almost succeeded. However, it was not just the failure to persevere with his attacks on the British which doomed him, but the very success of his advance to the River Marne which tempted him to undertake the final two operations (GNEISENAU and FRIEDENSTURM) which seriously weakened his whole army. Dazzled by the success of his third attack, Ludendorff failed to perceive the signs of recovery in the French Army. Furthermore, opting for the ill-prepared GNEISENAU offensive seriously delayed the start date for FRIEDENSTURM, which allowed the Allies to strengthen their defences and contributed to its failure.

General Friedrich von Lossberg was the chief of staff of the German Fourth Army, and considered an expert in defensive warfare. He was sent by Ludendorff to investigate the true situation of the Seventh and Ninth Armies, and he repeatedly recommended withdrawal from the Marne salient to prepared defence lines. Instead Ludendorff prevaricated and continued to throw reserves into desperate attempts to hold the salient to maintain the fiction of success until, finally, ignominious withdrawal became totally unavoidable. As Lossberg later wrote in his memoirs, 'July 18 1918 was the precise turning point in the conduct of the war.'

Hindenburg and Ludendorff continued to fantasize over clever counter-attacks to regain the initiative, but the five spring offensives had drained their reserves; and, having suffered almost one million casualties, the German Army was irretrievably weakened. Particularly as a result of their bloody attacks in June and July, the five armies of the centre section (the Eighteenth, Ninth, Seventh, First and Third) of the German line had sustained heavy casualties and were drained of supplies and manpower. Furthermore, the previous successes had left the German Army with far longer and less well fortified lines to defend.

Foch then inflicted a rapid series of body blows on an overstretched and weakened enemy, which never allowed the Germans time to recover. The full extent of the German weakness in its men, morale and supplies was to be amply demonstrated by the succession of defeats which began with the Amiens attack of 8 August. On the first day of this battle alone, the 'Black Day', the British attack virtually destroyed the German Second Army. Supported by the French First and Third Armies, this attack took back the southern end of the Somme salient and recaptured Montdidier. Eventually the Germans were thought to have suffered some 70,000 casualties. During August and September the Allies inflicted further defeats, as they recaptured the Somme, Aisne and St Mihiel salients, and pierced the Hindenburg Line. By launching his great counter-attack on 18 July, Foch signalled that the Allies had regained their battle strength along with the strategic initiative and demonstrated the value of being strengthened by the addition of 1,000,000 fresh American troops.

The formation of IX Corps and the training of Generals

In the course of two centuries of exercising colonial power, the British had gradually acquired the art of controlling a widespread empire using only a very small professional army, supported by a superlative navy. As such, their officers were used to conducting substantial campaigns in faraway places with comparatively small forces of infantry and cavalry arrayed against often huge numbers of native forces. British officers were expected to be resourceful and were well-acquainted with using their initiative. Indeed they were forced to, as they met the requirements of a parsimonious government, equipped only with relatively limited numbers of troops to set against huge masses of enemy forces. However, the second South African, or Boer, War (1899-1902), had revealed many weaknesses of organization and equipment as it pitted a comparatively large and professional British Army (supplemented by Militia and Yeomanry reserves) against the fast-moving superb light cavalry of Afrikaans farmers. The Boer War was therefore extremely useful in forcing the British Army to bring its organization, weapons and tactics up to date at the beginning of the twentieth century. In particular the standard of musketry, the mobility of artillery and the provision of logistical and medical services were much improved.

Although considerable numbers of British (and empire) troops were sent to South Africa and benefited from the campaigning experience, they rarely met large numbers of enemy soldiers in formal battle. Therefore the British were still not greatly adept at marshalling their forces to meet superior numbers of organized enemy as, in the autumn of 1914, the five divisions of Regular Army soldiers and reservists of the British Expeditionary Force (BEF) arrived in France. There this 'contemptible little army' (as the Kaiser dismissively named the small army of his cousin, King George V) found itself ranged against the 130 well-drilled infantry divisions, and eleven cavalry divisions of the German Army. Under successive Chiefs of Staff, Germany had planned for years to deliver a massive knockout blow against France within weeks of starting the war, by quickly invading Belgium and France with seven huge armies.

On the right of the advancing German forces was the largest, General von Kluck's First Army, comprising nineteen divisions heading for Paris. Initially von Kluck had seven infantry and two cavalry corps under command, each of which was fully capable of fighting a separate battle. Fortunately, as the First Army advanced through Belgium and France, it was reduced by two infantry corps (left behind or sent to East Prussia); otherwise von Kluck might have utterly annihilated the BEF on first contact.

Despite these reductions, the formidable German First Army still mustered ten infantry and five cavalry divisions, and its artillery heavily outgunned the British artillery as it arrived at Mons, and forced Sir John French's outnumbered BEF to withdraw. During the subsequent 'Retreat from Mons', it split into two corps columns and managed to stay just ahead of von Kluck's columns. The British and German troops got up early each morning and covered an average of twenty miles a day as they kept marching south. The danger of stopping to give battle (other than by delaying rearguards) against such large forces was demonstrated all too clearly at the Battle of le Cateau, which was forced on II Corps by the exhaustion of its troops. Le Cateau plainly revealed the lack of planning and control exercised by General Smith-Dorrien and his very small corps staff, and almost resulted in a complete disaster. However, despite suffering heavy casualties, the bulk of II Corps managed to march away, and then made even more strenuous efforts to stay clear of the pursuing Germans. Although the Expeditionary Force was organized into two corps (with a separate cavalry division) soon after it landed in France, it had never really exercised in this formation before. Thus the early battles of the First World War were to provide a dramatic learning experience for the senior British commanders and their staff. This 'on-the-job' training was largely in the school of adversity, and inevitably the price of this education was paid for by the frontline officers and soldiers. As Marshal Foch observed caustically, 'It takes 15,000 casualties to train a major general.' This lack of command skills applied even to those officers who had attended the British Army's small Staff College at Camberley.

British military thinking had, for many years, emphasized that in large-scale operations, the division was the main fighting formation of the British Army. A British infantry division comprised three brigades, and was designed to be a sufficiently large force to be capable of acting as an independent entity, and able to conduct a significant battle in a relatively large area. In modern parlance it was organized to comprise a mixture of manoeuvre elements, i.e. infantry and cavalry, together with force multipliers such as artillery and field engineers. However, most of the British army was stationed around the empire in small out stations, leaving only a few divisions in the United Kingdom, and they rarely had the opportunity to exercise together. Only Salisbury Plain, in the south of England, offered sufficient space for large numbers of troops to be exercised. Thus the annual pre-war summer exercises, which might involve one division being pitched against another, resulted in much marching by the infantry, but were often little more than social events for the senior commanders. Serious soldiering took place on the troubled borders of the empire, with comparatively small numbers of troops; and there was very little opportunity to develop experience and a military doctrine around the infantry corps level of command.

Napoleon had developed the corps level of command to manage his army as it ranged widely across Europe. It is a fundamental rule of war that one should never divide one's forces in the face of the enemy. However, Napoleon demonstrated repeatedly how he could outmanoeuvre his enemies, by relying on his marshals to move their corps along separate parallel routes and then combine them at the critical moment for decisive effect in battle. To this corps organization was linked the system of command using staff officers, which had been developed by Berthier in Italy, and then espoused by Napoleon. The emperor relied on Marshal Berthier as his principal staff officer in most of his successful campaigns (but Berthier died mysteriously just before Waterloo, and his organizational skills were sorely missed by Napoleon). The corps concept spread to most European powers, who fielded large unwieldy conscript armies and was particularly embraced by the Prussian army, where a powerful central general staff concept was also developed.

A British corps was organized in South Africa, and afterwards a skeleton I Army Corps was established in Aldershot. It was commanded by Lieutenant General Sir John French, who had commanded a cavalry division in the Boer War. However, exercises were usually conducted at divisional or lower level and there is no evidence that General French had any opportunity to practise or understand the difficulties of corps management, or for his limited staff to practise the complex tasks of managing orders, information flows and resources.

As they moved to France in 1914 British infantry divisions normally comprised three infantry brigades, each of four 1,000-man battalions, with three or four supporting battalion-sized units of artillery (confusingly named artillery brigades). A full division numbered some 17,000-20,000 men and had its own engineer and signals troops, as well as sufficient logistic and medical units necessary to be self-sustaining. Two to six divisions were normally grouped into a corps, and two or more corps formed an army. As most major decisions were taken by the army commander, there was usually very little for the corps headquarters to do, other than break down the commander's plan to divisional level, and it often seemed to act as little more than a post office between the army commander and its divisions. This continued to be true even when the opening phase, the war of movement, ended and the troops settled into the relatively static lines of trenches.

By 1918 things were very different. The British had several million men and some sixty infantry divisions in France (as well as other divisions campaigning in Italy, the Balkans and Palestine). In France they were organized into five armies and more than twenty corps. Although the imperial divisions from Australia, New Zealand, South Africa and Canada had maintained their full divisional strength, with some changes, the brigades of the British infantry divisions had been reduced to three battalions, which in any case, due to the heavy casualties and shortage of reinforcements, often had fewer than 750 fighting men. While divisional strength had fallen by around 5,000 men, its tactical firepower had been increased enormously. Each division now had its own battalion of sixty-four Vickers heavy machine guns, three batteries of light mortars, and its infantry were equipped with almost 400 Lewis medium machine guns. In addition, there had been a huge increase in fire support available from the phenomenal increase in the numbers of medium and heavy artillery units, held mostly at corps and army level.

By 1918 the Royal Artillery comprised almost a quarter of the British army, and in that year alone the British manufactured 10,680 heavy guns. The constant turnover of manpower and the implementation of new war technology, such as improved artillery, mortars, tanks and machine guns, had turned the BEF into a giant teaching as well as fighting organization. Basic infantry training was undertaken in England, but each of the British armies in France had well-established training and battle schools, which ensured that the latest tactical knowledge in the use and deployment of the new weapons such as gas, machine guns and mortars, or signalling and patrolling techniques were rapidly disseminated to the combat troops. The value of training in reducing casualties and ensuring success was so well understood that, in addition, every division and brigade had established its own training structure and war schools. Large numbers of officers and men were sent out of the line, whenever they could be spared, to attend a multitude of training courses.

It had also taken several years of bitter fighting and failure to build up the necessary competence amongst generals and staff officers to convert the British corps and divisions into battle-winning formations that were able to meet and overcome the well-organized and highly experienced German army which had, in turn, expanded to some 250 divisions. The initial lack of training and new thinking was all too obvious when, in July 1916, the British fielded a confident army of new divisions formed mainly from volunteers. Its heavily-encumbered infantry had been trained to advance steadily in well-drilled waves, after days of artillery bombardment, but on the first day of the Somme battles they were cut down unmercifully. Eventually the British gained perhaps seven miles (eleven kilometres) of territory in five months of waging the Battle of the Somme, at a cost of 420,000 casualties while the French suffered another 204,000.

Already by the spring of 1917, after absorbing the bitter lessons of the Somme battles, growing British competence in the organization of its artillery and training of its infantry was becoming steadily apparent. This was clearly demonstrated by the brilliantly successful attack of General Byng's Canadian Corps at Vimy Ridge on 9 April. Total casualties were some 10,000, which, while a heavy cost for taking this key feature, represented less than a 7 per cent casualty rate. By comparison, the French army had suffered some 150,000 casualties in 1915, attempting to take this same, virtually impregnable hill position. This increasing competence was further evidenced by Plumer's overwhelmingly successful attack on the Messines Ridge on 7 June, and his first three model attacks at Passchendaele in the autumn of 1917 (see page 50). However, not all British generals and staff officers had become as competent and economical with their men's lives, and the ensuing Passchendaele bloodbath in the late autumn of 1917 severely weakened the British Army.

IX Corps had originally been formed in England in 1915 to command additional reinforcements for the Gallipoli campaign. It was given six Territorial and New Army divisions to make a fresh decisive landing at

Suvla Bay against the Turkish defenders of the high ground at Gallipoli. Overall command of the British land forces at Gallipoli rested with General Sir Ian Hamilton, who commanded a mixed force of British infantry, Royal Marines, Australian and New Zealand troops (ANZAC), and some French colonial troops. The original invasion force had proved inadequate to the task of making significant territorial advances in the difficult terrain, and in the time-honoured tradition of the military, the commanders called for more troops, while the various British and ANZAC units already ashore were formed into a new VIII Corps.

These additional six divisions formed into IX Corps were under the command of Lieutenant General Sir Frederick Stopford. However, the organizational difficulties of landing troops direct from the sea in the face of a determined enemy was hardly understood in 1915. Stopford's poor handling of IX Corps during the August offensive at Gallipoli led to terrible casualties, with no tangible success, and his sacking after only nine days. Eventually he was replaced by Lieutenant General Julian Byng. The failure of even these additional six divisions, comprising over 80,000 men, to change the untenable situation on the inhospitable rocky terrain at Gallipoli eventually led to the decision to evacuate the peninsula, and Byng oversaw the successful withdrawal of IX Corps from Suvla Bay in December 1915. Many military reputations were destroyed at Gallipoli, including that of senior staff officers such as Generals Braithwaite and Reed, who later commanded divisions in the Champagne campaign.

Initially IX Corps was evacuated to Egypt but moved to France in the summer of 1916. There it was commanded by the lugubrious Lieutenant General Alexander Hamilton-Gordon, until he was relieved in 1918. Its first serious engagement was at Messines in June 1917, and it went on to fight in the Third Battle of Ypres. Then the corps headquarters was withdrawn into reserve without its constituent divisions. Following the German Somme offensive in March 1918, the corps headquarters was sent north to command new convalescent divisions in a quiet sector, and thus arrived at precisely the right moment to play an unexpectedly large role in the defence of the Lys valley, particularly the Kemmel Ridge. Very heavy casualties were incurred in the Lys battles, before IX Corps was sent to recover and rebuild its strength in yet another quiet sector, namely the French Army's Champagne front. This had been the scene of bloody battles in 1917 when General Nivelle's abortive spring offensive had resulted in such horrendous casualties that the French Army was brought to the edge of mutiny. After careful handling by

General Pétain some limited successes were achieved, and the soldiers on the Chemin des Dames front had settled down into a relatively quiet co-existence with the 'Boche'.

Many of the British Territorial Force and New Army divisions were recruited on a regional basis, whenever possible, and this was generally thought to have developed a sense of identity and cohesion of individual divisions. However, no such policy was followed with the British infantry corps. The corps organization would comprise a headquarters with its own communications units, controlling assets such as heavy artillery batteries and specialist engineer units. It would then be allocated infantry divisions as they became available, and it is difficult to identify any organizational logic in most of the corps groupings. It was well understood that there were differences between the fighting ability of different divisions, which was connected with their battle experience, composition and the development of a divisional ethos. However, there was a failure by senior officers to recognize the advantages of ensuring that corps and divisional staffs developed a level of expertise and professionalism which came from continuously working together within the same structure. It could be argued that, in the comparatively static conditions of trench warfare, there was sometimes a definite advantage in positioning a corps in a fixed geographical area, which the corps staff officers got to know well, and then rotating fresh divisions through it for operations.

There was some training for junior staff officers but very little for senior officers while corps commanders were chosen personally by the commander-in-chief, Haig. All too often, each corps worked in its own way, procedures being dictated by the whim of the corps commander, or his senior staff officers. Important battle preparations, such as the liaison between infantry, artillery, engineers and the air arm, rehearsals of movement in the attack and defence, were often treated quite differently in each corps, and could dramatically affect the outcome of an action. The clear exceptions were the Australian and Canadian corps, whose tough divisions trained, rehearsed and fought together. The advantages of this continuity, joined with thorough planning and preparation were exemplified, as mentioned, by General Byng's Canadian Corps at Vimy Ridge, and by General Monash's Australian Corps. Monash demonstrated frequently how success and low casualties could be achieved, by thorough planning and rehearsal as typified by the Australian-American 'stunt' at Hamel on 4 July 1918 (see page 93–6).

The painstaking preparation of the infantry and artillery for the Hamel operation was used as a model for the great British breakthrough attacks which followed swiftly in August and September of 1918. It is interesting to note, in the context of this history, that in September 1918, command of IX Corps passed to Lieutenant General Sir Walter Braithwaite, who had commanded 62nd Division in XXII Corps during the tough fighting in the Ardre valley. Braithwaite, who had been sent home with Stopford and Hamilton from Gallipoli in 1915, had re-established his reputation through his steady command of 62nd Division, and went on to lead IX Corps in the successful battles of the Hindenburg Line. In particular it was IX Corps, which commanded the dramatic crossing of the St Quentin Canal by its 46th (North Midland) Division on the morning of 29 September 1918. The crossing of this key feature, a deep canal obstacle and tunnels on which the Germans had lavished years of engineering effort to improve its defensive capabilities, was accomplished by the 46th Division in just a few hours. It not only crossed the canal and captured the defensive tunnels, but within three days had taken 4,000 prisoners and seventy guns. This dramatic feat of arms alongside the American II Corps, with its 27th and 30th Infantry Divisions pierced the impregnable German 'Siegfried' defences and opened the Bellenglise tunnels. Supported by the Australian Corps led by its 5th Division, the towns of Bellicourt and Nauroy were quickly captured and Fourth British Army was able to break through to the third and final Hindenburg system. When this was breached a few days later the whole German front had to pull back, and victory became certain. Braithwaite continued to command IX Corps successfully during the final advance in Picardy, which steadily pushed the Germans back to the Belgian border.

After landing in France in July 1914, the BEF had been organized into two distinct corps, but these corps were not well-organized to act as separate fighting organizations. Initially a British corps headquarters commanded just two divisions using a small staff of eighteen officers and about seventy soldiers, mostly line signalmen to maintain communications, together with cooks, clerks, drivers and orderlies. Only gradually did it become apparent that a corps headquarters could be both a planning and a command organization. While the day-to-day battles were fought by the divisions, the corps commander and his staff officers needed to concern themselves with the overall development of the battle, and events some twenty-four or forty-eight hours ahead, or sometimes longer. As such they needed to anticipate the enemy's attacks, or reaction to the British attacks, and plan to counter this by organizing the infantry divisions and the corps' assets, particularly its heavy artillery and engineer units. Those corps staffs that understood the problems of the fighting men, and were able to plan and rehearse well, generally experienced greater success than those corps that added little to the passing on of orders from army level.

Progressively the British corps staff grew in size as the headquarters acquired further assets and responsibilities. By 1918, the typical headquarters had grown to some fifty officers and 141 other ranks. Often the corps had a designated signals company and was assigned additional engineer units for tasks such as mining, bridging or road maintenance. It also had a reconnaissance element made up of a mounted cavalry regiment and a bicycle battalion. The cyclists were often used to improve the communications within the corps by carrying messages, marking routes or burying telephone cables more deeply in the ground. The corps would also have its own heavy artillery, usually comprising batteries of 60-pounder guns and 9.2-inch howitzers, as well as a heavy trench mortar battery and an air wing to help with reconnaissance and targeting. The senior artillery officer in the corps, a brigadier general (CCRA, or Corps Commander Royal Artillery), could take command of all its guns for use on specific targets or for specified purposes, such as counter-battery fire or a combined creeping barrage. Often, for a set-piece attack, artillery staff would produce printed maps which detailed the targets and fire missions to be completed by all the corps and divisional artillery during each stage of the battle. However, this tight control could mean a reduction in the ability of the gunners to respond to opportunity targets. In addition the corps would often have its own motor transport column to move the heavy ammunition, and associated maintenance facilities. As a result this could involve the corps headquarters in directly commanding a total of over 2,000 men.

Having served in General Plumer's Second Army for over a year, the staff officers of IX Corps were uniquely experienced by the spring of 1918. One of its most experienced officers was also actually one of the most junior officers on the corps staff. This was the General Staff Officer Class 2 responsible for planning and conducting military operations, GSO 2 (Operations), namely Captain Bernard Montgomery DSO. His extremely responsible post within the corps headquarters was normally held by an experienced and staff-trained major. In fact the other two GSO 2s were majors, but Montgomery, although holding the senior post, had not attended Staff College. He was just 29-years old and had been a captain for three years. He had experienced a pre-war career as a fairly ordinary regimental officer; however, his development as a staff officer in wartime was to endow him with a quite extraordinary range of experience.

After graduating from the Royal Military College at Sandhurst, Bernard Montgomery had joined the 1st Battalion of the Royal Warwickshire Regiment on the North-West Frontier in India in December 1908. Then as now, a century later, this notorious border area required frequent military patrolling to keep the warlike tribesmen and bandits under control. In addition to being a platoon commander, Bernard enjoyed other roles such as battalion sports officer, scout training officer, and served as temporary regimental quartermaster for a year. The battalion returned to the UK in 1913 and was based at Shorncliffe in Kent. After mobilization in 1914 it was used for home defence and Bernard served as adjutant. The battalion crossed the Channel to France on 23 August 1914, and joined the BEF in the retreat from Mons. It arrived just in time to take part in a badly organized attack at le Cateau, which shattered the battalion, leaving the split-up survivors to retreat as best they could. The battalion lost eight officers at le Cateau, and Lieutenant Bernard Montgomery was appointed a company commander as a temporary captain. After its harrowing retreat, the BEF then began to advance again on 5 September, arriving at the Aisne river front close to the Chemin des Dames on 13 September. There it found the Germans were already well dug-in on the high ground, where they resisted all British attempts to shift them.

On 10 October 1914, the 1st Royal Warwicks moved, with the whole BEF, from the Champagne to the Ypres area, near the Belgian border. The arrival of relief officers meant that Montgomery was soon reduced to being a platoon commander again. Within three days Lieutenant Montgomery led a bayonet charge at Meteren, during which he was wounded several times in the chest and knee and lay in the mud under sniper fire for four hours before being brought in. While recovering from his severe wounds in England, he was promoted to captain and awarded the Distinguished Service Order (DSO). Montgomery was keen to return to duty and was now regarded as a relatively experienced officer in a rapidly expanding army. After recovering he was posted on 12 February 1915 to be brigade major, the senior staff officer and brigade commander's right-hand man, of a newly formed brigade, 112 Infantry Brigade at Manchester, although he remained a captain. The brigade was soon broken up to provide reinforcements and was then reformed to become 104 Brigade of 35th Division, a 'Bantam' division, i.e. a division where all the men were below average height (5 feet 3 inches). In January 1916 it embarked for France.

Montgomery served as Brigade Major under two brigade commanders, the second being Brigadier General Sandilands, a 40-year-old Cameron Highlander, who took over from the much older Brigadier General Mackenzie in April 1916. Montgomery later acknowledged that he learnt a great many important lessons from Sandilands, particularly the need for co-ordination with the engineers and artillery, and the value of issuing clear orders. Sandilands was clearly a very competent young brigade commander, but was somewhat outspoken and was never promoted again, although his brigade was involved in much serious fighting throughout the rest of the war.

In January 1917, after almost two years as Brigade Major of 104 Brigade, Captain Montgomery was moved to the staff of 33rd Division. There, as GSO 2, he worked very closely with the GSO 1 (a lieutenant colonel), issuing orders for operations, that is battle orders, and training, including visiting the forward units in the trenches on a daily basis to check conditions. He attended a short locally-organized staff course and returned in time to be involved with his division in the Battle of Arras. This attack, which began on 9 April against the deep defences of the Hindenburg Line, came just two days after the United States entered the war. The 33rd Division was designated as a reserve division to exploit the success of the opening attacks. However, general progress was very limited, and the 33rd was moved to VII Corps to join the attack on 23 April. Despite the bravery of the soldiers (when the soldiers of the 1st Queen's Regiment found the enemy barbed wire intact, they famously contemptuously trampled it down with their feet), they were overcome by German counter-attacks, although 33rd Division achieved an advance of one mile at the cost of some 3,000 casualties.

On 6 July 1917 Captain Bernard Montgomery was promoted from GSO 2 of 33rd Division to the post of GSO 2 (Operations) of IX Corps, part of General Plumer's Second Army. Herbert Plumer was a 60-year-old general and with his white hair, white moustache and ruddy complexion looked like a caricature 'blimp'. However, Plumer was a wily bird, with vast military experience from his campaigning as an infantry officer in the Sudan, Matabeleland, and South Africa. He had spent two years commanding in the Ypres sector and had already established a reputation for being careful with his men's lives and planning every attack meticulously. At the beginning of

June 1917 Plumer's army was exhibiting obvious signs of launching a major infantry attack. It had begun a build-up of stores, reserves, and an artillery bombardment which went on for several weeks. The Germans had no difficulty reading these signs and had readied their own artillery and reserves to swamp the impending attack.

For the Allies in France, there were two overwhelming problems when seeking to eject the German army from France. Even before the war started, the German army reflected many of the virtues of the most populous and industrious country in Europe. It was a very large well-trained organization, whose units possessed a strong military and regional identity, and whose conscripted soldiers took naturally to their two years of military service, followed by many years on reserve. Its disciplined infantry were equipped with large numbers of machine guns, and were trained to entrench themselves quickly. It had abundant horse-drawn field artillery, but, following on from its experience in the Franco-Prussian War, it also made sure that it had large numbers of heavy large-calibre guns, which the British and the French lacked at the start of the war. These heavy guns had been acquired in preparation for reducing the fortresses which sealed Germany off from Belgium and France. However, they also gave them a real advantage in the siege conditions of trench warfare. Moreover, as this well-equipped army withdrew from its failed offensive on the River Marne in September 1914, it had chosen to occupy and dig in on the high ground and ridges facing largely south or west. This high ground was often shielded by river lines and allowed the Germans to observe all of the Allies' attack preparations, as well as providing excellent defensive features.

In addition to these natural advantages for the defence, the dutiful German officers and soldiers, would, whenever they lost ground, immediately, as a doctrinal imperative, launch a counter-attack. Invariably, this enabled the Germans to retake quickly their former position, from the few exhausted survivors of the attack. The British and French soldiers who had struggled bravely uphill though the murderous German machine-gun and artillery fire would, all too often, find themselves out of range of their support artillery, and occupying enemy trenches which faced the wrong way. Therefore they were vulnerable and could be overwhelmed easily by the German infantry counter-attacking, supported by heavy artillery fire. The result was all too frequently a failure to hold the dearly-won position, which invariably cost the Allies very high casualties for little eventual gain.

A clear example of these usually successful German tactics was demonstrated in the first serious attack mounted by the American Expeditionary Force (AEF) in the war. At 6.45am on 28 May 1918, the 28th Infantry Regiment of the 1st Infantry Division launched an attack to take the village of Cantigny and its observation point on the high ground that overlooked the Allied front. Cantigny lay some seventy miles (about 115 kilometres) north of Paris. It was strongly fortified and had a commanding position over the rolling countryside, just three miles to the east of Montdidier. The American attack had been minutely planned by the divisional operations officer, Major George C. Marshall Jr, and was supported by its own divisional field artillery, as well as by twelve French Schneider tanks, French flame-thrower teams, and more than a dozen batteries of French heavy guns. The attack took the defenders of the German 82nd Reserve Division by complete surprise, and the Americans rapidly occupied their objectives with minimal casualties and captured over 200 prisoners. Anticipating a counter-attack, the Americans then quickly established three strongpoints and strung barbed-wire barriers on their new front line.

Unfortunately, the timing of the American action coincided with the overwhelming attack by the Germans on the Chemin des Dames, and much of the supporting French artillery was soon withdrawn to counter that threat. In any event, the Germans had already decided to give the Americans a thorough pasting whenever their troops first appeared in battle, and their artillery kept up a constant barrage throughout 28th May and the two following days. In addition, the Germans launched seven counter-attacks. Some were locally organized impromptu attacks in company strength, which were easily repelled. However, at least three were regimental attacks, supported by artillery, with infantry waves in battalion strength following closely behind the barrage. Only when the seventh and final counter-attack was repelled on the morning of 30 May did the Germans appear to accept the loss of Cantigny. The German artillery had pounded the Americans throughout the three days and total casualties eventually totalled some 1,603 men of whom 199 were killed. The old, but extremely vigorous, Prime Minister Clemenceau visited the Americans to congratulate them, and the 28th Infantry Regiment, under Colonel Hanson Ely, was awarded the Croix de Guerre and the nickname 'Lions of Cantigny' for its exploit.

However, in June 1917, the cunning British General Plumer was only too well aware of the difficulties involved in attacking the high ground held by the Germans, and their propensity to counter-attack, and he had therefore prepared accordingly. Usually he eschewed relying on a long preliminary bombardment, because he believed this gave the Germans certain warning of an impending attack. Plumer's preference was for surprise assaults supported by heavy creeping barrages in multiple lines, which provided cover for his advancing infantry, and he also usually ordered preparatory counter-battery fire against the German artillery and reserves who usually occupied the rear of the German positions. In addition, he believed it was essential to have fresh reinforcements ready to follow on and support his original assault troops, who had been specifically trained to consolidate as soon as they had taken their objectives, and prepare to defeat the inevitable counter-attack. Thus for his attack on the German salient on the high ground of the Messines Ridge he had readied nine attack and three reserve divisions, under the command of three corps headquarters, IX Corps, X Corps, and II ANZAC Corps of General Godley. These corps assembled to attack on a ten-mile-wide front, but, in a typical Plumer 'bite and hold' operation, they were ordered to remain within range of covering artillery fire, and thus advance only to a depth of just two miles.

It was therefore a distinct departure from Plumer's normal practice to commence with a very heavy artillery bombardment by some 2,300 guns and 300 heavy mortars on 21 May; his preliminary bombardment actually began on 8 May. The bombardment lasted for almost three weeks and included knocking out most of the key German defensive positions sited in the stone village of Wijtschate and the mill at Spanbroekmolen. It was said that 90 per cent of the German field-gun positions on the Messines Ridge were destroyed by this devastating bombardment of over 3,500,000 shells. As mentioned, the Germans naturally observed this well-signalled attack and disposed their frontline soldiers in deep shelters while readying reserves for the counter-attack close behind the front line. As soon as the bombardment ceased, at 2.50am on 7 June, the concealed German troops rushed up from their deep bunkers and ran forward to man their weapons in the main defence positions.

However, General Plumer had planned a special surprise to make up for his all too obvious preliminary bombardment. Since the beginning of January 1916 (some eighteen months earlier) his engineers and tunnellers had been busy digging by hand, twenty-two deep saps under the German positions. These had been filled with 1,000,000 pounds (450,000 kilos) of ammonal explosive. At 3.10am, after twenty minutes of total silence, nineteen of these mines were blown in a ripple explosion which caused virtual earthquake conditions. The noise of these huge explosions was deafening and so loud that it was heard in London. Many of the German main defensive positions were totally annihilated, and it was estimated that some 10,000 soldiers were killed outright. The nine attacking divisions then moved forward against the dazed German survivors, under carefully-phased standing and creeping barrages and the covering fire of 700 heavy machine guns. In addition some 1,500 oil bombs were fired by Livens Projectors.

There was still some very tough fighting, particularly in the village of Messines, which was captured by the New Zealand Division, but all of Plumer's divisions were able to reach their initial objectives by 8.00am. Forty batteries of artillery were then brought forward to support the next phase of the attack by the follow-on divisions. As the troops consolidated on their new positions, German counter-attacks supported by heavy artillery bombardment began in the afternoon. These attacks continued for some days, but all were repelled, and the whole salient was retained, as well as some 7,000 prisoners. Subsidiary attacks by the British Fifth Army and the French First Army were equally successful. The German defence was thrown into disarray, and although Plumer's men had suffered some 24,000 casualties, particularly the New Zealanders, who suffered almost 5,000 casualties, the Germans were estimated to have lost at least 25,000 men and were considering retiring. However, Field Marshal Haig, the British commander-in-chief, refused to accept Plumer's plans for a further advance and handed over the Third Battle of Ypres to General Gough and his Fifth Army. Gough was a much younger general, and a cavalryman, and Haig considered him more of a 'thruster' than the phlegmatic Plumer.

This change of plans involved building communications and supply roads, as well as building ammunition stocks and there was a delay of more than a month before Haig's huge Ypres offensive, under the command of Gough, started. However, it began to fail under the heaviest August rain seen for almost thirty years. Meanwhile, the Germans had reacted to the British tactics by leaving their front line relatively thinly-manned and massing their reserves farther back where Gough's artillery bombardments failed to damage them. The consequent failure of Gough's offensive forced Haig to hand over command once again to Plumer's Second Army. Plumer immediately ordered a three-week pause in the offensive so that the troops, including IX Corps, could be properly prepared. Captain Montgomery was then responsible for issuing all the orders and training programmes for the subsequent three model attacks by IX Corps. His instructions ran to some hundred pages plus twelve pages of maps. It included the arrangements for the creeping barrage, the leapfrogging of fresh reserves through the advancing troops (known later as the 'expanding torrent'), and communications, as well as instructions for training and dress rehearsals. The attacks in September and early October 1917, which followed these careful preparations, were very successful and established British possession of the ridge east of Ypres. As the young Captain Montgomery wrote to his father, Bishop Montgomery, on 9 October:

> Things are going very well here and we are entirely successful every time we attack .... The attacks delivered on 20th Sept [Polygon Wood], 26th Sept [Menin Road], 4th Oct [Broodseinde], and today are really masterpieces and could not have been better.

Captain Montgomery undoubtedly enhanced his reputation as he discharged his key responsibilities for issuing all the IX Corps operational orders. Naturally Montgomery's orders reflected the Plumer Doctrine for dealing with the strong defence capabilities of the Germans. It not only included constantly feeding forward fresh troop reinforcements, but also taking up strong defensive positions on the objective, supported by artillery, ready to receive and destroy the inevitable German counter-attacks. Without doubt, this intimate experience of planning Plumer's successful 'bite and hold' tactics had a huge influence on Captain Montgomery's military thinking. It taught him the value of ensuring troops were properly trained and rehearsed for the tasks expected of them and that there were fresh troops continually available to pass through the advancing front line thereby maintaining momentum. Most essential of all, he ensured they were supported by adequate artillery. Montgomery had learnt to never underestimate the Germans, but undoubtedly his later reputation as Britain's most successful general in the Second World War, owed much to his careful planning and husbanding of his resources to ensure that lives were not wasted and to his habit of constantly creating fresh reserves to give himself tactical flexibility.

Weather conditions deteriorated, and after Plumer's three successes, Haig insisted on continuing with the offensives in appalling weather. The patient British infantry then plodded gamely forward through thick mud and rain-filled shell holes to face a prepared German defence, which included extra machine-gun bunkers and five lines of reserve trenches. In fairness to Haig, he was very aware that the other Allies were suffering very badly from their own losses, and he hoped his attacks would divert attention from weaknesses in the French and Italian armies, and make possible a breakthrough to the U-Boat pens at the Belgian ports. Equally it seems that the last Plumer offensive was not prepared with the same thoroughness or knowledge of actual conditions. As a result, the attacks, which went on in the mud, rain and misery of the Flanders marshes caused huge casualties to both sides, but particularly to the British and Canadian forces, including the single New Zealand division which suffered at least 3,500 casualties in the hopeless badly prepared attack on the Bellevue Spur on 12 October 1917. Total battle casualties were later variously estimated to be at least 250,000 on each side but possibly were as high as 400,000. At last Haig closed the offensive down on 10 November, after the final glorious attack by the Canadian Corps, which captured the town of Passchendaele and the high ground to its north.

The prolonged Battle of Passchendaele, despite eventual British successes in appalling weather against a determined enemy, then passed, somewhat unfairly, into British folklore as an example of poor generalship, and the senseless waste of lives in attritional trench warfare. Few observers comprehended that the battle had been at least just as punishing for the Germans, who had also suffered severely as they had been driven back from the commanding high ground. Moreover, the long defensive battle and suffering of the German soldiers convinced their leaders that it was vital for them to pre-empt further costly British attacks. Only by launching their own offensive could they seize the strategic initiative and have some hope of achieving a decisive advantage in exchange for all their losses. Ludendorff was thus led to plan his gamble of great spring attacks, which almost succeeded, but eventually led to comprehensive defeat.

On 30 January 1918 the constituent divisions of IX Corps were withdrawn into Army Reserve and IX Corps Headquarters moved to the British Fifth Army, holding the southern end of the extended line, which the British had recently taken over from the French, around the Somme river. There the corps headquarters staff studied the problems of defence and supporting the French Army should it be attacked. However, it was the British who were taken by surprise, when three reinforced German armies, comprising a total of ninety-three divisions, stormed forward on 21 March 1918. It was very different from a careful Plumer attack. Using storm-trooper infiltration tactics, preceded by an intense but short artillery barrage along a forty-five-mile front, they quickly pushed the Fifth Army and part of the Third Army back some twenty-five miles. IX Corps Headquarters was moved forward to Montdidier, and then on 25 March was ordered to lay out a new defensive line, the GHQ Line, some fifty miles in rear of the old front line. Despite prodigious efforts by the Germans to break through to Amiens, the British and French defenders eventually managed to seal the breach, and by 5 April the Germans had to admit the failure of their offensive. On 3 April IX Corps, with new divisions under command, moved back north to the quiescent Second Army sector where it relieved the Australian Corps.

The move back under command of Second Army was completed just in time to receive the second of the great German attacks, which began 100 miles farther north of the Somme battle, in the Lys valley on 9 April. For the Battle of the Lys the two attacking German armies, did not enjoy the same overwhelming force advantage as in the earlier Battle of the Somme, having only some forty-five divisions available, many of which had come up from the Somme. However, their attack struck a weak point, namely the two Portuguese divisions at Neuve Chappelle. These divisions formed a small Portuguese corps, which had been sent by Portugal, in an entirely voluntary gesture, to aid the Allied effort. Sadly, the Portuguese Corps suffered from a lack of home support, and the soldiers were in a weakened state, which was clearly apparent to the Germans. Once again the Germans took advantage of the heavy fog, which was intensified by a bombardment with gas shells. The Germans made significant advances in the first few days, and when Foch initially refused to send reserves to help the British, Haig was reduced to issuing his famous 'backs to the wall' message of encouragement to his troops. IX Corps, with six divisions under command, was directly involved in defending the key Kemmel Ridge feature overlooking the Lys valley. Captain Montgomery was once again responsible for issuing all the corps' operational orders throughout this intensive defensive battle, lasting some ten days, during which the British Army was pushed back some five miles.

As IX Corps successfully defended the Mont Kemmel Ridge, against strenuous German attacks, its six divisions paid a high price, and the corps suffered some 27,000 casualties in the ten days of this battle. Desperately, Haig had requested French reserves to come to his aid, but Foch feared that the attack was just a German ploy to draw away reserves before a major attack was launched against Paris and, at first, had refused to help. Eventually, when he realized it was essential to aid the British or face total Allied defeat, Foch did send substantial French reserves, seven French divisions grouped in *Détachement d'Armée du Nord* (DAN), to Ypres. This help came just in time and the last German attack was defeated on 29 April. However, this delay showed clearly that the Allies needed to co-operate better. After the Battle of the Lys, Foch and Haig finally agreed that the German threat was so serious that they should provide strategic reserves for each other's fronts. Accordingly, it was decided to send IX Corps, as a reserve formation, to a quiet area behind the French front where it could rest and rebuild some of its badly weakened divisions.

The destruction of IX Corps on the Chemin des Dames

After suffering appalling casualties in the Battle of the Lys, IX Corps was withdrawn from the line and, on 23 April 1918, was transferred to a quiet sector of the French front as a reserve formation in exchange for French reserves, placed behind the British sector. IX Corps was reorganized to command just four recuperating divisions, namely 8th, 21st, 25th, and 50th Divisions. A further British division, the 19th, was sent to the nearby area of Châlons-sur-Marne, the Aldershot of the French Army. It was under command of IX Corps but, after training of its replacements, it was envisaged that it might be used in the French Fourth Army area. Following a brief period of leave, Captain Montgomery, the GSO 2, rejoined the corps headquarters, which had started rebuilding and retraining its badly mauled divisions east of Soissons. Reinforcements were available, but time was needed to absorb the replacements and retrain the officers and soldiers, not only in technical fighting skills, but also to ensure that the newly-arrived officers got to know their men, who were increasingly under-age boys, or men of over thirty-five.

After the shock of meeting overwhelming numbers of German troops and artillery in 1914, the British had been forced into a rapid expansion of their army. Not unnaturally it was initially thought that only well-trained regular soldiers could take on the task of fighting in Europe, and the British had quickly formed twelve divisions based on Regular Army formations. In addition Britain expanded its Territorial Force of volunteer reservists, which eventually numbered some thirty-four divisions. But even this proved insufficient for a major war in Europe. It was the redoubtable Minister of War, Field Marshal Lord Kitchener, who foresaw the need for even larger forces to defeat the Germans, and began the creation of some thirty 'New Army' divisions in August of 1914. Three of these fine New Army Divisions, 19th (Western), 21st and 25th Divisions joined IX Corps in the Champagne. New Army divisions were all manned initially by volunteers, and it was only in

1917 that the British had to resort to national conscription of eligible males to fill the depleted ranks of its army.

Formed in September 1914, the 19th Division had arrived in France in April 1915. It took part in many of the key battles, particularly in 1916, as part of IX Corps, including the Messines Ridge battle, where the divisional memorial was later erected. During the course of the campaign in France it was to suffer almost 40,000 casualties. The two major German attacks of March and April 1918 cost it over 8,600 casualties, including 281 officers. Therefore it felt quite fortunate to be sent in early May to train in the beautiful, largely untouched Châlons area, just south of the River Marne. By the time it was called forward on 28 May, it had managed to rebuild its nine infantry battalions to a total of 237 officers and 7,214 men. In addition, its pioneer and machine-gun battalions numbered a further 1,700 men.

Both the 21st and 25th Divisions had arrived in France in September 1915 and were quickly initiated into the horrors of trench warfare. The heavy losses incurred in the British attacks of 1916 and 1917 were just the precursors to what followed in the spring of 1918. The two divisions were involved in the defence against the German attacks at Bapaume and Mount Kemmel. Unusually, no divisional history was ever written for the 21st Division, which had experienced some of the war's fiercest fighting with total casualties of 55,581 men. The heavy fighting around Mount Kemmel during the second German offensive on the Lys, also caused heavy losses for 25th Division, which suffered 7,000 casualties, including nine of its infantry battalion commanding officers. This had reduced it to just one third of its infantry strength, and was in addition to its losses of 3,350 suffered in the Battle of Bapaume (21–26 March) during Operation MICHAEL. Because of its heavy losses in the Aisne campaign, 25th Division was broken up to provide manpower for other divisions but was later reformed in England and sent back to France in September 1918.

The New Army divisions had suffered heavy losses, but they were even greater in the remaining two divisions. Composed of doughty Territorial soldiers from the north-east of England, the 50th (Northumbrian) Division had arrived in France in April 1915 with 572 officers and 16,858 men. By 1918 it had endured many tough battles and, on 2 April, barely numbered 6,000 soldiers as it was withdrawn north to a quieter front to recuperate from its hard-pressed role in the great retreat caused by MICHAEL. Within days it was moved forward to the town of Estaires where it was planned to relieve a Portuguese division. Unfortunately, this placed the 50th on the Lys river just in time to suffer the second great German offensive. Four days later, when finally withdrawn, after another horrendous fighting retreat, the division numbered just fifty-five officers and 1,100 other ranks.

Sad experience during the early battles of the war had taught the British that, whenever a serious engagement was anticipated, it was wise to ensure that a battle reserve was created. Thus each battalion made sure that at least two officers and fifty men were sent to the rear before each major action, so that the battalion and its ethos could be reconstructed afterwards. As a result, even after the most shattering engagements it was possible to re-build battalions. However, the fighting on the Chemin des Dames was so desperate and the enemy advance so catastrophic, that even these final battle reserves were committed, and lost. As a result, when 50th Division finally returned to the British zone, it was unable to rebuild its original Northumbrian battalions, which were reduced to cadres. The division was then reformed with entirely new infantry battalions; most of which contained soldiers recuperating from the ravages of malaria incurred during service in the Salonika campaign. Although 50th Division was reconstituted, it was no longer the 'Northumbrian' division.

Unlike the other four divisions, 8th Division was a Regular Army division which had been formed in November 1914 from Regular Army battalions (usually the 1st or 2nd battalions of infantry regiments), which were brought home from serving abroad in the Empire. For three and half years its brigades had remained largely unchanged, as replacements came out to France from the regimental depots, to serve in its original battalions. Also, unlike the others, it was the only division in IX Corps which had remained in the Somme area after it had been heavily involved in repelling the first German attack against Arras and Amiens. It had not been sent to recover in Flanders but remained in the south of Picardy. It was thus fated to be involved in the desperate fighting around Villers-Bretonneux (described on page 15) when Ludendorff attempted to draw British reserves from the north by a surprise diversionary attack against that small town on 24 April. The counter-attack by two Australian brigades (13 and 15 Brigades) supported by the troops of 8th Division was a brilliant action which recovered the town and stalemated Ludendorff's diversionary ploy. Foiled, Ludendorff was forced to recommence the battle in Flanders on the following day. Although the Germans had an early success against Mount Kemmel, they were unable to take control of the whole ridge against a stubborn British defence, and eventually, on 29 April, Ludendorff had to abandon his Operation GEORGETTE attack. Despite its absence from the Battle of the Lys, 8th Division had suffered total casualties of 390 officers and 8,200 men in the period from 23 March to 27 April and was in desperate need of time to rebuild its infantry brigades.

However, although designated a reserve formation and thus not intended to be used unless there was a serious emergency, IX Corps was not given much time to rebuild its units in the rear areas. On 10 May 1918 General Duchêne, the commander of French Sixth Army, ordered it forward to replace a French corps in the front line on the Chemin des Dames feature. By 13 May it was in position along the Chemin des Dames defences. Soon its sector from Hurtebise to Berry-au-Bac was extended farther south to the Aisne-Marne canal, and IX Corps had to hold a 'quiet' front of almost fifteen miles with just three of its recuperating divisions. The British sector was so wide that each of its three forward divisions was obliged to station all three brigades in the front line, and even then each frontline battalion had to hold a front of 2,500 yards.

Fiftieth Division was on the left, occupying the Californie Plateau opposite Corbény and adjacent to the French XI Corps which held the French line west as far as the important city of Soissons. In the centre, opposite the village of Juvincourt, was 8th Division while 21st Division held the right-hand side of the sector south of the River Aisne, which ran down from Berry-au-Bac to Cauroy. To its right was the French 45th Division and further to its right was II Colonial Corps, covering the defences of Reims. Twenty-fifth Division was in Army reserve, but later moved up to the area south of the Aisne so that each of its three brigades could support one of the forward divisions.

On deployment to the Champagne area IX Corps had its normal complement of eight brigades of divisional field artillery (a total of almost 200 18-pounder guns and 4.5-inch howitzers) and eight batteries of medium mortars (almost fifty tubes), to support its four divisions. In addition, IX Corps had two brigades of corps heavy artillery (41st and 77th Brigades RGA) comprising twenty-two 60-pounder guns, twenty-two 6-inch howitzers and five 8-inch howitzers. Also under its command were three 'groups' of heavy French artillery totalling some ninety-four 75mm and 155mm guns, which occupied strong defensive features behind and among the main frontline defences.

Properly positioned, forty battalions supported by 400 pieces of field and heavy artillery, and some 300 heavy machine guns, should have constituted a formidable obstacle to any enemy attack.

The Chemin des Dames position consisted of trenches stretching along and in front of the long ridge, which carried the famous historical road (the Ladies' Highway) which derived its name from having been surfaced to improve the travelling comfort of the two daughters of Louis XV in the eighteenth century. In accordance with the uncompromising orders of General Duchêne, the majority of the defenders and their artillery were obliged to defend the ground in front of the ridge. The position had great strength and had been captured at a heavy cost in French blood the previous year, so Duchêne was not prepared to give up even an inch of ground. He seems to have deliberately misunderstood the intentions of General Pétain, who had ordered the implementation of a more flexible defence posture to cope with the new German attack methods. Duchêne's explicit orders left the British and French frontline troops very exposed in the event of a serious attack, as almost all their artillery was also positioned very close to the front, and thus likely to be trapped north of the River Aisne.

Pétain had actually ordered that at least three defence lines should be constructed so that a deep flexible defence could be organized. The thinly manned forward line (the Red Line) was designed to maintain observation of the enemy and control of no man's land with the minimum of troops. Some naturally strong features and redoubts were to be defended fiercely in order to slow down any enemy advance. The main defensive line (the Yellow Line) was organized some 2,000-3,000 yards behind. It was supposed to be out of range of most of the enemy artillery and mortars and was designed to be held strongly with continuous wire and trenches. It should have included concrete strongpoints on commanding positions equipped with heavy machine guns, and supported by field artillery. A third defence line (the Green Line) farther behind was intended to defeat any breaches. Finally, battle reserves and heavy artillery were to be maintained even farther back, located behind natural obstacles from where they could also mount counter-attacks.

The main weakness of the Chemin des Dames position was that the immediate combat area was closely bisected by three major river lines running east to west. The long Chemin ridge was a 'hog's back' ridge, which ran straight and true due west from Craonne (just north of Reims) for some twenty miles (thirty kilometres), and was entrenched along its entire length. In front of the ridge, and closest to the enemy, was a narrow stream, the Aillette. Then behind the ridge came the substantial Aisne river and its parallel Aisne canal, while some five to ten miles farther south was the narrower Vesle river and its canal. Finally, some twenty-five miles away to the south, ran the deep and wide Marne river. Also crossing at an angle through the high plain between the Vesle and the Marne were the Ardre, Crise and Ourcq rivers. Because of the lack of depth the main defence line should have been organized behind (that is south of) the River Aisne, but General Duchêne's orders meant that almost all the artillery and infantry were stationed north of the river. Duchêne was an uncompromising and unpleasant man, who brooked no discussion of his orders. His defence also suffered from the fact that most of his French divisions were understrength, with only two infantry regiments and a few auxiliary battalions. The area immediately below the Aisne was heavily folded and, with its steep valleys and hillcrests, would have offered rich opportunities to create impregnable defence lines on rear slopes, but this was not done. Despite the protests of the British commanders, they too were forced to place most of their troops and guns far too close to the enemy, with the uncomfortable disadvantage of having an un-crossable river at their backs.

At the western end of the ridge, lay the ruined Fort de Malmaison. Originally constructed by General Séré de Rivières after the Franco-Prussian War, it was later used by the French to test the effect of their explosives on fortifications. Following these self-inflicted bombardments, it was considered unusable and abandoned in 1914 but was garrisoned by the invading Germans. In April 1917, after a week of diversionary attacks at Arras by the British, General Nivelle launched a major offensive between Soissons and Reims with nineteen French divisions supported by over 5,000 guns. However, von Boehn's Seventh Army was forewarned and had prepared well to defend its positions. The Germans were deeply entrenched along the high ground facing south on the banks of the Aisne river, and they were easily able to defeat most of the attacks. Eventually, by 5 May, part of the Chemin des Dames had been captured, but the price had been very high. On the first day of combat alone, the French suffered over 40,000 casualties and lost 150 tanks. Total losses were eventually estimated at 271,000, and these immense losses for small gain ended the career of Nivelle (and left his lieutenant, General Mangin, in disgrace for almost a year) as well as bringing the French Army to the verge of mutiny.

Some idea of the heavy losses suffered can be imagined from a visit to the eastern end of the ridge where the road runs down to Pontavert. There the huge Californe French Military Cemetery at Craonne contains over 5,000 graves. From a distance it seems to cover the sides of the hill in pretty white flowers, which on nearer examination, turn out to be white stone crosses. Actually on 23 October 1917 a well-prepared attack by three French corps, operating under General Pétain's careful plan, succeeded in capturing the Fort de Malmaison and the Germans were obliged to pull back off the ridge to the north side of the Ailette valley.

Ludendorff remained convinced that he would be able to achieve a decisive victory over the British in Flanders where he thought they were especially vulnerable after the partial success of his GEORGETTE attack, which had taken his armies to within six miles of the great rail junction at Hazebrouck and almost surrounded Ypres. This long-planned decisive battle, Operation HAGEN was postponed a number of times in May and June, as Ludendorff allowed himself to be distracted by the battles against the French. Nevertheless, Ludendorff had gathered most of his reserves ready for what was intended to be a decisive high-powered continuation of the Lys attack, with more than double the number of divisions and at least 1,400 batteries of artillery (5,000-6,000 guns). Already, at the beginning of May, thirty-two of the forty-seven divisions required for the attack had begun special training behind the front of the German Fourth and Sixth Armies.

Despite the success of the first two major attacks in Picardy and Flanders, Ludendorff realized that he had still failed to make a decisive breakthrough. For this he first needed to weaken the British defence by drawing reserves away from the north, and he felt this could well be achieved by another surprise attack in a new sector. Unfortunately for the recently-arrived British defenders his choice fell on the Chemin des Dames ridge possession of which would threaten both Reims and Paris. While the ridge line looked strong the Germans, who had occupied it the previous year, felt it could be outflanked easily and it would then become a trap for its over-extended defenders.

27 May 1918. First day of Operation BLÜCHER-YORCK, the overwhelming attack by German Seventh Army on the Chemin des Dames.
Given their experience of the Somme and Lys attacks, the British recognized clear signs of an impending German attack from the 22nd,

but Duchêne and his staff ignored their warnings. During the 26th the British became convinced that the Germans were preparing to attack that night, and the whole of IX Corps stood to while its artillery began a counter-preparation harassing bombardment of German positions at 9.00pm. Ominously, despite this provocative shelling, Bruchmüller's guns remained resolutely mute, until precisely at 1.00am on the 27th, when they opened their devastating barrage of gas and HE shells.

The bombardment began with every single gun firing as many gas shells as possible for the first ten minutes. This was to cause maximum shock and dislocation, and incidentally forcing all the defenders to don their restrictive gas masks. The three frontline divisions of IX Corps, and the three divisions of the neighbouring French XI Corps, were subjected to the heaviest artillery bombardment to that point in the war as 6,471 guns and 3,532 mortars fired off 2,000,000 shells in three hours on a front of thirty-eight miles (sixty kilometres). The focus of the attack was the central area, around the inter-corps boundary, which stretched some eleven and a half miles (eighteen kilometres) in front of the positions held by the British 50th Division and the French 22nd Division. Here were concentrated no less than 466 artillery batteries, that is more than forty batteries per mile, i.e. one gun for every ten yards. This was actually almost twice the density of guns that the British Fourth and French First Armies were to employ against the Germans in their successful attack on 8 August. Following this crushing artillery fire the Germans then assaulted the six battered Allied frontline divisions with twenty-three attack divisions. However, the very thickest concentration of troops was directed against those central 50th and 22nd Divisions, where eight attack divisions and three second-echelon divisions streamed forward in the early morning, under cover of a continuing artillery barrage.

Facing just the British IX Corps alone were elements of three German corps, Conta's and Schmettow's corps from Seventh Army and Borne's corps from First Army. They launched the specially-trained 5th Guard, 50th, 52nd, 7th Reserve, 86th and 33rd Reserve Divisions in the front line, with the 213th, 88th, 103rd and 232nd Divisions in their second echelon. The bulk of the German shells, mortars and infantry struck the six forward brigades of the 50th and 8th Divisions and their supporting artillery, almost all of whom were located forward of the Aisne. With the wide River Aisne at their backs, the eighteen British infantry battalions were particularly vulnerable to enveloping infantry attacks on their right, as well as to penetration on the left through the overrun positions of the French 22nd Division. Given the initial destructive artillery onslaught, only substantial re-engineering of the defence positions in depth would have given them any chance of surviving against the overwhelming odds that they faced.

At about 4.00am the artillery bombardment ceased, and a major assault with German tanks (mostly captured British tanks) and infantry was mounted at the right face of the British position, where it bent with the River Aisne, which enabled the Germans to use their infiltration tactics to outflank the shell-shocked troops of 8th Division. The right flank of 8th Division's salient was defended by 25 Brigade, commanded by an outstanding young Territorial officer, Brigadier General Hussey DSO MC. In principle 25 Brigade occupied a strong lozenge-shaped position, its eastern boundary sheltered behind the River Aisne and its canal, while its western boundary with 24 Brigade ran along the water-logged valley of the Mielle. At the back of the brigade area, just south of the river, was located the enormously strong Gernicourt position on sloping ground which overlooked most of Hussey's brigade front. Gernicourt had a permanent French garrison of a battalion of infantry, five companies of machine guns, and a 'group' of 75mm guns under Commander Paul. It had been further strengthened by the divisional pioneer battalion and by bringing forward 110th Field Artillery Brigade of 25th Division.

However, the stunned forward battalions of 25 Brigade were quickly overwhelmed and Brigadier General Hussey pulled back to the River Aisne where he tried to maintain a defensive line with survivors and his brigade headquarters while ensuring that all the bridges in his area were blown. Crossing over the river, he then tried to establish a defensive position on the higher ground west of the strongpoint at Gernicourt, but was overcome in hand-to-hand fighting and died from his wounds as a prisoner of the Germans a few days later. The substantial garrison on Gernicourt continued resisting gamely until the early afternoon, but was overcome by streams of Germans attacking them from the south-west – effectively from behind their position.

In the centre of the division's area, the 1st Northamptons of 24 Brigade held the outpost line, but were attacked at 5.00am and were soon forced back to the main battle line, where they and the 1st Worcesters mounted a stubborn defence. However, the Germans had broken through along the river line, and they were soon surrounded in their battle trenches and either killed or forced to surrender. The 1st Northamptons were commanded by Lieutenant Colonel Buckle. A last message from him to his battalion was found by his father, Major General Buckle, who visited the site of the battle shortly after the war ended. It typified the determination of the defenders. It read:

> All Platoon Commanders will remain with their platoons and ensure that the trenches are manned immediately the bombardment lifts. Send short situation wire every half-hour. No short bombardment can possibly cut our wire and if sentries are alert it cannot be cut by hand. If they try shoot the devils.

The Northamptons were overcome by 6.00am and Lieutenant Colonel Buckle's body was later found buried just outside his headquarters, together with those of some German soldiers. The headquarters of 24 Brigade pulled back to defend la Pecherie bridge, west of Pontavert, but was soon surrounded. By 9.00am the sole remnants of 24 Brigade, consisting of three officers and sixty-eight men, were holding a trench north-east of Roucy.

On the left of 8th Division's line it was a similar story for 23 Brigade, commanded by Brigadier General Grogan. The two lead battalions were attacked at 5.00am and resisted robustly in the main battle line until, by 7.00am, they were surrounded. The 2nd Devons, the reserve battalion of the brigade, occupied tunnels and deep bunkers in the Bois des Buttes position, which had been originally fortified and entrenched by the Germans, before being lost to the French in a bloody 1917 battle. The position was important as it covered the road to Pontavert and was so well protected that it shielded the Devons from the worst of the enemy shells and gas. When the shelling ceased, the Devons moved out to their fire trenches but discovered that German machine gunners were already beginning to take possession of the Bois de Buttes. A platoon commander of the Devons later wrote:

> We obliterated these before they knew what had happened, and this cheered up the troops who were young and rather demoralized by the shelling and general uncertainty.

However, the avalanche of grey-clad enemy troops could not be halted and, as the enemy broke through on both sides, the position was soon surrounded. The Devons continued to inflict heavy casualties but were steadily worn down. Their commanding officer, Lieutenant Colonel Anderson-Morshead DSO, understood the importance of defending the approach to the bridge at Pontavert and refused to retire any further. A battery commander, who had lost his guns, was falling back with a few of his men and came upon their position. He later wrote:

> At a late hour in the morning I, with those of my men who had escaped the enemy's ring of machine guns and his fearful barrage, found the CO of the 2nd Devon Regiment and a handful of men holding on to the last trench north of the Canal. They were in a position where they were entirely without hope of help, but were fighting on grimly. The Commanding Officer himself was calmly writing his orders with a perfect hell of HE falling round him. I spoke to him, and he told me that nothing could be done. He refused all offers of help from my artillerymen, who were unarmed, and sent them off to get through if they could. His magnificent bearing, dauntless courage and determination to carry on to the end moved one's emotion.

Lieutenant Colonel Anderson-Morshead was killed at about 9.30am leading the last fifty of his men in a charge down the hill to stop some German guns moving up the road from Juvincourt. Captain Montgomery at Corps Headquarters later recorded in a IX Corps' Special Order that, 'in obedience to their orders', the commanding officer, twenty-eight officers and 552 NCOs and men of the 2nd Devons had all perished 'en masse'. The self-sacrificing stand by the Devons granted some time to Brigadier General Grogan, who was thus able to organize a defence of the Aisne crossing until 25th Division came up. Moreover, a few men under Second Lieutenant Clarke did manage to fight their way out by moving back into the tunnels of the Bois des Buttes and escaping from the other side. Eventually some eighty survivors escaped the fate of the rest of the battalion and joined up with those who had been away on training courses, or were with the battalion transport, and were organized into a small company of about 140 men, who formed a defensive flank on the left at Ventelay, and later at Jonchery. This composite company then played a vital role on the evening of the 28th, when it mounted a fierce counter-attack, which drove the Germans back from a hill at Savigny and stabilized the front over-night.

A small stone cross memorial to the last stand by the 2nd Devons is situated opposite the church in la Ville-aux-Bois. The remarkable sacrifice by the Devons was acknowledged by the French in an

Army Order, in which it became one of the few British regiments to be awarded the Croix de Guerre. In 1918 the Bois des Buttes was a series of sandy hills filled with trenches and deep dugouts. Today it is a dark and dank place with bunkers hidden among the trees and rank undergrowth, and littered with signs warning visitors to stay out. Actually a very similar fate to that of the 2nd Devons befell all nine battalions of 8th Division, from which not one commanding officer or adjutant remained at the end of the action. Such was the scale of this military disaster that each of the field artillery batteries supporting the infantry shared their misfortune as their men fought their guns until overcome by enemy infantry, or slipped away taking their sights and breech blocks with them. Some attempted to defend their gun positions with rifles, but the devastating tide of enemy fire and soldiers overcame all resistance.

The fate of 5 (Gibraltar) Battery of 45th Brigade RFA, supporting 8th Division, was typical. The battery, under the command of Captain Massey, began firing harassing fire missions on likely enemy approach routes from 9.00pm on the 26th, and continued firing throughout the night. From 1.00am it was subjected to a German HE and gas barrage, but continued its fire. At 6.30am the German barrage on the battery ceased just as German infantry were spotted 200 metres from the position. Captain Massey ordered the guns to direct fire in defence of the position while he attempted to beat back the infantry with a Lewis gun and rifle fire, but the Germans soon broke into the rear of the gun position and most of the officers and men were killed in hand-to-hand fighting. Only six men escaped death or capture by fighting their way out.

Five (Gibraltar) Battery was also cited for its heroic stand in French Army Orders and awarded the Croix de Guerre. The battery's sacrifice is commemorated by a memorial plaque placed on the outside wall of the church of la Ville-aux-Bois, opposite the memorial to the Devons.

Captain Massey's body was discovered in 1935 and now lies buried at the Jonchery-sur-Vesle British Military Cemetery. Brigadier General Hussey is buried in the Vendresse Military Cemetery, which lies near the centre of the Chemin des Dames Ridge, on its south side. This cemetery also contains the bodies of the many soldiers who were killed in the first British offensive in this area, by the BEF under Sir John French who had established his headquarters in Fère-en-Tardenois in the autumn of 1914. Lieutenant Colonel Buckle is buried at the lonely

Ville-aux-Bois Cemetery, which still has bunkers built into its boundary wall, and is close to the Bois de Buttes position held by the Devons.

To the left of 8th Division, 50th Division held the strategically critical high ground around the Californie Plateau and it was subjected to the same crushing artillery barrage, which levelled trenches and destroyed communications. The experience of 149 Brigade, which commanded three battalions of the Northumberland Fusiliers on the right of the division, was typical. The forward companies of the 4th Northumberland Fusiliers, which was the right forward battalion, were shattered by the opening barrage of HE and gas. Visibility was extremely poor, which made the defence difficult when the first infantry attack developed at 3.30am. However, despite heavy casualties, the survivors withdrew to the line of posts and broke up the enemy attack with rifle and Lewis-gun fire. At 4.00am the attack came on again, supported by some German and captured British tanks, which drove the outposts back to the battle line. By 4.15am the battle line, which was located far too close to the outpost line, was in action and being outflanked. At 5.00am, Lieutenant Colonel Gibson, the battalion commander, reported that he was holding out with some forty men in the Centre Marceau strongpoint. Despite a desperate defence, the issue was never in doubt. Some survivors managed to reach the Butte de l'Edmond, just north of Pontavert, where, together with some divisional machine gunners, they made a final stand and Lieutenant Colonel Gibson was killed.

The 6th Northumberland Fusiliers, who were supporting the 4th in the battle line, were outflanked from the Bois des Buttes, and by 8.00am only a few remnants got away. The 5th Northumberland Fusiliers were in brigade reserve, and had begun to move up at 2.40am to establish a line between the Bois des Buttes and Butte de l'Edmond, but ran into heavy barrages which caused serious casualties. Reduced to just skeleton companies, the survivors attempted to hold the railway line near the Aisne crossing at Chaudardes, and various lines south of the Aisne. Brigadier General Riddell had already been wounded by an artillery salvo, and thus his 149 Brigade had virtually ceased to exist before midday, so the survivors fought on as an amalgamated 149/151 Brigade. It continued to support 74 Brigade of 25th Division, which was moving up during the morning to help the survivors of 50th Division establish a new defence line on the Aisne.

The centre of the 50th Division front was held by the three Durham Light Infantry battalions of 151 Brigade, with its headquarters in the Evreux defensive node. Its two advance battalions, the 6th and 7th, were both shattered by shellfire, and then overwhelmed by huge numbers of enemy. At the same time, the brigade headquarters was targeted by enemy artillery shelling, which killed Brigadier General Martin. The reserve battalion, the 5th Durham Light Infantry, attempted to establish a defence line in front of and east of Pontavert but was surrounded and captured by the floods of enemy troops. Nevertheless, groups of soldiers were gathered and defensive positions established at the Beaurieux, Chaudardes, and Concevreux crossings to hold back the hordes of enemy until the bridges could be blown by the Royal Engineers.

The left sector of the divisional front around the Californie Plateau, was held by 150 Brigade. It suffered the same overwhelming barrage, but was not subjected to a frontal assault. Instead, by 6.00am, its two lead battalions were overwhelmed by divisional assaults which came in from the western and eastern flanks, which had been opened up by the rapid German advance. As the barrage continued right up until the plateau was enveloped, many defenders were captured while still taking cover in their deep dugouts. The reserve battalion, the 4th Green Howards, attempted to move forward to hold a defence line, but they were overwhelmed as they advanced. The brigade headquarters then tried to pull back to the Aisne, but all the officers were wounded except Brigadier General Rees, who became exhausted and was captured. As a result, 150 Brigade was virtually obliterated and could not be reformed until 31 May, when the division was withdrawn to Vert la Gravelle.

Obedient to General Duchêne's uncompromising orders, the two field artillery brigades of 50th Division were subjected to the same unkind fate: 251st Brigade had been firing its SOS barrage in support of the infantry, when German troops broke into the back of its four battery positions and took them prisoner before they could react. Although 250th Brigade continued firing for a little longer, gradually each battery was overcome and all the guns were destroyed in situ or lost during the early morning. Only a few gunners managed to remove their gun-sights and make their way back to the wagon lines at Glennes.

Doggedly, survivors of 50th Division formed a number of composite units to continue fighting over the next few days, but its three brigades had ceased to exist as they had been completely outnumbered and overwhelmed during the first morning by three enemy divisions. Furthermore, the loss of the divisional artillery at the start of the battle meant that no temporary defensive position could be held for long against such overwhelming numbers. Even the divisional headquarters at Beaurieux was almost captured. The remnants of 50th Division, who answered the divisional roll call on 31 May, numbered just 700.

On the right of IX Corps was 21st Division, which was holding positions generally facing east when it was attacked by the divisions of German First Army. It fought an almost independent battle as it slowly withdrew in a south-westerly direction towards the River Vesle. Fortunately, its initial defence positions were located largely south of the River Aisne and its artillery was not destroyed in the initial barrage. Thus it was better able to protect its infantry and maintain its links with the French 45th Division on its right and pull back in contact with it to maintain the shoulder on the right of the French line, thus protecting Reims. Nevertheless, it was continually attacked by at least two enemy divisions, usually the 7th Reserve and 86th Divisions. In three days of fighting it lost 150 officers and 3,600 other ranks, and a number of its soldiers lie buried in the French Military Cemetery at Gernicourt near Berry au Bac. The 21st Division was then withdrawn to the Dormans area, but its field artillery and two heavy RGA batteries remained in support of the 45th Division until the 30th.

Although all the forty-two bridges across the Aisne river in the corps' sector were due to be blown by the engineers and covering parties on army orders, these orders were not given or received in time, and eight bridges were captured intact by the enemy, enabling the Germans to continue streaming south at a great pace. Observation balloons towed by trucks flew above the advancing German troops. Together with numerous squadrons of aircraft they enabled the artillery and trench mortars to deal quickly with any strong points or improvised defence positions.

Major General Heneker, commanding 8th Division, attempted to organize a new defensive line based on the second position, which ran along the high ground south of the River Aisne from Bouffignereux through Roucy to Concevreux. He manned this with survivors who had flowed back from his brigades, as well as reserves from the transport lines and some 600 men who had been attending the divisional Lewis-gun School. These scratch reserves were bolstered by the three brigades of 25th Division, which had been in corps reserve. However, 25th Division came up with only half its artillery, as its 110th Brigade RFA had initially been sent forward to the Bois de Gernicourt strongpoint. There it was assigned a low-lying position just south of the Aisne, without infantry protection, and, when attacked by enemy troops, lost most of its guns and howitzers by midday on the 27th. It managed to extract just enough guns to form a composite battery, which later joined 112th Brigade RFA. The latter brigade was initially in action south west of Cormicy, where its batteries began firing from 6.00am on the 27th, and remained in action all day despite heavy shelling. From there it covered the retirement of the artillery of 21st Division, but tarried too long and some of its guns were lost that evening as its positions were overrun.

The three infantry brigades of 25th Division had come forward during the morning of the 27th to establish a twelve-mile defence line south of the Aisne, from Maizy in the west through Concevreux and Bouffignereux to Cormicy on the Aisne canal. On the right was 7 Brigade, with 75 Brigade in the centre, and 74 Brigade holding the western end. The brigades were then placed under command of the three forward divisions to support their defence. However, the scale of the enemy attacks was still so overwhelming that these outnumbered troops were unable to block the enemy advance. For example, 74 Brigade had lost touch with the French regiment on its left, which had been forced back south of the Aisne, leaving a two-mile gap. Therefore it sent the brigade instructional platoon, a body of 100 picked and well-trained men, forward to cover this gap. The platoon then ran into a large group of enemy near Glennes and, despite putting up a gallant defence for over an hour, was surrounded as the majority became casualties; the remainder were forced to retire. The lesson was quite clear. No matter how well-trained, fine soldiers like these, when caught in the open, without the benefit of protective trenches and support weapons, had no chance against the machine guns and mortars of such overwhelming numbers of enemy. Only one officer and two men succeeded in rejoining 74 Brigade.

Although the British fought a determined defensive battle as they retreated southwards, their left flank always remained open, and they found themselves continually out-flanked by the enemy. The Germans pressed forward resolutely making successful use of their *stoss* infiltration tactics to exploit the river lines and folds in the ground, and to advance under cover of suppressing fire from their light machine guns and mortars. Valiant efforts by 74 Brigade to cover the open western flank were constantly frustrated and it suffered heavy casualties as it attempted to hold on to the Aisne crossing at Concevreux. It was forced back to Romain and Ventelay, and then pulled back during the night to the high ground north-west of Montigny. During the afternoon, Lance Corporal Halliwell of the 11th Lancashire Fusiliers became a legend, as he acquired a horse and rode out nine times, under heavy machine-gun fire, to rescue wounded men. He was awarded the Victoria Cross (VC) for his courageous action.

By the evening of the 27th the leading German troops had broken through in the centre of the Allied line and triumphantly advanced some twelve miles as they took possession of the ridges between the Aisne and the Vesle, finally crossing the Vesle between Braine, Bazoches and Fismes. The British and French troops on the shoulders of the German advance struggled to slow the advance in their sectors. Around Soissons, the outnumbered French fought hard to defend the city while, in the east, IX Corps pivoted on its 21st Division as it pulled back some six or seven miles in a south-easterly direction. During the evening the Germans managed to occupy the important crossroads at Ventelay and, nearby, the advanced dressing station (ADS), manned by the 77th Field Ambulance of 25th Division, was captured in the village of Bouvancourt. Nevertheless, the other two divisional field ambulances managed to evacuate some 800 wounded that night. Despite all efforts to stem the enemy advance with machine-gun and rifle fire; continued pressure drove the British back towards the line of the River Vesle.

28 May 1918. Second day of Operation BLÜCHER-YORCK against the remnants of IX Corps defending the River Vesle.
By early morning of the 28th the remnants of 8th and 50th Divisions, supported by two of the much-reduced brigades of 25th Division, held a number of bridgeheads around Jonchery on the River Vesle while 8th Divisional headquarters had moved back to Faverolles. On the right, the enemy attacks against 21st Division had damaged its forward positions, and reduced its artillery to some twenty-nine guns, but it was sustaining a vital hinge on the right of the Allied line, together with the French 45th Division. The forward defence of the Jonchery area was led by Brigadier General Grogan. He had commanded 23 Brigade which, like all six of the forward brigades, had been destroyed in the first morning by the artillery bombardment and overwhelming infantry assaults. Grogan was fortunate to be the only infantry brigadier to have survived in a condition to continue the fight; Hussey and Martin had been killed, Riddell and Haig had been wounded, and Rees had been taken prisoner. Martin's body was never identified and he is listed on the Soissons Memorial to the missing, as are three lieutenant colonels, including Anderson-Morshead of the Devons. Grogan's tireless and

brave leadership of the British troops during this retreat was later recognized by the award of the Victoria Cross.

The bridgehead at Montigny north of the Vesle was held by 74 Brigade, while the Prouilly bridgehead to the north-east was held by 75 Brigade. Heavy enemy attacks continued and, by 9.00am, 75 Brigade and part of 74 Brigade were forced to withdraw across the river. Their escape was largely thanks to the heroic last stand by the 11th Lancashire Fusiliers, which, although eventually surrounded, held the high ground north of the Vesle around Breuil until finally enveloped by the enemy. Only two fusiliers from the 11th Battalion managed to get back across the river. The attempt by the engineers to blow up the bridge at Jonchery failed, and some 300 prisoners were captured by the German 52nd Division. The remnants of 7 Brigade, supporting 21st Division, managed to hold their position on the high ground east of the Trigny-Prouilly ridge throughout the 28th. They made good use of their machine guns to inflict heavy casualties on the enemy until trench mortars were brought up which then forced 7 Brigade across the river at dusk. During the night, the British established a new line on the Ardre river, from Serzy through the high ground at Savigny to Faverolles.

Despite the French having sent a new corps (XXI Corps) to halt their advance, the Germans still managed to capture the key town of Fismes, where the Ardre joined the Vesle. The Germans then continued advancing in a south-easterly direction up the Ardre valley towards Savigny which enabled them to outflank all the British defensive positions. As one Jonchery survivor later wrote:

> Fighting became very monotonous now. We would hold a position till we were outflanked, when we withdrew to the next ridge, and the same thing happened again. Our left flank was in the air the whole time and he always concentrated upon it.

By the evening of the 28th an overwhelming German victory looked inevitable, and Ludendorff was acclaimed for having found another weak point in the Allied front line. Nine German divisions, mostly from General Conta's IV Reserve Corps, had broken through the centre of the Vesle line, and were racing for the River Marne. The shoulders of the deep German penetration had been widened on both flanks, and included the approaches to Savigny in the east, and the outskirts of Soissons in the west. Despite resisting fiercely, the understrength French

74th Division had lost the key fortress of Condé, which commanded all the eastern approaches to Soissons.

That evening, the Kaiser held a War Council with the German Crown Prince, Hindenburg and Ludendorff. It was then decided, in view of its unexpectedly dramatic success, to change this Aisne attack from a diversion into a principal attack and continue all the way to the River Marne. Only Ludendorff voted against continuing the advance to the Marne. Originally it had been hoped that Operation BLÜCHER would be sufficiently successful to allow the Germans to cross the River Aisne, and to establish a new defensive line along the north bank of the Vesle. However, when their jubilant troops had advanced so much further so quickly, thereby capturing huge quantities of food stores, booty, guns and prisoners, they became beguiled by the glorious prospect of once again reaching the Marne, and cutting the Paris to Nancy railway. It seemed quite possible that Germany was on the verge of being able to attack and occupy Paris, as Marshal Blücher had done in 1814, and General Moltke in 1870.

Perversely, the very success of BLÜCHER-YORCK had the disastrous consequence of enticing the Germans to commit many of their precious reserves to expand the Aisne salient into the Marne salient. This was in spite of the fact that the new salient suffered from poor communications and, more importantly, that their primary intent still remained to attack the British army in the Flanders sector.

29 May 1918. Third day of Operation BLÜCHER-YORCK against the remnants of IX Corps, as it is reinforced by the arrival of 19th Division.
The third day of the German advance began with a heavy bombardment of British positions at 8.00am, followed by new infantry attacks mainly on the open left flank. In the meantime the two leading brigades of 19th Division had been bussed up from the Châlons area during the night and bivouacked around the village of Chambrecy. As divisional headquarters opened at Chaumuzy it had been sensibly decided that, rather than throwing the arriving brigades of 19th Division straight into the battle, they should establish a new defensive line in rear of the current forward line of troops, from Lhéry on the left through Coemy to Faverolles. At the same time, the IX Corps Cyclist Battalion was ordered forward early on the morning of the 29th to hold the planned Lhéry line until 58 and 57 Brigades could come up. Eventually, at around midday, 57 Brigade dug in its positions from Lhéry to Coemy,

and 58 Brigade held from Coemy to Faverolles. At first 58 Brigade tried to make contact with the French 154th Division on its right, but, when it failed to find them, it was decided to push the 2nd Wiltshires forward to occupy the key high ground north of Bouleuse, just behind Treslon.

In the meantime, under the command of Brigadier General Grogan, the thin covering front was maintained by the remnants of the 8th, 50th and 25th Divisions and some French troops from 154th Division, with many units being totally intermixed. The forward British line had been reinforced during the 28th by composite units made up from stragglers and B Echelon men and by a fresh infantry battalion, the 6th Cheshires, which had just been sent into the area. The Cheshires marched up to join 23 Brigade, and, later, 75 Brigade. Still holding on the far right were the three brigades of 21st Division, maintaining its link to the French defenders of Reims. Then the railway line south of the Vesle near Branscourt was held by 7 Brigade, with 75 Brigade on its left. The centre was held by some details from 21st Division and the remnants of 23 Brigade. On their left were a few fresh French reinforcements dug in along the Treslonne road, and farther to their left were the remnants of 74 Brigade holding the high ground north of Savigny.

At midday the senior command changed as General Micheler and his French Fifth Army Headquarters was brought up to command the French sector to the west of Reims. The British then ceased to report to the irascible General Duchêne who, not surprisingly, was soon sacked.

Heavy German mortaring at midday caused serious casualties, and was followed by numerous infantry attacks. The German 86th (recently transferred from Russia) and 7th Reserve Divisions were now advancing in a south-westerly direction, under orders to secure the high ground south-east of Lhéry (close to the Bois d'Aulnay) and they launched multiple attacks during the afternoon and evening. This eventually forced the advanced British line to withdraw across the wooded Treslon valley to the high ground around Bouleuse and Rossigny, where they fell back on the 2nd Wiltshires from 58 Brigade who were now well dug in and supported by four Vickers machine guns. During the evening the 19th Divisional Artillery arrived and began to provide covering fire from 8.00pm. This reinforcement by the forty-eight guns and howitzers of 19th Division was very welcome, as it more than doubled the artillery available to defend the widely-spread British positions.

On the right, 21st Division was shelled heavily as it tried to hang on to its shallow trenches on Hill 202, while 7 Brigade, on the high ground at Savigny, covered the retirement of the French and British troops to Bouleuse, when it withdrew to the high ground south of Rossigny. The shelling wounded its commander, Brigadier General Griffin, and killed the last of his brigade staff, which left 7 Brigade without a command element.

The defensive position on the Bouleuse Ridge was not good. Although occupying a forward slope, its field of fire was restricted by woods, which covered the advance by the German 7th Reserve Division from the Treslon valley. Repeated attacks were beaten off, and the defensive line was strengthened during the night by two battalions from 56 Brigade. Nevertheless, the heavy shelling on the right forced 21st Division to fall back from Hill 202 to form a line around Germigny.

30 May 1918. Fourth day of Operation BLÜCHER-YORCK as it strikes 19th Division and the remnants of IX Corps.
During the night of the 29th, Brigadier-General Heath, commanding 56 Brigade, relieved the tireless Brigadier-General Grogan and took command of all the troops on the Bouleuse Ridge. At the same time 19th Division, sandwiched between the French 13th Division on its left and 154th Division on its right, assumed command of all remaining British troops in the area. Also during the night, the French 45th Division, which had been relieved on the 28th, came up from reserve to relieve the remnants of 21st Division around Germigny. The division assembled at Pourcy before withdrawing to the area around Dormans, although its artillery remained in support of the 45th Division. On consolidation at Dormans, the 21st Division had only sufficient troops left to form one composite battalion from each brigade. These three battalions were then formed into a single 21 Independent Brigade under Brigadier General Gater, which then marched back to the Tardenois area to act as a reserve to 19th Division.

The remnants of the two thoroughly worn-out brigades, 7 and 75, of 25th Division had also been withdrawn during the night. Thus only 74 Brigade remained in the line. Actually, 74 Brigade was largely a composite formation made up of men from the 25th, 8th, and 50th Divisions. It had remained in position on the high ground around the Bois des Limons, south-west of Lhéry, as it covered the left of 19th Division. The 19th continued holding either side of the Ardre river, with 74 and 57 Brigades on the left around Coemy, and 58 Brigade on the right around Faverolles. To its right was a line of French Senegalese *tirailleurs*, from 154th Division, and then, finally, maintaining a strong position on the Bouleuse Ridge, were the 2nd Wiltshires and 56 Brigade.

During the early morning of 30 May it was the turn of 19th Division to suffer overwhelming attacks by four German divisions, preceded by violent artillery and trench-mortar fire. German infiltration patrols began advancing very early against the left of the division around Lhéry and the centre of the division around Faverolles. In the west a regiment of the German 7th Reserve Division and two regiments from the newly-arrived 103rd Division launched a strong attack on the junction of 74 and 57 Brigades at 6.00am. As a result 74 Brigade was driven back towards Romigny where it formed a defensive flank on the left of the British line. It received some reinforcements during the morning and managed to cling on to the high ground south of Romigny until midday, when it was forced back to the high ground south-west of Ville-en-Tardenois. As the enemy occupied Lhéry, heavy casualties were inflicted on 57 Brigade and it too was forced successively backwards until it reached Ville-en-Tardenois, where it was once again able to link up with 74 Brigade.

At 3.30am eight lines of German troops from another regiment of 7th Reserve Division began successive attacks on the centre of 19th Division's front. By this stage these attacks seemed to reflect an abandonment of *sturmtruppen* tactics and a reversion to traditional massed assaults. In any event, they managed to penetrate on the right of 58 Brigade around Faverolles. There the Senegalese troops were driven in, which caused almost two whole battalions, the 9th Welch and 9th Royal Welsh Fusiliers, to be outflanked and surrounded, most of the men being either killed or captured. As a result, the remainder of 58 Brigade had to fall back towards the Sarcy-Bouleuse road. During the afternoon, its commander, Brigadier General Glasgow, was wounded and Brigadier General Heath of 56 Brigade also took command of the remnants of 58 Brigade.

A third attack was launched by the German 86th Division and the newly-arrived 232nd Division, against the 56 Brigade position on Bouleuse Ridge. At first each assault was beaten back, until at about midday it became necessary to withdraw almost a mile to the next ridge, west of Aubilly. Fifty-six Brigade held that position until the evening, when it was relieved by the French 28th Division, which had taken over from 154th Division, although some of its fragmented units remained in position. The survivors of 56 Brigade then marched back about two miles to the village of Bligny, but remained in support of 28th Division.

During the morning of the 30th, the headquarters of IX Corps, together with all the other divisional headquarters, withdrew and command of 19th Division passed to the French V Corps, although General Gordon kindly left some of his overworked staff to assist General Pellé, commanding V Corps. Farther south, in the centre of their new salient, the German advance troops had made much better progress and actually reached the banks of the River Marne in the early afternoon. Although all the bridges had been blown, the Germans managed to secure a small bridgehead on the south side of the Marne at the Jaulgonne bend.

In the afternoon, a further series of enemy attacks was mounted in the centre of the position around the River Ardre, but were broken up by the divisional artillery and machine guns. During the evening fresh attacks were launched in the west, where 74 Composite Brigade and the pioneers of 5th South Wales Borderers managed to hold the high ground, inflicting heavy casualties, and, because contact had been lost with the French, extended their front somewhat to the west. Finally the French 40th Division came up and relieved 13th Division, and later that night they occupied the positions of parts of 74 Brigade, which was withdrawn into reserve.

31 May 1918. Fifth day of Operation BLÜCHER-YORCK, against 19th Division and the remnants of IX Corps.
Heavy enemy shellfire during the morning of the 31st caused considerable casualties and the line had to be drawn back from Sarcy. A further attack at about midday was made on the remaining part of 74 Brigade, which was driven in and eventually Ville-en-Tardenois was lost, and the whole centre of the 19th Division was threatened. On the right of the division, an attack against the French drove them off the Aubilly Ridge, although they later mounted a counter-attack which recovered the ridge. A counter-attack by the 9th Cheshires recovered the high ground north of Chambrecy, which helped a counter-attack by the 2nd Wiltshires, against heavy enemy fire, to recover the Montagne de Bligny position. Other developing enemy attacks, particularly along the road from Ville-en-Tardenois to Chambrecy, were broken up by artillery and machine-gun fire.

1 June 1918. Sixth day of Operation BLÜCHER-YORCK, against 19th Division and the remnants of IX Corps.
The front held by 19th Division was now much narrower, running either side of the River Ardre from the road just south of Ville-en-Tardenois to the south-west of Aubilly. However, the division could scarcely muster a single brigade's worth of men, having just 2,500 men left. The remnants of 57 Brigade on the left and 56 Brigade on the right were sandwiched between the French 40th Division to its left and 28th Division on the right.

During the morning of 1 June the enemy was seen massing south of the Bois d'Aulney. Eventually, at 4.00pm, a heavy attack was launched against the French 40th Division on the left, which drove them back through the Bois de la Cochette. At the same time a heavy attack also fell upon the 8th Gloucesters, which penetrated their front and pushed them down the hill towards Chambrecy. However, Captain Pope of B Company rallied his men and led a counter-attack, driving the enemy back and regaining the position as well as taking twenty prisoners. Nevertheless, it became necessary that evening to conform to 40th Division's new positions and pull the line back on the left to just north of Chantereine, thence north-westwards along the western edge of the Bois d'Eclisse and round the northern slope of the Montagne de Bligny to the crossroads, a mile north of Bligny village.

2 to 6 June 1918. Build-up of German artillery to support continued operations against 19th Division and the remnants of IX Corps.
These last attacks had exhausted the Germans, and no further attacks were mounted by the enemy from 2 to 5 June. However, the German artillery continued to pound the British and French positions with increasing ferocity as more of their heavy 15 and 21cm howitzers were brought up, and it became clear the enemy was preparing a major new attack. Fifteen miles away at Jaulgonne, on the River Marne, a German battalion had established a bridgehead on the south side of the river. It did not stay long. A strong counter-attack, mounted by the American 3rd and French 10th Colonial Divisions, drove it back across the river.

On the Ardre the Allied defence line remained largely unchanged, although, on 4 June, the French 28th Division had taken over part of the line to the north of Bligny on the right of 19th Division. Thus in the early morning of 6 June the line was held by a mixture of Allied units indicative of the chaotic and ferocious battle which had been fought since 27 May. On the left was the 161st Regiment of the French 40th Division; then came a composite battalion of the 8th Division, with another composite battalion of 25th Division in close support. Next, along the edge of the Bois d'Eclisse and the Montagne de Bligny, was 57 Brigade which included a composite battalion of 50th Division; to its right was 56 Brigade which included a composite battalion of 58 Brigade; finally the French 28th Division held the right of the line. In divisional reserve were elements of the French 134th Division – about 1,200 men.

From 2.00am on 6 June the 19th Divisional artillery and attached batteries began a counter-preparatory fire against the German positions. At 3.00am the German artillery opened up with a very heavy bombardment against the whole of the 19th and 28th Divisional fronts. After an hour of this heavy shelling the enemy launched an infantry attack against the two British brigades holding the line around the Montagne de Bligny. The hill was an extremely important feature and the defenders had been ordered to hold it 'at all costs', since possession of it would give the Germans 'direct observation and command of the Ardre Valley and so all our battery positions in the valley would become untenable and communications extremely precarious'.

Strong infantry attacks were launched against various parts of the British line. On the right of 56 Brigade, the composite battalion of 58 Brigade – all that was left of the 2nd Wiltshires, the 9th Royal Welsh Fusiliers and the 9th Welch Regiment, climbed out of their trenches and fell upon the enemy with their bayonets and completely shattered his assault. Two bodies of the enemy advanced against the remnants of the 10th Worcesters and 8th Gloucesters of 57 Brigade along the edge of the Bois d'Eclisse, who held their fire until the Germans had advanced to within a short distance of the line. Finally, when the enemy were almost upon them they opened up with heavy machine-gun and Lewis-gun fire, which killed many of the attackers and dispersed the remainder. The 9th Cheshires and 8th North Staffords, holding the line of 56 Brigade, also repelled enemy attacks. By 8.00am the fighting had died down in front of the British, but, on the right, heavy attacks against the French 28th Division had driven them back from the village of Bligny.

Just prior to 11.00am the Germans began an intense bombardment against positions on the Montagne de Bligny and then launched a further determined attack against the crucial 56 Brigade trench line on its summit, which drove the 9th Cheshires and 8th North Staffords off the hill. An immediate counter-attack by the 9th Cheshires was mounted, but did not succeed. At that stage the 4th King's Shropshire Light Infantry (KSLI), who were in reserve about a mile south at Chaumuzy, were ordered forward. An attack at 12.45pm supported by an artillery barrage was planned. However, as the KSLI came forward over a mile of open ground, they were exposed to enemy observation, and were subjected to heavy shell and rifle fire from the top of the hill, causing them severe casualties. By the time the KSLI gathered in the dead ground at the base of the hill, the 200 men who had left Chaumuzy had been reduced to 120 effectives.

On arrival near the base of the Montagne de Bligny, the remnants of the KSLI met with the survivors of the earlier failed counter-attack, and organized for a fresh assault in four lines or waves. Lieutenant Bright led the first A Company wave, Lieutenant Graves led the second B Company wave, and Lieutenant Derbyshire led the C Company wave. The remainder of the 9th Cheshires and 8th North Staffords formed a fourth wave. In the absence of the planned artillery barrage, the four thin waves then charged forward. Unbelievably, they braved the German rifle fire and quickly ascended the steep hill driving the surprised Germans from the hill-top trenches and dugouts. More than thirty prisoners were taken, while the remaining defenders were killed or fled the hill. As Bright re-organized on the position with just 150 men to hold this brigade position, a new bombardment fell on them. This turned out to be the late British barrage. Despite the helpful barrage, Lieutenant Bright managed to organize an active defence of the vital hilltop until his men were eventually relieved at midnight. Later that same day the French 28th Division was able to re-take the village of Bligny and re-establish the front line.

The capture of the Montagne de Bligny by such a weak force was a remarkable feat of arms and attracted a great deal of attention. The whole of 56 Brigade was awarded the Croix de Guerre with Silver Star. The 4th Battalion King's Shropshire Light Infantry was awarded the Croix de Guerre with Palms, as was Lieutenant Bright. Field Marshal Haig was so impressed that he issued a special order citing their heroism to be read out in front of every British unit, and also ordered that the Croix de Guerre should be carried on the colours of the 4th King's Shropshire LI.

The stubborn defence by the 19th Division and its composite units on 6 June seems to have finally put an end to all the German attempts to advance up the Ardre valley and capture Épernay. The German divisions, which had failed to complete the encirclement of Reims, were criticized for their lack of aggression and Ludendorff regretfully commented, 'It was a strategic disadvantage to us that we had been unable to take Reims and get our armies forward into the hilly country in that region.' Shelling continued fitfully and one more assault was mounted on 9 June; but when this was easily repelled, the Germans settled into a defensive mode. As such the failed assault on the Montagne de Bligny seems to have marked the high-water mark of the German Aisne attack in the Reims area. The 19th Division remained in its positions holding the Ardre valley and the Montagne de Bligny until 19 June, when it was relieved by the 8th Italian Division. It then marched to the south of Épernay, where units were sorted out and it began to receive new drafts, before 19th Division returned to the British zone.

During the next German offensive, which began on 15 July (FRIEDENSTURM), the Italian II Corps was pushed back from Bligny, and in subsequent operations, suffered severe casualties. Today a large Italian Military Cemetery lies near the top of the Montagne de Bligny, occupying both sides of the D980 road, which then winds down to the small British Cemetery at Chaumuzy. The Italians have recreated a beautiful but poignant corner of Italy, with cedar trees and marble monuments to the 5,000 Italians who fell fighting for France. Running along the right side of the cemetery is a small path which leads up to the very summit of the hill, where, hidden amongst the trees, stands a simple cruciform memorial to the units of 19th Division, who had taken and held this hill during June 1918.

Overall, although the British had suffered severely, they had contributed significantly to slowing and then halting the German advance as it attempted to surround Reims from the west. However, the price of being unable to make effective use of the Chemin des Dames terrain to mount a more flexible defence had been very heavy. Two-thirds of the artillery of IX Corps had been lost, and five infantry divisions had been reduced to the combat equivalent of less than half a division. In all the British suffered 28,703 casualties in the five divisions, including no fewer than seven brigadier generals. Proportionately, this was a considerably greater loss than IX Corps had suffered in the Lys battle.

The greatest losses were naturally suffered by the two forward divisions, 8th and 50th, whose destruction by shellfire in the opening barrages came on top of the losses suffered in the previous two battles.

In ten weeks of fighting the 8th Division lost a little short of 17,000 men. These losses were just exceeded by the total losses suffered by 50th Division in the same period. Both divisions had been involved in three major battles and suffered the highest losses recorded by any of the divisions in the British army during this critical period when total Allied defeat seemed all too possible. The 8th, 19th and 21st Divisions required six weeks to refit and retrain their reinforcements. However, both 50th and the 25th Division had to be totally reconstructed with new infantry battalions after the Champagne battle, and almost four months passed before they were able to come into action again, during the final drive against the German Army.

Losses to the many French divisions fighting in the Champagne were also devastating. The French suffered some 98,630 casualties along the whole Aisne front, but were to suffer a further 35,000 casualties in the Matz campaign. German losses were probably similar (they were estimated at some 130,000), but their offensive had gained significant territory, including the north bank of the Marne, and they still retained the strategic initiative. The Germans also benefited from seizing the huge stores of ammunition, food and war supplies which had been held in depots behind the Aisne. Additionally, Ludendorff had succeeded in successfully resurrecting the bogeyman of a military threat directed at capturing Paris.

Pétain was heavily criticized for his lack of foresight and poor handling of the defence, and came very close to being sacked. With his position threatened, he became obsessed with the threat to Paris above all other considerations, and arbitrarily moved reserves from behind Amiens to block the German advance, thereby falling for Ludendorff's strategy. But for the steadfast opposition of Foch, Pétain would have also taken all the carefully-husbanded troops being gathered for Mangin's counter-attack and used them to guard Paris. Fortunately, two American divisions (the 2nd and 3rd), which were supposedly still in training, were able to be brought forward to block the attempt by Conta and Winckler's corps to secure the Paris-Metz road west of Château-Thierry. By blocking these attacks, the Americans demonstrated the vigour and courage of their young soldiers, and gave the French time to strengthen their defences. Thus German efforts to attract reserves away from the northern front, by developing this threat to Paris in the early part of June, were only partially successful.

The British also suffered a significant loss of manpower and equipment from their five divisions, which had been sent to the Champagne area with the intention of refitting and retraining. These wholly unexpected losses were very worrying for Haig as they came on top of the heavy losses already suffered in the first two great German attacks. To make things worse, reinforcements were still being retained in England by Lloyd George's policy, and only three of the five divisions could be brought up to strength immediately to face a presumed new German attack.

The extremely unlucky fate of moving from one unanticipated battle area to another was a personal disaster for most of the men of IX Corps, but definitely not for the GSO 2. The contribution made by Captain Montgomery in his key role of GSO 2 (Operations) of IX Corps throughout its terrible retreat from the Chemins des Dames position was finally recognized and on 3 June 1918 he was promoted brevet major. A month later, Bernard Montgomery left IX Corps on promotion again as he joined he joined 47th (London) Division as the GSO 1 with the rank of temporary lieutenant colonel. The 47th Division was commanded by the most senior major general in the British army, Major General Sir George Gorringe. The GSO 1 has to work very closely with his commander and not everyone would have welcomed being close to someone so notoriously difficult, nicknamed 'Bloody Orange'. However, Montgomery got along well with Gorringe who gave Montgomery full authority to act in his name. This enabled Montgomery to develop another important aspect of his command philosophy, namely the use of a chief of staff (COS) as the commander's right-hand man, and his empowerment to act as the commander's effective deputy. Much later, as a general, Montgomery considered this a key aspect of his exercise of command, and believed this left him free to devote his whole attention to the prime task of preparing for or fighting the next battle.

The French Army had fared little better than the British when faced with the overwhelming German spring attacks. Now at least there was a greater common understanding of the peril faced by all the Allies. Significantly, the inexperienced Americans had begun to demonstrate their fighting qualities in combat against the veteran German divisions. Moreover, the Americans had also agreed to accelerate their transfer of troops by bringing over to Europe a further 500,000 men during the months of June and July, including ten huge infantry divisions.

The Foch Offensive and the arrival of the Americans

As a young man of just 18, Ferdinand Foch had served briefly as a volunteer in the infantry during the disastrous Franco-Prussian War of 1870-71. He had witnessed the fall of the regime of Napoleon III, as well as the resulting dramatic conversion of his college town of Metz into a German city, which turned him into an implacable enemy of Germany. In 1873 he was commissioned into the artillery and began an illustrious military career. He held a succession of staff and regimental appointments until, by 1895, he was a major and was appointed to serve for six years at the French Staff College, where he proved to be a very gifted instructor. His analysis of the French defeat in 1870, and his writings on military history and theory, became extremely influential, and led to the regeneration of the French Army. Although he firmly believed that the attack was the key to victory, he did not recommend recklessness in military strategy. Nevertheless, his reputation for blind espousal of the attack, above all else, blighted his later reputation. However, it was his unfailing optimism during the crises of the dark days of 1918, partnered by the courage of the equally indomitable Prime Minister Georges Clemenceau, which ensured the eventual triumph of the Allies.

General Foch was no stranger to the River Marne area. In 1914 the courageous attacks by his XX Corps had held up the advancing Germans in Lorraine, and caused General Joffre to promote him to command the newly-formed Ninth Army. He was then able to liberate Châlons on the River Marne from the Germans, and went on to co-ordinate the northern French armies and liaise with the British during the 'Race to the Sea'. Eventually he was placed in command of the Northern Army Group of French and British armies. However, he was blamed for the heavy loss of life in the campaigns of 1915 and 1916, fell out of favour, and was posted to Italy. In 1917 he was rehabilitated by General Pétain, who, taking over from General Nivelle as the French Commander-in-Chief, brought Foch back to be Chief of the General Staff of the French

Army. In the crisis of March 1918 he continued to show determination and fighting spirit and was selected by the Allies to be the Supreme Allied Commander with responsibility for ensuring that reserves were available to guarantee there would be no breakthrough of the Allied front in France.

In later years Foch was frequently criticized for always favouring the offensive in battle, but it is undeniable that conducting skilful defensive battles and withdrawals, while absolutely necessary, does not actually win wars. Nevertheless, while the Germans held the strategic initiative, as they did during the early part of 1918, it was essential for the Allies to defend themselves as economically as possible. Experience through much of the war showed that an elastic defence, bolstered by reserves, artillery and machine guns, would always overcome the attacker. Every German or Allied offensive, no matter how successfully launched, was doomed to run out of fresh troops and supplies and then flounder in the debris of the battle zone. Eventually the offensive would succumb to enemy counter-attacks, thus making it impossible to administer a single mighty knock-out blow. Aware that the key to blocking powerful German attacks was the ready availability of reserves, Foch spent much of his effort as 'Supremo' persuading his allies to make reserves available to support each other.

To achieve Allied victory General Foch envisaged that they would need both to recover the strategic initiative, and then mount a succession of repeated attacks to wear down the great German war machine. Therefore, during the crisis summer months of 1918, Foch had to steer carefully between the competing needs of his two major commanders. Pétain was under serious political threat, and sought to draw reserves to Paris for its immediate defence, while Haig was desperate to attract more reserves to ensure the survival of the British Army against a repeat of the hammer blows of March and April. While balancing these needs, Foch was continually pressing the Allies to build up their troop numbers and to think about mounting offensives as soon as conditions would allow.

The role of Supreme Allied Commander was not easy. Foch had no direct powers of command and had to work through the senior Allied commanders, Pétain, Haig, and Pershing. He could demand control of reserves, but had to negotiate to persuade the commanders to undertake offensives where he thought it would have best effect. It was also natural for the Allies to feel that more was being demanded of them than the Supreme Commander was asking of his own nation.

Fortunately, Foch was a commander with unique qualifications. Not only did he have outstanding abilities as a military thinker, he had also repeatedly demonstrated his outstanding leadership and determination through four years of war. He had shown his ability to command successfully major French formations in the field and had worked closely with the British in the northern sector. Moreover, Foch was usually supported by the equally pugnacious veteran French prime minister, Georges Clemenceau, who was able to prevail upon the reluctant British prime minister, Lloyd George, to send more troops to France. The Allies were fortunate that in Foch, they had chosen a supremo who was strong enough to hold the alliance together and to inspire the Allies to make sacrifices to help each other to withstand the challenging reverses inflicted by the victorious German Army.

Fortuitously, Foch recognized the vulnerability of the German positions around Soissons, and was primarily responsible for championing and initiating the Second Battle of the Marne. Following its success, it was he, not Pétain, the French Commander-in-Chief, who was rewarded by promotion to maréchal on 6 August 1918; Pétain was promoted a few months later. Marshal Foch, by his vision and determination, became the undoubted architect of the succession of heavy Allied attacks across the whole front, which defeated and threatened to encircle the German forces in France. In outline his strategy was based on two major thrusts, one from the south-east, the Franco-American St Mihiel-Meuse-Argonne offensive, and one from the north-west, the Belgian, British and French offensives in Flanders. Despite heavy casualties, both offensives succeeded, and were only halted close to the borders of Germany by the German requested Armistice.

Nevertheless, despite his belief in eventual victory, there seems little doubt that the rapid success of the third German offensive on 27 May 1918 took Foch, as well as the other senior French commanders, by surprise. The first two offensives had struck the British, and it was confidently expected that the third attack would also be in Flanders, where most of the reserve divisions had been gathered. As a result, many sections of the 450-kilometre French front line had been thinned out. Therefore, Ludendorff's brilliant decision to switch his attack from Flanders to a weakly-held section of the French line in the Champagne area richly deserved the total strategic and tactical surprise that it achieved. The French Intelligence service, normally clever and well-informed, was duped and failed to detect the movement of thousands of guns and more than a dozen divisions to the Reims area. As a result, the violent initial artillery barrage on 27 May achieved complete surprise as it shattered the forward positions of the French XI and British IX Corps on the thinly-held Chemin des Dames line. Then the great tide of rampaging German infantry swamped all French attempts to plug the gap, enabling the Germans to advance almost thirty miles and reach the River Marne within three days. Ludendorff was within an ace of achieving his aim of drawing sufficient reserves away from his preferred attack area, which remained Flanders.

The Germans appeared to be on the cusp of achieving total victory in the early summer of 1918 as their infiltration tactics and commitment of fresh divisions repeatedly surprised the Allies and gained them huge swathes of territory. The swingeing losses also badly undermined Allied civilian and military morale. However, these signal victories were all achieved at a huge cost in casualties to the German Army, which then required additional troops to garrison the new longer and less easily defendable front lines. The loss of so much territory was a stunning shock to the Allies, and it initially overshadowed the realization that they had actually managed to contain the best the Germans could throw at them. Moreover, the prospect of imminent defeat forced them to sink their differences and combine their resources under Foch as the single Supreme Commander.

While the three spring defeats had been bitter, the Allies now knew how to recognize the indicators of the German preparations for a surprise attack, and how to counter these new German tactics with a deeper, more flexible defence. It was abundantly clear that as long as the Germans retained the strategic initiative they would be able to make a significant impact on almost any part of the front, but actually breaking through into the open area behind the front would remain very difficult for them. As a result the subsequent two major German attacks, in June and July, were held comfortably by the French, who had quickly gathered sufficient reserves to meet these attacks. In addition, for the first time, the French benefited from the significant support provided by a few of the new divisions of the American Army.

Having contained the fifth great German offensive of 15 July, Foch immediately exploited the opportunity to strike the over-extended German divisions, particularly in the west of the Marne salient. There is little doubt that, supported by their tanks, aircraft and artillery, the French, attacking with their Tenth, Sixth, Ninth and Fifth Armies would have achieved surprise and a degree of success with their co-ordinated counter-attacks on the 18th. However, the French Army was generally very short of trained reserves, and, under Pétain's pessimistic leadership, had adopted a largely defensive posture in front of Paris. Moreover, after four years of bitter war and huge debilitating losses, many French soldiers had lost their appetite for sacrifice. They were prepared to defend France to the death, but few believed that further offensive action would make any real difference against the proven ability of the Germans to seal off every breach in their defences.

Foch's genius was to appoint one of his best attack generals, Charles Mangin, to command the troops of the enlarged Tenth Army that he was carefully husbanding in the thick Forest of Villers-Cotterêts. Then he negotiated with Pershing to add American troops to Mangin's Army. The addition of two divisions of fresh American troops, brave to the point of recklessness, added enormous punch, vitality and momentum to Mangin's attack. The sheer power and sacrifice of these fresh American troops ensured that Tenth Army was able to break through the thickest lines of German wire, trenches and artillery barrages, to threaten the neck of the salient at Soissons.

When the United States declared war against Germany on 6 April 1917 it was dependent, like the pre-war British, on a small regular army and a back-up territorial force, namely the state-based National Guard. Some steps had already been taken to increase both forces, but the regular army had only 127,588 officers and men, supplemented by a National Guard of about 180,000 men. This was a very small force in the context of a European war. Interestingly enough, when George Marshall became Acting Chief of Staff in July 1939 the enlisted strength of the active regular army was still only 174,000 men, with just 12,000 officers. Bitterly Marshall complained to Congress in 1939 that the Americans, once again, had no field army, while the Germans had ninety divisions available and the Japanese deployed fifty divisions in China alone.

However, in 1917, almost 1,000,000 men immediately volunteered for service, and another 3,000,000 were drafted. The dramatic expansion of the army and the training of so many officers and men represented an enormous training commitment, which needed time to produce results. The very first soldiers of the 1st Division were shipped in June and July 1917, but were only a token of the forces to follow. By the summer of 1918, 250,000 men were being shipped each month; actually, 313,410 landed in France in July 1918. More than 2,000,000 'doughboys' (as the American soldiers were nicknamed) sailed to France before the end of hostilities, and, despite the best efforts of German submarines, very few were lost at sea; some 230 men were lost in the sinking of the British SS *Tuscania* by *UB-77* in February 1918, and another fifty-six were lost when the British SS *Moldavia* was sunk by *UB-57* in May 1918. By the Armistice, the Americans had created an enormous logistical support base, and brought forty divisions to France, of which twenty-nine had been in combat. Generally it was the early divisions which saw most action and, accordingly, suffered the greatest losses. Altogether 50,280 American soldiers were killed in battle; more than half of these (26,277) were killed in the bloody Argonne offensive while another 56,000 died from other causes in France, principally influenza, and some 205,690 were wounded or gassed.

It was planned that each newly-formed division should be given six months' training in the United States before being sent abroad. This was to be followed by two months more continuation training and exposure in quiet sectors of the front in France before commitment to intensive operations in an active sector. However, many units did not receive any training on their artillery or infantry support weapons until they actually got to Europe. Indeed, in the rush to send sixteen divisions to France in May and June of 1918, many only partially-trained men were embarked precipitately. For example, when Buster Keaton, the famous Hollywood actor, enlisted in July 1918, he said he was given just two weeks' training before being shipped overseas with the 40th 'Sunshine' Division.

It was felt necessary to show the Allies some early benefit from the American participation in the war, and the first four regular divisions were quickly formed from a mixture of regular army personnel and volunteers and then rushed to France, often with the minimum of training, two in 1917 and two in early 1918. In addition a number of divisions based on National Guard formations were also hurried to France, including the famous 26th (Yankee) and 42nd (Rainbow) Divisions, which both arrived in late 1917.

As mentioned earlier both Bernard Montgomery and George C. Marshall were young captains serving as operational staff officers in 1917, but both were destined to play huge and significant roles in winning the Second World War for the Allies. Each acknowledged the debt they owed their war service in France in preparing them for the later conflict. Perhaps Montgomery's most important was the realization that one needed to possess the strategic initiative in order to launch a successful attack, as he did at El Alamein. Marshall's talents were significantly different from Montgomery's. He was never given the chance to lead a field army, but his organizational talents and single-minded determination created an army of eight million men, which was equipped and trained to defeat all of America's enemies. His experience fighting in Europe convinced him that Germany needed to be defeated before Japan, and could be defeated by an attack delivered from Britain into northern Europe.

As the war began for the United States, Captain Marshall was already a relatively experienced officer, who had graduated from the prestigious Virginia Military Institute in 1901, and been commissioned in the Army the following year. He quickly distinguished himself as an extremely competent officer whose wide experience included service in the Philippines. He graduated from the Infantry/Cavalry School in 1907 and from the Army Staff College in 1908. In 1915 he became a staff officer, and as the United States mobilized for war he was heavily involved in training new officers and the newly-formed units. He accompanied the first American formation to be sent to France, where he was responsible for organizing the accommodation, organization and training, evolution of tactics and operations of the 1st Division, as it adapted to conditions in France. Although supposedly a regular army unit, 1st Division lacked training and experienced men. Marshall was responsible for organizing everything needed to turn this green force into a combat-ready organization which could be pitched against the highly-experienced Imperial German Army.

In October 1917, at the same time as Montgomery was organising IX Corps for its attacks in the Passchendaele area, Marshall found himself recklessly challenging his ultimate boss. Marshall was always a fiercely loyal man, who stood by his friends and commanders, and this quality caused him to contradict General Jack Pershing, whom he thought was unjustly criticizing the training and preparedness of the American 1st Division, and implicitly its commander, Major General Sibert. Major Marshall had just been promoted and was the acting Chief of Staff (COS) of the 1st Division, which was Pershing's showpiece unit. Not only was Marshall responsible for organizing its training alongside the French 47th Chasseur Division but, at the same time, was also bearing heavy responsibilities for organizing many other things, such as the reception arrangements for the next three divisions (the 2nd, 26th and 42nd) due to arrive at short notice, and Marshall was working long hours as he attempted to meet all the requirements of the new American command structure.

Training conditions had not been easy for the 1st Division, which had to undertake long marches to reach its training areas, and constantly saw talented men taken from its ranks to build up the American command organization. In preparation for the visit by General Pershing, Marshall had personally arranged for Major Teddy Roosevelt Jr to march his 2nd Battalion, from the 26th Regiment, to a training area, where it could give a demonstration of trench clearing. Teddy's battalion had marched all night to be at the training area and then gave an enthusiastic and noisy demonstration. However, this did not satisfy General Pershing as it was not according to the book. Actually 'the book' had not reached the 1st Division, and the officers of 2nd Battalion had done their best with what they had learnt from the French. Marshall therefore felt that the criticism aimed at the division's level of training was unfair, and said so plainly to the general. Pershing was forced to admit that his people had not actually produced or printed 'the book', due to 'certain difficulties'. Marshall by then was thoroughly warmed up, and launched another attack on his general saying that despite 'his difficulties', he was expected to constantly deal with fresh demands from Pershing's headquarters.

Everyone expected Marshall to be sacked for his outburst, but surprisingly Pershing tolerated his candour. Fortunately, this habit of speaking his mind did him no harm with Pershing, who came to value his forthrightness and eventually moved him to his headquarters and later made him his ADC, and indeed remained a friend for life. However, Marshall always thought that his famously short temper had held back his career for many years after the war, and he may well have had a point. Pershing soon sacked Sibert, and when a new divisional commander took over, he eschewed promoting the experienced but difficult subordinate Marshall who had initially filled the role of acting COS. As a result, in November 1917; when Colonel Hanson Ely, who had actually taken over as COS from Marshall, left to take command of the 28th Infantry Regiment, Major General Robert Bullard chose Lieutenant Colonel Campbell King to be his divisional chief of staff, and Marshall remained as the Operations Officer. Marshall was quite aware of his own high level of competence and always regretted that he did not get a field command during the First World War, because he felt that he could easily have risen to general rank like MacArthur or Ely by the end of the war. As it was he had to wait another eighteen years, until October 1936, to make brigadier general. Montgomery waited even longer, not getting his first brigade command until August 1937, on his return to England from India.

While Marshall went on with the exhausting work of planning the training of the men and combat operations, including all the preparations for the attack at Cantigny, Colonel Hanson Ely actually commanded the 28th in the battle (see page 47). There he acquired the nickname of 'Ely of Cantigny'. Later Ely commanded 3 Brigade in the 2nd Division, and eventually as a major general commanded the 5th Division when it successfully forced the Meuse crossings as part of the Argonne offensive.

Although Marshall desperately wanted a field command he was far too useful in his role as a staff officer. Indeed he was often invited to work in other branches, such as supply, and offered accelerated promotion, but he could not be spared from the 1st Division. In January 1918 he was promoted to lieutenant colonel as he planned operations for 1st Division, including its successful defence at Seicheprey, and numerous raids culminating in its first independent attack at Cantigny on 28 May. Once the attack at Cantigny had been completed successfully, Marshall felt free to apply for a combat post. His request for a combat command was brief, if not terse, and based on the grounds that he had been on staff duty since February 1915, and 'was tired of the incessant strain of staff work'.

Major General Bullard had no option but to pass on the request. Bullard had grown to admire Marshall's talents and had indeed recommended him for accelerated promotion to colonel but this had been turned down. However, he withheld his support for the request, stating that Marshall's 'special fitness is for staff work and because I doubt that in this, whether it be teaching or practice, he has an equal in the Army today'. Since his boss had not added his recommendation to his request, Marshall was not given the field command he desired. However, his talents for staff work were recognized. The following month he left 1st Division on posting to AEF Headquarters at Chaumont. There he began working for General Fox Conner planning the St Mihiel operation. Marshall later wrote that he left the 1st Division with considerable sadness. It was not just that he had been a prime mover in ensuring its organization and movement to France. He had dealt with innumerable obstacles to its formation and training, and then nursed it through its early exposure to the dangers and boredom of life in the trenches. Although not in a direct command position, he had worked continually on their behalf and concerned himself for the safety and welfare of the frontline troops. In later life he wrote about his emotional farewell to 1st Division, and the pain of severing the connection and bonds with the men who had accompanied him to France. Although he would experience other problems and triumphs, he would never again enjoy 'that feeling of comradeship which grows out of an intimate relationship among those in immediate contact with fighting troops'. Twenty-one years later, speaking as Army Chief of Staff at a 1st Division Dinner, he acknowledged how important this major formative experience had been for him: 'The greatest experience of my life as a professional soldier remains in my recollection of those days and my contacts with the splendid young lieutenants and captains of the First Division.'

St Mihiel was the very successful first attack by the First US Army, which used seventeen divisions to capture the St Mihiel Salient in just two days. In August Marshall was again promoted to colonel, and to be Assistant Chief of Staff of First US Army. He was then ordered to begin planning for the great American Meuse-Argonne offensive, even before the St Mihiel attack was launched on 12 September. This required him to switch 400,000 men, 3,000 guns and 900,000 tons of supplies from the St Mihiel sector to the Argonne front for an attack to be launched on 26 September, while some 220,000 French and Italian troops had to be withdrawn from the same area. There were only three railway lines and three roads to make this switch and to bring in 200,000 extra American soldiers. The eventual success of this switch to the Argonne, which surprised the Germans, was due largely to Marshall's planning genius.

There were serious divergences of view between the Americans and their allies on the best employment of this enormous reservoir of manpower. The principal one was that the French and British senior officers considered themselves, after more than three years of fighting, to be seasoned practitioners of the art of war and wanted the Americans to provide 'fill-in' manpower, of which they were crucially short, while they continued to organize their armies for victory. Not unnaturally, the Americans did not want to provide 'cannon fodder', but did want to run their own show under their very determined commander General John 'Black Jack' Pershing. The Allies were also keen for the Americans to prioritize the scarce shipping resources for moving manpower and not for transporting equipment and stores.

For his part, Pershing seemed oblivious of the frightful combat conditions, particularly artillery shelling, which had forced both sides to seek shelter in trenches. He wanted to demonstrate to the unconvinced French and British generals that the Americans would not get bogged down in trench warfare, but would be able to break out of the trenches and win a convincing victory by manoeuvre warfare. He therefore sought to have his men trained for a war of movement. Newly arriving divisions were sent for battlefield exposure and training to the British and French armies but were discouraged from becoming too 'trench-minded' or from absorbing 'bad habits' from their teachers. Pershing's overriding concern was to ensure that his boys gained combat experience, and were not used as trench fodder.

The Battle of Cantigny, which was a classic test piece attack by the American 1st Division on 28 May, was the first divisional attack organized by Americans and is justly famous as an example of American military prowess. However, the 1st Division had, by this time, been in France for almost a year. It had served with different French formations in the trenches and was becoming a quite experienced fighting unit. Perhaps a better example of the quality and capabilities of the Americans was demonstrated some five weeks later by just four green companies, about 1,000 men, of the 33rd Illinois National Guard Division. The 33rd was new to France, and had been sent to gain battlefield experience by training with the Australians in the south of the British sector. The Australian Corps, with its five large divisions, occupied the most southern end of the British line as the right wing of Fourth Army, commanded by the intelligent and very competent General Rawlinson. Part of its front extended south of the River Somme, which put it next to French General Debeney's First Army.

The 33rd 'Prairie' Division had been activated in July 1917 but did not begin training until September. It had begun to assemble in France in May 1918 and moved in June to the Australian sector near Amiens. Volunteers from the division then rehearsed enthusiastically for their part in the well-prepared attack by the Australian 4th Division on le Hamel, a heavily-defended German spur located a couple of miles north-east of Villers-Bretonneux. Under the careful plan devised by General Monash, the 4th Division stormed the German trenches on 4 July 1918, supported by the four companies of Americans, and sixty Mark V fighting tanks. In support were 600 guns and howitzers as well as the machine-gun battalions of three other Australian divisions. The whole operation was planned to take ninety minutes and the objectives were actually carried in just ninety-three minutes. Some six square miles of land was occupied with relatively light casualties of 1,062 Australians and 176 Americans. Captured that morning were forty-one German officers, 1,431 soldiers, two field guns, twenty-six trench mortars, and 171 machine guns; another 631 Germans were taken prisoner during the diversionary attack on Ville-sur-Ancre.

This truly model attack demonstrated not only the outstanding planning ability of one of the most able corps staffs, but also the proficiency that the British and their Dominion troops had acquired in organizing their artillery. This battle was totally different to the great staged battles of June 1916. It was a deliberately contained 'bite and hold' operation. There was no preliminary barrage lasting many days and no intention of achieving a break through. However, for the Illinois National Guardsmen, the short creeping barrage, which initiated the attack, would have been a revelation, particularly for their own gunners. Unfortunately for the 33rd Division, its own 58th Field Artillery Brigade was separated from it in the United States and supported other divisions during the war, particularly the 1st Division at St Mihiel, and did not rejoin the division until it reached Luxembourg in January 1919.

At 3.10am on 4 July the German 13th Division was woken by one of the biggest bangs ever to welcome an Independence Day. On a front of just over three miles, 326 field guns and 302 heavies opened up with a barrage fired in three lines. Six hundred yards out from the start line, the HE shells of the heavy 6-inch howitzers rained down. Some 200 yards closer in landed the 4.5-inch howitzer shells containing 90 per cent HE and 10 per cent smoke. Finally, closest to the start line, just 200 yards away, a barrage from 240 18-pounder field guns, firing 60 per cent shrapnel, 30 per cent HE and 10 per cent smoke fell on the enemy forward trenches. The barrage was continued for some distance up and down the line to confuse the enemy, and some heavies were tasked to provide counter-battery fire beyond the attack area to hinder enfilade fire. The barrage then moved forward in 100 yard lifts every three minutes. Critical to the success of this short operation (or 'stunt' as the Australians called it) was the innovative use of tanks, both to break into the enemy lines and to carry forward supporting stores and extra ammunition. Some aircraft were also used to drop ammunition to the forward troops.

Despite the thorough planning and rehearsal, and the 'glorious' barrage, not everything goes right in war. The close-in barrage hit some of the Australian infantrymen and tanks, perhaps due to the inclusion of 30 per cent HE in this line of the barrage, as it is usually considered safer to fire just shrapnel close to one's own troops. Also, despite its intensity, the barrage failed to destroy the crucial trench in the centre of the German line. The Pear Trench was left only partially damaged, and most of the casualties were caused by the German machine gunners regaining their positions in that trench after the first artillery lift. However, what did work effectively was the counter-battery fire from the heavy guns which ensured that the Germans found it very difficult to respond effectively with enfilade fire from the flanks.

Two Australian soldiers, Lance Corporal Thomas Axford and Private Henry Dalziel were both awarded the Victoria Cross for their bravery in charging enemy machine-gun nests. Private Dalziel was the Number 2 on the Lewis gun and, when held up by the defenders of Pear Trench, silenced one machine gun and then dashed forward with just a pistol in his hand and killed or captured another machine-gun crew. Also the green American soldiers from the 131st and 132nd Infantry Regiments, who had trained and rehearsed intensively with the Australians, proved their mettle to the Australians that day. As one impressed Australian company commander later reported, 'United States troops are now classified as Diggers.' Corporal Thomas Pope of E Company, from the 131st Infantry Regiment, charged a German machine-gun nest and bayoneted its defenders. He was awarded a British Distinguished Conduct Medal (DCM), which was presented to him by King George V when he visited the 33rd Division in August 1918. Corporal Pope and seven other American soldiers were awarded Distinguished Service Crosses, and Pope also became the first recipient of the Medal of Honor in France; which was presented to him by General Pershing in 1919.

There were many important lessons to be learnt from this short battle, which removed the German threat to Villers-Bretonneux, and clearly demonstrated the fighting qualities of both the experienced Australian and the green American troops. Not least for the Americans, there were many valuable lessons learnt on how to co-operate with artillery, tanks, and aircraft. This included staying close to the barrage, and particularly the importance of making sure that the infantry consolidated on the objective having thoroughly cleared the area taken of snipers and machine guns. The Battle of Hamel, like Cantigny, provided a clear demonstration of the ability of the Allies to attack successfully and hold any part of the front they chose, no matter how well defended by the Germans. The orders for the Hamel attack were quickly copied and became the model for later British attacks, particularly the three-corps attack by Fourth Army just four weeks later, on 8 August, which caused so much damage to German morale.

However, despite their signal success on 4 July, of all days, Pershing was aggrieved and regarded even this extremely limited diversion of manpower, all of whom had volunteered, as a dangerous example of how his allies were intent on 'abusing' his soldiers, although perhaps there was also a degree of chagrin involved. The well-planned and well-executed attack at Cantigny by the 1st Division, said to be Pershing's favourite division, did not get the public attention it deserved, compared to the success of the 33rd Division at Hamel, or the determined battles around Château-Thierry by the marines of 2nd Division and the machine gunners of 3rd Division. Pershing was reinforced in his belief that only by establishing independent command and getting full control of his troops, could he avoid this kind of 'exploitation' and prevent his soldiers from becoming as 'trench-minded' as the other Allies.

The 131st Infantry Regiment of 33rd Division was able to render one more service to its tutors before moving east to join the American Army assembling for its Argonne offensive. The British 18th and 58th Divisions of III Corps, on the left of the British Fourth Army's great attack at Amiens on 8 August 1918, faced a particularly tough task against the alerted Germans of the 27th Division, holding the Chipilly Spur dominating the Somme river valley. On 9 August the 131st Regiment joined the assault, which had fallen behind schedule, and captured Gressaire Wood and finally the key Chipilly Spur, thereby enabling the whole offensive to continue going forward. By the 27th the British had advanced twelve miles and the Allies had captured 500 guns and 50,000 prisoners, and taken back much of the Somme salient, which had been lost in the March attack.

The 33rd Division then fought for eleven days in the first phase of the Argonne offensive. It served in Bullard's III Corps on the far right of the American line, where it captured the Bois des Forges on the first day. In October it moved to the French XVII Corps for its offensive astride the River Meuse, thereby establishing the unique record of being the only American division to fight directly under British, French and American command. It was still attacking the Hindenburg Line guarding the western approaches to Metz when hostilities ceased on 11 November. During its busy campaign, the 33rd served in eleven different army corps and suffered some 8,000 casualties, of whom over 800 were killed.

A serious obstacle to achieving Pershing's aim of independence was that, although the Americans came with huge manpower resources, they arrived without heavy weapons, and with only limited quantities of transport. American industry in the First World War provided small arms and copious quantities of ammunition, but developed only limited capacity to manufacture heavy weapons, such as the British 18-pounder, before the war ended. As a result, most artillery pieces had to be provided by French and British industry and they could only be towed by reducing the number of horses available to move the French and British artillery. Cars and trucks were shipped to France, but the lack of sufficient logistic support for American divisions became apparent even as early as the Marne battles and would severely handicap the Argonne offensive.

American soldiers wore the same steel helmet as the British, and pictures of their respective soldiers are often confused. Although both armies spoke English, it rapidly became obvious that there were very many similarities in name, but a great many differences in fact, between the organization, equipment and tactics of the British and American armies. Important terms such as division, brigade and regiment often refer to quite different sizes of formations within each army. There are numerous references to both armies in this history and it is important to clarify the differences in the size, equipment, and performance of the armies of these two English-speaking allies to understand their capabilities, and to appreciate both their similarities and differences.

As in most armies of the period, American divisions were established with twelve infantry battalions, each of about 1,000 men, and with three battalions per regiment. It was organized as a so-called 'square' division, with two infantry brigades, each commanding two infantry regiments. This enabled the division to mount a very strong attack with two brigades side by side, or one behind the other. This was similar to the original organization of the German divisions, which had also begun the war as square divisions with four regiments. However, in spring 1915, the Germans adopted a triangular organization, with each division comprising only a single infantry brigade of three regiments, each of three battalions. This reduction to nine battalions was said to allow the Germans to effect a significant manpower saving, by reducing divisional strength from 17,500 to 12,500 men and accordingly allowing them to expand significantly their total number of divisions (for more detail on German and French divisions see pages 152-4). Battle losses and German manpower shortages reduced this figure to well below

10,000 men, while the fresh American divisions usually numbered close to their official establishment of 28,000 men (with 979 officers and 27,082 soldiers).

Each of the four regiments in an American division had 112 officers and 3,720 soldiers, and was considerably larger than a comparable British infantry brigade of 1918. In addition to its three infantry battalions, of four rifle companies, it was organized with a headquarters company, a supply company, and a machine-gun company, with sixteen 8mm Hotchkiss machine guns, or later the .30-inch Browning machine guns.

The headquarters comprised the regimental staff, as well as the intelligence and signal detachments and the pioneer platoon. It also contained the regimental commander's own two units of close-support artillery, grouped in the howitzer company. Half of this dedicated close-fire support was provided by the mortar support platoon, equipped with six 3-inch Stokes mortars. The Stokes light trench mortar (LTM) had been adopted from the British, who had begun using the simple and reliable Stokes mortar in 1916. It was a 'light' weapon, and easily man-portable, provided the men could carry the 43lb barrel, 28lb base plate, and 37lb bipod, as well as plenty of its 11lb bombs, and thus could provide close support to the infantry advance. The Stokes LTM could launch ten bombs a minute up to 800 yards, and was very effective against massed troops, as well as in the indirect-fire role against enemy trenches and machine-gun nests. The regiment's other close-support unit had been adopted from the French army. This was the 37mm cannon platoon, equipped with three rifled guns, which fired one pound shells in a flat trajectory up to 1,500 yards. Also known as the 'one pounder', this was a really effective weapon against machine-gun nests, fortified buildings and bunkers and remained in use with the American army for almost twenty years. Finally, in order to move its basic equipment, each regiment needed at least 120 wagons, sixty-five horses and 325 mules.

By comparison a British division was much smaller, and had a triangular organization of three infantry brigades, each comparable but rather smaller than an American regiment. Due to the lack of manpower, these brigades had all been reduced from four to three infantry battalions early in 1918. Each battalion was nominally supposed to number 1,000, later 900, men. However when shortfalls, training courses, sickness and leave were taken into account, most battalions considered themselves fortunate if they had 600 effectives. As a result most British divisions could barely muster a total of 10,000 men including all support units, often less. Generally, each infantry battalion was recruited on a geographical basis as part of a much larger county regiment, e.g. the Gloucestershire Regiment raised twenty-five battalions during the war, which were largely recruited from Gloucestershire. British soldiers identified strongly with their regiments, all of which were marked by wide variations in tradition, culture, uniform, footwear and headdress, not to mention the soldier's regional dialect, although these differences could become camouflaged by the mud of the trenches. The British soldiers took enormous pride in these differences of uniform, which contributed to their sense of history of the unit and its *esprit de corps* and were fiercely loyal to their regiments, as well as to their individual battalions. The differences in footwear and uniform between regiments can be seen quite clearly in the picture of blinded gas casualties from the 55th (West Lancashire) Division taken on 10 April 1918 (see plate section).

Each British infantry battalion was consecutively numbered within its regiment as it was raised and, as the war progressed, more and more battalions were formed or split to form two battalions. In peacetime most county regiments had two battalions but, during the course of the war, many regiments raised more than thirty battalions. The battalion was organized with four rifle companies, normally each of four platoons. Each platoon was made up of four sections, plus a small command section comprising the platoon officer and two or three men. One section was designated the Lewis Machine-Gun Section. As a minimum the Lewis gun would require a two-man crew (one to fire and one to help load the ammunition drums, which sat on top of the weapon), although more men were needed to carry the extra boxes of ammunition drums.

The Lewis gun could fire 500 rounds per minute and thus was the most significant source of firepower at the disposal of the platoon commander, who could deploy the gun for defence or attack, particularly against enemy machine guns. The air-cooled Lewis gun was not really light; it weighed 28lbs (12.7kg) but was considerably lighter than the water-cooled Vickers gun and could be carried easily by one man and even fired from the hip. In more open warfare, of the kind experienced in Champagne, Lewis guns could be used to engage the German machine guns, suppressing them with rapid fire, while the rifle sections worked in closer to the gun position, from where they could then bombard the gun nest with hand or rifle grenades. By 1918 most platoons were actually equipped with two Lewis guns, usually in two four-man sections. Thus, with an additional four Lewis guns for the anti-aircraft role, each British infantry battalion could have available a total of thirty-six Lewis guns.

British military doctrine also laid great emphasis on the firepower available from the quite accurate soldier's rifle (the SMLE) which, with its bayonet fixed, could also be a deadly close-quarter weapon. In addition, at least half the riflemen would be trained to project the No. 36 Mills grenade, which had a detachable base plate, and was fired from a cup-shaped discharger fitted on the end of the rifle. This had a range of up to 240 yards when fired using a ballistite cartridge. With two dischargers per section, it gave the infantry extra range when stalking the enemy, and proved very useful against enemy trenches, pill-boxes and machine-gun nests, particularly when they were protected by deep belts of barbed wire. Although the British infantry did not have flamethrowers, much the same effect could be achieved against German bunkers, full of ammunition, by the hand-thrown phosphorous grenade.

Unlike the Germans, the British, particularly their senior commanders, had been slow to appreciate the value of the heavy machine gun. Nevertheless, by 1918, each division had its own heavy machine-gun battalion of four companies, each equipped with sixteen Vickers machine guns. In 1914 a division deployed with just twenty-four heavy machine guns. By 1918 a much smaller British infantry division had a total of sixty-four Vickers guns. The heavy machine guns played an absolutely vital role in defence, but were less useful in the advance because of their weight and comparative immobility. In time it would be realized that the required mobile heavy supporting fire could only be provided effectively by tanks. However, the British divisional infantry could deploy some 350 of their far more mobile Lewis machine guns.

Each British division also had three light mortar batteries, one for each brigade, equipped, like the Americans, with eight 3-inch Stokes mortars. Communications within the division were provided by a signals company. Combat engineering support was provided by a pioneer battalion and three Royal Engineer companies. The pioneer battalion was trained in basic infantry tactics, and it could be used as the division's tenth infantry battalion, but its prime purpose was to provide troops who could undertake military labouring tasks such as road-building or trench-digging, including basic carpentry or brickwork. The Royal Engineers could support the combat brigades by undertaking more technical tasks such as building defensive works, roads and bridges, minelaying and demolitions as well as dealing with enemy booby traps. Of no less importance for the support of the division were the three field ambulances, the British name for a forward medical unit used to evacuate and treat battle casualties, and the Army Service Corps train units, which collected stores from the railhead and used its hundreds of wagons, mules and horses to distribute all food, ammunition, water and supplies needed for the division's soldiers.

In the earlier years of the war, heavy guns and howitzers had been found in the divisional artillery, but by 1918 these had been concentrated at the corps or army level. So, for their close artillery support, British infantry divisions would rely on their own two field artillery brigades, each with almost 800 men manning four horse-drawn gun batteries. Three batteries were equipped with six 18-pounder guns, which fired a 3.3-inch (84mm) shell weighing 18.3lbs (8.4kg), with an effective range up to five miles (eight kilometres), and the fourth battery usually had six 4.5-inch howitzers. There were also two medium mortar batteries, each with six 2-inch mortars (or six 6-inch Newton mortars), plus the divisional ammunition column. Organizing the fire plan, movement and replenishment of ten batteries with thirty-six field guns, twelve howitzers and twelve medium mortars was a complex task. It was not easy to ensure that the infantry were properly supported as they faced different types of terrain, weather conditions and enemy defences. Nevertheless, by 1918, British commanders and gunners in each division had the benefit of almost four years of experience in deploying direct supporting fire and ammunition, HE, shrapnel, gas or smoke, to fit the tactical situation, and were considered particularly expert in providing counter-battery fire and covering barrages.

American infantry divisions were not just significantly larger in infantry, but disposed greater artillery resources. The divisional field artillery brigade (FAB) commanded three artillery regiments. The two field regiments, each having two battalions of three batteries, each with four guns, were equipped with the superb French 75mm field guns firing a 15lb shell for barrage and harassing fire in close support of the infantry, one battalion ideally working in close co-operation with each infantry regiment. Its medium artillery regiment was equipped with twenty-four 155mm howitzers (the famous *'cent cinquante cinq'*). This formidable weapon fired almost the same weight of shell as the British 6-inch howitzer at 95lbs, but it could reach out thirteen miles to provide counter-battery and interdiction fire across the division's whole front. In addition to its seventy-two guns and howitzers, the American

FAB also commanded a heavy trench mortar battery with twelve 58mm mortars. These heavy mortars, with a range of 1,300 yards, provided extra punch to the offensive and were not only effective against wire entanglements, machine-gun shelters and trenches, but could provide smoke and gas cover. The American FAB of some 5,000 men was almost three times the size of the two field artillery brigades that supported each British division, and could take up almost the same road space as a whole British division – say fourteen miles or around twenty kilometres.

In addition to its field artillery, an American division could deploy some 260 Hotchkiss heavy machine guns. Each infantry regiment had its own machine-gun company with sixteen machine guns, and each brigade had its own machine-gun battalion, equipped with sixty-four heavy machine guns. The air-cooled (Mle 1914) 8mm Hotchkiss heavy machine gun had a range of 3,600 yards and was extremely reliable. It could provide sustained fire of 400-500 rounds a minute using 250-round belts, but was usually fired in bursts of ten to fifteen rounds. It weighed just over 53lbs (24kgs), which was light enough to join the offensive, although it had to be mounted on a heavy tripod to provide sustained supporting firepower. When used in the offensive, each American infantry battalion could have a whole company of sixteen Hotchkiss machine guns attached for fire support. Even allowing for four guns to be kept as a reserve, this could actually mean having a four-gun platoon available to support each of its three attack companies, leaving the reserve company to pick up support as it came forward.

The third divisional machine-gun battalion comprised just two companies and thirty-two guns. It served as the divisional reserve and was usually motorized. This advantage explains how the 7th Machine Gun Battalion could get itself to Château-Thierry on 31 May and hold up the German 10th Division for fully two days before the rest of the American 3rd Division, travelling by train and on foot, could arrive. The American machine gunners stiffened the French defence of Château-Thierry and contested the streets of the town and its bridges. It received the following well-deserved French Army citation for its action:

> Prevented the enemy from crossing the Marne. In the course of violent combats, particularly on May 31 and June 1, this battalion disputed the northern suburbs of Château-Thierry foot by foot,

inflicted severe losses on the enemy, and covered itself with glory by its bravery and ability.

Actually part of the 7th Machine Gun Battalion had simply piled into some twenty Ford vans, which they normally used to take them and their heavy weapons and ammunition to and from the practice range, and drove non-stop for thirty-six hours to get to Château-Thierry in time to halt the German advance.

Finally the American infantry division included an engineer regiment, with two battalions, a signal battalion, and divisional supply and medical trains. It was thus a very formidable self-contained fighting formation with tremendous firepower. It had almost four times as many heavy machine guns and twice the number of infantry of a British division. In addition, its divisional infantry were equipped with anything up to 768 of the Chauchat automatic rifles, obtained from the French Army and later replaced by the far more reliable Browning machine guns. The British infantry considered their 350 relatively light and reliable Lewis machine guns, which had actually been developed by the American Colonel Lewis, markedly superior to the Chauchat which suffered from stoppages caused by soil and dirt.

The confusion over names of military formations adds to the difficulty of making direct comparisons of firepower. Although the American division had only one FAB compared to a British division with its two field artillery brigades it actually had about the same number of close-support field artillery pieces. However, with its twelve full-strength infantry battalions and the additional regiment of 155mm howitzers, each American division was almost comparable to a small British corps. Even so, with twice the infantry and much wider fronts, the artillery support was often found to be inadequate. Early experience in France showed that the American division could not fully capitalize on its assets in a longer advance, and was often hindered by insufficient numbers of combat support troops and transport. Co-ordination between infantry and artillery was often poor, hampered by unreliable communications, and by having had too little joint training, which meant it was difficult for the artillery to keep track of the movement of infantry units they were supposed to be supporting. This was a problem for all armies at the time, and American divisions often resolved this by attacking with at least two FABs in support. For example, when the American 5th Division attacked to capture the Frapelle salient on 17 August 1918, its integral FAB had actually only joined the division two weeks earlier.

However, it had the additional support of forty-three French artillery batteries.

American commanders were frustrated to find that offensive actions quickly ran into support and supply problems, which often prevented the rapid exploitation of the successful initial attack. This was partially due to the terrible condition of the roads and terrain after heavy artillery bombardments. A shortage of personnel and equipment specifically reserved for medical evacuation, and general logistical requirements, such as transporting rations and water, and dealing with the dead, further slowed the advance. These disadvantages came to the fore particularly in longer difficult campaigns such as the Argonne offensive, and would have needed to be addressed, if the war had continued into 1919.

The organization of American divisions had been developed by trial and error during late 1917 and early 1918. Pershing had wanted his divisions to be strong enough to be able to continue pressing the attack in manoeuvre warfare, and not to falter due to lack of manpower. However, even he realized, after the war, that the big square divisions lacked co-ordination and were unwieldy and were moreover difficult to support logistically; as Army Chief of Staff, he accepted an army of smaller, but still square, divisions. It was not until September 1939 that the new Chief of Staff, General George Marshall, ordered the American army to change to a triangular organization of three regiments per division.

Pershing was clearly determined to establish an independent army, not least because this would enable the Americans to play an appropriate political role in the eventual peace negotiations. However, he was not blind to the necessity of ensuring his allies were not defeated. In the crisis days of March 1918, when it looked as if the Germans would achieve a surprise victory over the British, he went directly to Foch's HQ at Clermont-sur-Oise and made a dramatic declaration: 'At this moment there are no other questions but of fight. Infantry, artillery, aviation, all that we have is yours; use them as you wish. More will come, in numbers equal to the requirements.' The generosity of this gesture has few parallels in history. It was perhaps only equalled by Secretary of State George Marshall's offer of economic help to all the prostrate European nations under the Marshall Plan in 1947.

Despite General Pershing's prevailing determination to achieve independence of action, he repeatedly showed himself ready to lend some of his soldiers to bolster the French and British armies. He was even prepared to send a regiment to support the Italians. This was the 332nd Infantry Regiment from 83rd Division, which joined the British XVI Corps as part of the Italian Tenth Army and took part in the Battle of Vittorio-Veneto in October 1918. Indeed, he also sent contingents of troops to Vladivostok and Murmansk, as well as 'lending' a whole corps permanently to the British.

This American II Corps comprised the 27th and 30th Divisions, which had only begun to arrive in France in May 1918. The inexperienced American soldiers were given four weeks of concentrated training and schooling by the British 39th and 49th Divisions. II Corps was then sent to join Plumer's British Second Army in preparation for its 28 August offensive at Ypres-Lys. The infantry were gradually accustomed to combat conditions by attachment to British units, before taking independent command of their sector for the offensive. The American II Corps, supported eventually by the American 301st Heavy Tank Battalion, which was equipped with the British Mark V tanks, then moved south to reinforce the British Fourth Army and made a huge contribution to the breakthrough of the Hindenburg Line at Bellenglise in September 1918. In October, II Corps moved north again to attack towards the River Selle. Altogether the 27th and 30th Divisions suffered almost 16,000 casualties in their battles under British command.

By early October 1918, the AEF was suffering from the heavy casualties incurred in the extremely arduous Argonne offensive. For many of the Argonne divisions it had been their baptism of fire, and the totally inexperienced officers and men had suffered heavy casualties, and, as a result, some 90,000 reinforcements were needed. Pershing actually needed to break up arriving divisions in order to make good the shortfall. Nevertheless, Pershing realized that, to maintain the momentum of the Allied advance, the northern Allied offensive also needed bolstering and agreed to lend two of his divisions (37th and 91st) to the French Sixth Army in Flanders to support its attacks. Both divisions had already fought in the opening phase of the Argonne campaign but were swiftly transferred and by 1 November were attacking Germans positions on the Escaut where they achieved an advance of ten miles, continuing to attack right up to the Armistice.

Perhaps most famously, during the crisis defence of the Marne valley in June 1918, following the third great German attack, Pershing sent the partially-trained 2nd and 3rd Divisions to help the French. Both divisions were supposedly drawn from regular soldiers, but had only a smattering of regulars, the ranks being made up largely of raw recruits lacking in combat experience. However, they were soon to earn immortal fame as they stopped the German advance at Château-Thierry, and then recaptured the woods at Belleau and Bouresches. The resolute actions of these green American divisions halted the westward advance of the German forces, which would otherwise have registered an even greater success following victory in their rapid Aisne offensive.

Even after the crisis was over both divisions remained in the Marne area. The 3rd Division went on to hold an eight-mile stretch of the River Marne for a month. It was still holding on to these positions when it played a crucial role in the defence of the River Marne against the German 'Peace Offensive' of 15 July. While the German attacks east of Reims failed on the first morning, the massive attack along some ten miles of the Marne by its Seventh Army, supported by overwhelming Bruchmüller artillery barrages, had much more success. Using makeshift boats and temporary bridges, its soldiers managed to carve out a new threatening salient south of the Marne, centred on the town of Dormans. However, it was singularly unsuccessful at the western end of its offensive, where it suffered very heavy losses in 3rd Division's area.

Ludendorff's own account attempted to portray the outcome of the attack as a victory, but demonstrated how the Germans had completely underestimated the fighting ability of the newly-arrived Americans.

> All divisions [along the Marne] achieved brilliant successes, with the exception of the one division on our right wing. This encountered American units! Here only did the Seventh Army, in the course of the first day of the offensive, confront serious difficulties. It met with the unexpectedly stubborn and active resistance of fresh American troops. While the rest of the divisions of the Seventh Army succeeded in gaining ground and gaining tremendous booty, it proved impossible for us to move the right apex of our line, to the south of the Marne, into a position advantageous for the development of the ensuing fight. The check we thus received was one result of the stupendous fighting between our 10th Division of infantry and American troops.

Apparently, one of the regiments of 10th Division broke in the river crossing, and its losses in this assault were so serious that the whole division had to be withdrawn across the Marne by the evening of the 15th.

The 3rd occupied the centre of the French XVIII Corps area and was sandwiched between the French 39th and 125th Divisions. All four of its regiments were well dug in to hold the southern banks of the Marne and the area around the Surmelin valley near Mezy. Each regiment had a battalion forward on the river, another battalion in the main defensive line (MDL) on the steep forested slope behind, and a third battalion in reserve behind the hill. The Allies had discovered that the German artillery preparation would commence just after midnight at 12.10am. So from 11.45pm Allied artillery bombarded the anticipated enemy forming-up points and artillery positions.

Despite the Allied spoiling bombardment, the German attack began, as predicted, with the usual heavy Bruchmüller barrage at 12.10am. In the 3rd Division area alone, eighty-four batteries of German artillery began firing some 100,000 shells into the American positions, the majority of which were gas shells, with over half being fired in the first three hours. Unlike Gouraud's troops east of Reims, the defenders of the Marne were dug in along the southern bank of the river and were therefore far too close to the enemy artillery. As a result, they took heavy casualties before most of the French defenders pulled back out of range. However, despite suffering heavy casualties, the American 3rd Division defence remained solid and they shot down the enemy infantry as they crossed the river in boats or on pontoon bridges. Eventually some of the German infantry struggled forward up the southern bank. However, none of the enemy attackers got much farther forward than the railway line, which ran parallel with the river in 3rd Division's area, and there was no need to call upon the two reserve divisions (the American 28th and the French 73rd) which lay some three to five miles farther back.

The following account by Captain Jesse Woolridge, a company commander with the 38th Infantry Regiment, 3rd Division, portrays vividly the fierceness of the assault and the incredible defence by the 3rd, which stopped the German 10th and 36th Divisions.

> a grand offensive was to be made [where] the Marne was only about 50 yards wide ... . We had 600 yards of [this] front all to ourselves ... . [When it began] it seemed [the Germans] expected their artillery to eliminate all resistance ... . French Officers attached to our Brigade stated positively there was never a bombardment to equal it at Verdun. At 3:30am the general fire ceased and their creeping barrage started – behind which at 40 yards only, mind you, they came – with more

machine guns than I thought the German Army owned ... . The enemy had to battle their way through the first platoon on the river bank – then they took on the second platoon on the forward edge of the railway where we had a thousand times the best of it – but the [Germans] gradually wiped it out. My third platoon [took] their place in desperate hand to hand fighting, in which some got through only to be picked up by the fourth platoon which was deployed simultaneously with the third ... . By the time they struck the fourth platoon they were all in and easy prey. It's God's truth that one Company of American soldiers beat and routed a full regiment of picked shock troops of the German Army ... . At ten o'clock ... the Germans were carrying back wounded and dead [from] the river bank and we in our exhaustion let them do it – they carried back all but six hundred which we counted later and fifty-two machine guns ... . We had started with 251 men and 5 lieutenants ... . I had left 51 men and 2 second lieutenants ... .

The intensity of the heavy Bruchmüller shelling from across the river was so fierce that it almost shattered the experienced French 125th Division, on their right. Although it had been reinforced with two companies of the American 28th Division, the French were not able to resist the fierce German onslaught, and were forced away from the river, and the two companies of Pennsylvanian National Guard were virtually destroyed. The steadfast defence by the 38th Regiment also owed much to the dedicated artillery support of the 75mm guns of its own 10th Field Artillery Regiment, which were sometimes overrun as they engaged the German infantry. Very fierce fighting continued at the western boundary of the German advance for several days as the Americans prevented the Germans from expanding their bridgehead. This lack of progress in the direction of Paris, despite bloody sacrifice, blunted the German attack, and left them with little choice but to execute a withdrawal back across the Marne.

To this day the Second Battle of the Marne, which involved the first wholesale utilization of American troops in the attack under French command, is described as a Franco-American battle. This seems perfectly just since the battle included combat for eight American divisions; 1st, 2nd, 3rd, 4th, 26th (NG), 28th (NG), 32nd (NG), and 42nd (NG) Divisions. Actually a ninth, the 77th (Liberty) Division, became involved in the closing stage of the Vesle campaign after 12 August. To field these nine combat divisions so quickly was a magnificent achievement. It took a mighty national effort to train millions of civilians as officers and soldiers in such a short time, while organizing and equipping some eighty brand-new divisions for war. The Second Battle of the Marne also provided the first opportunity for American formations to fight as part of the first two newly-organized American corps formations in combat, thereby giving valuable experience to a higher level of staff officers and commanders.

The first four Marne divisions were ostensibly veteran American divisions nominally based around regular army cadres although, as stated, they actually included largely raw recruits. They had arrived in France, almost as soon as they could be organized, put into uniform and shipped. The 1st and 2nd Divisions arrived in late 1917, and the 3rd and 4th in early 1918. The equipment and training of these young divisions was poor and lacking many essentials, but the morale of the troops was very high and the United States was keen to demonstrate its commitment to its new allies by an early transfer of troops. Some of the soldiers from the 1st Division (2nd Battalion of the 16th Infantry Regiment) went straight from landing on the quay in France to appearing in a parade through Paris, still wearing their slouch hats, as a positive morale-boosting demonstration to the French that the Americans had finally arrived. The American 3rd Division was actually still undergoing its continuation training when it was thrown into the defence of Château-Thierry during the third German offensive in May 1918.

The other four Marne divisions were based on National Guard formations, some of which had been mobilized in 1916 for service along the Mexican border. Two of them, the 26th (Yankee) and the 42nd (Rainbow) had arrived during the autumn of 1917, and had already gained considerable combat experience. They were committed as part of the American I Corps. The 28th (Pennsylvania) and 32nd (Red Arrow) Divisions had arrived in the spring of 1918 and were committed to combat for the first time in the Marne battle, and eventually became part of the newly-formed American III Corps.

A prime mover in the establishment of the 42nd (Rainbow) Division, which arrived in France in November and December 1917, was Major Douglas MacArthur. The majority of regular army officers felt that only regular formations should be involved in the difficult combat conditions in France, but MacArthur believed that National Guard units could acquit themselves well. He therefore sought to form a new National Guard formation representing men drawn from all the

American states and accordingly the 'Rainbow' was formed. By the time it sailed, Colonel MacArthur was its chief staff officer. He went on to command its 84 Brigade as the youngest brigadier general in the US Army; he was just 37. Finally, just the day before the Armistice he was promoted to serve briefly as commander of the 42nd Division (until 22 November). He established a reputation as a fearless commander who actually accompanied his troops into action and was awarded seven Silver Stars, two Distinguished Service Crosses, and two Purple Hearts.

Another famous member of 42nd Division was Colonel 'Wild Bill' Donovan who was an outstanding and highly-decorated commander of the 1st Battalion of the 'New York Irish' 165th Infantry Regiment. Donovan, a lawyer, was awarded the Medal of Honor, the Distinguished Service Cross and the Distinguished Service Medal. After the war he became very influential in American public life. General Donovan went on to establish the OSS (the American espionage and sabotage organization) during the Second World War and, later, the CIA. He was also awarded a British Knighthood.

It has often been claimed that the 42nd was the second American division to arrive in France, but actually this honour would appear to have gone to the 26th (Yankee) Division. The 26th Division had been formed from National Guard units drawn from the New England states. It was so keen to get to Europe that, under its redoubtable commander, Major General Clarence Edwards, it had made private arrangements to obtain Canadian shipping and got itself to France in record time, via England in some cases, in September and October 1917. It then went into training at Neufchâteau, and was introduced to life, and death, in the trenches on the Chemin des Dames ridge in January 1918.

The 26th was fated to serve in some of the hottest fighting spots, spending some 210 days in combat. This hazardous exposure started when it took over the Seicheprey sector, in the south of the St Mihiel salient, on 3 April, from the more experienced 1st Division. The 1st Division had already suffered probing patrols and several bouts of gas shelling in its position, but the 26th was to experience the first combat action by a full American formation on 20 and 21 April 1918, as some 3,200 German soldiers, including 1,400 stormtroopers, attacked the 102nd and part of the 104th Regiments of the division in the village of Seicheprey. Despite being totally surprised and isolated by the German artillery firing a cordon barrage, the inexperienced soldiers of 26th Division held their position and eventually retook the village and woods, suffering some 670 casualties. It proved a bloody but important lesson for the division, as it learned it could never afford to relax in the trenches opposite such professional and experienced soldiers as the Germans. Unfortunately, the 26th was often compared unfavourably with the 1st Division, and its early problems embarrassed Pershing, who wanted desperately to show the experienced Allied commanders just how useful his troops would be.

Between 5 and 8 July 1918 the 26th Division relieved the 2nd Division near the Belleau Wood position and was then involved in action to clear parts of the village of Bouresches and Bouresches Wood. The division played a key part in the counter-attack of 18 July, when it advanced north of Château-Thierry as part of the American I Corps. The 26th also played a significant role in the St Mihiel campaign, when, on the second day of the battle, its 102nd Infantry Regiment formed up and marched at high speed to capture the critical village of Vigneulles, thus completing the encirclement of German forces. However, General Clarence Edwards did not get along with either Pershing or, later, General Liggett, who both frequently criticized the performance of his division, and eventually they found the excuse to sack him just before the third phase of the Argonne offensive.

The American soldiers were often criticized for their enthusiasm bordering on recklessness in combat, and this was signalled when over 1,000,000 men volunteered for service before the Draft Law made service compulsory. This enthusiasm to join the cause of freedom was typified by all the sons of the twenty-sixth president, Theodore (Teddy) Roosevelt (TR), three of whom established a close connection with the fighting in the Champagne area.[1] TR himself, who liked to be called 'Colonel', was quite old by 1917 but that did not stop him from writing to Pershing requesting, unsuccessfully, a post with the AEF.

TR's youngest son, Quentin, was a 20-year old pilot with the American 1st Pursuit Group. On 14 July 1918 Lieutenant Roosevelt was shot down very close to the village of Chamery, on the Montagne de Reims, and he was, for a time, the most famous casualty of the American forces. Chamery was in enemy hands at the time, and the

---

[1] The fearless President Roosevelt actually had four sons. The second oldest, a famous explorer, writer and linguist named Kermit, actually served with the British Army as a captain and was awarded the Military Cross during his service in Iraq in 1918. He was later commissioned into the American Army. During the Second World War he again served in both the British and American armies before dying in 1943. An annual Anglo-American Seminar is held to commemorate the memory of Major Kermit Roosevelt MC.

news of Quentin's death was reported by the Germans, who gave him a full military funeral. It is said the news of the death of his youngest and most favourite son hastened the death of the former president in January 1919. Chamery was liberated by the French counter-attack on 18 July, and it was where the British 62nd Division rested a few days later, before joining the battle on the Ardre. Quentin's mother, Edith, visited the village later and paid for the erection of a commemorative fountain.

Two other sons of the former president actually served in the 1st Division. Roosevelt's fifth child, Archibald, was a captain in 1st Division but, after being wounded three times, he was invalided out of the army with 100 per cent disability. This in no way deterred him from volunteering again when the Second World War broke out, and he went on to serve as a lieutenant colonel, commanding an infantry battalion in 41st Division in New Guinea. In August 1943, while fighting in the Salamaua campaign, he had the misfortune to be struck by a Japanese grenade, which once again damaged his knee and he was again invalided out with 100 per cent disability, thereby establishing a unique record of being 100 per cent disabled in both wars. Archie was awarded the Croix de Guerre by the French government, as were both his brothers, as well as the Bronze Star, Purple Heart, and two Silver Stars with Oak Leaf Cluster.

However, the president's oldest son, also called Teddy, established an even more impressive record of service in this patrician warrior-family. As a major, Theodore Roosevelt Jr commanded the 2nd battalion in the 26th Regiment, and was said by the divisional commander to be the best battalion commander in 1st Division. He was wounded on 19 July, during the counter-attack at Soissons, but recovered and, as a lieutenant colonel, commanded the 26th Regiment in the Argonne campaign in November 1918. Just before the Armistice, there arose a famous conflict between the 1st and 42nd Divisions and the French Army about boundaries, and who should have the honour of taking Sedan. Teddy, despite needing to lean on a stick due to his injuries, received orders to take the 26th through the lines of soldiers from the French 40th Division. They were lying down awaiting their orders to attack; and the French protested that it was their sector. Teddy Roosevelt rejoined, 'Well, you aren't advancing' and continued to lead his troops forward. However, when the French soldiers heard it was the famous Theodore Roosevelt leading the attack, they stood up and cheered him.

Actually, in contravention of normal military procedures, the 1st Division, which had been in reserve to the V Corps, commanded by General Summerall, had been ordered to cross behind General Dickman's I Corps and across the supply routes for 42nd Division into the area of the French Fourth Army. During this unusual manoeuvre, Teddy's soldiers had actually 'captured' Brigadier General MacArthur at his headquarters. The move had effectively been ordered by the Army Group Commander, General Pershing, who apparently, having expended so much effort in the Argonne fighting, wanted to claim the honour of liberating Sedan. A storm of high level protests followed from the French and not least from the irascible Dickman; shortly afterwards, Pershing rescinded his order for the Americans to take Sedan. The 26th Regiment returned to its former area, while the French Army went on to capture the town, which it had lost to the Prussians in 1870.

Theodore Roosevelt Jr continued his service and training as a reserve officer between the wars, and was also a successful businessman and politician although, as a Republican, he was a political opponent of his cousins, Franklin (FDR) and Eleanor Roosevelt. He served as Assistant Secretary of the Navy, Governor of Puerto Rico and Governor General of the Philippines, and was a leading founder of the American Legion. When war came again in 1941, Teddy, despite being 54, returned to active service with the 1st Division. Once again he was given command of the 26th Regiment, which he led ashore in the beach landings at Oran in Algeria on 8 November 1942. The 1st Division then fought in the Tunisian campaign. Teddy was promoted to brigadier general and, as the assistant commander of the 1st Division, went ashore and campaigned with them in Sicily.

Teddy Roosevelt Jr did not stand on ceremony. He was a popular leader who insisted on visiting his troops in the front line. He had somewhat informal ways (he was known to everyone by his nickname of Teddy and his jeep was emblazoned with the slogan 'Rough Rider'), which did not endear him to the martinet General George Patton, who wanted to sack him. However, Patton was himself dismissed for striking sick soldiers, and it was his successor, General Bradley, who eventually sacked both Teddy and his divisional commander, Major General Terry Allen, who had served with the 90th Division in France in 1918. Despite his legacy of wounds, a heart condition and arthritis, Teddy then served as an important senior liaison and staff officer, while continuing to petition for a return to combat command. Eventually he was appointed as the deputy commander of the 4th Infantry Division, which, as part of the American VII Corps, was designated to land on Utah Beach on D Day.

Teddy Roosevelt's direct experience of landing with his troops at Oran and in Sicily, as well as the bloody landings on the mainland of Italy, had convinced him of the certainty of chaos during amphibious operations, and he feared what might befall his soldiers on the Normandy beaches in June 1944. In addition, Teddy had also witnessed the training tragedy off Slapton Sands in England during late April 1944. This appalling disaster during a night-time landing exercise was concealed at the time but almost 1,000 American soldiers, many from 4th Division, were killed or drowned by enemy E-boat action and friendly fire. As a result, Teddy repeatedly requested to be allowed to land with his troops on D Day. Eventually permission was granted for him to go ashore in the first assault craft, which predictably landed in the wrong part of Utah Beach.

Despite this mishap, Teddy's personal leadership and bravery did much to ensure the success of the amphibious landings on Utah Beach. Famously, when he realized that his vessel had landed far from their intended destination, he said, 'We will start the war from right here'. He was the only general officer to lead his men ashore on 6 June, and his bravery became legendary as he greeted and re-organized each group of the landing troops to attack the German defences. By early afternoon, the 4th Infantry Division had succeeded in linking up with elements of 101st Airborne and had suffered only some 200 casualties from the 23,000 landed on Utah Beach. However, one cannot help thinking that he would have preferred to have gone ashore with his beloved 1st Division at the much bloodier Omaha Beach. There, the veteran 1st Division landed alongside the 29th National Guard Division and both sustained extremely heavy casualties as their craft were sunk or landed them in the wrong places and their supporting tanks were swamped by waves.

General Eisenhower had already decided to promote Theodore Roosevelt Jr to major general, but Teddy endured poor health due to his earlier war service, and died of a heart attack on 12 July 1944. He was buried in the American Normandy Cemetery at Colville-sur-Mer. Later, after the Second World War, Quentin Roosevelt's body was moved to the same cemetery in Normandy, so that he could lie next to his older brother. Brigadier General Roosevelt's leadership during this critical phase of the Normandy landings was eventually recognized by the posthumous award of the Medal of Honor in September 1944. In

2001 Teddy's father was also awarded a posthumous Medal of Honor for his intrepid leadership of the assault on San Juan Hill. Thus, the two Roosevelts joined the MacArthurs as the only two pairs of fathers and sons to have been awarded the Medal of Honor.

The 1st and 2nd Divisions were the two most combat-experienced American divisions. Since each was more than twice the size of a French division, they made a huge impact against the over-stretched Germans on 18 July as they attacked on either side of the RICM (*Regiment d'infanterie coloniale du Maroc*) (see page 230), one of the fiercest French attack units. The 2nd Division was a temporary last-minute addition to Mangin's command, and came literally hotfoot from its battles outside Château-Thierry, as it had to march in double time to get to its start line. It had attacked without its normal logistical support, lacking even water for its men to drink but, in less than two days, before being withdrawn, had advanced five miles (eight kilometres) and captured 3,000 prisoners at the cost of some 4,000 casualties.

The RICM also advanced rapidly through the thick Forest of Retz and captured the hamlet of Longpont within forty-five minutes of launching its attack at 4.35am. Two hours later the regiment had advanced a further two and a half miles (four kilometres) and seized Mont Rambœf. By midday on 19 July, it had taken the small village of Parcy and was close to the road leading south from Soissons, which was stubbornly defended by Germans occupying the village of Hartennes. During its advance of almost five miles (seven kilometres), the RICM had suffered 754 casualties, including Captain van Vollenhoven, a famous colonial administrator, but had captured 825 prisoners, twenty-four guns, and 120 machine guns. On 22 July 1918 the RICM and part of its division, the French 38th Division, was relieved by the British 34th Division.

The 1st Division, which attacked on the left of Mangin's Tenth Army, had maintained the momentum of its attack continuously for four days and nights against stiffening German opposition. As a result it suffered 8,500 casualties, including 2,213 killed, as it advanced seven miles (eleven kilometres) until relieved by 15th (Scottish) Division. It captured 3,500 prisoners from seven German divisions and, in particular, totally destroyed the 11th Bavarian Division. Although the vital road from Soissons to Château-Thierry (now the D1) was not quite reached by the Americans it was brought within French artillery range, and the German threat to Paris, was lifted, as their main supply route into the salient became practically unusable. This threat to its continuity of supplies accelerated the German decision to evacuate its short-lived salient south of the Marne. The 1st Division Memorial of stone and bronze, which stands with its closely-packed list of names, on the side of the D1, just between Berzy and Buzancy, illustrates vividly the heavy mortalities suffered in its attack.

Teilhard de Chardin, the French Jesuit priest who later became a world-renowned palaeontologist and philosopher, was serving with the Moroccan Division as a stretcher-bearer, and wrote about his impressions of the American troops:

> We had the Americans as neighbours and I had a close-up view of them. Everyone says the same: they're first-rate troops, fighting with intense individual passion (concentrated on the enemy) and wonderful courage. The only complaint one would make about them is that they don't take sufficient care; they're too apt to get themselves killed. When they're wounded, they make their way back holding themselves upright, almost stiff, impassive, and uncomplaining. I don't think I've ever seen such pride and dignity in suffering. There's complete comradeship between them and us, born fully-fledged under fire.

Attacking further south of Mangin's Tenth Army was General Degoutte's Sixth Army. He had also been given two American divisions (4th and 26th) to support his attack. Parts of the 4th Division were split up and were included in the attacks by French divisions along both banks of the River Ourcq, until 26 July. Lieutenant Bedell Smith, who was Eisenhower's chief of staff in the Second World War, was wounded in this battle. Within Sixth Army was also established the first Americans corps headquarters to exercise tactical command; it was located just north of Château-Thierry, and initially commanded the French 167th and American 26th Divisions.

The task of the American I Corps was to engage the Germans in the nose of the salient and prevent them withdrawing troops to strengthen their vulnerable flanks. I Corps moved east along the ridge north of Château-Thierry, and then pivoted to continue advancing in a northerly direction towards Fère-en-Tardenois. The 26th Division, advanced for an astounding eleven miles (eighteen kilometres) at high tempo through Torcy, Belleau and Epieds, to reach Trugny, north-west of Château-Thierry on 26 July. For all the criticism it endured from General Pershing, this was a magnificent feat and cost the division some 5,300 casualties. It was then relieved by the 42nd (Rainbow) Division, which also joined the attack at short notice, having already helped to halt the German attack east of Reims as part of Gouraud's Fourth Army. The 42nd Division continued the attack and by the 28th had crossed the Ourcq and taken Sergy. There was desperate fighting around Sergy, which was held by the Americans until the Germans pulled back on 2 August. The 42nd was then in turn relieved by the re-assembled 4th Division, which carried on attacking north alongside the 32nd Division, as part of the newly-formed American III Corps, until 6 August. The 4th Division has left its marker, in splendid isolation, just one kilometre west of Fismes on the N31 road.

Farther to the east of Château-Thierry, the 3rd Division had advanced from its famous defence of the city and the River Marne to join the counter-attack, and by 22 July had crossed over the Marne near Jaulgonne. For the next three days it was involved in heavy fighting on the wooded slopes of le Charmel, which it eventually took on the evening of the 25th. The division continued advancing to take Roncheres until finally being relieved, on the 30th, by 32nd Division, which had just come up from Belfort. In all, 3rd Division suffered total casualties of almost 7,900 in the defence of Château-Thierry, and in its advance across the Marne.

By 7 August the American I and III Corps had finally reached the River Vesle, and this is usually considered the conclusion of the Second Battle of the Marne, but it did not mean an end to the fighting for the American divisions. As the French army prepared for its next offensive, at Amiens and Montdidier, it handed over the pursuit of the retreating Germans almost completely to the Americans. The two lead divisions of I and III Corps had driven the Germans back to the critical crossings at Bazoches and Fismes on the River Vesle, where the Germans attempted to establish a new defensive line. From early August the 28th and 77th Divisions took over the front along the Vesle and fought for almost a month to gain possession of the Vesle bridgeheads from St Thibaut to Fismes. The Germans fought just as stubbornly to hold their ground and the front swung backwards and forwards. The fierce fighting at Fismes, nicknamed the 'Valley of Death' by the men of 28th Division, resulted in heavy American casualties as the German artillery bombarded them repeatedly with HE and Gas.

Finally, a fresh offensive by Mangin's Tenth Army was launched on 18 August, which took the Germans in the flank. The American 32nd Division participated and eventually captured the key village of Juvigny in bitter fighting. This cut the Soissons to St Quentin road and made the German positions on the Vesle untenable. As a result they retreated to a new defensive line just south of the River Aisne, and the 28th and 77th Divisions were finally able to cross the Vesle and close up to the new German defence line. The 28th later commemorated its liberation of Fismes, by donating to the town the ornate bridge over the Vesle, bearing its 'Keystone' emblem.

Undoubtedly the 300,000 soldiers of the fledgling United States Army who gathered around the River Marne in the summer of 1918 had made a unique contribution to the success of the Allied counter-attack. They had fought in company lots, regiments, divisions and then corps under French command. They had subjected the German army to continuous attacks and defeats, which had left it with no choice but to retreat to the more defensible river lines, close to where it had started its remarkable advance on 27 May. Even as Pershing wished, they had forced a war of movement on the Germans. The young Americans had proved their ability as soldiers and were shortly to administer another shock to the Germans, moving east to attack the large St Mihiel salient, which they had held for almost four years.

While the continually expanding American army left two of its divisions on the Vesle river, it mounted its first army level operation at St Mihiel. On 12 August the American First Army, with three American corps, I, IV, and V, and the French II Colonial Corps under command, attacked and liberated the St Mihiel salient. In four days First Army took 15,000 prisoners and 257 guns at a cost of barely 7,000 casualties. Of the 419 French tanks used to support the St Mihiel attack, 144 were manned by Americans in two newly-trained tank battalions, commanded by Major Patton.

George Patton, who had trained as a cavalry officer, had served under Pershing in the Mexican campaign, during which he quickly earned a reputation as a bold soldier. In 1917, when the AEF went to France, Patton was determined to see action and petitioned Pershing to join his staff in France as a captain. Pershing eventually gave him the task of training American tank crews. Patton grasped the opportunity firmly, and revelled in the task of forming the first American tank school. He personally learnt how to drive the French tanks at their training school at Champlieu and his commitment and success in training his tankers resulted in further promotion. In August 1918 he was given command of 304 Tank Brigade, with two battalions of FT-17 Renault tanks, to support the American St Mihiel operation.

While the St Mihiel attack was a military success, Patton's tanks suffered severely from breakdowns, ditching and enemy gunfire, as did all the British and French tanks at this time. Patton also came very close to being disciplined for disobedience, due to his habit of going forward to where the action was, rather than sitting back at his headquarters waiting for reports. However, by personally embracing exposure to combat, Patton gained an intimate understanding of combat realities for the new tank weapon with its attendant problems of poor visibility, breakdowns, and difficult inter-tank communication.

In September 1918, as a lieutenant colonel, Patton led his tanks in the American Meuse-Argonne offensive and once again moved to the front, leading an attack on a German machine-gun post on foot. During this attack his tanks were supposed to be supported by Captain Harry Truman's battery of 75mm guns but, despite Truman making a reconnaissance on foot to find him, Patton could not be found. Truman's 35th Division was also supported by a cavalry squadron under Captain Ernest Harmon, probably the finest American armoured commander in the Second World War. Patton had actually been wounded in the thigh on the first day of the battle, and finished the war in hospital. Nevertheless, he was promoted to colonel and awarded a Distinguished Service Cross and a Purple Heart.

While Patton trained his tank force in France, Captain Dwight Eisenhower had begun training men for the embryonic tank force in the United States. His job quickly grew in importance as some 10,000 men were trained at Camp Mead in Maryland, and Eisenhower was promoted to lieutenant colonel. After the war, Patton and Eisenhower worked together closely in an attempt to develop an armoured force for the American army, but soon fell victims to conservatism and peacetime reductions. Eventually most of their tank force was disbanded and they were both reduced to their pre-war ranks.

A frustrated Patton went back to a career with the cavalry. However, with the approach of another war, armoured forces were re-established and Patton eventually took command of the 2nd Armoured Division in 1941. He commanded the Western Task Force landing at Casablanca as part of Operation TORCH in November 1942. In 1943 Eisenhower gave him command of the American II Corps, to replace Lloyd Fredendall, after its salutary defeat at the Kasserine Pass by Rommel. Patton then demonstrated his capabilities as a courageous and hard-driving corps commander, retraining his men and inflicting swift defeats on German armoured forces. This contributed to the rapid defeat of large Axis forces and their final surrender to the Allies in Tunisia. He then led the American Seventh Army, alongside Montgomery and his British Eighth Army, in their successful occupation of Sicily. Patton was not exactly a team player, and insisted on driving west to capture Palermo rather than attacking alongside Montgomery to defeat the main German defences. Moreover, Patton's impetuousness again asserted itself, and he was removed from command after striking some sick soldiers, to be succeeded by his deputy, Omar Bradley.

Eventually Patton was given a second chance and command of the American Third Army for its breakout from Normandy in July 1944. Driven hard by Patton, Third Army surged through France and Germany, finally liberating western Czechoslovakia, just short of Prague, in May 1945. He unbalanced and outmanoeuvred the Germans by pushing his troops to move faster than the enemy. George Patton constantly exposed himself to danger during both wars and believed that he was destined by fate to achieve great fame. He certainly became the most colourful and outspoken general among all the senior Allied commanders. In December 1945, shortly after succeeding Eisenhower as military governor of the American zone, Patton was injured in an unlucky car accident and died.

Patton's character was totally opposite to that of William H. Simpson, who was a quiet and thoughtful Texan. He had joined the 33rd Division as a captain in 1917 but finished the war as its chief of staff. By May 1944 he was organizing the American Ninth Army in the UK, and was to lead it throughout its successful campaign in Europe. Fighting through France alongside the Ninth Army was the First Army commanded by Courtney Hodges. Hodges began his service as a cadet at West Point, but flunked his course and then decided to join the army as a private soldier in 1906. He was commissioned from the ranks some three years later and by 1918 Major Hodges was a battalion commander in the 6th Infantry Regiment of 5th Division. The 5th was a new regular division, which came into being in December 1917. In May 1918 it became the eighth American division to arrive in France, and soon went into the line in the Vosges Mountains. On 17 August its 6th Infantry Regiment launched a small operation to capture the long-held German salient at Frapelle. Despite vigorous German shelling for three days and numerous counter-attacks, the salient was successfully taken and held. Fifth Division then moved to the Verdun area for its participation in I Corps' successful attack on the right-hand face of the St Mihiel salient. Having crossed the start line at 5.00am on 12 September, it took all its objectives within nine hours.

St Mihiel was a comparatively gentle preparation for its next task in the Argonne, where it was deployed without its own artillery, which stayed behind in St Mihiel. The first Argonne attacks had quickly run into difficulties, and the 5th Division was inserted as part of the second phase, to attack near Montfaucon on 11 October. Major Hodges was fortunate not to be killed or injured during the vicious eleven-day battle to take the Bois-des-Rappes, when 5th Division suffered almost 5,000 casualties. Perhaps this may have been due to its attacking through overgrown woods without proper artillery support. Under General Ely, the division again attacked on 26 October to force a crossing of the Meuse river. Hodges was promoted and awarded a Distinguished Service Cross for his leadership during its successful crossing of the Meuse during a thirteen-mile (twenty-one kilometres) advance.

After the war Hodges continued his military career and was no doubt extremely gratified to be appointed as an instructor at West Point, where he had once failed to graduate. In 1943 he assumed command of the Third US Army forming in Texas and, in August 1944, he took over command of First US Army from General Omar Bradley. During the Battle of the Bulge in December 1944 Eisenhower placed the First and Ninth Armies under the temporary command of Field Marshal Montgomery, who co-ordinated the operations north of the Bulge. Hodges then led First Army across the Rhine to occupy the Ruhr area, and final victory in Germany.

Also with 5th Division was Captain Mark Clark who graduated from West Point in April 1917 and, as a company commander, seemed to be on the fast track to promotion. He took part in the St Mihiel operation, but, whilst serving in the bloody Argonne offensive, he was seriously wounded by shrapnel, and when he recovered, was moved to the staff of First Army. His subsequent career during peacetime was extremely slow. It took him fifteen years to gain promotion to major, in 1933. However, with the advent of the next war, his career once again took off, and he received swift promotion to command the US Fifth Army for its invasion of Italy in September 1943. He later succeeded the British General Alexander as commander of 15th Army Group in Italy, becoming the youngest officer to be promoted four-star general in March 1945. General Clark was famous for ordering the bombing of the great monastery on Monte Cassino (although he always denied responsibility), as well as for being the much-photographed liberator of Rome. Eventually, he commanded the United Nations Forces in the Korean War, before retiring in 1954.

Of the huge supporting fleet of 1,500 aircraft deployed for the St Mihiel operation, 604 were flown by American pilots under the command of Colonel Billy Mitchell, who was designated Chief of Air Service for the First Army. Mitchell became a controversial figure as he campaigned unceasingly for the development of American air power. He was an enthusiastic visionary who was later court martialled for expressing his undiplomatic views. He died in 1936 before he could see the vindication of many of his ideas.

Many other distinguished leaders of American forces in the Second World War gained valuable experience with the American Expeditionary Force (AEF) without necessarily establishing such flamboyant reputations. As mentioned earlier, Captain Harry Truman led his battery through the bloody carnage of the opening Argonne offensive, where his 35th Division suffered some 5,000 casualties. Despite this bloody baptism, Truman did not lose a single man from his battery. Truman had been a reserve officer before the war and in peacetime went on to serve as a colonel in the National Guard. He often said that everything he had learnt about leadership, he had learnt during his war service. In 1944 he was, rather unexpectedly, chosen to be Franklin Roosevelt's vice president and, equally unexpectedly, became the president when FDR died in April 1945. Roosevelt had done little to inform Truman about his war policies, or indeed such important issues as his health and the secret development of the atomic bomb. As a result, he left President Truman to deal with many contentious issues for which he was ill-prepared, particularly the increasingly difficult relationship with the Russians, as well as the best way to end the war with Japan.

Despite his soft image, President Truman had experienced combat at first hand and had few illusions about the bloody realities of attempting to land on and occupy the islands of Japan. Given a fanatical defence by soldiers and civilians, it was estimated that this would cost the Allies at least a million casualties and certainly many more millions of Japanese casualties. Nevertheless, it was an awesome burden to have to take the ultimate decision to employ devastating atomic weapons to end the war against Japan. Truman stated later that he fully understood the terrible nature of the choice he faced in using the atomic bomb, but that he never wavered in making his decision.

Truman faced many other difficult decisions during his presidency, of which possibly the most challenging was opposing the march of the communist regimes across eastern Europe and Asia. He therefore chose to rely heavily on George Marshall, who served as his Chief of Staff of the Army until he retired in November 1945. Truman then asked Marshall to undertake a special mission to China, as his personal representative, to try to sort out the intractable problems of that enormous country. For almost a year Marshall endeavoured to reconcile the nationalists and communists, but it was a task beyond him, or perhaps any man.

When Marshall returned home, Truman nominated him as his Secretary of State, where he served very successfully until January 1949. It was during this period that Truman and Marshall launched the economic aid programme for Europe, known as Marshall Aid, which enabled Europe to begin rebuilding its business and banking structures. This farsighted and generous programme of aid, totalling over US$13 billion, helped the shattered economies of Europe to recover and led eventually to the formation of the European Union. In 1949 George Marshall left office to become chairman of the American Red Cross, but within a year was recalled by Truman to serve as Secretary of Defense, tasked once again with building up the American Army for the Korean War. To Marshall's exasperation, he discovered there had been a precipitate decline in the numbers of American troops, and the defence budget. These had fallen so far that he was, for the third time in his life, faced with the awesome task of rapidly rebuilding America's national army from almost nothing.

Montgomery and Marshall met on only two occasions during the actual war. The first time was on the third day of the Algiers Conference, which was held in Eisenhower's villa in May 1943. Montgomery joined the conference that day and, despite his fame as the conqueror of Rommel, was very much the junior general compared to the senior Allied commanders of their respective naval, army and air forces. Marshall then paid Monty the courtesy of visiting him at his field headquarters in Belgium in April 1945. By then Montgomery was a field marshal and the famous victor of the Normandy landings. Marshall seems to have understood how disappointed Montgomery was to not be allowed to go on commanding the Allied ground forces after Eisenhower established himself on the mainland of Europe. However, Montgomery did himself few favours. Rather stupidly, Montgomery spent the bulk of his time criticizing Marshall's protégée, Eisenhower. Marshall later wrote that it was only with difficulty that he was able to control his temper and avoid admonishing Montgomery. However, the experience added to the very considerable sympathy Marshall felt for Eisenhower's difficulties in dealing with his French and British allies.

Marshall was willing to serve the American people whenever called upon to do so, but was never interested in pursuing a political career, seeing it as no part of a soldier's life. Indeed he did not support Eisenhower's bid for political office. Eventually Marshall took final retirement in September 1951 but continued to hold the honorary (five-star) title of general of the army until he died in October 1959.

XXII Corps with 51st and 62nd Divisions joins French Fifth Army in the Ardre Valley

On 15 July the failure of the fifth great German attack in the area east of Reims had become quite clear from early on the first morning, although unsuccessful attempts were made to re-launch the offensive on the 16th and 17th. The failure to capture the rail centre of Reims meant that, while they trumpeted the success of Seventh Army south of the Marne, a new danger had been created for the Germans. They had acquired an additional salient, which was being choked of supplies by French air and artillery attacks and could not be expanded. Originally, it had been intended to close around Reims from the east and the west in a wide pincer movement. However, the early failure of the eastern attack meant that it was even more important to show some strategic success by advancing towards Épernay through the Ardre valley and along both banks of the Marne from the new salient. Therefore fresh attacks were launched by the Germans on the afternoon of the 16th.

The area west of Reims, around the Ardre valley, had been defended by the Italian II Corps, which comprised two Italian divisions and the French 120th Division. The first German attack on the 15th made a rapid advance of almost five miles from their positions north of the Montagne de Bligny, and captured Chambrecy and Marfaux. By the evening of the 15th, all the Italian and French troops in the first line of defence had been overcome and the Germans had reached the second line of defence which lay in the Forest of Courton, close to Pourcy. The troops in the second line of defence, manning defensive positions in the Bois de Courton, included the other two battalions of the 408th Regiment and a battalion of the Italian 52nd Regiment.

The renewed German attack on the afternoon of the 16th was so fierce that the 2nd Battalion of 408th Regiment was virtually destroyed, and German troops flooded through the breach. The Germans, of 123rd Division, apparently made good use of their light machine guns and quickly occupied the Saint Denis Farm, the Moulin de l'Ardre and Liberty Wood. Fortunately, the French 14th Division had arrived in the area on the morning of the 16th and finally managed to halt the German advance. However, the 3rd Battalion of 408th Regiment, which had collected some survivors from the other battalions, and the Italian battalion, were totally surrounded in positions in the Bois de Gallinettes, close to Pourcy, and seemed in real danger of being captured. On the 17th French aircraft managed to drop some supplies to the cut-off troops. Counter-attacks were mounted on the 18th by the 35th and 44th Regiments of 14th Division, in an unsuccessful attempt to relieve them. To assist the encircled troops, the French artillery fired an interdiction barrage, which unfortunately also struck and killed some of their own men. Finally, on the 19th, the German 123rd Division, which, by this time had become quite weakened, was ordered to withdraw to defensive positions in the Bois de Courton, and the remnants of the 3rd Battalion could be relieved.

As the 51st and 62nd Divisions marched from their railheads and temporary camps on 19 July 1918 it was clear that the defenders of Reims had managed to prevent the Germans from taking that city, despite repeated heavy German attacks. Furthermore, the French and Italians had managed to halt the German offensive in the high heavily wooded area of the Montagne de Reims, and had thereby prevented the two wings of German Seventh Army from linking up and occupying Épernay, which would have isolated Reims. However, General Bertholet's Fifth Army lacked the strength to drive the Germans back from their advanced positions in the Bois de Courton and in the Ardre valley, and it seemed possible that the Germans could renew their offensive at any time.

General Foch had shown an initial slow response to the British requests for assistance and reserves during the second great German offensive, GEORGETTE, in April on the Lys valley. Foch now feared that, after the success of their third attack in May on the Aisne front, and its limited follow-up in June on the Matz river, the GNEISENAU offensive, the Germans were planning a series of significant attacks farther east against the French army and, accordingly, he wanted to move some of the Allied reserves farther east. He therefore asked Haig to replace some of these French reserves with four British divisions. Haig agreed, rather reluctantly, not least because he had serious manpower problems of his own, and had good grounds for anticipating another German attack in Flanders, and selected the relatively adjacent XXII

Corps, which had been moved in early June to the Somme area, southwest of Amiens. XXII Corps, under Lieutenant General Sir Alexander Godley, had two divisions under command, 51st (Highland) and 62nd (2nd West Riding) and was then reinforced with the 15th (Scottish) Division from First Army, and 34th (Tyneside) Division from Second Army.

Godley was a very experienced officer. He had joined the army at Sandhurst in 1885, and was commissioned into the Royal Dublin Fusiliers. He then served as a staff officer in South Africa during the Boer War. His grandfather had been very influential in founding the Canterbury Company, which promoted the establishment of the New Zealand colony of Canterbury, and Godley retained an interest in New Zealand. Following the recommendation of Lord Kitchener for the setting-up of the New Zealand armed forces, Godley was appointed in 1910 to establish and command the New Zealand Territorial Forces, which he did with considerable energy and success. Having formed and trained the units, he was a natural choice to command New Zealand troops, as they were mobilized to join the war effort and were sent to Egypt in 1914. He commanded the Australian and New Zealand Division at Gallipoli in 1915, although not altogether successfully. He evinced genuine concern for his troops' welfare, but he was a tall thin cadaverous man with a cool and distant manner to all under his command and usually appeared aloof and uncaring. His wife, Louise, who established a hospital for soldiers in Egypt, was considered even less sympathetic, particularly to those she considered malingerers.

In 1916 the New Zealand Division went to France as part of II Anzac Corps, which was commanded by Godley. During September 1917, the division established a remarkable fighting reputation during extremely successful attacks organized by General Plumer at Polygon Wood and Broodseinde, which benefited from multiple covering barrages by artillery and machine guns. However, Godley was not considered a natural or successful field commander, and was blamed for the heavy losses sustained by the Australian and New Zealand troops at Passchendaele in October 1917. On a single unhappy day, 12 October 1917, in the First Battle of Passchendaele, some 2,735 New Zealand troops became casualties in the attack on the well-fortified German lines at Poelcappelle. Of these some forty-five officers and 800 men were killed or mortally wounded. The artillery were unable to provide the usual strong covering barrages due to the awful weather conditions and it took two days to clear the huge number of casualties. Godley, rather than the appalling rain and mud, was blamed for the disaster, the worst in New Zealand history. One senior officer commented on the conditions in his private diary:

> October 11th – We all hope for the best tomorrow, but I do not feel as confident as usual. Things are being rushed too much. The weather is rotten, the roads very bad, and the objectives have not been properly bombarded. However, we will hope for the best.
>
> October 12th – Today has been a very bad day for us. We were hung up a very short way from the starting point. The situation is not yet very clear, but it is almost certain our men came up against a lot of pillboxes, concrete and ferro-concrete constructions, very strong and with machine guns. No guns can smash them up except with much concentrated fire. They are very small and strong and hard to hit. They are arranged chequer-wise and form a very stiff obstacle. My opinion is that the senior generals who direct these operations are not conversant with the conditions, mud, cold, rain and no shelter for the men. Finally, the Germans are not so played out as they make out. All our attacks recently lack preparations, and the whole history of the war is that when thorough preparation is not made, we fail. ... You cannot afford to take liberties with the Germans. Exhausted men struggling through mud cannot compete against dry men with machine guns in ferro-concrete boxes waiting for them.

A photograph of Godley reviewing New Zealand troops soon afterwards appears to show clearly the disdain felt for him by many of his troops. Efforts were made by some New Zealand politicians to get rid of him, but foundered on the concern that they might well get someone worse. He therefore retained the title and duties of commander of the New Zealand Expeditionary Force (NZEF). In February 1918 II Anzac Corps lost most of its Anzac units and was re-designated XXII Corps. This was the last British combat corps to be formed, although a reserve XXIII Corps was formed in Britain in 1918. Despite no longer having any New Zealand infantry, Godley retained some of his Australian and New Zealand Corps cavalry reconnaissance units, as well as the XXII Corps New Zealand Cyclist Battalion, which went on to play a vital role in the 1918 battles.

Godley's personal memoirs provide little insight into military matters. Rather they indicate that as the commander of XXII Corps, he was a self-obsessed officer who enjoyed living in a Champagne château and was much involved with visits, lunches, dinners and social contact with other military commanders and influential civilians. He complained that this socializing left little time for planning, which he seems in any case to have left largely to his staff officers, and visiting his troops. It is clear he seems to have had little in common with those under his command, and in his brief mention of the Ardre valley campaign he makes only limited reference to the key role played by his New Zealand cyclists at Marfaux, and none to the role played by the Anzac cavalry on the advance to contact on 27 July as the Germans retreated. Moreover he barely refers to the corps' very heavy casualties, and gives the distinct impression that he only had time to get up to the front just once. This was right at the end of the main battle, when he found conditions rather shocking:

> We fought continuously for nine days, gradually driving the Germans back, and when I got up to the front I found the men in great heart, but very tired. They had been perfectly splendid and done more than their share. Hampden, who I found in a filthy cellar in a most filthy, desolate and ruined village, was commanding the most advanced brigade, which had taken the Montagne de Bligny.

This is a reference to Brigadier General Viscount Hampden commanding 185 Brigade from his temporary headquarters in Bligny village, and the final courageous attack of the campaign, when the 8th West Yorkshires captured Bligny Hill.

Perhaps this criticism of a lack of apparent insight into the battle is unfair. During a ten-day battle, Godley's small corps suffered more than 7,000 casualties, but almost half its casualties occurred on the first day. Under French orders, it had attacked with inadequate preparation and a poor artillery barrage, and his real view of that situation might have been interesting. Perhaps the good readers of 1939 were actually more interested to know that, on his pre-battle liaison visit to Paris, he had lunch at the Ritz and took tea with Lady Hartington, who later became the Duchess of Devonshire. Godley managed to establish good relations with his French commanders, but undoubtedly his troops would have appreciated more thorough preparations before they were launched against the deadly German machine guns. Godley was not actually a diplomat, he was the senior British officer serving under foreign command and responsible for the lives of his men.

The French had expected that the British would insist upon more deliberate arrangements before that first attack, so his ready acceptance of the French plan may well have made him popular with the French commanders, but it cost many lives, and certainly deserves criticism on strictly military grounds.

After the campaign in the Tardenois, XXII Corps returned to Fourth Army and was involved in many of the final battles. This included approaching and breaching the Hindenburg Line and, although commanding different divisions, it was generally successful. When the war ended, Godley was promoted to general and eventually commanded the British Army of the Rhine, after which he served as governor of Gibraltar. Despite his numerous connections, he was never invited to hold any public office in New Zealand. During the Second World War he was an enthusiastic Home Guard commander.

Haig had agreed that the reinforced XXII Corps would move to the Marne area as a strategic reserve to be ready to counter the anticipated new German offensive. However, as it became clearer that the Germans were planning new offensives in the Reims area, Foch wanted to have the independent ability to smother these attacks and quickly move onto the counter-offensive. Accordingly, on 13 July, Foch requested that these four divisions should be placed directly under his orders, and indeed asked that four more reserve divisions should be sent to take their place. Haig agreed to the former but was not keen on this latter idea, although he did eventually send two more divisions, but they arrived too late to play any role in the fighting.

The 62nd (2nd West Riding) Division was one of seven second-line Territorial divisions, which were originally raised in 1914, and then kept in the UK to provide home defence and to feed reinforcements to frontline units. Its commander was Major General Walter Braithwaite, who had also earned a poor reputation at Gallipoli, for which he had been sacked in 1915.

Braithwaite was commissioned into the Somerset Light Infantry in 1886. His only son was commissioned into the same regiment but, as a 20-year old, was killed in action during the Battle of the Somme on 1 July 1916. Braithwaite saw active service in Burma and entered Staff College in 1898. When the South African War broke out he had not quite completed his studies and, together with the college's other students, he was sent out as a special serving officer, later becoming a brigade major. After the Boer War he had a series of staff appointments which brought him into contact with some of the British Army's leading figures, including Ian Hamilton, Henry Wilson and Douglas Haig. Haig, in particular, held him in high regard. In 1911 Braithwaite became Commandant of the Staff College at Quetta (where Bernard Montgomery became chief instructor in 1934). In March 1915, he was appointed chief of staff, as a lieutenant general, to Sir Ian Hamilton's Mediterranean Expeditionary Force.

Braithwaite appears to have been a loyal subordinate, and much of the blame for the Gallipoli campaign's failings fell on his head, perhaps unfairly. When the Suvla Bay attack by IX Corps failed, Hamilton was recalled in October 1915, and Braithwaite soon suffered the same fate. However, possibly because of Haig's support, he received a second chance. In December 1915 he was given command of 62nd Division which was, at the time, still very much a second-line division, being kept in the UK for home defence. Although this was not a particularly distinguished command, Braithwaite eventually earned the respect of his men, and took pains to turn the 62nd into one of the best fighting divisions in the British Army.

The 62nd (2nd West Riding) Division had been formed in the war enthusiasm of 1914 as a reserve to the 49th (1st West Riding) Division, a Territorial division recruited from the Yorkshire area, which was sent to France in April 1915. As a reserve formation it had difficulty getting resources and proper training, while it lost many of its best officers and NCOs who were transferred to units already fighting in France. Eventually it was allowed an independent existence, and was finally sent to France in January 1917. After a difficult baptism at Bullecourt in May 1917 the division performed well at Cambrai in November 1917, alongside the 51st Division, where it famously stormed the village of Havrincourt. In April 1918 it helped check the German spring offensive at Bucquoy where Braithwaite's personal leadership was conspicuous. The 62nd Division distinguished itself further in the fighting in the Ardre valley and went on to play a full role in the final advance. This included being given the 'honour' of storming Havrincourt again on 12 September 1918 and thereby breaking into the Hindenburg Line. On 7 June 1922 the Divisional Memorial was unveiled at Havrincourt by General Berthelot.

After a brief period as temporary commander of XXII Corps, Braithwaite was promoted to command IX Corps on 13 September 1918. Sixteen days later IX Corps used its 46th Division to spearhead Fourth Army's crossing of the St Quentin Canal in the Hindenburg Line at Bellenglise. It was a bold coup which, together with the attacks by the

Australian 5th and American 30th Divisions, peeled open an immensely strong section of the Hindenburg Line. This significant victory meant there were no important defensive obstacles left to pushing the Germans out of France. IX Corps continued to lead the advance on the extreme right of the British line. Although Braithwaite was accused of lacking imagination – the future Australian general, John Gellibrand, who was a student of his at the Quetta Staff College, opined 'Imagination is as foreign to him as independence' – his leadership of IX Corps was quite impressive. During the final advance he showed himself open to new ideas and sympathetic to technological solutions to tactical problems. Fittingly, Lieutenant General Sir Walter Braithwaite KCB organized Haig's funeral in 1928. He retired as a general in 1931 and died in 1945.

In common with most British formations, 62nd Division had suffered severely during the spring attacks by the Germans. It had been particularly active in defending the Bucquoy sector, south of Arras close to Bapaume, and was frequently in and out of the line until 24 June, when it was moved back to the Pas area west of Doullens for a rest. However, rumours soon spread of a new mission, and on 14 July the division began entraining at Doullens. By the 17th its infantry had detrained in the area east of Épernay, and were originally bussed to areas slightly farther east ready to support the French Fourth Army under the courageous General Gouraud. However, Gouraud had fully embraced the new flexible French defence tactics and, using them, soundly defeated the German First and Third Armies within hours of their opening attack on 15 July. Therefore Gouraud felt he did not need additional reinforcements, and 62nd Division then received orders to move to the French Fifth Army and concentrate behind the Italian II Corps at St Imoges, just north of Épernay.

Despite its clear Yorkshire origins, two of 62nd Division's battalions were not actually 'Yorkshire lads'. Due to the losses suffered in the great German attacks, and the lack of reinforcements from the UK, two of its original battalions had been reduced to cadre at the beginning of June 1918. To everyone's great regret, the 2/7th West Yorkshires of 185 Brigade and the 2/7th West Ridings of 186 Brigade had ceased to exist as battalions. They were replaced by two 'southern' battalions of tough experienced territorials, who had been sent directly from Palestine.

The 2/4th Battalion of the Hampshire Regiment had been formed soon after the outbreak of the war in 1914, as a second-line home defence battalion. In December 1914 its soldiers volunteered for overseas service and went out to India with 45th (2nd Wessex) Division. In April 1917 the battalion left India for Egypt and, by September 1917, found itself fighting the Turks in the Gaza front line. In December it took part in the successful advance on Jerusalem and, after its capture, moved to invest Jaffa. It remained campaigning against Turkish forces near Rafat and Berulin until ordered to France, with no home leave, in May 1918 where it joined 62nd Division.

The 5th Battalion of the Devonshire Regiment was also formed in September 1914. Two months later it sailed to India and was stationed in the Lahore Garrison area. In April 1917 it too sailed from India and landed at Suez to join the campaign against the Turkish army in Palestine. The battalion was then ordered to France and landed at Marseille on 1 June 1918. Both battalions had been made up to full strength of almost 1,000 men before leaving Egypt. As 5th Devons marched and attacked in the French summer's heat, they were probably grateful for the fact that there had been no time to replace their tropical uniforms, which therefore still included the khaki shorts, seen clearly in photographs taken at the time.

The 62nd Division's three infantry brigades were organized as follows:

185 Brigade
    5th Battalion Devonshire Regiment
    2/5th Battalion West Yorkshire Regiment
    8th Battalion West Yorkshire Regiment

186 Brigade
    2/4th Battalion Duke of Wellington's Regiment
    5th Battalion Duke of Wellington's Regiment
    2/4th Battalion Hampshire Regiment

187 Brigade
    2/4th Battalion King's Own Yorkshire Light Infantry (KOYLI)
    5th Battalion King's Own Yorkshire Light Infantry (KOYLI)
    2/4th (Hallamshire) Battalion Yorkshire & Lancashire Regiment

In direct support of each brigade was a light trench mortar battery. In addition, for close support, the 62nd had available a divisional pioneer battalion, namely the 9th Battalion Durham Light Infantry (DLI), three Royal Engineer field companies (Nos. 457, 460 and 461) and 62nd

Machine Gun Battalion. The heavy fire support was provided by 310th and 312th Brigades Royal Field Artillery and its two medium mortar batteries. Divisional communications were provided by the small signals company. Equally critical to the fighting ability of the division was its divisional ammunition column and the supply train, which brought supplies forward from the rail heads with horse and mule carts to individual units or brigade dumps. Just as vital, each brigade received medical cover from a field ambulance unit.

XXII Corps also commanded another famous territorial division. The 51st (Highland) Division had been formed as a Territorial Force (TF) division in 1908, as a result of the Haldane reforms. On the outbreak of war it was quickly mobilized but was used to provide home defence and reinforcements to other divisions serving in France until it went out to France, as the first TF division to go, early in 1915. Its infantry component was nine, originally twelve, battalions of kilted Scottish highland regiments. Its first commander was Major General Harper. The divisional sign was HD and, as the 51st did not do very well at first, due mainly to losing some of its best battalions to other divisions, it was often maligned as 'Harper's Duds', a nickname which the division took perverse pride in for many years. It fought in the Third Battle of Ypres in July 1916, and then distinguished itself with its famous action on 13 November 1916 when it stormed the heavily-fortified village of Beaumont-Hamel, thereby establishing its reputation as one of the fiercest assault divisions in the BEF.

In April 1917 it made a significant advance of 10,000 yards in the Battle of Arras alongside the Canadians who captured Vimy Ridge. It also achieved a significant advance at Cambrai in November 1917 and took part in the defence of this area against the heavy German counter-attacks in December 1917. In 1918 it was still in the Cambrai area near Flesquières when the Germans launched their first Somme offensive on 21 March and drenched the division with gas. It then fought a long withdrawal action, suffering some 4,900 casualties, until it was moved north to the Béthune area to recuperate on 1 April. There it was supposed to retrain its badly depleted battalions, but fate had placed it precisely in Flanders just in time to receive the second of the great German attacks on 9 April. Fighting grimly alongside the 55th (West Lancashire) Division, its young soldiers managed to hold the right shoulder of the British line and halt the German offensive near Richebourg Saint Vaast. At the beginning of May it moved to the Oppy area, south of Arras, but was frequently back in the front line, where it rebuilt a series of trench defences designed to provide all-round defence and to withstand the German's new infiltration tactics.

For the campaign in Champagne, the 51st Division commanded the following:

152 Brigade
 5th Battalion Seaforth Highlanders
 6th Battalion Seaforth Highlanders
 6th Battalion Gordon Highlanders

153 Brigade
 6th Battalion Black Watch (The Royal Highlanders)
 7th Battalion Black Watch (The Royal Highlanders)
 7th Battalion Gordon Highlanders

154 Brigade
 4th Battalion Seaforth Highlanders
 4th Battalion Gordon Highlanders
 7th Battalion Argyll and Sutherland Highlanders

Each brigade also had its own light trench mortar battery and the divisional pioneers were the 8th Battalion Royal Scots while 400, 401, 404 Field Companies Royal Engineers provided engineer support. Direct divisional fire support was provided by its own 51st Machine Gun Battalion, and 255th and 256th Brigades RFA. Together with the X.51, and Y.51 Medium Mortar Batteries this gave the division a total of sixty-four Vickers machine guns, thirty-six 18-pounder guns, twelve 4.5-inch howitzers, and twelve 6-inch mortars. Communications were provided by 51st Divisional Signals Company. Ammunition supply was the responsibility of 51st Divisional Ammunition Column RFA, and the 51st Divisional Train ASC took care of transporting the rest of the division's supplies from the rail heads to individual units.

Arrangements for medical support and evacuation are often unreported, but acquire huge importance when serious combat conditions are met. For the 51st, this was provided by the division's own three medical units, 2nd, 3rd, and 2/1st Highland Field Ambulances. The ten officers and 224 men of each field ambulance carried no weapons, but played a vital role in the collection, initial treatment and evacuation of wounded from the regimental aid posts (RAPs) of their assigned brigade. A field ambulance was organized with three sections, which included a tent sub-section, stretcher bearers and ward orderlies, and theoretically each field ambulance was capable of dealing with some 150 casualties per day.

The two British divisions were to suffer a total of some 8,000 casualties over the ten days of the battle in the Ardre valley, and the resources of the British medical services were undoubtedly stretched to the limit. Moreover, they had to deal with this enormous number of casualties while operating in very difficult hilly and wooded terrain, and while marooned in a sea of French army forces, far removed from their normal back-up of medical supplies, motor ambulance convoys and base hospitals. That they did this so successfully, day after day, in the difficult terrain of the area was a tremendous tribute to the men of the medical services, who also treated enemy wounded. Significantly, identified mortalities were only about 10 per cent of total casualties.

During a battle the normal evacuation procedure was for casualties to either walk back or be stretchered back from where they fell to the RAP at each battalion. There wounds would be dealt with first by the battalion's own doctor and small medical staff. The injured would then be sent or carried back to Advanced Dressing Stations (ADS) or Casualty Clearing Stations (CCS) maintained by each field ambulance, and then back to a divisional Main Dressing Station (MDS). In the Ardre valley the route back for the wounded or stretcher bearers was marked by bandages tied around trees. XXII Corps itself had no additional medical services in its structure, and there was initially no depot of medical stores available, so each field ambulance had to rely on its mobilization stocks of tents, stretchers, dressings and medicines.

Given the necessity to provide a medical service for the British troops in this difficult situation, the two senior directors of medical services in the 51st and the 62nd Divisions decided to pool their resources and organize joint facilities. A major CCS was opened at Sezanne by 62nd Division where patient transfers to rail were undertaken. The tent sub-section of a 51st Division field ambulance opened an advanced operating centre for serious cases at the Hôpital Auban Moet in Épernay. The MDS of the 62nd Division was opened at St Imoges, and the 2/2nd West Riding Field Ambulance opened a walking wounded dressing station further south at Champillon. It was a thirty-one-mile (fifty kilometres) journey from the MDS at St Imoges to the CCS at Sezanne, so passing transport was stopped and cases loaded and transferred back, in stages, to Champillon or Sezanne. A casualty control point had been established in Épernay, but both the

Lieutenant General Sir Alexander Godley.

Lieutenant General Godley inspects the New Zealand Division after the unsuccessful attack at Passchendaele in October 1917.

Major General Sir Walter Braithwaite.

General Ferdinand Foch.

General Charles 'Butcher' Mangin.

King George V presenting medals to American soldiers with General Plumer behind him.

British, American and Australian troops resting after the attack at Hamel.

British 55th Division gas casualties, 10 April 1918.

General Bertholet's review of XXII Corps and the 51st Highland and 63rd Division after the Ardre Campaign, 1 August 1918.

The *Fanion* Party of New Zealand Cyclists, which returned to France in 1919.

Memorial to the 2nd Devons at La Ville-aux-Bois.

Original Camp Flag of the 2nd Devons with the original Croix de Guerre.

Memorial to the 5th (Gibraltar) Battery RA at La Ville-aux-Bois.

5 (GIBRALTAR) FIELD BATTERY ROYAL ARTILLERY

IN MEMORY OF THE MEMBERS OF THE BATTERY WHO GAVE THEIR LIVES AT LA VILLE AUX BOIS LES PONTAVERT ON 27TH MAY 1918.

DURING THE OFFENSIVE OF MAY 1918 THE BATTERY WAS ATTACKED BY AN OVERWHELMING FORCE. THE GUNS CONTINUED TO FIRE AND RESISTANCE DID NOT CEASE UNTIL EVERY MAN WAS KILLED OR CAPTURED. FOR THIS ACTION THE BATTERY WAS AWARDED THE CROIX DE GUERRE.

A LA MÉMOIRE DES ARTILLEURS QUI DONNÈRENT LEUR VIE, A LA VILLE AUX BOIS LES PONTAVERT, LE 27 MAI 1918.

PENDANT L'OFFENSIVE DE MAI 1918, LA BATTERIE FUT SUBMERGÉE PAR UN ENNEMI TRÈS SUPÉRIEUR EN NOMBRE. LES PIÈCES CONTINUÈRENT LEUR TIR, ET LA RÉSISTANCE NE CESSA QUE LORSQUE LES HOMMES EURENT ÉTÉ TUÉS OU FAITS PRISONNIERS JUSQU'AU DERNIER. POUR CETTE ACTION, LA BATTERIE REÇUT LA CROIX DE GUERRE.

The memorial in the centre of Soissons to the 3,987 officers and men who fell in Champagne and have no known graves.

Divisional Memorial to the 62nd Division in Havrincourt.

British CWGC Cemetery at Marfaux.

Memorial in Marfaux Cemetery to the lost New Zealanders with no named graves.

British CWGC Cemetery beside the Château at Buzancy, containing mainly Scottish graves.

Memorial to the 15th Scottish Division made by the 17th French Division.

Memorial at Buzancy to those 2,200 soldiers lost from the 1st Division, 18–23 July 1918.

Memorial to the 4th Division just outside Fismes.

The huge memorial to the 9 Divisions of the AEF who took part in the Second Battle of the Marne on Hill 204 overlooking Château-Thierry.

Aisne-Marne American Cemetery at Belleau Wood.

Oise-Aisne American Military Cemetery near Fère-en-Tardenois contains the graves of 6,012 American soldiers, many from the 1st and 42nd Rainbow Division.

The 'American Memorial Bridge' at Fismes presented by the 28th Division.

Arch commemorates 5,000 Italians who died for France.

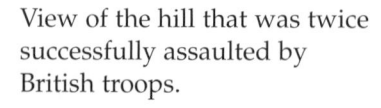

View of the hill that was twice successfully assaulted by British troops.

Memorial to the 19th Division and 56 Brigade, who took this hill.

Close-up of the 19th Division Monument.

TO THE GLORIOUS MEMORY OF THE OFFICERS AND MEN OF THE 19TH (BRITISH) DIVISION WHO FELL IN ACTION IN THE CHAMPAGNE MAY-JUNE 1918 THIS MEMORIAL IS ERECTED ON THE MONTAGNE DE BLIGNY WHICH WAS RECAPTURED AND HELD BY THE 19TH DIVISION JUNE 6TH 1918

Château de Commétreuil today.

Dormans Memorial today.

Fort de Condé, near Soissons.

Crown Prince Rupprecht's battle headquarters.

French living quarters carved into the rock below the front-line near Vic-sur-Aisne

German bunker cut into the chalk at Buzancy.

Rock carving made by soldiers in the French caves near Vic-sur-Aisne.

Entrance to Hitler's mess.

Telephone exchange and world-wide communications centre at Hitler's HQ.

men manning it were killed by an air-dropped bomb during the night of the 20th. The divisional histories reported that the French medical services were ungrudging in the help they provided to the British with stretchers and care. Although the British doctors tried to ensure that all British patients were taken care of by their own services and kept out of the French hospitals, some of the ever-resourceful British walking wounded managed to get themselves into the French hospital at Épernay.

As described earlier, 51st (Highland) Division had played a key role in the British defence of the Somme and the Lys, and as a result suffered some 7,480 casualties in the four weeks before it came out of action on 15 April 1918. The British Army was so stretched that there was no time for leisurely recovery by its damaged units. Divisions had to assimilate and train reinforcements, many of them straight from the training depots, whilst continuing to stand their turn in the trenches. Between 24 April and 11 July, the division was only out of the line for a total of just ten days. Commanders noted that the young men replacements, often mere boys who had lied about their true age, simply did not have the physical strength necessary to undertake the hard work of labouring in the trenches to build new defence systems. In addition, the young officers and men had to be trained to make the best use of their infantry weapons, as well as learning to patrol aggressively the no man's land in front of the division, where they aimed to have some six to eight patrols out every night.

The division went back into the line between Bailleul and Willerval on 6 May, when great efforts were made to build extensive dugouts to protect the men, under the guidance of the Royal Engineers. These structures were so successful that, for example during the night of 25 May, over 800 heavy shells were fired by the Germans into the divisional area at Thelus without causing a single casualty. However, earlier, on the night of 16 May, the Germans had fired three half-hour bursts of mustard gas shells at three hour intervals, causing 142 casualties among the men of the 7th Argyll and Sutherland Highlanders. Usually the men were protected by breathing through the small box respirator (SBR), which they carried slung around their chests, but some chemical gases also attacked exposed skin. This same SBR was also adopted by the American soldiers when they came to France.

The Germans relied heavily on the incapacitating effect of gas to increase the shock effect of their intense artillery barrages in their spring 1918 attacks. Gas had the great advantage that it could incapacitate the defenders without physically destroying the ground and buildings, which allowed the attacking troops to advance faster. It certainly made the task of the Allied counter-bombardment artillery much more difficult, as the gunners had to wear their masks while serving the guns. Gas usually comprised more than 50 per cent of the shells fired in Bruchmüller's barrages, but it clung to low ground and could be a very blunt weapon. Crucially, its effectiveness depended upon the weather conditions and wind strength. However, the British soon learnt how to protect themselves and gradually became equally expert in the aggressive use of gas. Unsurprisingly, having suffered from the attack of 16 May, the Scots were not displeased to see a 'gas beam' attack delivered on their front on 10 June. This was an attack mounted from a forty-carriage narrow-gauge train, loaded with long metal gas cylinders. The use of this miniature train enabled a large number of the heavy gas cylinders to be brought at short notice into position immediately behind the foremost British trenches. Then, when the wind was in the right direction, the gas from all forty of the cylinders could be released electronically at the same moment.

At the appropriate moment, just before the attack started, the Scottish trenches were evacuated. Then the 'gas beam' was released and rolled slowly forward silently at a steady walking pace some 5,000 yards (five kilometres) into the German lines towards Douai. Later, it was possible from the air to see a broad belt of discoloured grass extending far into the German lines. The gas was apparently very potent and returning Scottish troops found large numbers of dead rats and beetles at the bottoms of their trenches. At any rate, this vicious attack seems to have kept the German batteries silent for some days afterwards. On 11 July the division was once again relieved by the 4th Canadian Division.

After just a few days out of the trenches, the division was warned to pack for a special 'move' and began to entrain at Bryas and Pernes near St Lô. The move of the division to the Champagne area required thirty-four separate trains, which left every hour between the 14th and 16th. The circuitous journey, by way of the southern outskirts of Paris, took about thirty hours for each train, and was considered a thrilling adventure by the Scottish soldiers. Whilst the divisional move was still underway, the Germans launched their fifth great 'Peace Offensive' on 15 July, which threatened Paris and seemed very likely to involve the 51st as it began detraining at Épernay, just south of the Marne on the 16th. However, it took almost another two days of hard travelling by bus and marching on foot for the brigades to assemble fully. Marching during the day was uncomfortably hot and dusty, but a great storm on the night of the 18th ensured that the soldiers were also drenched during the night and their routes were blocked by fallen trees.

In addition to its three infantry battalions, each brigade needed to gather all the vehicles and stores of its regimental transport carrying the vital food, clothing, and ammunition for its troops. Hundreds of horses, mules and carts were needed for the mortars and ammunition of its light mortar battery, its attached Royal Engineer field company, and its supporting field ambulance. The horse-drawn divisional artillery, which had been the last to entrain on the 16th, and thus the last to detrain, had a long march from Nogent-sur-Seine to its assembly point and did not arrive until the 18th. During the 17th the German attacks in the Fifth Army area were finally halted, and General Bertholet could begin to plan his part in the French counter-attack. An initial attack on the 18th by the weakened Italian corps had made only limited progress, and the Italians needed to be relieved.

Having begun entraining at Doullens on 14 July, the 62nd Division had by the 16th, reached the area of Mailly-le-Camp, a long-established French garrison area south of Châlons. (German forces occupied Mailly-le-Camp during the Second World War and several panzer battalions were famously bombed by the RAF in an ill-fated attack on the night of 3 May 1944, when the camp was totally destroyed. However, the bomber force was delayed over the target and tragically forty-two Lancasters out of 332 in the attack force were lost.) On 17 July the 62nd Division moved north to the Tours-sur-Marne area and then, by the 19th, had marched or bussed to its concentration area around Chamery. XXII Corps' headquarters opened at Vertus, but later moved to the château of the Comte de Chandon.

Some eight months earlier, on 20 November 1917, the 62nd Division had fought alongside the 51st Division as part of IV Corps in Third Army, which attacked at Cambrai with six infantry divisions and 381 tanks. The Battle of Cambrai was a superb opportunity to break through the Hindenburg Line using the power of a sudden artillery barrage and overwhelming numbers of tanks. Unfortunately, one of the strongest parts of the German defence was around Flesquières, where the 51st attacked alongside the British tanks, but was held by a stubborn German defence. The 62nd Division had advanced on the left of the 51st and quickly swept through Havrincourt and Graincourt up to Bourlon Wood. The Germans were deeply concerned by the success at Cambrai and were determined to recover the ground lost. Heavy counter-attacks over the next two weeks eventually drove the British back to their start lines, although Havrincourt was actually retained by the British until it was lost during the German advance on 23 March 1918. However, on 12 September 1918, the 62nd Division returned to the area and retook the town in spectacular fashion. Cambrai remains a famous if controversial battle to this day, but fully demonstrated the battle-winning potential of the new British Tank Corps.

The most remarkable feature of the powerful Mangin attack on the morning of 18 July was that it came as such a complete shock to the Germans. Mangin had launched a large number of small counter-attacks during July to straighten the line in preparation for the major attack, but managed to keep secret the strength of the forces, including particularly tanks and artillery, that he was quietly assembling in the Forest of Villers-Cotterêts. Some degree of threat was apparent to the nearby German commanders, but the attention of the OHL was focused on the preparations for its own major attacks around Reims. They had anticipated some action by the French on 14 July (Bastille Day), but when the French army did not launch even a token attack they assumed they could launch their own great attack with impunity, the following day. After the 'success' of their four earlier attacks, they had confidently built up very high expectations around this great 'Peace Offensive' by three and a half German armies with which they hoped to compel the French to the negotiating table. In preparation for their offensive, the Germans had spent four weeks covertly gathering additional forces in the area behind the front and building up huge stocks of ammunition and battle supplies. They therefore hoped to achieve both strategic and tactical surprise, which would give them a signal victory, including the capture of Reims, before turning their attention again to defeating their implacable British enemy in Flanders.

An additional well-planned feature of the German attack was that they had moved the so-called 'Paris gun' from the Beaumont site to the woods around Fère-en-Tardenois, which brought it even closer to Paris. In order to preserve the secrecy of its location, overhead camouflage was erected to protect the sites and railway lines from air observation. It was clearly a massive engineering undertaking for the Germans and a further heavy burden on their supply network, and they could only justify this effort if it could induce panic in the civil population. When the gun did open fire from the completely new site on the morning of 15 July, after being silent since 11 June, it brought shock and terror to civilians and contributed to the panic which gripped Paris on that day and caused thousands to flee from the city. However, the physical damage inflicted was very limited, and its overall impact seems to have been far less than its heavy cost, particularly in maintenance and re-supply terms.

The ancient royal coronation city of Reims had enormous significance for both protagonists. The Germans had captured Reims in 1870 during the Franco-Prussian War. They almost captured it again in 1914, before retreating to the Aisne river line in September 1914. Having been successful in their two previous attacks on the French, in the Aisne and Matz battles of May and June, the Germans planned to seal their victories over the French Army by a general advance either side of Reims using three German armies. This attack was intended finally to pinch out the Reims salient and allow the Kaiser to lead his long-postponed Reims victory parade. As before, the Germans had secretly assembled some fifty infantry divisions, supported by almost two-thirds of their artillery, namely 6,353 guns, and 2,200 mortars, together with almost 900 aircraft. Expectations were high for this attack, which, perhaps unwisely, was named the 'Peace Offensive'. It was clearly anything but peaceful, and was actually the second largest of the German spring attacks of 1918, as it commenced with immense Bruchmüller artillery barrages of gas and high explosive shells along two separate fronts.

Ludendorff was, as ever, confident that he could inflict such a severe blow on them that the French would have no option but to open negotiations; he seems to have completely underestimated the fortitude and determination of both Clemenceau and Foch. On 7 July he had confided to the Foreign Secretary, Admiral von Hintze, that his next great offensive would 'finally and decisively conquer the enemy'. During the intensive pre-battle preparations, German officers and soldiers came to believe that victory in this battle could signal a much desired successful and rapid end to the war. However, aerial reconnaissance of the German preparations, and human intelligence gained from captured prisoners and espionage, alerted the French and they were thoroughly prepared for the great attacks. An intense spoiling barrage was put down on the German lines just ten minutes before the opening gas bombardment, at 1.00am, which signalled the start of the battle, and this French bombardment, which then continued throughout the night, undoubtedly aimed at weakening the German attack.

East of Reims, the Germans had readied twenty-three attack divisions. At 3.40am, after a thorough pounding of the French forward trenches, von Mudra's First Army and von Einem's Third Army advanced into the French forward zone of General Gouraud's Fourth Army, meeting little resistance. Gouraud had organized his defences in accordance with the latest flexible defence doctrine ordered by Pétain, with the majority of troops held back from the forward front line, apart from a few sacrificial strongpoints, and this had quickly proved its value. The forward zone had been thoroughly gassed and pulverized by the German artillery, and the assault troops had little difficulty picking their way through it. However, when out of range of their own support artillery, they finally came up against the bulk of the French forces entrenched in the main battle zone and were hammered terribly by the dreadfully accurate French artillery. Lying well out of range of the German artillery, the French guns were able to bring down interdiction fire in front of and behind the waves of German infantry, jammed into the bare killing zone. By 9.00am on the 15th, it was obvious to all that the attackers could make no real progress and their situation was totally hopeless. Gouraud's army had repelled waves of attackers and suffered casualties of around 5,000, compared to von Einem's losses of at least 40,000.

To the south-west of Reims, von Boehn's Seventh Army was much more successful against the French Fifth and Sixth Armies. In particular, the German gas shells proved very effective against the French defence lines, which lay close by just across the River Marne and were less deep and sturdy. As a result, despite the French counter-bombardment, three German corps forced crossings of the Marne, at Dormans particularly and elsewhere, using numerous pontoon bridges and quickly spread out in a bridgehead nine miles long and almost four miles deep. However, the Germans actually lacked sufficient horses and road transport to move their heavier supplies and artillery, and they were limited in the support they could provide to their troops.

News of the huge attacks surprised civilians and caused tremendous panic to spread in Paris. The panic was heightened by renewed shelling from the 'Paris gun', which had begun firing from the Bois de Bruyéres on the 15th. However, the American 3rd Division, which had been deployed around Château-Thierry for almost six weeks, held its positions steadfastly and halted all attempts by the German 10th Division to cross the Marne east of Château-Thierry. The Americans thereby prevented a complete break-through, its 38th Infantry Regiment deservedly earning its nickname as the 'Rock of the Marne'. Farther east along the river at Varennes, the German 36th Division had suffered from the heavy Allied counter-barrage, which outshelled their own and caused many casualties. Finally, it managed to put some of its pontoon bridges into the Marne and cross, but suffered crippling losses as it met two companies of the American 28th Division, the Pennsylvania National Guard, who, although without any previous combat experience, poured a hail of rifle and machine-gun bullets into the Germans, and curbed their advance before they were finally overcome. One German officer wrote feelingly about the shock of finding Americans waiting for their approach to the Marne:

> 'The Americans kill everything!' That was the cry of horror of July 15th, which long took hold of our men. At home meanwhile they were sarcastic about the imperfect training of this enemy, about the American 'bluff' and the like. The fact that on July 15th more than 60 per cent of our troops led to battle were left dead or wounded upon the battlefield may substantially be charged to his credit.

Although six German divisions eventually managed to cross the river and achieved an apparent German success in the 'Marne elbow', they had moved away from the direct support of their artillery and their advance was soon contained by the surrounding French and American divisions, including the new French Ninth Army.

In the high Ardre valley, just west of Reims, the Germans had launched their attack from their positions just north of the Montagne de Bligny. This was the area where they had been halted, just six weeks earlier, by the counter-attack of the British 19th Division on 6 June. The French normally established three lines of defence, but it was difficult to establish continuous positions in the densely forested country, which was overlooked by the Montagne de Bligny. The first line of defence closest to the Germans was the outpost line held by the Italian II Corps, which ran from Champlat through the Bois des Eclisses to Bligny and St Euphraise.

Following the Italian defeat by the Austro-German Fourteenth Army at Caporetto, France and Britain had sent eleven Allied divisions to bolster the Italian front. Actually Caporetto had provided an early example of the successful implementation of the Hutier infiltration tactics by a number of German units. Among them was Captain Erwin Rommel's *Jäger* company, which he led against vastly superior numbers of Italian troops to take Mount Matajurer on 26 October 1917, thereby earning himself the award of the *Pour le Mérite* decoration.

When the German spring offensives began in 1918 the Italians decided to reciprocate the earlier help by sending an infantry corps to the French front. The Italian II Corps consisted of the 3rd and 8th Italian Divisions, plus corps troops including heavy artillery, cavalry, medical and service units. After some combat exposure in the Argonne region, the Italian II Corps had moved to the high Ardre valley in mid-June to relieve the British 19th Division holding around Bligny. At the beginning of July the French 120th Infantry Division had joined the corps and been placed in its second defence line. On the right of the Italian II Corps was the French I Colonial Corps which held the flank of French Fifth Army, closest to Reims.

The Italian II Corps, particularly its 8th Division, bore the brunt of the German attack in the Ardre valley. Early on 15 July the Germans advanced, led by the 22nd, 103rd and 123rd Divisions, under a very heavy artillery barrage of shells and gas, supported by tanks. They quickly took the trench line on the Montagne de Bligny and, during the morning, the villages of Chaumuzy and Marfaux fell. By the afternoon the Germans had arrived at the second position in the Bois de Courton. On the 16th they began an attack on the French and Italian units in the centre of the Bois de Courton. Unless halted, the German divisions threatened to be able to continue down the mountain of Reims and occupy Épernay, thereby completing the encirclement of the city of Reims.

The Germans had achieved a huge success as three other corps of von Boehn's Seventh Army had crossed the Marne river despite heavy casualties and had created a new salient south of the Marne. However, these troops were quickly blocked by French and American reserves and were unable to expand their bridgehead significantly. Moreover, they suffered heavy continuing casualties amongst their engineers as the supply bridges were subjected to continuous air and artillery attack. They quickly discovered that their narrow supply routes across the Marne were actually dangerous chokepoints. As a result, Ludendorff was forced to restrain the stream of German troops flooding across the river, as it quickly became clear that, far from threatening Paris, the Germans had effectively created another, even more vulnerable, salient.

Although fierce attacks were delivered on either side of Reims on the 16th, these also made only limited progress. Multiple attacks were launched against Fort de la Pompelle, which guarded the approaches to Reims from the south, without success. The fort had been briefly occupied by the Germans in September 1914, but was quickly retaken by the French Army. It remained the cornerstone of the defence of Reims for the next four years and its shattered ruins, off RN44, can still be seen and visited today.

Another attempt was made to envelop Reims the following day, but by the afternoon of the 17th it was clear that the 'Peace Offensive' had totally failed to achieve its aims. Moreover, the Germans south of the Marne were suffering severely as their temporary bridges across the river endured heavy French and Allied air attacks, and they faced strong ground attacks by French and American forces. Even before Mangin's counter-attack, the German High Command had recognized the inevitability of an early termination to von Boehn's offensive and the necessity for a withdrawal back across the Marne.

However, Ludendorff himself stubbornly refused to accept this reality and wanted to hold on to the territory gained, while continuing to plan for a fresh attack to begin on 21 July. Eventually, given the success of Mangin's attack on the 18th, which threatened the whole Marne salient, he had no alternative but to agree to a complete German withdrawal back across the Marne.

This situation had its parallel with events in early September 1914. Then the three armies of the German right wing, which had overwhelmed the British Expeditionary Force and the French Fifth Army, forcing them to retreat from Belgium, had brought their advance cavalry to within nineteen miles (thirty kilometres) of Paris. The whole German army and civil population expected their victorious soldiers to be marching triumphantly through Paris within days. Suddenly, General von Kluck's First Army was struck by a surprise attack on its western flank from the newly-formed French Sixth Army, advancing from Paris. This threat forced him to order his leading divisions, which were already well south of the Marne, to turn around and make forced marches north to meet the dangerous flank attacks in the Ourcq valley. Consequently, his unexpected withdrawal from south of the River Marne opened-up a large gap with the German Second Army into which the British Expeditionary Force advanced. Recognizing this danger, General von Moltke, through his emissary Colonel Hentsch, ordered his army commanders to pull their forces back to the Aisne river and dig in. This first withdrawal from the Marne in September 1914, precisely when victory seemed assured and imminent, had struck a tremendous blow to German morale. History was repeated in July 1918 as the Germans again crossed the Marne. Once again, Mangin's attack caught the Germans on a vulnerable flank. German hopes, including the Kaiser's personal expectations, had been raised precipitately, only to be crushed and subjected to the same unexpected disappointment and humiliation.

No one was more astonished than Ludendorff himself. He had already moved his headquarters to Tournai and was actually holding a HAGEN staff planning meeting there on the morning of 18th. He had just dismissed the suggestion that the French could possibly gather sufficient forces to do battle when news was brought of Mangin's great attack towards Soissons. He admitted later that he finished his talk in a state of great nervousness. While he still clung to the idea of launching HAGEN, Ludendorff had to admit reluctantly, to both Hindenburg and the Kaiser, that the attack by Mangin in the Soissons area was a really serious threat, particularly to the large element of Seventh Army which was fighting south of the Marne, as its major resupply artery came under enemy fire. Ludendorff later wrote:

> The danger in which we are placed by the depth of the enemy's penetration makes it our first task to strengthen the lines at this point – at any cost against further assault. It is a pivotal position defending the whole Seventh Army, fighting in the Marne elbow. Unless we can feel certain of our Western flank, we cannot undertake further operations around Reims, or withdraw in an orderly way from the South bank of the Marne. So long as we are not in safety at that point, or until we can erect a new front which is safe from the assaults of the enemy, we are not complete masters of the situation and cannot resume the initiative. Here is where we have got to settle things. Here we must decide our further plan of campaign.

Despite the heavy air attacks on its troop concentrations and bridges, the Germans were nevertheless able to exercise all their usual skills to withdraw their exposed troops south of the river. On 18 and 19 July, under cover of night, the Germans managed to withdraw all their wounded and stores and then their fighting troops across the Marne. The fact that they were able to complete this withdrawal in two nights using makeshift bridges and boats seems to indicate that only the vulnerable infantry and light artillery had actually managed to cross the Marne. For heavier fire support they had relied on the artillery stationed north of the river. However, to secure this withdrawal, they were forced to reinforce their defences on the shoulders of the Aisne salient, particularly south of Soissons and west of Reims, and it was this strengthened defence that the attacking American, British and French divisions met after 19 July. No Germans could relax until the last of their rearguard troops had been pulled back across the river. Finally their Marne evacuation was completed by 4.00am on the 20th.

Foch had recognized that the layout of the German Aisne salient made it vulnerable, and that a great victory could be achieved if the Germans could be enveloped by co-ordinated attacks coming from several directions. A swift advance onto the central plain around Fère-en-Tardenois would make possible a significant encirclement of German troops. In order to achieve this, he ordered that the main encircling attacks were to be made by the Tenth Army in the west, in order to reach the Vesle river, and the Fifth Army in the east to attack up the Ardre valley, also to reach the Vesle. Sixth Army was to engage the face of the salient and push the Germans away from Château-Thierry, while tying down enemy troops and preventing them from assisting on the flanks. However, General Bertholet, commanding French Fifth Army, was short of fresh troops and, to assist him, he was promised the British XXII Corps, which started detraining at Épernay on the 17th. After an arduous march during the stormy night of the 18th, the two divisions of XXII Corps gathered in the early morning of the 19th in the southern part of the Montagne de Reims.

General Mangin's Tenth Army and the western part of Degoutte's Sixth Army had achieved astounding progress with their surprise attacks between Château-Thierry and Longpont on the morning of the 18th. They were still attacking fiercely on the 19th, but no longer with the benefit of surprise, as General Berthelot met Godley and his two divisional commanders at the Italian II Corps headquarters.

Ludendorff reluctantly admitted the vulnerability of the German position:

> South of Soissons our infantry did not resist this attack as firmly as I had hoped, although we had a division in line there which had been considered particularly reliable. A gap was made in our line, and this soon widened. This situation north of the Ourcq River made it necessary to withdraw our troops further south. The success of the enemy came to me as a shock, and I sent immediate reinforcements, which, however, owing to the difficulties of transport, were slow in arriving. On July 19th our situation was much more satisfactory. Even the troops who had been surprised on the preceding day now

rallied and fought well. The reason they gave for their former failure was the wholly unexpected nature of the attack. One General of a division told me he had personally visited our foremost line on July 17th, and there had been not the slightest sign of the enemy's activity.

It was impressed on the British that it was necessary to maintain the pressure on the Germans to prevent them withdrawing troops to meet the Tenth Army attack. It was already apparent that the Germans had been hit hard by Mangin's attack, and that they were therefore in the process of withdrawing from their bridgehead south of the Marne. The French commanders anticipated that the German withdrawal could well continue elsewhere. However, unknown to the Allies, the German commanders had recovered quickly from their surprise and, being competent soldiers, were taking measures to harden their defence. They had actually moved two divisions which they had been saving for the proposed HAGEN attack to defend Soissons and the high ground south-east of it, which they considered the key to holding on to the Aisne and Marne pockets. Fresh divisions were also on their way to relieve the over-extended Germans to the west of Reims in the Ardre valley.

Despite the Allied success elsewhere, it was also obvious that the immediate situation of the Italian corps was precarious and threatened the viability of Fifth Army. The Italian II Corps, under General Albricci, had borne the brunt of a fierce attack by two German corps between 15 and 17 July and, despite having been bombarded and attacked severely, it had made some progress with its counter-attacks on the 18th. However, it was reported the Italian troops were 'in an exhausted and shaken condition'. The Italians had suffered some 9,000 casualties and needed to be relieved. The British generals were then prevailed upon to agree that, rather than undertake a deliberate relief of the Italians, they should attack through them on the next morning, the 20th. The attack was planned to be a powerful punch delivered up the Ardre valley by four hard-fighting Allied divisions.

The attack on the right of the small Ardre stream was to be led by the 62nd Division, with the French 2nd Colonial Division, a mixture of Algerian, Senegalese and French colonial troops, on its right. On the left of the stream, 51st Division was to attack with the crack French 9th Division, commanded by General Gamelin, on its left. The ground was totally new to the British, and there had been no opportunities for reconnaissance, but the strength of this assault sounded promising,

XXII Corps with 51st and 62nd Divisions joins French Fifth Army 149

and the British generals were keen to appear co-operative and dispel the perception that the British would only act with deliberation. Furthermore they placed reliance on the expectation that the French would have good intelligence about the enemy intentions, as well as large quantities of their own well-registered artillery.

The reality soon proved very different; and their lack of experience of the peculiar fighting conditions they faced was to cost the British infantry many casualties over the first days of the battle. Despite the pressing circumstances, the British commanders, particularly the corps commander, Lieutenant General Godley, should take most of the blame for agreeing to launch a major attack without reconnaissance, and without proper artillery support, against a virtually unknown enemy. In the event, the four British and French divisions fought heroically to drive back a stubborn foe, but it was to take the Allied soldiers virtually ten days to attain the final objectives given for their initial attack on the 20th.

The 51st (Highland) and 62nd (West Riding) Divisions fight their way up the Ardre Valley

Saturday 20 July 1918. The opening attack of the Battle of Tardenois in the Ardre valley against Marfaux and Chaumuzy.
The two British divisions had very little time in which to shake themselves out for a four brigade attack on a four-mile (six kilometres) wide front, which was scheduled to commence at 8.00am on the 20th. They had already completed an arduous night approach march along pitch-black forest paths through streams of retiring French and Italian troops. Thousands of troops from the three divisions already in the area were on the move, and there was enormous congestion on all the approaches to the front. As a result, many of the footsore and weary troops did not get into position until 4.00am. Because they believed that the Germans were vulnerable as they pulled back the French commanders had set ambitious objectives. The final objective for the first day's advance (the Brown Line) was set some six miles (nine and a half kilometres) from the start line. The intermediate Blue Line objective was set two and a half to four (four to six kilometres) ahead, and the initial objective (the Green Line) ran from Chaumuzy to the north-western edge of the Bois de Courton.

The basic battle plan was that each British division would advance with two brigades forward and one in reserve. For 51st Division on the left of the Ardre river, 153 and 154 Brigades were to lead the advance, leaving 152 Brigade in reserve. Although hardly more than a shallow stream in this area, the Ardre flowed northwards through the wide Ardre valley to join the River Vesle at Fismes. It provided a general direction of advance, and was the obvious inter-divisional boundary. Each attacking brigade was to advance on a one-battalion front, intending to rotate its lead battalions to take each of the objective lines in succession. The artillery fireplan was substantial with opening barrages to be provided by French and Italian artillery (fourteen

The 51st and 62nd Divisions fight their way up the Ardre Valley

batteries of 155mm howitzers and thirty-nine batteries of 75mm guns) to cover the advance up to the Green Line, and then for the respective divisional field artillery batteries to move forward and cover the rest of the advance. The British divisional artillery, which had been unloaded last from the trains, had been on the march for three days. With its heavy horse-drawn guns and mule-drawn ammunition wagons, it had struggled heroically to cover some eighty miles (120 kilometres) in three days, but could not get all the guns into position ready for the start of the battle. Although they were unable to get into position to take part in the opening barrage, it was hoped that the field gunners would be able to support the further advances by the infantry.

On the left bank of the Ardre, closest to the stream as it faced a hill which was partially wooded, was 154 Brigade with 4th Seaforth Highlanders leading. The hill sloped up to the dominating villages of Marfaux and Courmas, and on its eastern side it sloped down to the Ardre stream. On the left of 154 Brigade, 6th Black Watch led 153 Brigade, as it faced the huge, impenetrable and dark Bois de Courton. The 6th Black Watch quickly captured the German outpost line and then plunged into the Bois de Courton. The two follow-on battalions, 7th Black Watch and 7th Gordon Highlanders, should have kept their distance, but came under a heavy German barrage aimed at the start line and, to avoid the deluge of shells, the troops pressed forward into the south-western corner of the wood.

The British had been told that the Germans were in full retreat. Unfortunately, as mentioned earlier, although the Germans were retreating from their enclave south of the Marne, they were determined not to give ground easily and their commanders were indeed trying to strengthen their defences in certain critical areas, such as on the shoulders of the Aisne salient. They were only too aware that their positions in the Marne pocket offered a golden opportunity to the French to complete an encirclement of substantial German forces, particularly if they could break through at Soissons and Reims.

In point of fact 51st Division faced elements of four enemy divisions. Actually occupying the front opposite them were three divisions, the 103rd Saxe-Meiningen, the 123rd Royal Saxon and the 22nd Hessian Divisions. The 123rd had been one of the original assault divisions for the great attack on 15 July, and had been substantially reinforced with engineers and artillery for this task. However, by the 20th it had suffered significant casualties and was being relieved in the line by the 50th Prussian Division.

During the course of the First World War the German Army formed some 250 infantry divisions, which, by the beginning of 1918, were rather similar in size and equipment to British divisions. Most divisions contained three infantry regiments, recruited, like the British battalions, on a geographical basis. During the war, more than 700 German infantry regiments, excluding *Jäger* and *Landsturm*, were formed. Each German infantry regiment comprised a mortar company and three infantry battalions. Within each battalion were four infantry companies, numbered 1 to 12 within the regiment (late in 1918 this was reduced to just three companies per battalion), plus a heavy machine-gun company. Usually the battalion's machine-gun company was equipped with twelve MG 08 heavy machine guns, while each infantry company had six light machine guns. Thus by 1918 each German infantry battalion was well adapted for the defensive role, with twelve heavy machine guns and twenty-four light machine guns, usually the MG 08/15. The MG 08/15 was the same gun as the 08, but was mounted on a bipod instead of having a tripod mounted on a heavy metal sleigh. It was lighter but still weighed some eighteen kilograms. The regimental mortar company had three medium and nine light mortars, or *Minenwerfer*, but each of the twelve infantry companies was also equipped with two light mortars, *Granatenwerfer*.

As a minimum, each regiment would be accompanied by at least 100 wagons for its heavy weapons, field kitchens, ambulances, ammunition stores etc., although this still does not include the many additional wagons which would be needed for the regiment's full heavy baggage. Significantly, each infantry battalion had a designated wagon, *Bataillon-Schanzzeugwagen*, which contained entrenching tools and defence stores. During the course of the war, the strength of an infantry battalion was gradually reduced from just over 1,000 to about 650 men, but the addition of light machine guns, which were gradually increased from two to six per company, compensated for the reduction in manpower. As a result each German regiment was roughly the same size as a British brigade and, after some three years of Allied attacks, highly experienced in entrenching its 100 machine guns to mount a formidable defence. It was a very tough nut to crack.

The three German infantry regiments were grouped into a single infantry brigade, which was closely supported by the division's artillery brigade. Within the artillery brigade was a close support artillery regiment with three battalions firing either 77mm field guns or 105mm light howitzers. It also commanded a heavier *Fuss* (foot) artillery battalion with two batteries of 150mm howitzers and one battery of 100mm guns. Often an assault division would have an additional specially-trained 'Marksman' heavy machine-gun company, *Maschinengewehr-Scharfschützen-Abteilung*. Finally there was at least one pioneer (combat engineer) battalion, a mortar company and an anti-aircraft element. The division would have its own field hospital and medical companies, with the regimental bandsmen doubling as stretcher-bearers. In addition there were transport, signals and ammunition supply units. A field recruit depot was also established at each division to improve the training of newly-arrived drafts. At full strength a German division had about 12,500 men. As such, it was usually just slightly larger than a French division.

French divisions had also started the war as square formations, with two brigades and four regiments. Despite huge manpower losses, the French army had gradually increased to a force of over 100 divisions, but had reduced each division to three infantry regiments, totalling about 10,000 men. Even so, by 1918 some divisions had been further reduced to just two infantry regiments, plus two or three battalions of auxiliary troops, such as dismounted cavalry or light infantry – *Batallions de Chasseurs à Pied* (BCP), somewhat similar to German *Jägers*. Each French regiment had about 2,200 men organized in three battalions, each of three infantry companies and one machine-gun company equipped with eight machine guns. It also had a 37mm cannon platoon. The division remained strong in artillery with a field regiment of artillery consisting of three 'groups' each of three batteries of four 75mm guns giving them a total of thirty-six guns. In addition there would be one or two groups of heavy artillery, providing a further twelve to twenty-four 155mm howitzers, plus a battery of trench artillery. This resulted in a far higher ratio of artillery to infantry, and the fierce fire of the French 75mm and 155mm guns often terminated many German assaults. French divisions usually had an air wing, a cavalry detachment and one or two companies of engineers, as well as supply and medical units.

The structure of ordinary German infantry battalions, described above, was designed primarily for defence. It was not the same as that of a German storm (*Stoss*) battalion, which was designed for the offensive and was generally rather larger. The *Sturmtruppen* contained up to 1,400 specially trained soldiers divided into five assault companies, and two machine-gun companies each with twelve Maxim MG 08 machine guns. In addition to its copious supplies of rifles, grenades, sub-machine guns and light machine guns, the storm battalion had three support platoons equipped with four flamethrowers, four to six 37mm cannon and eight mortars.

The German troops in the Ardre valley had not had a lot of time to construct substantial defence positions, probably because, on the 19th, it was still planned that they would continue their advance; a new attack to close around Épernay was scheduled for 22 July. However, they had quickly established interlocking networks of machine-gun nests to block all the routes through the forest. These guns were either ensconced in the woods or in the small stone villages which overlooked all the approaches in the area. Machine guns were either placed in individual nests, or often they were combined for mutual protection and then they occupied quite large wired-in defensive posts. Naturally these large nests were very difficult to approach and attack. Major defensive positions were created in the villages of Marfaux, Espilly and at Paradis Farm, which controlled the exits from the northern end of the Bois de Courton. Individual German snipers, equipped with telescopic sights, added to the problem for the attackers. In addition, the enemy disposed of sizeable quantities of artillery, which had been gathered for the 'Peace Offensive' just five days earlier, and some of which were still available to be used to spoil the Allied attacks. The German divisions on the Montagne de Reims, far from retreating rapidly in this area, were reinforcing their forward positions and preparing to fight a brave and determined defensive battle centred around their network of some 1,000 machine guns, supported by artillery barrages and infantry counter-attacks.

As they attacked on the left of the 51st Division, the whole of 153 Brigade quickly found itself enmeshed in the wood, desperately trying to keep direction, but constantly being split up and diverted by the need to attack the well-concealed machine-gun posts. On the far left, men of the 6th Black Watch linked up with some Senegalese troops and reached the north-western edge of the Bois de Courton. They actually passed on into the Bois des Eclisses. Soldiers of the German 83rd Infantry Regiment, 22nd Division, reported that they were attacked by 'Scots and Blacks in a wood one kilometre north of Paradis'. Eventually the Senegalese realized that Paradis had still not been taken and fell back towards their own lines. This left the 6th Black Watch exposed, holding a very narrow part of the front against the 83rd Regiment, and they too were obliged to fall back.

The 4th Seaforth Highlanders, leading 154 Brigade, carried the hill in front of them and then on the far side of that hill came under heavy machine-gun fire from Marfaux and Espilly. They occupied Bullin Farm but, despite a number of gallant and desperate attempts to get forward, were held off by the fire from numerous enemy machine guns, probably manned by the German 32nd Regiment of 103rd Division. As a result they also lost the cover of the supporting barrage, which had moved ahead of them. Frustrated by the delaying fire of one machine gun, a 19-year-old sergeant, John Meikle, raced forward armed only with a revolver and a stick and put it out of action. Shortly afterwards he seized a rifle and bayonet from a fallen comrade and charged another machine-gun post. He was killed just in front of the position but his charge enabled the two men with him to capture the gun. Sergeant Meikle was awarded the Victoria Cross posthumously for his action, and lies buried in Marfaux cemetery.

Some of the Seaforth companies mistook Marfaux for their true objective, Chaumuzy, and angled towards it. Two companies of 4th Gordon Highlanders came forward to support the Seaforth Highlanders, and two companies filled the gap on the left of the brigade. The officers of one company had all become casualties and Lieutenant Colonel David Bickmore DSO, the 26-year-old commanding officer of 4th Gordons, took command and led a two-company assault against the German soldiers who had fallen back into a wood just behind the Bullin road, which ran north to south some 700 yards east of Espilly. As they charged forward they came under intense machine-gun and rifle grenade fire, which shattered their attack, Lieutenant Colonel Bickmore falling mortally wounded.

The three battalions of 153 Brigade had become hopelessly enmeshed and disorganized in the Bois de Courton and could not get forward against the very heavy machine-gun fire from the Espilly strongpoint. Guns from the 51st Machine Gun Battalion and light trench mortars from 153 Battery were brought forward in the afternoon, but the forest was so dense that the sheer physical labour of moving forward heavy weapons and ammunition meant they could not be used effectively until very late in the day. The 6th Seaforth Highlanders from 152 Brigade were brought forward to take over the front line and maintain touch with the French on the left, so that the survivors of 153 Brigade could re-organize during the night.

A second French attack during the afternoon was mounted against Paradis but failed. At 4.30pm the Germans mounted a counter-attack against the right of 51st Division, where 154 Brigade was holding around the ridge of the hill. It was dispersed with rifle and Lewis-gun fire, but at 6.00pm a more serious attack threatened the flanks of the depleted lead battalions and they were withdrawn to the line of the la Neauville to les Haies road. At 6.30pm an even more serious enemy counter-attack on 154 Brigade was mounted, preceded by an intense artillery barrage. This appears to have been the final phase of two attacks by elements from the 71st and 116th Regiments of the 103rd Division, from different directions. As the enemy companies got to within a few yards of the position held by the 7th Argyll and Sutherland Highlanders, they were caught in enfilade fire. They were finally dispersed by a wild bayonet charge, and the survivors fled down the hill.

The divisional artillery moved forward to provide close support during the morning. By 11.00am 256th Brigade RFA was in action near Pourcy on the right and 255th Brigade in front of Nanteuil. Because of the enemy counter-attacks most of the guns were soon moved back behind Nanteuil. However, forward sections, two guns each, of each brigade were left in position just 1,000 yards from the enemy to provide close support and suppress enemy machine-gun nests. The artillery continued to provide harassing fire all night.

In summing up the first day's attack by 51st (Highland) Division, it was clear that its costly attacks had largely failed as it had faced a far tougher defence by the Germans than expected by the French higher command. On the 20th, as the last of the encircled troops south of the Marne had withdrawn from their bridgehead, the Germans had mounted a desperate defence of their flanks to protect this operation and leave them in command of the critical ground. Even at this stage General Ludendorff still hoped to defeat the Foch counter-attack and mount a new offensive, although his focus had already turned to the planned HAGEN operation in Flanders. Moreover, due to the wish to get forward quickly, the British infantry battalions had only taken their own light weapons – rifles, grenades and Lewis guns with them – and had not burdened themselves with heavier support weapons. As a result, the British soldiers had neither a tactical plan nor the means to subdue the numerous enemy machine guns with much more than their own blind courage.

Nevertheless, the entry of the British into the battle had given additional impetus to the Allied attack and had achieved some success. The two highland brigades had carried the German outpost line and dealt with many machine-gun posts. They had captured more than 368 German prisoners and about thirty machine guns, eight trench mortars and a battery of 75s, previously taken from the French. This included the remarkable capture of two German officers and fifty soldiers from just one wired-in post in the Bois de Courton, probably the headquarters of the 1st Battalion of 178th Regiment of 123rd Division. The 178th had to be relieved by 158th Regiment of 50th Division the following morning. Moreover, the fierce attacks during the day had taught the Scottish infantry many lessons about fighting in the woods and now, with their support weapons and artillery moving forward, they hoped to be better placed to continue the attack the following day.

Attacking across more open ground, the men of the 62nd Division had, if anything, an even tougher day. Their orders were to advance on the right bank of the Ardre valley, and the two lead brigades were to attack at 8.00am behind a heavy French and Italian barrage. On the left, closest to the Ardre stream, 185 Brigade was to attack and take the villages of Marfaux and Cuitron; 187 Brigade, on the right, was to capture the small village of Courmas and the Bois de Petit Champ. On reaching those first objectives, it was planned that 186 Brigade, in reserve, would pass through the leading brigades and take the second objective. Each brigade was reinforced with a company of the 62nd Machine Gun Battalion, each of which was equipped with sixteen heavy Vickers machine guns. The fourth machine-gun company, with the three Royal Engineer field companies and the pioneers of 9th Durham LI, remained in divisional reserve in Courtagnon Wood.

Most of the units of 187 Brigade were already assembled at Ferme d'Ecueil and had only a short distance to move to their jumping-off points for the next morning. However, the other lead brigade, 185 Brigade, faced a nightmare approach march as it struggled to arrive in time for the battle. It had actually set out at 5.00am on the 19th from Plivot and had already spent all day marching along crowded dusty roads in the hot sun to reach its intended bivouac area in the woods around St Imoges. Barely had the tired battalions arrived before they received new orders to march to Courtagnon by midnight to meet French guides, who would lead them to their assembly area around Pourcy, for their morning attack on Cuitron and Marfaux. They had set off immediately on the evening of the 19th and endured a frightful night approach march through congested roads and paths before meeting their guides at Courtagnon Farm, who then led them through the woods. Thus three very tired and exhausted battalions finally got to their jumping-off points by 5.30am, and prepared for an attack commencing at 8.00am.

The reserve brigade, 186 Brigade, had spent the morning of the 19th marching to the woods south of Germaine, which it reached at midday. The men were then able to rest until the brigade set out at midnight to march from Germaine to its assembly point in the wood east of Courtagnon, about 4,000 yards short of the front line, which it reached without incident. At zero hour on the 20th the three battalions formed up and began to advance, following in the wake of the two lead brigades.

The desperately tired 185 Brigade advanced on the left, closest to the Ardre. Its objective that morning was the high ground along the line Chaumuzy–Bligny–Aubilly, a line which was eventually reached some eight days later. On reaching this line the two lead battalions of the West Yorkshire Regiment were supposed to halt and allow the 5th Devons to pass through and capture the final objective, the line Sarcy–le Gros Termie. However, the morning's attack was doomed. Despite liaison visits by divisional staff officers to the French 120th Division providing the creeping barrage, it actually fell some 1,000 yards ahead of the forming-up position. Tragically this left completely untouched the German machine-gun nests skilfully concealed in the woods and fields immediately ahead of the British jumping-off line.

On the far left of 185 Brigade, the 2/5th West Yorkshires attacked with A Company on the far left and D Company on the right; C Company was in support and B in reserve. Its immediate objective was the village of Marfaux and it had to cross mainly open cornfields to reach it. However, the stone cottages of Marfaux, the woods ahead, and the commanding hillsides contained dozens of German machine-gun nests, which had been untouched by the barrage. Hundreds of the courageous soldiers of the 2/5th West Yorkshires were mown down by direct and enfilade fire as they attempted to brave the enemy bullets and get forward. Amazingly, some men did reach a position just short of the village, but the battalion had taken very heavy casualties, and the two lead companies had been almost wiped out. The situation report from A Company at 10.07am said that only twenty men remained. The D Company commander reported at 11.00am, 'Am occupying two shell holes south-east of Chaumuzy, only six men of ours left and eight men and one officer of the Devons; in touch with Hants [2/4th Hampshires] on right, but nobody on left. What am I to do? At present holding on and consolidating.'

On the brigade right, 8th West Yorkshires had advanced with its A Company on the right and B on the left. C Company was in support and D in reserve. Despite the comforting scream of the French shells passing overhead, it was soon obvious that they were landing far too far ahead, and the German machine guns began exacting a heavy toll of the British infantrymen advancing through the golden corn. This was added to by hidden snipers and a heavy German artillery barrage. The commanders of A and B Companies were soon killed, together with many of their men, and C and D Companies were advanced into the line. German machine-gun fire came from Marfaux and Cuitron, from the woods high above the right flank, mainly in the Bois de Petit Champ, as well as from many nests hidden directly ahead in the corn fields. As one officer wrote later, 'It was an invisible foe we were pitted against, and very few of us ever caught sight of a Boche.'

The men struggled to advance against the hidden enemy, but soon so many were killed or wounded that the survivors just took whatever cover they could find. The commander of D Company later wrote:

> I crouched in a small pool of water ... not knowing where my enemies were. I lay 'doggo' in this two feet of water, surrounded by rank undergrowth and rushes, with the hot sun scorching the little of me which was above water. Any slight movement I made was immediately rewarded by a sharp crack from my attentive sniper and a neat little furrow curved along the rim of my shell-hole refuge. They suddenly began to shell this corner of the copse. Heavies and gas shells followed each other in quick succession and I became covered with wet muddy earth and almost choked with poison gas. This nightmare ceased after about twenty minutes.

At last the officer could begin to crawl away collecting wounded as he went, although still harried by invisible snipers.

> I looked at my garrison of wounded and decided to make an attempt to get back to our own lines ... . Still we crawled on and on, helping each other over bad places, before we reached the edge of the copse and out again into the cornfields.

Eventually, at midnight, he got his party of exhausted wounded back to battalion headquarters.

The support battalion of 185 Brigade, 5th Devons, had already suffered some twenty-five casualties from shellfire while waiting to advance. Eventually, seeing that both West Yorkshire battalions were unable to make any more progress, the commanding officer, Lieutenant Colonel Bastow, sent two companies forward to support the 2/5th West Yorkshires in front of Marfaux, and then put out outposts to link all three battalions.

On the right of the division, 187 Brigade attacked at 8.00am with the 2/4th York and Lancaster Regiment, also known as the Hallamshires, on the right, and the 5th KOYLI on the left. The Hallamshires stormed forward towards the small village of Courmas with D Company on the right, A on the left and C Company in support. The Germans attempted to spoil this attack with a defensive barrage, which fell in front of Courmas at 8.10am causing considerable casualties in D Company, but the attack still went forward and Courmas was cleared.

The two companies of Hallamshires then pressed on to the Château de Commétreuil which was surrounded by a park-like wood. However, although the château was a burnt-out wreck, the German 39th Lower Rhine Fusilier Regiment, from 50th Division, had filled its upper floors with riflemen and garrisoned its cellars with machine guns which swept the ground over which they were advancing. The two Hallamshire companies chose to pass around the château and move on to the village of Bouilly, which they cleared of enemy, capturing several machine guns and twenty prisoners, including an officer. Eventually, contact was gained with the French 86th Regiment at Bouilly and the Hallamshires formed a defensive flank along the Courmas–Bouilly road, with a strongpoint at the crossroads between Bouilly and Onrezy.

The left-hand battalion of 187 Brigade, the 5th KOYLI, had been tasked with the clearance of the western edge of the Bois de Petit Champ. Its left-hand company fought its way through part of the wood, but was then held up by heavy machine-gun fire which swept down the drives of the Château de Commétreuil. This intense machine-gun fire also caught the centre company, and both companies were withdrawn and re-organized with the reserve company. They then attacked again but, after attempting to establish a line along the south-eastern edge of the wood, they were forced to withdraw by the sustained machine-gun fire from the château.

On the far right of the 5th KOYLI was B Company. Its two left-hand platoons were held up at the south-east corner of the Château de Commétreuil Wood. However, the two right-hand platoons under Second Lieutenant Moore attacked the wood to the west of Courmas. Moore then led a party of ten men against the wood. All except one were killed or wounded as the Germans withdrew to the north-east corner of the wood, but Moore went after them and, charging the machine gun, killed the gunners, captured the gun and two prisoners. Using the German machine gun he cut off a party retiring along a track and captured two more prisoners and another machine gun, which he then turned on other retreating Germans until it stopped firing. These troops were probably from the 5th or 6th Companies of the 39th Fusiliers (50th Division). Moore then gathered his troops and attempted to move on to take Bouilly. However, his party was too weak to take and hold the village, so he retired and consolidated along the road on the north-eastern side of the château lake.

The support battalion of 187 Brigade, the 2/4th KOYLI, had suffered heavy enemy shelling for an hour and a half before zero hour, which caused some casualties. Obviously the Germans were expecting an attack, and were trying to spoil it by bombarding the likely assembly areas. The battalion went forward about 500 yards behind the Hallamshires, with A Company on the right, C on the left and B in support. It passed through another heavy German artillery barrage with almost no casualties, and then A Company came up against machine-gun fire from the Bois de Reims as it crested the ridge south-east of Courmas. On the Courmas–Onrezy road a German machine gun was captured. As they came up to the Hallamshires, who were being held up by enfilade fire, they captured another machine gun, killing its crew and taking prisoner the German officer in command. On the left, C Company reached a copse and cornfield west of Courmas and attempted to get forward through the cornfield by section rushes, but was held up by machine-gun fire, which wounded most of the officers. B Company then came forward, and a section led by Sergeant Housley engaged a machine-gun nest and eventually captured the nest with its four guns. An officer and two soldiers were also taken prisoner. Eventually the remnants of the 2/4th KOYLI consolidated on the left of the Hallamshires.

By midday, as it became clear that both assault brigades had been halted, divisional headquarters decided it wanted to commit the reserve brigade to reinforce the attack on the right, around Courmas, which seemed to be having some success. However, it gradually became clear that, due to the heavy shelling and machine-gun fire, 186 Brigade, which should have been in reserve, had become dispersed and its battalions had already become involved in some of the fighting alongside the lead battalions.

On the right the 5th Duke of Wellingtons had soon split into two groups with HQ, B and C Companies following 187 Brigade into the area around Courmas, while A and D Companies had advanced along the Courtagnon to Pourcy road until heavy shellfire forced them to take cover in the western edge of the Bois de Poucy. The centre battalion, the 2/4th Hampshires, had come up to 185 Brigade and attempted to support their attack on Marfaux. Small bodies of Hampshires did manage to reach the outskirts of Marfaux, but were forced to retire and dig in some 500 yards east of the village. On the left of the brigade, the 2/4th Duke of Wellingtons had also split into two groups. The two companies on the right became merged with 185 Brigade as they moved through the Bois de Pourcy and attempted to assault Marfaux. On the far left, two companies pressed along the northern bank of the River Ardre, taking out strongpoints and capturing the Moulin d'Ardre farm, where many Germans were killed and fourteen prisoners were captured together with four machine guns. Then the two companies split into smaller groups and approached to within seventy yards of Marfaux, and one platoon even entered the village. However, they were eventually forced to retire to a line some 200 yards east of the village.

By 3.00pm it was evident that the whole attack by a very tired division had completely broken down. Most battalions had suffered very heavy casualties and were badly intermixed. In the evening 185 Brigade was ordered to withdraw behind the line of 186 Brigade, but it was unable to establish contact with all its soldiers, and still had many wounded men lying out under enemy machine guns in front of Marfaux, where they remained until they could be reached the following evening.

The first day of combat had been a very disappointing experience for 62nd Division. The planned rapid advance through apparently peaceful woods and golden cornfields had foundered on a tenacious German defence based on interlocking machine-gun fire supported by field artillery. The attractive woods and cornfields revealed themselves to contain the certain promise of violent injury and death. It should now have been clear to the three senior British generals, Godley, Braithwaite, and Carter-Campbell, as well as their senior staff officers, that there was a price to be paid for being too ready to comply with a French plan which was based on the rapid deployment of troops without any opportunity for reconnaissance, proper artillery support or sufficient intelligence about enemy intentions. There had been no concrete information about German intentions to retire – in fact there was plenty of evidence to the contrary – but General Berthelot was under pressure to show some success in his area. The French and Italian defenders had only just managed to halt the German attacks in the Ardre valley on the 15th to the 17th. Their own counter-attacks on 18 and 19 July had made only limited progress against the hardening German defences and, as a result, not only the British, but also the French troops suffered just as badly in their attacks on the 20th.

There is no criticism of the French plan or tactics reflected in the divisional history of the 62nd. The account does state that over 800 officers and men had been killed or injured by shellfire, machine guns or hidden snipers. It acknowledges that this figure relates to just six of the infantry battalions in close combat that day, most of which had suffered grievously, and some battalions had lost half their effectives. However, in reality, this report of losses was an almost deliberate underestimation. It did not include the losses of 185 Brigade, where its two battalions of West Yorkshires alone had suffered over 700 casualties. The 8th Battalion had fifty officers and men killed and over 250 wounded, gassed and missing. The 2/5th was even worse off having been practically shattered as a battalion. Exact losses could only be estimated at first, because many of its casualties could not be contacted during the night of the 20th, and were left exposed and untended all the following day in front of Marfaux. The battalion's own estimate was that it had lost eleven officers killed and wounded, and over 400 men killed, wounded and missing. Only the third battalion of 185 Brigade, 5th Devons, which had joined from Palestine with a full strength of 978 officers and men, could still field four infantry companies. Even so, the Devons had suffered more than 250 casualties.

Realistically, 62nd Division had suffered at least 1,750 casualties in the first day of contact with the enemy. This represents almost half of its total casualties of 118 officers and 3,865 other ranks which it endured during the whole of its ten days of fighting in the Tardenois campaign. The division had barely advanced a mile and its losses were akin to a major defeat, which meant it was left very short of fighting manpower until reinforcements could arrive. Of course there were many reasons for this dreadful outcome. The men were new to this kind of combat, and the artillery barrage, although fierce, had missed the main forward enemy locations. It was not until the evening of the 20th that the 62nd had its own field artillery in position to support its troops. Finally, the outnumbered British now realized from interrogated prisoners that they faced elements of four German divisions who were fighting desperately on ground they knew, to protect the retreat of their comrades farther south from the potentially lethal Marne salient trap.

Nevertheless, despite these odds, the men of 62nd Division had managed to achieve some success. By their courage and doggedness they had secured some important ground on the division's right, including occupying the village of Courmas and the approaches to Bouilly. On the left they had taken the Moulin d'Ardre farm, bringing them fairly close to Marfaux. They had clarified that the Germans were fighting determinedly in all the stone villages and woods, as well as in the burnt-out Château de Commétreuil. In spite of facing devastating numbers of well-concealed machine guns, they had managed to kill many defenders and captured a dozen machine guns as well as three officers and fifty men. Important lessons were in the process of being learnt, and some soldiers had already learnt how to tackle successfully even the largest machine-gun nests. Moreover, the British artillery had finally arrived after their exhausting approach march and taken up fire positions, and would now be able to provide direct supporting fire for the infantry. The gunners had little time to rest, as ammunition had to be readied for the following day's barrage, while they continued with harassing fire during the night. However, it was not enough to just fire in the general direction of the enemy. To cause meaningful damage they still needed to know exactly where the main enemy positions were located. They still needed to prepare an effective fire-plan and put out their forward observation officers (FOOs) to identify targets.

The ambitious French plan had clearly failed; nevertheless the commanding generals still wanted action. General Foch believed in the power of the attack against all odds. General Pétain, Commander-in-Chief of the French armies, ordered Fifth Army to continue to attack on both sides of the River Ardre towards Fismes: 'no respite must be allowed to the enemy until the objectives have been attained.' General Bertholet, commanding Fifth Army, ordered his troops to advance without stopping on the whole front: 'An opportunity to obtain important results has arisen; it must not be allowed to escape ... . The General counts upon the will and energy of all to give the enemy a blow which may be decisive.' General Godley ordered XXII Corps to continue the offensive 'by a process of successively reducing the enemy's points of resistance until the objectives are gained'. These exhortations from the senior commanders left the two divisional commanders with little choice but to press on with the offensive despite their reduced manpower.

After the attacks of the first day, the Allied commanders and their staffs knew their troops were facing large numbers of dug-in Germans, but not exactly where they were or how to overcome them. The British tactic of using four brigades to attack blindly in virtually line abreast had clearly proved extremely costly. The situation required new tactics and Brigadier General Gwynn, the senior staff officer of the XXII Corps HQ staff, suggested that, rather than attempting to advance through the Ardre valley, which was thoroughly laced by fire from machine guns placed high and low, they should take the commanding ridges first. Gaining control of the high ground should enable the British and French to outflank the stone villages as well as the deadly machine-gun fortress established in the ruins of Château de Commétreuil.

Therefore, despite the appalling losses of the first day, the intention was announced for each of the Allied divisions to maintain pressure by mounting another attack on the 21st. On the far left, the French 9th Division was to attack once again the fearsomely strong defensive position in Paradis. In the centre, 51st (Highland) Division was to continue to fight forward through the Bois de Courton, engaging the defenders in Espilly, and was promised another heavy artillery barrage designed to fall much closer to the British troops. On the right, 62nd Division was to attack the Château de Commétreuil and attempt to outflank Marfaux by taking the high ground in the Bois de Petit Champ, while the 2nd French Colonial Division was to attack in the direction of St Euphraise.

Meanwhile, during that evening, the German 39th Fusilier Regiment of 50th Division had withdrawn its worn-down garrison, the 5th and 6th Companies of 2nd Battalion, which had been defending the Château de Commétreuil and its grounds, and replaced them with a fresh garrison of the 7th and 8th Companies.

Since the two lead brigades of both British divisions had been severely mauled, this did not leave many options for the following day. The new, much more modest, plan of attack was for 152 Highland Brigade to advance the next morning on a one-battalion front, led by the 6th Gordon Highlanders and followed by the 6th Seaforth. The Scots were to advance at 8.00am under cover of a barrage which would also cover the French 9th Division on their left, who would attack as soon as it could to deal with the Paradis strongpoint and thus threaten Espilly from the west. Behind them, 153 Brigade was to form defensive flanks.

Sixty-second Division was also to continue the attack with its 186 Brigade, the follow-up brigade from the day before. However, as even 186 Brigade was no longer fresh, an attack on the high ground in the Bois de Petit Champ was to be mounted by the divisional pioneer battalion, while the Hallamshires from 187 Brigade were once again to attack the Château de Commétreuil. Although a better barrage was planned, there was actually very little evidence of fresh thinking and better planning by the British staff officers, who, unknown to them, faced a strengthened stubborn foe.

Sunday 21 July 1918. The second day of the Battle of Tardenois in the Ardre Valley.
The 6th Seaforth had taken over the front line from the exhausted 153 Brigade units and entered into a firefight with some of the German machine guns. Eventually the whole of 152 Brigade came forward and took over the line, allowing 153 Brigade to move back during the night into a close support position. However, far from falling back during the night, the Germans had continued to maintain pressure on the Scots and mounted a counter-attack by two German battalions, supported by a very heavy artillery barrage, which had pressed the line back more than half a mile south of the Neuville–les Haies road. As a result the supporting Allied artillery barrage fell where planned just south of the Neuville–les Haies road but, as the Germans had taken advantage of their successful counter-attack against the Scots to move many of their outlying machine-gun posts forward, these were again missed by the morning barrage.

As a result, although the 6th Gordons were supported by the very heavy barrage when they commenced their attack at 8.00am, they once again faced a hail of bullets as soon as they showed themselves. Despite their losses, the Gordons pressed forward, taking out individual machine-gun posts until they encountered a carefully prepared German line of resistance about 200 yards short of the north-western boundary of the Bois de Courton. The 6th Gordons were unable to break through this line, which was composed of numerous well-sited machine guns and trench mortars. Indeed, the Gordons found themselves threatened by Germans filtering through gaps in the advance and on the right flank, which caused them to fall back to a new defensive line established only some 200 yards in advance of their start line.

On the right, 154 Brigade had put out strong patrols on its front, but these were harassed and held up by the fire from machine-gun posts.

Eventually, a Stokes LTM was brought forward to fire forty rounds at a number of particularly troublesome machine-gun nests to silence them. Later a patrol came upon one of these strongpoints, where some twelve Germans were found dead.

The results on the left bank of the Ardre were that, after some very hard fighting, eighty-one prisoners had been captured together with machine guns and trench mortars. A clear line now linked all the forward positions of the 51st Division, but no real progress had been made. Although the advanced guns of the divisional artillery were very active in trying to support the infantry, they too were severely hampered by the difficult country. The Germans, far from retreating from this vital area of the Ardre valley, were employing up to six divisions to continue the struggle to retain this important flank. The Germans in Paradis, 167th Regiment of 22nd Division, also resisted all attempts by the French to take it, and thus the forward divisional line curved around the village of Espilly, about 300 yards short of it.

On the right of the Ardre, 62nd Division planned to launch its prime attack at 10.30am, using 187 Brigade. On its left, opposite Marfaux, 185 Brigade had been relieved by 186 Brigade, which left scores of wounded men from the 2/5th West Yorkshires still lying out in front of the village, exposed to snipers and numerous enemy machine guns. Only when night fell could they finally be brought in. On the right, the main objective was a second attack on the Bois de Petit Champ, which included the high ground overlooking Marfaux. The previous day the 5th KOYLI had been badly cut up attempting to attack the wood, and it had been decided to use the only fresh troops remaining in the division, the pioneer battalion, for this task. The pioneers of the 9th Durham LI were to filter through the 5th KOYLI position and attack the wood, supported by an enhanced barrage. The first day's barrage had been found to be relatively ineffective against the thick woods, and the shell fuzes needed to be altered. The creeping barrage, which was to include the British divisional artillery as well as the supporting French and Italian guns, was slowed from 100 yards every six minutes to 100 yards every ten minutes.

During the morning, the Durham pioneers were moved forward into the positions occupied by the 5th KOYLI, ready for their attack to start at 10.30am. Unfortunately, the three lead companies of the Durhams were led to a position 600 yards short of where they should have been. Therefore, although they raced forward at Zero hour, they missed the barrage and confronted an inferno of machine-gun fire when they finally debouched from cover. They later recorded that they faced 'hundreds of machine guns' and accordingly suffered heavy casualties. Although the survivors actually managed to enter the Bois de Petit Champ, they were unable to make any progress and were ordered to consolidate their positions. It was a brave but botched attack by the pioneers, and evidenced lack of staff co-ordination.

To their right the 2/4th York and Lancs attempted once again to attack the Château de Commétreuil and Bouilly Ridge. Sadly they found that the grounds and ruins of the château were still thick with machine guns and, although the Hallamshires captured several machine guns and some prisoners, they were unable to make any forward progress.

The Germans had anticipated another heavy day of attacks. They were therefore considerably relieved by the absence of a major attack, and found it comparatively easy to deal with what they perceived as only patrol activity although they continued to suffer from the undiminished Allied artillery fire. However, on the right, the 2nd French Colonial Division did make some progress, retaking Bouilly from the Germans and capturing other important ground towards St Euphraise.

Monday 22 July 1918. The third day of the Battle of Tardenois in the Ardre Valley.

After two days of bloody combat it was abundantly clear that the Allies faced far greater numbers of enemy units than first anticipated, and that the Germans were in no mood to retreat. The Germans had assembled significant quantities of troops and artillery to support their successful Aisne offensive on 27 May, as well as for their great Marne offensive of 15 July, and were now prepared to use all these resources to hold their ground. In the immediate area fronting XXII Corps, troops from six German divisions were identified during the battle, namely 22nd, 50th, 86th, 103rd, 123rd, and the 240th Divisions.

The history of these six divisions represents a cross-section of the history of many of the German Army's 250 divisions in the First World War. Five out of six of them, the exception being 123rd Saxon Division, were designated Prussian infantry formations, most of which had been in the Champagne area for some time. The 123rd Saxon Division had been formed in early 1915 and fought on the Western Front until it was savaged in the British Somme offensive of June 1916. In July 1916 it was sent to the Eastern Front to recuperate and continued fighting there until November 1917, when it was brought back to the

Western Front and served at Verdun. On 2 June it was brought to the Champagne front and took part in the 'Peace Offensive' of 15-17 July. Only at midday on the 18th was it informed that the offensive had been terminated, and the division should adopt a defensive position in the woods south of Marfaux and around Espilly. The Allied attacks on the 19th and 20th caused it further heavy losses, and the remnants of 123rd Division were relieved by 50th Division on the 21st.

The 22nd Prussian Infantry Division had been a regular division formed in 1866, with units from Thuringia and Hesse. It had fought in the Franco-Prussian War of 1870. In 1914 it had taken part in the invasion of Belgium until early September, when it was moved to East Prussia. It had been triangularized in 1915, when it had been reduced to two Hessian infantry regiments and one regiment from Alsace, and then served continuously on the Eastern Front until October 1917 when the armistice with the Russians allowed it to be brought to the west. It fought at Verdun until it was brought to the Champagne area on 25 May 1918. Used as a follow-up division during the Aisne offensive, it then took part in the 'Peace Offensive'. It was withdrawn from the front on 2 August when its 2nd Kurhessische Regiment No. 82, which had been defending the area east of Paradis against the French 9th Division and 51st (Highland) Division, reported that it had suffered over 1,000 casualties. As mentioned earlier (pages 152-4), a German regiment by this stage of 1918 probably numbered considerably less than 1,800 infantry when it first went into action.

The 103rd Division was also largely recruited from central Germany, having been formed in 1915 from two Thuringian regiments from Saxe-Meiningen and one Hessian regiment. It served on the Serbian and Macedonian fronts until April 1916 when it moved to the Western Front where it fought in the Battle of Verdun and the 1917 Battles of the Chemin des Dames. In March 1918 it moved to the Somme for the surprise MICHAEL offensive against the British. In April it was brought back to the Champagne area and took part in the Chemin des Dames operation in May, when it attacked the British 19th Division on 30 May. It then became part of the assault force for the 'Peace Offensive'. It was now defending the northern area of the Courton Wood around Espilly and Marfaux. On the 20th, its 32nd Regiment was relieved by the 53rd Regiment of 50th Division but was kept as divisional reserve due to the heavy Allied attacks. After the main German retreat on 26 July to the defence line called the *Dora Stellung* 103rd Division was finally withdrawn.

These three divisions, 103rd, 123rd and 22nd, had led the main assault against the Italian II Corps. Their attack in the direction of Épernay was initially successful but then failed to make progress beyond Hill 230.3, just south-east of Pourcy. Hill 230.3 was then lost against French counter-attacks on the 18th, and the divisions pulled back into the Bois de Courton around Paradis. Although in a weakened state, the three German divisions had quickly and professionally switched from an offensive to a defensive posture, as the French and Italians attacked on the 18th and 19th. They then defended stubbornly the strong defence line that they had established in the Bois de Courton.

The 50th Division had just arrived hotfoot in the River Ardre area to buttress the German defence. It had been formed in March 1915, as the German Army reduced to three regiments per division, from a Lorraine regiment and two Westphalian regiments, grouped as 100 Infantry Brigade. It had served mainly on the Champagne and Verdun fronts, where it experienced heavy fighting in 1916 and 1917. In January 1918 it was withdrawn for special training and then took part in MICHAEL on 21 March 1918. In May it returned to the Champagne area and stormed the Chemin des Dames on the 27th as part of Schmettow's corps. It remained in reserve for the 'Peace Offensive' and was earmarked for the HAGEN operation but was then ordered forward, mainly by night marches, to relieve the depleted units of 123rd and 103rd Divisions. On the 19th its 53rd Regiment occupied the Bois de Petit Champ and its 39th Fusilier Regiment (commanded by Ludendorff himself in 1912) occupied the Château de Commétreuil. Its third regiment, the 158th, was held in reserve until the 21st when it took over from the worn-down 178th Regiment of 123rd Division, which had been holding the woods south of Marfaux and Espilly.

The 86th had been originally formed in 1914 as the Temporary Division Wernitz. In 1915 it became the 86th Division and continued fighting on the Eastern Front until February 1918 when it was moved to the Western Front. After re-training it joined the army in Champagne at the beginning of April 1918, and was used as a line division in the area. Together with 232nd Division it had made frequent attacks against the British 19th Division positions around the Bouleuse Ridge on 30 May, and they had both been driven from the Montagne de Bligny by the 4th KSLI counter-attack. It then took part in the offensive on 15 July and was stationed on the left of 103rd and 50th Divisions around Courmas, Bouilly and St Euphraise where it was attacked fiercely by French and British troops, until relieved by the 8th Bavarian Reserve

Infantry Division on the night of 22 July when it withdrew across the Vesle river.

The 240th had not been formed until January 1917, after which it fought in Flanders. It had been re-trained as a *Stoss* division, and was committed on 23 March 1918 to attack Vimy and Arras. In May it was moved to the Argonne front to recuperate, and then transferred to the Champagne area on 13 July just in time for the 'Peace Offensive' two days later. It relieved the exhausted 50th Division during the night of 23 July.

Faced by such determined and experienced German units, equipped with their abundant machine guns and support weapons, the British commanders needed to exercise considerable imagination, supported by a detailed attack and fire-plan to overcome them. After two days of brave, but amateurish frontal attacks, the staff finally began producing plans which made better use of the corps' capabilities and the ground. It was decided that 62nd Division would launch a co-ordinated two-part attack by its reinforced 186 Brigade. The intention was to concentrate initially on capturing the Bois de Petit Champ on the first day (that afternoon), to be followed by assaults on the villages of Marfaux and Cuitron early on the following day.

Twenty-five of the small French light tanks (Renault FT17), which had proved very effective against machine guns, were placed at the disposal of XXII Corps. Some reports stated that they were generally found to be too heavy for the soft going in the wooded areas, but they were certainly to prove of great value to the British and French attacks on the 23rd. Sections of the 6th Light Battalion were attached to 51st Division and tanks of the 4th Light Battalion with placed with 62nd Division. Sections of the 4th Battalion also attacked alongside the 56th and 60th Battalions of the *Chasseurs-a-Pied* from 77th Division as part of their attack against the Château de Commétreuil, where they proved particularly effective against the emplaced German machine guns. Meanwhile, on the left, it was decided that pressure was to be maintained by the 51st (Highland) Division on the Germans in the Bois de Courton, although no large infantry attacks would take place until the late afternoon.

During the morning strong patrols were put out in front of 51st Division but immediately suffered from the enemy machine-gun fire, which appeared, if anything, to have been reinforced. It was intended that the 7th Black Watch should attempt to get forward to a position on the south-west edge of the Bois de Courton from where they would provide covering fire for another attack on Paradis by the French. At 4.00pm the 6th Black Watch, in an effort to assist the 7th Battalion, attempted to move the line forward by a series of individual rushes, but the enemy fire was so intense that all attempts were knocked back. As a result, the 7th Black Watch were unable to assist the French attack, which came at 5.00pm, and inevitably the French were unable to make any real progress against the continuing stubborn German resistance in Paradis. So fierce was the German firing that the French troops suffered very heavy losses immediately and were compelled to dig themselves in after advancing only some 100 metres.

During the night of the 22nd, the Highland Division re-organized itself; 152 Brigade was relieved by 153 Brigade and moved to the 154 Brigade front where it prepared to launch an attack early the next morning. The aim was to make an ambitious right-flanking attack by two brigades, designed to get 152 Brigade forward to the Bois de l'Aulnay and attacking the German defence node of Espilly from the east. At the same time the 7th Argyll and Sutherland Highlanders and 4th Gordons from 154 Brigade were to move forward through the Bois de Courton and clear the enemy positions to the west of Espilly. On the far left of 153 Brigade the firing line was taken over by two companies of the pioneers of 8th Royal Scots, and two companies of the 7th Black Watch.

On 62nd Division's side of the Ardre there was a shortage of formations strong enough to undertake a serious attack, and corps headquarters placed the XXII Corps Cyclist Battalion of New Zealanders, as well as a section of tanks, at the disposal of Brigadier General Burnett for his major 186 Brigade operation on the 23rd. The divisional pioneers, having rested for a day, were also added to the assault force.

Capture of the key spur in the woods overlooking Marfaux and Cuitron was considered an essential preliminary, and very detailed plans were laid by 186 Brigade for a third attack to capture the Bois de Petit Champ. It ordered a methodical flanking attack by the 5th Battalion the Duke of Wellington's Regiment, supported by massive artillery fire. The full battalion attack was to begin at 12.15pm on 22 July, supported by a creeping barrage of the British 18-pounders and French 75s, which would come down just 250 yards in front of the start line and creep forward at a rate of 100 yards every ten minutes until clear of the wood. In addition the heavies were to pound certain selected areas while British machine guns were to sweep the southern slopes of the hill, and French machine guns would cover the northern slopes.

The double-pronged infantry wood-clearing plan was to be deliberate and astute. A and D Companies were to advance along the northern edge of the woods on a platoon front of fifty yards, and C and B Companies were to advance along the southern edge of the woods. While pressing forward, the columns were to drop off a platoon every thirty yards to establish a strongpoint capable of all-round defence. Once these were established, section patrols were to be sent out to search the woods for enemy personnel or machine-gun nests located between themselves and the adjoining posts.

A Company led the northern assault and was the first to meet opposition, which was quickly overcome, and then pressed on until, some 250 yards farther into the woods, it came upon a strongpoint manned by twenty Germans with four machine guns. The strongpoint was only overcome after a desperate struggle, and some prisoners taken. After a further 200 yards another strongpoint was discovered and six more machine guns and thirty-five prisoners captured. A Company was now joined by D Company, since it had been severely reduced by casualties. Another 300 yards was covered yielding isolated single guns with small crews. The two companies then came under very heavy fire from a strongpoint hidden in the centre of the wood. When this post could not be located, the Dukes fell back to consolidate their series of posts extending along the northern edge and into the central part of the wood.

On the southern side, even before it entered the wood, C Company had come under fire from an enemy strongpoint, which it immediately engaged. Eventually, aided by B Company, who encircled it from both flanks, this major defensive post was overcome and a garrison of fifty Germans and eight machine guns was captured, almost certainly the headquarters of the 2nd Battalion of 53rd Regiment. Five more strongpoints were encountered and a total of twenty machine guns and eighty prisoners taken. C Company went on to capture a number of smaller posts until it reached the north-western edge of the woods where it began establishing a number of its own platoon posts. However, these posts were soon counter-attacked by overwhelming numbers of enemy, and their defenders either killed or captured; the Germans reported an officer and twenty-five men captured from one British post. The German infantry counter-attack was very fierce, underlining the importance of the woods to their defence of Marfaux, and included the employment of artillery fire, stick bombs and bayonet charges. Eventually all the C Company posts fell to the German counter-attacks and the remnants, two officers and six men under Captain Cockhill, finally withdrew to the B Company positions. The German counter-attacks continued, and A and B Companies from the 5th Devons were sent up to consolidate the defence of a line of posts extending from the north to the south of the wood. However, the German counter-attacks had regained possession of the critical south-western corner of the Bois de Petit Champ, which overlooked Marfaux.

Despite being driven from the western edge of the wood, the 5th Duke of Wellingtons had achieved a most remarkable success against greatly superior numbers of Germans, at the cost of five officers and 150 men in casualties. They had inflicted a severe reverse on the German defenders, who had also suffered many casualties from the accurate artillery barrage. In an unconfirmed, and probably exaggerated, claim, one of the German machine-gun posts reported holding its fire until the British soldiers were twenty metres from the gun and then shooting down some seventy men. Nevertheless, the 5th Dukes had succeeded in clearing over half of the Bois de Petit Champ, and had captured some forty-one machine guns as well as two officers and 206 men from the 53rd Prussian Regiment. This was a very remarkable demonstration of not only their bravery, but increasingly expert infantry skills.

Coincidentally, the 53rd Regiment was also known as the 5th Royal Prussian Westphalian Regiment, and recruited from the Cologne area. It was one of the three regiments of the 50th Prussian Infantry Division, which had relieved parts of 103rd and 123rd Divisions on the 19th and 20th. Prisoners revealed that the 53rd Prussians had been holding the Bois de Petit Champ with its 1st and 2nd Battalions occupying the wood, and the 3rd in close support. It was this 3rd Battalion which had mounted the first counter-attack in the afternoon. When this failed to stop the Dukes, a new counter-attack was mounted by the 3rd Battalion of the 158th Regiment. By the evening the 53rd Regiment had been so reduced that the 3rd Battalion of the 158th was obliged to remain with it in support.

During the evening, the left flank of the 5th KOYLI was pushed forward to link up with the 5th Dukes in the Bois de Petit Champ, thus strengthening the British front line. The capture of so many prisoners and machine guns was a clear tribute to the successful wood-clearing skills of the 5th Dukes, who had also benefited from the well-planned collaboration with its artillery and resulted in the

5th Dukes receiving many messages of congratulation from the corps and divisional commanders.

Fighting patrols from the 2/4th Duke of Wellingtons also attempted to enter Marfaux, but were repelled with 50 per cent casualties. However, they managed to pick up a prisoner who revealed that Marfaux was garrisoned by a battalion of infantry and many machine guns. To deal with the risk posed by the Germans controlling the south-western spur of the Bois de Petit Champ, 62nd Division decided to mount a fourth attack on the wood in the early morning, using two companies of the 8th West Yorkshires from 185 Brigade.

Tuesday 23 July 1918. The fourth day of the Battle of Tardenois in the Ardre Valley and the main attack on Marfaux.
The ambitious objectives set for the Allied attacks on 23 July fell largely on the British that day. In Mangin's Tenth Army the two newly-arrived British divisions were used to maintain the pressure on the Germans and to relieve the American 1st Division and the French 38th Division, which had played such a key role in the initial success of the Mangin offensive. In Berthelot's Fifth Army, the two British divisions were deployed to make a fresh co-ordinated attack either side of the Ardre, supported by the combined Allied artillery and the French 77th Division, which was to make a supporting attack on their right.

The new attack by the whole of 51st Division was planned for early the next morning with a covering barrage from the French batteries and the divisional artillery, supported by the fire of the 51st Machine Gun Battalion. The barrage, set for 6.10am, was to fall just ahead of the forming-up line, and then to advance 100 yards every five minutes. This time, after the bad experience of the 22nd, the opening barrage was brought much closer to the front line, actually set at zero to 200 yards. Unfortunately this was a bit too close. Shells from some of the French batteries fell on both lead battalions of 152 Brigade, causing casualties and severely disorganizing the planned attack. For example, all the remaining officers of one company of the 6th Gordon Highlanders became casualties. Even farther back, in the 154 Brigade assembly area, shells fell short amongst the 7th Argylls and caused many casualties.

Despite these clear dangers, the 5th and 6th Seaforth Highlanders stayed close to the advancing barrage, known as 'keeping your nose in the barrage', and, having dealt with six machine-gun posts in the Bois de Courton, they followed the barrage into the Bois de l'Aulnay. By 8.30am they had subdued the Germans in that wood and reached its northern end very close to the Ardre. There they had to form a defensive flank to the east, as the Germans still held the opposite bank of the Ardre. Some men of 6th Seaforth actually got forward to a spur south-west of the Bois de l'Aulnay, but most of them, and the 6th Gordons, came under very heavy fire in the sunken road which led up to Espilly. Despite taking heavy casualties they were still unable to get any closer to the stubbornly defended stone hamlet of Espilly.

The inside flanking attack against Espilly from the west by the 4th Gordons and 7th Argylls of 154 Brigade was also unsuccessful. The two battalions had come under heavy German artillery shelling as they attempted to advance through the Bois de Courton, and heavy machine-gun fire from those posts which had survived the barrage. As a result their advance was held up and little progress made. At 11.00am two companies of 7th Argylls attempted a fresh advance through the wood to the left of the 6th Gordons. After strenuous efforts the two companies managed to move the line forward some 400 yards through the dense undergrowth and take out two enemy machine-gun nests. Despite numerous attempts, all other efforts at getting forward to Espilly failed under the scourging fire of the German machine guns. However, vigorous patrol activity by the 7th Argylls during the evening and night located further machine-gun posts and forced the Germans to pull back, allowing the line to advance a further 100 yards.

On the far left the two companies of pioneers from 8th Royal Scots had followed the barrage closely and, despite not being trained infantry, had, by 7.00am, captured two machine-gun posts. During the morning, although unsupported on either flank, they fought their way 500 yards into the Bois de Courton. However, their totally unsupported position was vulnerable and eventually they were forced to withdraw slowly, taking their bag of twenty-eight prisoners with them as they returned to their start line.

The 51st Divisional artillery had come under heavy gas attack during the night of the 22nd but had still fired their support and harassing fire barrages. During the morning, the two batteries, which had established themselves west of Nanteuil to support the infantry advances, again came under mustard gas attack, causing casualties to men and horses.

Despite the frustrations of continuing to make only limited progress against the determined German defence in the thickly-wooded Bois de Courton, the day's attacks had achieved some success. The Bois de l'Aulnay had been occupied as well as eastern and central parts of the Bois de Courton. However, the price of this magnificent attack by the 5th and 6th Seaforth had been very heavy casualties, leaving 152 Brigade with sharply reduced numbers of effectives.

During the night of 23 July, the 51st and 62nd Divisional headquarters moved up to Hautvillers Château, the home of the Comte de Chandon, owner of the famous champagne vineyards.

On the eastern side of the Ardre, 62nd Division had organized a co-ordinated attack by its 186 Brigade, which had been reinforced with three additional but undersized battalions. The line-up included the divisional pioneers (9th DLI), the New Zealand Corps Cyclist Battalion, reinforced by a small company of the 2/4th Hampshires, and the 8th West Yorkshires from 185 Brigade. The objectives set for the day's attack were to clear the villages of Cuitron and Marfaux, and then gain the high ground about 500 yards beyond the road which connected them. To support this operation, the remainder of the enemy machine guns in the salient of the Bois de Petit Champ, which overlooked Marfaux, were to be cleared by the 8th West Yorkshires, while the corps cyclist battalion was ordered to take Marfaux itself. On their right the 9th Durham Light Infantry were to take Cuitron, and supporting them were the five small tanks of the French 4th Battalion, commanded by Lieutenant de Ravel.

In a clear example of co-ordinated operations organized by rapidly learning officers, the successful artillery barrage was provided by French and Italian artillery as well as the 62nd Divisional artillery. Target spotting and artillery support was provided by No. 82 Squadron of the Royal Air Force. The barrage was said to be particularly accurate, intense and effective. However, it was unable to prevent the Germans putting down their own counter-barrage on what they anticipated to be an assembly area, which actually caused some seventy casualties, mostly amongst one company of the 9th Durhams.

It should not be forgotten that, by this stage of the battle, virtually all twenty battalions of the two British divisions were severely worn down. The 8th West Yorkshires had already suffered very heavy casualties on the 20th when, in the first hour of the attack on Marfaux, it had lost seven officers and forty-three men killed and more than 220 officers and men wounded and missing. For the wood attack on the 23rd, the battalion had been re-organized into two small companies; No. 1 Company was drawn from A and B Companies, and No. 2 Company from C and D Companies. The battalion had moved up during the night to its jumping off points, although there had been no time for reconnaissance. There was no preliminary bombardment, and at 6.00am it advanced behind a creeping barrage provided by some of the guns of the 62nd Divisional artillery, before they switched to support the attack on Marfaux.

No. 2 Company, advancing on the left side around the south-western edge of the wood, immediately came under heavy machine-gun fire. Within half an hour, all its officers were out of action, and command passed to Sergeant J. Horne. He then led his men in some stiff fighting through the wood and eventually established a firing post which overlooked Marfaux. No. 1 Company advanced in small sections on the north-western side, fighting its way through the wood until it was cleared. For casualties of eight killed and thirty-five wounded, the small battalion captured eighteen prisoners and nine machine guns. Patrols the following day reported the Bois de Petit Champ clear of enemy soldiers, but a great many dead Germans left in the woods provided evidence of their stubborn defence. Most importantly, by successfully clearing the woods, the 8th West Yorkshires had ensured that the troops who assaulted Marfaux and Cuitron were not enfiladed with fire from German machine guns.

Led by Major Evans, the small New Zealander Cyclist Battalion, which was normally used for reconnaissance and route tasks, had been chosen to add its weight and reputation for dash to the attack on Marfaux. In preparation for the attack, the New Zealanders had parked their bicycles and marched for three hours to arrive at the assembly trenches by 2.00am on the 23rd. For the actual assault on Marfaux the several hundred men of the Cyclist Battalion were reinforced with an under-strength company of 2/4th Hampshires. Even so, they numbered a total of just 340 men as they set off behind the creeping barrage at 6.00am. Once they reached the top of the slope in front of Marfaux, the approach was almost completely devoid of cover for 300 yards and was continually swept by enemy machine-gun fire. Although the artillery barrage helped to subdue the machine guns, they still caused many casualties, and the attack might have failed but for the five tiny Renault FT17 tanks which provided vital support by suppressing machine-gun nests.

The light Renault two-man tank, although primitive, had proved itself to be an extremely useful weapon for the Allies, and over 3,000 were produced during 1918. It was the first tank with a rotating turret and was usually equipped with a 7.92mm Hotchkiss machine gun. Weighing only 6.5 tons, it could travel at about 4mph (7km/h). The tanks from AS312, commanded by Lieutenant de Ravel, had assembled at the crossroads just outside Pourcy, very close to where the National Park Information Centre is now located, and then advanced between the Durhams and New Zealanders. The infantry assault was mounted in two waves. The first wave swept into the village at 6.50am and quickly mopped up the opposition. They took prisoner a German doctor and a captain, and released two wounded British prisoners who had been in Marfaux since the first attack on Saturday.

The second wave followed swiftly and finished clearing the village. By 8.00am it had consolidated some 300 yards beyond the village. The first wave then dug in as support some 100 yards in rear of the forward line. Amongst the hardware captured were nine enemy machine guns, several French and British Lewis guns, and a battery of 75s. Although two of the tanks had been knocked out, they had played a critical role in suppressing enemy machine guns. Nevertheless, the infantry assault had been made under heavy fire and the New Zealanders had suffered almost 50 per cent casualties in their brief battle.

On the right the 9th Durham Light Infantry had, as mentioned, already suffered some 100 casualties from shell and machine-gun fire, while waiting to commence its attack at 6.00am. Its objective, Cuitron, was also stuffed with deadly German machine guns, and without the help of the suppressing fire of the French tanks the Germans might not have been overcome. Brigadier General Burnett sent a personal message to Lieutenant Ravel at 8.00am congratulating him and his tanks for their contribution to the success of the action. They had helped to ensure the assault by the pioneers was also completely successful. Total Durham casualties were 116, in addition to the earlier losses, of which fifteen were men killed. Eighty-nine prisoners were taken altogether by the Durhams and New Zealanders.

The New Zealand losses amounted to two officers and nineteen men killed and three officers and some seventy men wounded. This may seem a relatively small number but it was a major loss for a unit which had arrived in France with just 217 officers and men, although for part of their time in France some 200 Australians served with the battalion. The brave and bloody assault on Marfaux caused half the officer casualties and almost one third of the other rank casualties that the battalion suffered during its entire service in France from 21 July 1916 to the Armistice. Absolutely no recriminations were expressed as the battalion's history summed up the campaign in Champagne, and remarked sadly that 'The whole trip was an experience of value to us all, and if not for the fact of leaving so many of our dear comrades behind us, it would remain as a pleasant memory.' In the well-kept British cemetery located just south of Marfaux, next to the even larger German cemetery, a special plaque was erected to commemorate the memory of ten of the New Zealand soldiers who fell gallantly capturing Marfaux, so far from their island home, and whose bodies could not be identified.

The New Zealanders remained occupying their trenches for a further three days, continuing to see off numerous counter-attacks and enemy patrols which attempted to enter their positions. Finally, on Friday the 26th, they were withdrawn into the reserve line. The following day they recovered their bicycles and then, on the 27th, took part in the reconnaissance of the area forward to the Montagne de Bligny. They continued to play an active role until British troops were relieved by French units on Wednesday 31 July. Finally, on 1 August 1918, they took a well-deserved place in the Farewell Review march in front of General Bertholet.

Presentation of the *Fanion* Postscript.
The municipality of Épernay later decided to express its gratitude by presenting *Fanions* or banners to some of the units who had turned the enemy back when they came so close to threatening to occupy Épernay in July 1918. One *Fanion* was earmarked for XXII Corps, and General Godley decided that this should be awarded to the New Zealand Cyclists. Accordingly, Lieutenant Colonel Evans DSO and some fourteen members of the unit returned to France from New Zealand to be presented with the embroidered *Fanion* in a great military and civilian ceremony on Sunday 27 July 1919. A photograph of the *Fanion* party is shown in the Plates Section.

On the far right, the French 77th Division was also successful in its attack which commenced at 11.00am. The division succeeded in taking the Bois de Rouvroy and half of the Bois d'Hyermont, as well as finally subduing the machine guns in the Château de Commétreuil with flame-throwers and tanks. The German 39th Fusilier Regiment reported that there were no survivors from its 7th and 8th Companies, which had been occupying the château and its park; when withdrawn that evening its three battalions listed just 360 soldiers available for action. It was relieved by the 470th and 471st Regiments of 240th Infantry Division.

The French success had ensured that the Bois de Petit Champ was now completely sealed off, but it was felt that there were still some

Germans concealed in the wood. Therefore a fifth attack, against any German remnants, was mounted in the late afternoon by some platoons of 187 Brigade and the French. Working together, the Anglo-French operation cleared the pocket and established contact with the 8th West Yorkshires in the south-west corner of the wood. Finally, during the night of the 23rd, the 8th West Yorkshires succeeded in occupying the strongpoint on the spur where they captured two mortars and a searchlight mounted on a cart. The German 53rd Regiment reported that it had been surrounded in the wood by the success of the Allied attacks against Marfaux and Bouilly. It was only the evening counter-attacks against Marfaux by the newly arrived 470th and 471st Regiments of 240th Infantry Division which had allowed the survivors of the 53rd Regiment to escape in the darkness.

Usually German accounts are sparing in providing details of their exact strength and losses suffered following an action. However, on the following day, when the survivors of the 53rd Westphalian Regiment assembled in Chambrecy, it reported it had been reduced to the strength of a half-battalion, say about 350 men. This was a similar number of effectives to that reported by the 39th Regiment of 50th Division, which had been defending the Château de Commétreuil. The division's third regiment, the 158th, from Lorraine, had originally been in reserve but had also suffered severe losses as it was used to plug gaps in the German defence line. Thus the defence of the Marfaux area had reduced the whole 50th Division to barely more than a battalion's worth of infantry.

Ludendorff had been desperately keen to gather as strong a reserve force as possible to ensure that the HAGEN offensive against the British would be a success. Therefore he had only very reluctantly, on 18 July, allowed the 50th, rated a first-class assault division by Allied Intelligence, to be released to support defensive operations in the Aisne salient. Now, after enduring four days of attacks by the British and French, the 50th Division had been so worn down that it had to be relieved by 240th Division to avoid total destruction. After all these years, one cannot help but be impressed by the toughness of the soldiers, on both sides, and appreciate their ability to continue marching and fighting, while suffering such incredibly heavy levels of attrition. However, the fate of 50th Prussian Infantry Division provides a clear illustration of the change in fortune of the German forces. It, like others, had a desperate need for time and a degree of freedom from operations to recuperate and rebuild its units. This respite was precisely what Foch was determined not to give the Germans. Ludendorff, like a bad gambler, was being forced to commit good divisions after bad, as the Allies continued to press them back.

Although the British battalions were now significantly understrength, the combined attack by the two British divisions on the 23rd had finally been successful. The concentration of forces on clear objectives, supported by tanks and artillery, had proved unstoppable. The divisional field artillery had provided tremendous support for the infantry attacks. Some British batteries reported that they had fired 600 rounds per gun, and the German prisoners confirmed that their losses from artillery fire had been enormous. Nearly 200 prisoners had been captured in Marfaux, Cuitron, the Bois du Petit Champ and the Bois d'Aulnay. Significantly the German defence line had been broken through on the right, and the two divisions had achieved an advance of almost a mile. The British were only concerned with their own severe losses but, in fact, the four enemy divisions they faced, the 123rd, 103rd, 22nd and 50th, had become so worn down that they all needed to be relieved. Critically, having lost the key village line at Marfaux and Cuitron, the whole German defence line needed to prepare to pull back to their next reserve line, the *Dora Stellung*, while continuing to pull in fresh reserves from the north.

Wednesday 24 July 1918. The fifth day of the Battle of Tardenois in the Ardre Valley.
Although it had been intended to mount another attack on the Bois de Courton on the 24th, it was decided to postpone this until after Espilly had been captured. Accordingly the day was used by the 7th Argylls to continue strong patrol activity to gain ground against the very determined enemy troops continuing to defend to the southeast of Espilly. On the right, 152 Brigade, which continued to hold the Bois de l'Aulnay, spent the day re-organizing its battalions. The 5th Seaforth were so reduced in manpower they had to be reorganized as two companies and the 6th Seaforth as just one company. Reinforcements arrived during the night, which allowed each of the battalions to send back some 100 of their most exhausted men to rest.

Occupying the ground won by the patrolling of its 7th Argyll and Sutherland Highlanders, 154 Brigade moved up to its left. During the night of the 24th, the divisional front was reduced as 153 Brigade was relieved by the 35th Regiment of the French 14th Division and moved into reserve. The brigade had lost 30 per cent of its men as casualties up to its relief, and was to suffer a further 500 casualties over the next four days.

The divisional front for 62nd Division was also shortened on the 24th, and the right divisional and corps boundary became the southern edge of the Bois de Petit Champ and the western edge of the woods: Bois de Rouvroy, Bois d'Hyermont, and Bois de Dix Hommes. The division was required to station a battalion on the spur on the south-western corner of the Bois de Petit Champ to ensure it was not retaken by the Germans. As 62nd Division re-organized, the opportunity was taken to pull out 187 Brigade and place it entirely in divisional reserve; 186 Brigade then took over holding the front, with 185 Brigade in support. After five days in combat, the division had suffered casualties of ninety-eight officers and 3,053 men. Nevertheless, it could pride itself on having made significant advances against very stiff opposition, causing many enemy casualties, while seven German officers and 428 men had been captured.

Just after midday the 8th West Yorkshires were relieved in the Bois de Petit Champ and marched back to their bivouacs in Ecueil Farm. They, like most of the other British battalions, were tired and far below normal strength but, on the following day, were moved forward into the Bois de Cuitron as a support battalion. On the evening of the 26th the remnants of the two companies moved back to Ecueil Farm for a well-deserved rest. Late that night, a very welcome, but wet and tired reinforcement draft of ten officers and 200 men joined the battalion, which could once again re-organize on a four-company basis.

Despite having lost their key positions in the villages, the Germans kept up their pressure on the victors by heavy shelling of Marfaux, Cuitron and Pourcy, and vigorous patrolling, but were unable to prevent 62nd Division from consolidating its gains. A constant feature of combat, for both sides, was that nights were often busier than days; this applied also in the Ardre valley. The cover of night was used to bring up supplies of hot food and ammunition to the fighting units. Units also used the night hours to move up to relieve other units, who could then move back under cover of darkness. Night working parties evacuated the wounded and repaired the defences while fighting or listening patrols hunted for prisoners and reconnoitred enemy positions. Night did not provide total cover from observation and attack. The primitive aircraft of the period were able to glide quite slowly and silently, while listening for the sounds of movement or incautious lights below them, and when identified they were not slow to bomb them. In addition, the artillery of both sides kept up a harassing fire on suspected enemy positions or movements.

During the night of the 24th heavy German bombing raids were made on Épernay and Châlons, perhaps as a precursor to the infantry attack ordered by Ludendorff for the 25th, and raging fires lit up the night as buildings and a nearby French ammunition dump caught fire. The bombing caused casualties amongst the field artillery brigades, where several men were injured and nine horses killed. The 62nd Divisional Ammunition Column (DAC) was also hit by night bombing, which struck some of their prized draught horses, twenty-six horses being killed and twenty injured. Lieutenant W. H. House, United States Army, who was attached to the DAC as Medical Officer, was awarded the MC for his gallantry in saving and treating some of the injured men.

Thursday and Friday, 25 and 26 July 1918. The sixth and seventh days of the Battle of Tardenois in the Ardre Valley.
During the next two days no major attack was mounted, although strong pressure was maintained against the German positions by fighting patrols actively combing through the woods. The 5th Seaforth established eight posts some sixty yards clear of the Bois de l'Aulnay and reached the Moulin de Voipreux; 4th Seaforth pushed their line forward some 100 yards into the Bois de Courton. The 7th Argylls also kept up the pressure, trying to force a way forward through the forest although the enemy continued to deny them any progress.

At the same time the German artillery kept up an intensive bombardment of tactical features which had been captured, and of possible forming-up points for new infantry assaults. Indeed the Germans reported that Borne's corps, VI Reserve Corps, had mounted an offensive on the 25th, involving five divisions, to retake the ground lost at Marfaux. This assault was mounted in response to a desperate order from Ludendorff, who needed to show some success and actually hoped this last throw might lead to them gaining sufficient jumping-off points to consider taking Reims. Actually, the defenders of Marfaux were able to defeat all the attacks against them, without reporting any evidence of particularly strong assaults.

The failure of the attack on the 25th left Ludendorff with little option but to withdraw his troops. He was encouraged to do so by his defence expert General von Lossberg, although Ludendorff remained very reluctant to admit defeat and order a withdrawal. Lossberg, who had spent several days with Seventh Army and witnessed their desperate situation, advised that it was better to conduct a clean break and withdraw to prepared defences, rather than throw in fresh reserves to be destroyed by the Allies. Finally Hindenburg asserted himself and ordered Ludendorff to withdraw the Seventh Army.

A fresh British attack was planned for the 26th, but it was postponed to give the hard-pressed soldiers twenty-four hours' rest. Unfortunately, deluges of rain, which fell incessantly during the night of the 26th, largely nullified this benefit. Perversely, the Germans reported that this same deluge of rain favoured their withdrawal. Apparently the British did not have sufficient patrols out to notice the German withdrawal under cover of that wet night.

Finally, the Allied preparations for a major attack to be mounted early on the morning of the 27th were complete. Having learnt from the lessons of the first few days, it had been decided that the high ridge in the Bois de Courton was the key commanding feature and that no more progress could be made until it was occupied. Therefore it was planned that 62nd Division would maintain its front to the east of the Ardre, but be prepared to advance in line with the 51st as its attack progressed, while its 187 Brigade would move to come under orders of 51st Division, to add weight to its attack.

The line-up for the 51st Division's attack was: 153 Brigade on the left, 187 Brigade, from 62nd Division, in the centre and 152 Brigade on the right beside the Ardre, with 154 Brigade in reserve. The attack would commence with a heavy echeloned barrage by some thirty French and British field and heavy batteries. This would allow the French 14th Division, with la Neuville and Paradis as objectives, and 153 Brigade, clearing the Bois de Courton, to attack first at 6.10am; 187 Brigade would attack at 6.56am and 152 Brigade at 7.30am. Dumps at battery positions were made up to 600 rounds per 18-pounder, and 500 rounds per howitzer. In addition the 51st Machine Gun Battalion was to task twenty-four of its guns to fire an intensive 120,000-round barrage against the edge of the Bois de Courton, west of Espilly. Once again some of the small French tanks were to have taken part but, after the heavy rain of the 26th, the ground was found to be just too wet for their use.

Saturday 27 July 1918. The eighth day of the Battle of Tardenois in the Ardre Valley with the major assault towards Chaumuzy and Bligny.

Promptly at 6.00 next morning a powerful artillery barrage from almost 150 guns of three divisions commenced and was met ten minutes later by desultory enemy artillery shelling of the banks of the Ardre river and the Bois d'Aulnay. However, apart from some long-range machine-gun fire, no real infantry opposition was met. In fact the intricately-planned artillery barrage turned out to be completely superfluous. During the night, the Germans had carried out a skilful withdrawal to a new defence line based on holding the high ground north of Bligny village. By an enormous coincidence of history, the Germans were once again occupying the area where they had been halted by the British IX Corps in June. Bizarrely, they were again facing British infantry in the French sector, but the tide of events had changed, and those British troops were now advancing as part of a determined offensive.

At 7.45am, on 51st Division's front, 187 Brigade reported that Espilly had been captured and passed through with hardly any opposition. By 10.00am the attacking brigades reached Chaumuzy, just in time to see the last enemy transport hurriedly leaving. The seemingly impregnable defence nodes at Paradis and Espilly, which had cost so many French and Scottish casualties, were now liberated. The British and French were somewhat surprised and suspicious of the German withdrawal, thinking it might be a trap, and needed time to confirm this, as well as re-plan their artillery support. The British could have benefited from a system for the rapid reporting of battlefield situations to the headquarters, such as some American units had achieved by establishing a divisional observation group, which reported directly to the divisional staff and which, for example, worked so well for the American 26th Division at St Mihiel. However, the British were used to the conditions of static trench warfare and tended to rely exclusively on the slower formal reporting lines through their command chain, using mainly runners and field telephones. The British did have cavalry reconnaissance capabilities, so these were ordered forward to determine the extent of the German withdrawal.

In fact, unknown to the Allies, on the orders of OHL, the entire German front had withdrawn from its last pocket on the Marne and from swathes of the Tardenois to the line of the River Ourcq. Actually, during the night of the 26th, the Germans had skilfully withdrawn in most places some five to eight miles. In the Ardre valley the Germans

The 51st and 62nd Divisions fight their way up the Ardre Valley 187

had not fallen back so far, but were holding a new defensive position which ran from just north of Chaumuzy through the Montagne de Bligny and Bligny village, and on to Vrigny, just outside Reims.

As soon as it became apparent that the enemy had pulled back, mounted patrols and the cyclists were sent forward to locate the enemy and check for possible traps. Suddenly there was a large unfamiliar area of undamaged rolling fields, woods and hills to check, which proved an ideal task for cavalry. As mentioned, each corps of the British army included a small mounted element among its corps troops. In the case of XXII Corps it consisted of a combined Australian and New Zealand cavalry unit and the XXII Corps New Zealand Cyclists Battalion, which had already played a significant role in the capture of Marfaux. This was a relic of the fact that both these units had belonged to the former II Anzac Corps under the command of Lieutenant General Godley, who had retained them when most of his corps was merged with I Anzac Corps. The XXII Corps Mounted Regiment was a composite unit containing the regimental headquarters and B and D Squadrons of the Australian 4th Light Horse Regiment, and a squadron of the New Zealand Otago Mounted Rifles.

At last an opportunity had arisen for the cavalry to prove its value in carrying out a rapid reconnaissance of the large area, partially vacated by the enemy. A composite reconnaissance force was quickly established comprising the XXII Corps Mounted Regiment, the New Zealand Cyclist Battalion and a French tank battalion. B Squadron of the Light Horse operated on the left of the Ardre in front of 153 Brigade and D Squadron operated on the right in front of 186 Brigade, while the Otago Mounted Rifles were retained in reserve.

Initially the cavalry split into small patrol groups of four men, who spread out rapidly to cover as much territory as possible and uncover the enemy positions. These patrols quickly proved effective in scouting the positions of the enemy covering force, which lay in ambush along the front, by either engaging them or reporting their positions to the artillery. One group of defenders was found to be some 100 strong, and was engaged using the cavalry's Hotchkiss gun sections. Patrols from D Squadron came under fire from machine guns in the Bois des Dix Hommes and the Bois de Hyermont. Another patrol entered Bligny village and found it occupied by a strong enemy force.

Patrols from B Squadron found sizeable German forces north of the Bois des Eclisses and Nardi Farm and, using their own Hotchkiss machine guns, soon cleared them. Then, supported by the advance infantry of 153 Brigade, who had cleared the Bois des Eclisses, they linked up with the French 14th Division. Some patrols crossed the Ardre and attempted to secure the left flank of the Montagne de Bligny. Although they established a position and captured a 77mm gun, they were unable to resist strong German counter-attacks and were forced to retire. The Germans were clearly determined to maintain a very strong defensive position on their new line through Bligny and its dominating feature, the Montagne de Bligny.

Towards evening the reserve squadron, the Otago Mounted Rifles, came forward to strengthen the Light Horse Squadrons, which were coming under heavy pressure from the Germans counter-attacking between the Montagne de Bligny and Bligny itself. During the night the Mounted Rifles relieved B Squadron and, early the next morning, carried out a mounted reconnaissance of the villages of Aubilly and Sarcy, which were found to be still strongly held by the Germans.

By dealing so quickly with the rearguards and German covering force, the cavalry allowed the two British divisions to advance relatively quickly and securely, which caught the Germans somewhat off-balance. Most of the covering force troops were from the German 123rd Division, which was being relieved by the newly-arrived 240th Division, which had marched hastily from the Argonne front. The Australian and New Zealand troopers continued to support the advance boldly, uncovering enemy strongpoints, although not without cost. Three of the ANZAC cavalrymen were killed and twelve wounded in their rapid reconnaissance.

Chaumuzy was occupied at 2.00pm as the enemy were reported falling back behind the line of the road from Bligny to Chambrecy and the Bois des Eclisses was reported clear of enemy. Eventually, 51st Division occupied the old French trench line with a line through Chambrecy as its left boundary and the road through Chaumuzy to Sarcy, now the D386, as its right boundary with 62nd Division. While the Scottish troops moved into their new positions, effectively facing west in the old French trench line, 187 Brigade was returned to 62nd Division.

Despite the long advance, which had begun early that morning, the men of both divisions were kept busy taking up new positions during the night, ready for the following day's operations. The 62nd Division moved forward to positions north of Chaumuzy preparing for a further attack the next morning by two of its brigades on the small stone village of Bligny and the vital Montagne de Bligny, which commanded the high ground to the west of Bligny.

Sixty-second Divisional Headquarters moved forward to Nanteuil, from where it could see practically the whole battlefield. On the right was positioned 186 Brigade, with Bligny as its objective; 185 Brigade occupied the left, with the old French and British trenches on the summit of Montagne de Bligny as its objective; 187 Brigade moved back into divisional reserve. At the same time the forward brigades of 51st Division, 152 on the right and 153 on the left, closed up and prepared to move up through the woods of the Bois des Eclisses, in line with the Yorkshiremen. By complete coincidence, 62nd Division had therefore placed its forward units close behind the same positions as 19th Division had occupied at the beginning of June, just seven weeks earlier. At that time, the decimated battalions of 19th Division had stubbornly resisted all attempts by the Germans to re-occupy the Montagne de Bligny.

Sunday 28 July 1918. The ninth day of the Battle of Tardenois in the Ardre Valley with attacks on Chambrecy, Bligny and the Montagne de Bligny.
After the exhilaration of the advance on the 27th, conditions during the night were extremely unpleasant for these tough soldiers. Most had very little cover from the weather and, after an exhausting day, were forced to spend the night hours moving to new positions, as they took over the front line from the cavalry covering force. They also suffered from the heavy rain which fell all night and soaked them. This made the fields and roads extremely heavy going, and then formed a cold mist in the morning.

In the 51st Division area patrols reported that the Bois des Eclisses was clear at midnight. In pouring rain, 153 Brigade then moved forward to occupy the old French trenches. Next morning, when it was reported that the French had occupied Chambrecy, 152 Brigade was ordered to occupy the line from Chambrecy to the Michel Renaut Farm. However, it soon found that the Germans were still occupying Chambrecy, and the brigade could not get forward. Then 153 Brigade was ordered to support a French attack on Ville-en-Tardenois by advancing to the high ground north of Chambrecy.

To support the attack B Battery of 255th Brigade RFA dashed smartly through enemy fire from 5.9mm howitzers, which fell on the village of Chaumuzy, to an area north of the village. The French attack was launched at 3.00pm but failed under heavy enemy fire. Nevertheless, 7th Gordon Highlanders and 6th Black Watch attacked across the valley towards Chambrecy. As soon as they left the trenches in the Bois des Eclisses, they too were subjected to heavy machine-gun and shell fire. Despite heavy losses, the two battalions continued their advance and struggled to enter the Michel Renaut Farm. Eventually they were forced to withdraw back to the trench line, but the 6th Black Watch established a line from the Bois des Eclisses to a point 200 yards south of Chambrecy. During that Sunday night, 154 Brigade took over the front and the 4th Gordon Highlanders relieved 6th Black Watch in their line, and 4th Seaforth Highlanders relieved the 7th Gordons on the right, resting their right flank just south of the Montagne de Bligny.

At 4.00am, although desperately tired, the troops of 62nd Division began moving forward for an attack with a zero hour set for 4.30am. On the right 186 Brigade advanced with the 2/4th Duke of Wellingtons and the 2/4th Hampshires leading. The Hampshires were tasked with taking the village of Bligny, and the Duke of Wellingtons were to occupy the old French trench line north-east of Bligny. Both battalions immediately ran into an enemy artillery barrage and suffered heavy machine-gun fire from the high woods of the Bois de Dix Hommes on their right. There was little they could do about this, as the clearing of the Bois de Dix Hommes itself was the objective for the French 77th Division, which was advancing on their right.

Initially the Hampshires took cover in a sunken road. Then one party of twenty men, under Lieutenant Holbrooke, divested themselves of all equipment except for rifles and bandoliers of ammunition, and crept slowly forward using every bit of cover they could find until they reached the north-eastern part of the village, where they could establish a strongpoint. Next, four patrols left the sunken road and crept forward until they could establish four covering posts in the village itself. Only then could the rest of the battalion move forward and take possession of Bligny. The 2/4th Duke of Wellingtons also pushed forward small parties, moving right around the Bois de Dix Hommes and Bligny village until they reached the old French line, and could consolidate there. The British infantry had quickly adapted their progress to make tactical use of the ground cover, a vastly different tactic from that employed eight days earlier, when they had advanced steadily in line and suffered such horrendous casualties.

The attack by 185 Brigade also began at 4.30am. Its two lead battalions had moved up to the assembly positions just clear of Chaumuzy village.

The 5th Devons were on the right, with their right flank resting on the Ardre stream; 8th West Yorkshires were on the left, assembled on the immediate left of the Chaumuzy-Sarcy road, the D386 today. The brigade supporting battalion, 2/5th West Yorkshires, remained at Nardi Farm, just north of Chaumuzy. The 8th West Yorkshires were to take the old French trenches on the summit of the Montagne de Bligny, and the 5th Devons were to occupy the trenches which stretched from there towards Bligny.

The two lead battalions advanced together in the dark and wet mist without the benefit of a barrage. This absence of a supporting barrage may have been due to a lack of liaison with the supporting 312th Brigade RFA as it had also been ordered to move forward at dawn from its position west of Pourcy to a new position west of Marfaux, and therefore it could not support the infantry until later in the morning. However, the 62nd Machine Gun Battalion did provide supporting fire for the attack. The 5th Devons came under machine-gun fire from Bligny as they advanced, but they continued advancing doggedly and by 7.00am had occupied their objective. However, as they had lost touch with 186 Brigade on their right, which was still fully occupied in subduing the enemy in Bligny, 2/5th West Yorkshires sent forward A Company at 10.30am to form a defensive flank on their right. The 5th Devons had advanced with only about 350 men. During the assault, and for the next two days that they remained on the objective, they suffered severe shelling and gas attacks which caused them a further seventy casualties.

The 8th West Yorkshires, as mentioned earlier, had suffered severely in the original attack on Marfaux on the 20th, and during the subsequent clearing of the Bois de Petit Champ on the 23rd. As a result, the battalion had very few officers left and had been reduced to just two small composite companies. Fortuitously, on the 27th, it had received a fresh draft of ten officers and 200 men, which had allowed it to reform into four companies, each of three small platoons. However, most of these reinforcements were green troops straight from the depot in England, many of them just boys. As such, the battalion lacked experienced officers, NCOs and men. There were only sufficient trained Lewis gunners to have two per gun team, and platoon sergeants were mostly drawn from among the young lance corporals. Given the terrible weather conditions, the exhaustion of the men, and their level of inexperience, this makeshift battalion was to about to execute a remarkable military feat.

Initially the battalion moved forward by companies in artillery formation, well spread out small groups, designed to avoid suffering too many casualties from shellfire. Dawn was just breaking as they approached the base of the Montagne, but it was still misty. Suddenly rifle and machine-gun fire broke out from the hill's defenders, who were concealed in emplacements on the hillside. Initially this checked the advance, but then the West Yorkshires changed from a steady advance to quick rushes by sections. Small groups of men, in some twenty separate section groups, darted up in the cornfield, ran forward a short way, and then took cover. The commander of B Company wrote an account of this action:

> The sharp report of a Mauser rifle rang out 'crack'! Then rifles and machine guns sputtered and cracked from scores of hidden emplacements in the hill sides. Two guns were spurting out destruction from the high ground on the left. Were we going to be caught within a deadly zone of machine gun cross-fire? Our advance received a decided check. The delay did not last long, for each section changed its hitherto steady marching programme to one of quick rushes and short rests ... . Forgetting their fatigue, section after section darted up in the corn, rushed a few yards, dropped down and opened fire, all obeying orders which rang out from the impromptu section commander, above the spluttering of machine guns and the crack of snipers, and in the face of a heavy enemy fire coming from a hill with steep and treacherous sides. But we were making headway, though only a slow one against this strong resistance. Then up the road on which our right flank was resting and where we joined with the Devons a cavalry patrol galloped majestically towards us and amid the cheers of our men dashed past us.

This was undoubtedly the New Zealand Otago Mounted Rifles riding out on their early morning reconnaissance patrol to Sarcy.

Gradually, the line of sections crept up the hill until the doughty West Yorkshires could put the entrenched enemy to flight, using their bayonets. The dugouts and woods on top of the hill were cleared and the defenders forced to surrender or flee. The account continues, 'a few of our sections had won through to the crest. Sections reassembled and carried on up the hill, through the vines, and over the side and into the old disused trenches, where a few lingering Bosches were captured.'

Without doubt the capture of the hill was a most remarkable feat for this small battalion. Amazingly the 8th West Yorkshires lost only one officer, Captain Muller commanding C Company, which led on the left, and thirteen men killed. In addition five officers and 104 men were casualties due to wounds, gassing or missing. Despite these losses, the battalion not only occupied its objective, but captured sixty-nine prisoners and nine machine guns. The battalion diary paid tribute to Captain Muller, who had been commanding the left-hand company, when the hitherto silent hillside suddenly erupted into a sheet of fire:

> realising that the success of the operation depended upon the immediate capture of the high ground on his front, led his company forward, and after a short but stiff struggle gained the position. The whole line then pressed on and drove the enemy from the crown of the hill.

The 8th West Yorkshires then consolidated on the hill, together with two companies of 2/5th West Yorkshires, who came up to support them. Later on in the evening the 2/5th West Yorkshires carried out a small attack to complete the capture of the Montagne de Bligny. By the most incredible of historical coincidences, the scratch force of the 8th West Yorkshires found itself occupying exactly the same hill, and after performing exactly the same courageous military feat, as the 4th Kings Shropshire LI had done just seven weeks earlier.

During the late morning of the 29th, the 8th West Yorkshires were relieved by the full battalion of the 2/5th West Yorkshires, and moved back to Nardi Farm as support battalion. Meanwhile 185 Brigade remained holding on to the Montagne for two days during which they were subjected to constant shelling. It seems that the Germans had assumed they would be able to hold their strong positions on the top of the Montagne de Bligny with their newly-arrived 240th Division while they conducted a gradual withdrawal in other areas. Ludendorff, particularly, was extremely loathe to abandon the line, which lay so close to Reims, and repeatedly requested that it be held for a longer period. However, the surprise success of the attack on the 28th unbalanced the German eastern defence line and they could initially respond only with artillery fire. Later, on the 30th and 31st, the Germans made further strong counter-attacks against the British line but without success. On the 30th, OHL fixed the date for the withdrawal to the Blücher Line for the night of 1/2 August. The Montagne de Bligny had been the key feature of their eastern hinge and, once it was lost, they had little alternative but to pull back to the River Vesle.

The extraordinary exploit of the 8th West Yorkshires in capturing the Montagne de Bligny was even more remarkable given that the battalion had only just received, in the early hours of the 27th, a reinforcement draft of 200 men and boys. This draft, coming straight from the training depots and convalescent hospitals, had already been travelling and marching for several tiring days. Having joined the battalion, these exhausted men had then marched forward all day on the 27th, and, with very little sleep, re-organized for the assault on the Montagne, which commenced at 4.30am on the 28th. This great feat of military determination was recognized by the award of the Croix de Guerre to the West Yorkshire Regiment, an award which is still proudly borne by its successor unit.

Equally remarkably, this magnificent achievement took place alongside the successful attack by the 5th Devons. The two battalions were thus fighting in exactly the same area as where the composite remnants of IX Corps and 19th Division had put up such a stout defence, and thereby brought the first German Aisne offensive to a halt on 6 June 1918. After part of 56 Brigade had been driven from the hill, it was the ferocious assault by the remnants of the 4th KSLI which had cleared the Germans from the vital trenches at the top of the Montagne de Bligny and resulted in the award of the Croix de Guerre to that regiment. The sister battalion of 5th Devons, the 2nd Devons, had been awarded the Croix de Guerre for its sacrificial defence of the bridge at Pontavert during the morning of the opening attack on 27 May 1918. The 6th Black Watch, which had been attacking towards Chambrecy that morning, on the left of the Montagne de Bligny, was also awarded the Croix de Guerre for its courageous action at Chambrecy. It was thus a quite extraordinary coincidence that three of those regiments should find themselves fighting in the neighbourhood of the Montagne de Bligny on 28 July 1918.

During that night 187 Brigade came forward and took over the ground gained by 186 Brigade. The brigade continued to support the attack by the French 77th Division on its right by pushing forward liaison posts and patrols to support their attack through the Bois de Honleux. At one critical stage the French ran low on ammunition, and the British passed rifles and ammunition, taken from their own casualties, to them. However, a serious counter-attack mounted by the Germans finally drove the French out of the Bois de Honleux and 187

Brigade had to withdraw in conformance with them, back to the old French trench line.

Monday 29 July 1918. The tenth day of the Battle of Tardenois in the Ardre Valley and the defence of the Montagne de Bligny position.
At dawn on the 29th, 310th Brigade RFA moved its batteries forward to positions north of Cuitron, which enabled it to engage opportunity enemy targets. It was later reported that the batteries had engaged many moving targets and each fired some 1,500 rounds. D Battery engaged three enemy batteries from its position at Cuitron, while A and C Batteries moved forward in full view of the enemy to positions near the Moulin de Chaumuzy and engaged enemy machine guns 'which were annoying the infantry'. Although this was undoubtedly helpful, one cannot help thinking that the batteries were using every excuse to get rid of surplus shells rather than having to take back their unused ones.

At 8.00pm, D Company of the 2/5th West Yorkshires mounted an attack to clear a wood containing a strip of the old French line on the left of the Montagne de Bligny, which was still occupied by the enemy. This successful attack by two platoons of D Company was supported by 310th Brigade. Two other platoons of D Company then passed through with the aim of establishing an observation point overlooking the village of Sarcy about 150 yards north-west of the wood. Tragically, the two observation platoons seem to have lost direction and disappeared; apparently they were captured by the enemy.

Orders had been received for 62nd Division to be relieved on 30 July and 310th Brigade, after firing its support barrage, was then ordered to return to its wagon lines at Ecueil Farm during the evening. Meanwhile 312th Brigade had moved some batteries forward to Chaumuzy, and remained there to support the infantry.

During the evening 154 Brigade relieved 153 Brigade on the 51st Divisional front. The 4th Gordon Highlanders were on the left and the 4th Seaforth Highlanders on the right, with their right flank just touching the Montagne de Bligny. The 7th Argyll and Sutherland Highlanders were in support in the Bois des Eclisses. Later that evening, after the 2/5th West Yorkshires had completed their attack, the 51st Division was ordered to extend its front to cover the Montagne de Bligny, and 7th Argylls came forward to relieve 2/5th West Yorkshires, who then marched back to Eceuil Farm. The 7th Argylls spent the rest of the night digging themselves into the hillside. Thus only 154 Brigade was left holding the much-reduced XXII Corps front.

Tuesday 30 July 1918. The eleventh day of the Battle of Tardenois in the Ardre Valley as the British Divisions withdraw from the Ardre Valley.
On the Montagne de Bligny 154 Brigade remained in position, holding the front with the 7th Argyll and Sutherland Highlanders manning their trenches. There they were subjected to shell fire all day. Then at 8.00pm, after an intense fifteen-minute bombardment, an infantry assault was launched against them from the west. However, the 7th Argylls stood their ground and, with their rifles and Lewis guns, dispersed this attack by about fifty Germans. The divisional artillery of the 51st (Highland) Division provided full support until midday, when 255th Brigade was relieved. The last artillery batteries of 256th Brigade were relieved during the night, as the French 14th Division arrived to take over the position.

During the morning of the 30th, 312th Brigade RFA supported an early morning attack by the French 77th Division on the Bois de Honleux. Then at 10.00am it withdrew to St Imoges. Later, the divisional artillery marched to Châlons, where they entrained on 1 and 2 August, eventually returning to the old divisional locations around Pas. The 62nd Division was relieved on this day, and began moving south, apart from 186 Brigade, which stayed to be reviewed by General Bertholet. General Bertholet had asked to review a brigade from each division as a mark of his respect for the British troops, which had contributed significantly to driving the Germans from their positions in the Ardre valley.

Wednesday 31 July 1918. The twelfth day of the Battle of Tardenois in the Ardre Valley and the final actions in defence of the Montagne de Bligny.
Throughout 31 July 154 Brigade continued manning its positions on the Montagne de Bligny. No further enemy attacks were launched but the battalions remained in position continuing active patrolling until dusk. Command was finally handed over to the French 14th Division at 10.00pm on the 31st.

On 1 August a final Troop Review took place before General Bertholet and General Godley. The troops reviewed included the ANZAC Cavalry Regiment and the New Zealand Cyclist Battalion, as well as the marching contingent of an infantry brigade from each division. The soldiers, who came virtually straight from the battlefield, did their best to smarten themselves up for the parade and to clean and polish their transport. This task was not easy, but was made a little lighter by only burnishing the wheel hubs on the sides of the wagons which faced General Bertholet.

At last the British marched away feeling very satisfied with the contribution they had made to driving the Germans back, and not a little sad that they could not continue to experience the satisfaction of driving the Germans all the way back to the River Vesle. However, the divisions had suffered severe casualties as they winkled the Germans out of their two major defence lines and, although some reinforcements had been received, the divisions were in a very weakened state. They had experienced some very tough fighting, but an advance of some three miles (five kilometres) against a stubborn enemy had provided great satisfaction. General Godley recorded in his memoirs that having seen how tired his men were, and in view of their heavy casualties, he had been responsible for asking the French army commander, General Bertholet for his divisions to be relieved.

However, the truth was perhaps more prosaic. After the success of the Marne offensive, Maréchal Foch desperately wanted to maintain the momentum of attacks against the Germans and pressed the British to begin their next attack as soon as humanly possible. In response, Haig had promised Foch that he would be able to start his great attack at Amiens on 10 August. However, he was prepared to try to advance this attack, if the four divisions of XXII Corps were returned to him two days earlier. As a result Maréchal Foch ordered that XXII Corps be relieved and returned expeditiously. Furthermore, he ordered that the French First Army would be placed under command of the British General Rawlinson for the attack south of the Somme. This was a clear expression of the new spirit of closer co-operation and, as a result, Sir Douglas Haig was able to launch his momentous Fourth Army attack on 8 August.

Ludendorff was busy focusing on the re-organization of his forces and, as with the French assault on 18 July, was completely surprised by the British attack at Amiens. In an appreciation, which he sent out on 2 August, he pointed out that since the Allies had 'engaged large forces between the Vesle and the Marne, full-dress attacks by the enemy within a short time at another place are as little to be expected as is a counter-attack by us to be taken into account by him'. Just six days later his predictions were again contradicted by events. Moreover, the rapid collapse of six frontline German divisions on 8 August demonstrated how seriously German morale had been weakened. Strong Allied attacks then continued all through August as Foch was determined to give the Germans no rest, while he exploited the advantage conferred by possession of the strategic initiative.

On 4 August 51st Division opened its headquarters at Villers-Chatel, although many of its units and their equipment were still en route back to the British lines. It was said that each Scottish soldier was seen entraining with a large tin of bully beef in one hand and a bottle of Champagne in the other. The 51st (Highland) Division sorely needed adequate time to recuperate. During its twelve days of combat in the Tardenois, it had suffered total casualties of 115 officers and 2,950 other ranks. However, there was not much rest for such formidable warriors. By 14 August the troops were once again moving into the forward trenches in the Bailleul and Fampoux area close to Arras. This great division had been given less than ten days to refit and recuperate.

Most of the losses experienced by the division had been incurred while facing concealed German machine guns in the dreadful fighting conditions in the Bois de Courton. The 6th Black Watch, which had suffered total casualties of twenty-six officers and 428 men, was given special mention in the orders of Fifth Army and was decorated with the Croix de Guerre for its action at Chambrecy. The battalion had been originally raised as a Perthshire Territorial Force battalion and this award is still worn by the successor territorial units, sadly now reduced to a single company of the Royal Regiment of Scotland. However, although richly deserved, this honour, with some justification, could have been awarded to any of the Scottish battalions. All had taken part in repeated attacks against well-concealed enemy positions and, despite the difficult conditions in the woods in which they largely fought, they had bravely continued to advance and seek ways of overcoming the enemy's resistance.

The 51st Division continued to serve under command of XXII Corps as it rejoined First Army. Then, towards the end of August, it fought in the Second Battle of Arras including the storming of Greenland Hill, when the British recaptured many of the positions which had been lost in the spring. The Scots attacked alongside the Canadian Corps and the New Zealand Division in the re-capture of Bapaume. This frustrated a German plan to establish a new defence line on the Somme and forced the Germans to fall back to the Hindenburg Line. After that formidable obstacle had been breached at the end of September, the 51st took part in the pursuit to the River Selle and the advance in Picardy during October. After the Armistice most of the division was demobilized, but three of its battalions were chosen to serve in the British Army of Occupation in Germany, including the 6th Black Watch.

The losses suffered by the 62nd Division were even heavier. It had rushed forward to the battle in Champagne with a strength of some 226 officers and 5,536 other ranks in its nine infantry battalions. It then suffered total casualties of 118 officer and 3,865 other ranks in the ten days of its campaign, although the heaviest casualties were suffered in the badly-prepared very first morning of attacks against Marfaux. This loss of almost 4,000 men constituted practically two-thirds of its combat numbers. Even though it received reinforcements of sixty-nine officers and 1,712 soldiers during the course of the fighting, its battalions remained seriously below strength. Moreover, many of its men desperately needed training, as the reinforcements included largely newly-trained recruits and hospital returnees.

The losses of the two southern battalions in the 62nd Division were heavy but, because their starting strength was greater, perhaps not as severe as those suffered by the other infantry battalions on the Ardre. The 5th Battalion Devonshire Regiment had sailed from Egypt with thirty-five officers and 943 men. It had been trans-shipped in England, but the men had been allowed no home leave, although their families had waited on the quayside, before they joined 62nd Division in the area of Bucquoy in June 1918. The battalion had sustained thirty casualties in the move up to Pourcy on the 20th. Then in the first major action, although it had started as the support battalion, it had suffered casualties from shellfire and from sending troops forward to support the lead battalions. By the end of the first day of combat, a further two officers and thirty-four men had been killed and seven officers and 185 men wounded. Its next major action was on 28 July, when 5th Devons captured part of the ridge of the Montagne de Bligny, alongside the 8th West Yorkshires, suffering another seventy casualties. As a result, for the whole ten days of the Ardre battle, the battalion suffered eighty-seven officers and men killed and missing and over 300 wounded. As with the other battalions on the Ardre, it was the first day of the attack which had caused the major losses to the Devons; almost two thirds of those it suffered in the whole ten days.

The other battalion, which had joined from Palestine, the 2/5th Hampshires, suffered similar losses. Like the Devons, it had also been made up to full-strength of close to 1,000 men on leaving Egypt. During the Ardre campaign, two officers and 172 men were killed or reported missing; in addition nine officers and 170 men were wounded, reducing the strength of the battalion by more than a third.

The casualties amongst the division's supporting artillery were caused mainly by enemy shellfire, but were far less severe than in the infantry. This was attributed partly to the indifferent counter-battery work of the Germans, but also to the well-trained batteries digging themselves in directly a position was occupied. However, due to the frequent changes of location, stockpiling of ammunition and frequent barrages, this also meant very little rest for the gunners during the whole campaign. The total losses in the divisional artillery in the ten days of fighting were nine men killed, and five officers and sixty men wounded.

Another casualty did not appear until 8 August. On that day divisional headquarters communicated an order for the disbandment of 2/5th West Yorkshires. Due to the continuing lack of reinforcements, this fine battalion was disbanded on 13 August. It was acknowledged that the 2/5th West Yorkshires had been one of the smartest and best-fighting battalions in the division, but too many men had been lost in the first attack on Marfaux, exacerbated by the losses on the Montagne de Bligny. After a final parade, its remaining soldiers were split up among the other Yorkshire battalions.

The 62nd had returned to Third Army and immediately begun re-training its officers and men. By 26 August it was ready to take part in the Battle of the Scarpe. During this battle, the 5th Duke of Wellingtons once again demonstrated their superior skills in infantry tactics, when two companies dealt with some difficult German trenches. Supported by teams of Lewis guns, two bomber parties, each of nine men, attacked the trenches and finally cleared them with the bayonet. For slight casualties, they killed thirty-five Germans and captured ninety-three prisoners and fifteen machine guns.

On 12 September 1918, the 62nd Division was granted the privilege of attacking Havrincourt in the Hindenburg Line alongside the New Zealand Division and the 2nd Division. The division was being offered the opportunity to enhance its fighting reputation by, once again, regaining possession of the town, which it had taken the previous year. For this attack against four German divisions it was moved to

VI Corps under Lieutenant General Haldane. The attack was brilliantly successful and Havrincourt was occupied by the end of the first day. Marking the change in the tide of events for the Allies, this was the same day as the US Army demonstrated its growing competence by sealing off and occupying the huge St Mihiel Salient within three days. The two victories at Havrincourt are fittingly commemorated by the 62nd Divisional Monument, which still stands just outside the Château at Havrincourt. It was unveiled by General Berthelot in June 1922.

The great success of Second Havrincourt emboldened the British generals to consider closing up to the outpost systems of the Hindenburg Line, and General Rawlinson was allowed to launch the Battle of Épehy on 18 September, which again included 62nd Division. It continued to serve under command of VI Corps for the crossing of the Hindenburg Line in the Battle of the Canal du Nord on 29 September. During October it took part in the final advance in Picardy, including the Battle of Selle, and in November the Battle of the Sambre. Fittingly, after the Armistice, the 62nd Division was then selected to advance across Belgium and form part of the garrison of the Rhine bridgeheads. It was the only Territorial Force division to form part of the occupation army.

The 15th (Scottish) Division joins XX Corps in Tenth Army

In early July 1918 the 15th (Scottish) Division found that it was receiving orders to entrain for the French front as one of the four divisions selected to strengthen the French line east of Reims. It was to join XXII Corps, as a special reserve under the direction of General Foch. Even as the units of XXII Corps began moving south, Foch recognized an opportunity to deliver a crushing blow against the Germans in the Oise-Marne salient. Therefore he asked the British Commander-in-Chief for authority to use these divisions unreservedly under his orders, to which Haig agreed. As a result 15th (Scottish) received changes to its orders en route and began to detrain in the Clermont-Laigneville area by 18 July, where it was placed under the direct command of the French Third Army.

Up until the time of their excursion to the Champagne region, the Scots had been enjoying a relatively quiet time east of Arras. The 15th (Scottish) Division had of course been heavily involved in the Somme battles of the German spring offensive. Actually no fewer than forty-six out of the fifty-eight British divisions stationed in France had been involved in repelling the Germans during the great Somme battle. A separate Scottish corps was never formed, although that might well have created an interesting fighting formation to rival the exploits of the Australian and Canadian corps. However, unusually, during part of its time on the Somme front, it had been one of three Scottish divisions holding the line together when it was placed to the right of the 51st (Highland) Division, which had on its left 52nd (Lowland) Division. Just like the other divisions, which had withstood the German attacks, it had suffered huge casualties and had been kept busy after the battle rebuilding and training its units. It was also required, at the same time, to physically rebuild the defensive British trench lines and dugouts in a way which would defeat the new German tactics, with particular emphasis on constructing strongpoints which provided mutual support and all-round defence.

The division had been formed quickly in the war enthusiasm of 1914 as one of Kitchener's New Army divisions. Initially, the organization was somewhat chaotic and, when the division paraded for inspection before King George V in September 1914 it was still in civilian clothes. However, it was ready for active service by the following summer and landed in France in July 1915. It was considered a formidable attack division and was involved in many battles and actions throughout the rest of the war. By the end of the war it had suffered total casualties of 1,561 officers and 40,456 men, of whom some 5,000 were killed.

The division was commanded by Major General H. L. Reed VC. General Reed had been awarded the Victoria Cross for an action at Colenso during the Boer War. There, as a captain in 7 Battery, Royal Field Artillery, he had attempted to bring up three teams of horses to get the guns away after they had come under very heavy fire from the Boers. He was wounded, as were most of the men with him, and thirteen of the horses were killed under them before Captain Reed was forced to withdraw. As a lieutenant colonel he had been the GSO 1 of the newly formed 27th Division from November 1914 until June 1915, and was then promoted to brigadier general as the senior staff officer to Lieutenant General Stopford's unfortunate IX Corps, which went out to Gallipoli in 1915. As such his career suffered when Stopford was sacked following the failure of the Suvla Bay operation, for which he was also blamed and sacked. He then filled a number of Royal Artillery appointments, until he was given a second chance, and in November 1917 was made General Officer Commanding 15th Division. He continued to serve in that capacity until the end of the war and the final disbandment of the division in March 1919. He retired from the Army in 1927, having spent four years commanding the Territorial 52nd (Lowland) Division in Scotland.

The division mustered nine battalions of infantry drawn from some of the famous highland and lowland infantry regiments, most of whom wore either kilts or trews (tartan trousers). Some had served continuously with the division and fought in many battles since its arrival in France in 1915. However, due to the sweeping manpower changes following the losses caused by the German spring offensives, many of its battalions were actually new to service with the 15th Division:

44 Brigade
    4/5th Battalion Black Watch (The Royal Highlanders)*
    8th Battalion Seaforth Highlanders

5th Battalion Gordon Highlanders***

45 Brigade
13th Battalion Royal Scots (The Lothian Regiment)
6th Battalion Queen's Own Cameron Highlanders
8th Battalion Argyll and Sutherland Highlanders** ***

46 Brigade
9th Battalion Royal Scots (The Lothian Regiment)***
7/8th Battalion King's Own Scottish Borderers (KOSB)
10th Battalion Cameronians (Scottish Rifles)

Divisional Pioneers
9th Battalion Gordon Highlanders

* The 4/5th Battalion of the Black Watch was the result of a merger of two Black Watch battalions; it had also absorbed the 9th Battalion.
** The 8th Battalion of the Argylls was in fact a composite battalion, as it was merged with part of the 11th Battalion, which had fought as part of the original 15th Division but had just been reduced to cadre.
***These three battalions had joined from the 61st Division in June 1918.

The support elements of the division included the 70th and 71st Brigades of the Royal Field Artillery, with X.15 and Y.15 Batteries of 6-inch medium mortars. Close fire support came from the three light trench mortar batteries and the 15th Divisional Machine Gun Battalion. The Royal Engineers provided 73, 74 and 91 Field Companies together with the 15th Divisional Signals Company. Medical support was provided by 45th, 46th and 47th Field Ambulances. Keeping the division supplied with its food and equipment was the 15th Divisional Train. The total divisional strength on 15 June 1918 was 10,035.

In mid-July 15th Division had begun moving its troops and equipment to the Reims area with the rest of XXII Corps when its orders were changed and it was told to detrain farther west at Clermont. Accordingly, by 18 July, 15th Division was concentrated in that area. Initially its role was likely to be halting the final, as became apparent later, German attack to widen the Aisne salient around Reims. Launched at 1.00am on 15 July, this 'Peace Offensive' was supported by the heaviest artillery concentration ever put together by the Germans, but the attack failed to achieve strategic or tactical surprise, and was abandoned on 17 July.

Foch was not satisfied with just halting the Germans. He had been gathering counter-attack forces secretly in the huge Forest of Villers-Cotterêts. At last Foch saw the opportunity to take advantage of the over-extended Germans, particularly west of Soissons, and ordered General Mangin to launch his great Franco-American offensive on the 18th. The Germans were totally surprised, but recovered quickly as they realized their great danger and desperately threw in substantial reinforcements to prevent the Allies reaching the railway bottleneck at Soissons. Mangin continued pressing his offensive, and had given the French XX Corps, commanded by General Berdoulat, the objective of taking Soissons. However, after two days of fighting the original attack divisions were heavily worn down by their costly attacks, and the advance stalled as the French were short of further reserves.

Whilst this great battle raged ahead of them, long columns of Scots on foot or in horse-drawn vehicles and lorries moved up slowly along crowded and dusty roads into the Montigny area. There was mounting excitement as the division moved through the areas which had been briefly occupied by the Germans. They could see the debris and heard rumours of the successful Allied counter-attack, which they were joining, as the division came under command of Mangin's Tenth Army. On the evening of the 20th they were ordered to march the following day to join XX Corps in the Montgobert area. As is usual in such fast-developing situations, there were many bewildering orders and counter-orders. Eventually, at 9.00pm on the 21st, the 15th Division was ordered to commence a night march to St-Pierre-Aigle-le-Jardin, the small village behind the centre of Mangin's attack. This was another slow, halting, dusty night approach march, made worse by the activities of enemy aircraft, which buzzed the columns and twice managed to bomb the troops, causing casualties. However, by early morning, the division was concentrated around Coeuvres, just five miles (eight kilometres) west of Soissons.

In a typically surprise Mangin operation, General Reed received orders at short notice, namely 9.20pm on the 22nd, that Tenth Army would resume the offensive the following morning. The new assault required fresh troops, which was where the 15th (Scottish) came in, and small parties of Scottish officers had already been briefed by the Americans on the 22nd. The effort and success achieved by the Americans could not be underestimated. The American 1st Division had advanced from Cuitry through Missy-en-Bois to Berzy-le-Sec, a total of seven miles (eleven kilometres) in five days, during which it captured 3,500 prisoners, and sixty-eight guns but had suffered 8,365 casualties, including 60 percent of its infantry officers. For example the 26th Infantry Regiment had commenced its attack with ninety-six officers and 3,100 men. All its field officers had been killed or wounded, and the regiment came out of the line under command of a junior captain. It had lost 1,560 men and sixty-two officers killed or wounded. Among the casualties was its commander, Colonel Hamilton A. Smith, who was killed supervising an attack against the Sugar Mill at Noyant on the 22nd. Major Theodore Roosevelt Jr, the commander of the 2nd Battalion, had also been wounded in the fierce fighting around Ploisy during the afternoon of 19 July.

The American 2nd Division had made exhausting forced marches from the desperate fighting around Château-Thierry, in order to reach the battlefield in time to join the attack. Then, it had advanced five miles (eight kilometres) in the first twenty-six hours, capturing some 3,000 prisoners, two batteries of 150mm guns, and sixty-six light guns, as well as stocks of ammunition and military stores. Without question this was an immensely fine achievement by its soldiers who fought fiercely, despite being inadequately supplied and supported, and suffered 4,319 casualties in just two days of fighting. The troops of 2nd Division had their last proper meal on the evening of the 16th and were not supplied with food or water until they came out of combat on the 20th. This was a clear and early warning to the American staff officers about the problems of ensuring the logistics support kept up with the fighting troops. The brave efforts of these two American divisions had been more than matched by the courage of the multi-national 1st Moroccan Colonial Regiment (RICM), which suffered just as heavily, as it advanced between the two American divisions.

Accordingly, 15th (Scottish) Division, supported by its two field artillery brigades, was ordered to relieve the American 1st Division that night (the 22nd) and be ready for an attack to commence at 5.00am next day. The difficulties contained within such an order were breathtaking. Within eight hours, the 15th Division was expected to complete an exhausting night approach march, take over new positions and then attack an unknown enemy over unseen terrain. Its task was made even more complex by having to take over from both American and French troops on poorly-identified ground, *at night*. There was no clear front line and parts of the handover were very poorly executed by the departing units, some of whom barely identified enemy positions.

One platoon of Argylls actually stumbled onto a German post which alerted the enemy to the change of units – the Scots in their kilts were clearly very different from the French soldiers they relieved – and brought an avalanche of artillery and machine-gun fire onto the division's positions.

This was very much a hurried relief of forces, undertaken without allowing time for a proper Scottish reconnaissance. The Americans had not even had time to collect and bury their dead before leaving. As a result, 15th Division then dealt with many of the American bodies that they found, and forwarded the identity tags of the American dead to General Summerall. The division recorded that it 'was their privilege and sacred duty to render the last rites to their most gallant Allies'. To assist the attack the next day, the 1st American Artillery Brigade, under Colonel Holbrook, remained in position. It was, according to Colonel Holbrook, the first time that French, British and American artillery had ever worked together under the same command.

Despite the disparities and the huge difficulties involved in a night relief over unknown ground, 15th Division had completed the relief of the American and French units by 3.00am and was in position to make its preparations for the dawn attack. Its new front line extended from the outskirts of Berzy to the western edge of Rozières. The Scots were to mount a two-brigade attack with 45 Brigade on the left, 46 Brigade on the right, and 44 Brigade in reserve. Covering its flanks were newly-arrived French troops from the 69th Division on the left and the 87th Division on the right.

Tuesday 23 July 1918. 15th Division's opening attack at Berzy-le-Sec.
Supported by the joint Allied artillery bombardment, 15th (Scottish) was to attack the German positions between Berzy-le-Sec and the northwest corner of Buzancy, deploying four infantry battalions from the two assault brigades. On the division's left, the task of 45 Brigade was to capture le Sucrerie (the Sugar Mill) and the crossings on the River Crise north and east of Noyant with the 8th Argyll and Sutherland Highlanders (Argylls) on its left and 6th Cameron Highlanders on its right, with 13th Royal Scots in reserve. On the division's right, 46 Brigade was to capture the village of Rozières and the high ground between Rozières and Buzancy. Its attack was to be led by the 10th Scottish Rifles on its left and the 7/8th King's Own Scottish Borderers on the right, with 9th Royal Scots in reserve.

The artillery bombardment, which opened up from the tri-national artillery at 5.00am on 23 July, was fierce. Unfortunately, it was patchy and based on misconceptions about the exact location of the front line. Accordingly it fell 600 yards beyond the foremost German positions, thereby missing many of their most dangerous machine-gun posts, which were located close to the Scots. On the centre right, in front of 10th Scottish Rifles there was a complete absence of shelling. The result was predictable; as the Scottish battalions moved forward through the open country they suffered severely from enemy fire, particularly from the German artillery and the undamaged machine-gun nests.

Good progress was made by the two centre battalions, but the Scots quickly discovered that the two flanking French divisions had been unable to get forward. As a result the two battalions advancing on the outer flanks were left very exposed. Although the Camerons managed to capture the Sucrerie, they were forced to extend their line northwards to the railway crossing over the River Crise. Farther north the forward companies of 8th Argylls, who had suffered from the German artillery fire during the relief, were largely out of touch and suffering from more enemy shelling. They were unable to make much progress. Half the battalion remained stuck around Berzy, where they managed to find scattered cover and maintain some contact with the flanking French 69th Division. The divisional history records that the situation on the left flank was obscure for most of the day until a Lieutenant McKay went forward and checked the whole area of the Argylls' front and reported back to headquarters. He was under enemy observation and fire for much of this time. Fortunately, he kept a diary of his experiences, and the record of his brave reconnaissance amid the prevailing military chaos, still survives:

> About 11.15am I went out again, taking Corporal Langridge with me. My orders were to establish, if possible, a bridgehead over the Crise River, on the Eastern side of the Railway, and to collect information, and to help things on. As soon as Langridge and I got to the top of the ridge we were machine gunned at long range, so there was nothing for it – some of the shots were very near – but to bolt in the direction of the firing which was coming from the Sucrerie. This we did in a slightly zig-zag course until we reached lower ground when the firing became more intense. So we lay down in a shell hole to consider the situation. I had not met a single Argyll of A or B or D Coys on this journey.

A Coy, by this time, with McIntosh and several others killed, had fallen back north west about 200 yards to some very slight cuttings or banks which gave some degree of shelter from the machine gun fire. I noted A Coy's disappearance, but thought at the time that they had gone forward (and might be in front of us). B and D were non-existent, and there was not a B or D casualty to be seen on the ridge or on the ground below on the right half of the battalion front. From what I had heard, our front line as it had been 'handed over' ran from Berzy (inclusive) S.W. to the corner of the steep ridge, and then S.E. along the front of the ridge in the direction of l'Etang.

I watched the areas being shelled by the Boche, and concluded he had given up the ground West of the Railway. So with Langridge I worked along until I came into the Camerons' [6th Cameron Highlanders] area at the very S.E. corner of the ridge, got down, turned, and came back as towards Berzy at the foot of the ridge, on level ground. Not a single casualty, or sign of life could I see. The whole southern half was untenanted. We therefore made a bolt across the open for the little wood S.E. of Berzy village – and searched it, its edges, and its centre. Found no one.

Then I decided to work over to the Railway Embankment which was some 200 yards further on. As we were moving over, I saw the first sign of life – a small post of Camerons – 2-3 of them, holding a part of the embankment 200 yards south of the river. They told us we were the first Argylls they had seen. By this time I was sure that our fellows must be behind in Berzy or else had lost their direction of advance, and gone through the village in a North-East direction. Langridge and I therefore worked our way along the Railway, northwards. Boche was quieter now, although he machine gunned the top of the Railway Embankment from time to time, as from the Sucrerie.

We entered an orchard near the crossing of the road and railway, and I filled my pockets with peapods. I then searched a house nearby. Then we spotted some Camerons across the road alongside the Railway, and one or two dead Camerons in the road. They had been shot from under the railway bridge. Therefore we made a detour back and crossed the road at a point hidden from enemy view, came up again to the Railway and found Pat Fraser of the Camerons. His position was well inside our battalion area, and yet he had not seen an Argyll! I got some information from him about his own battalion, the 6th. His was the left hand flank post of the 6th.

I then went a bit north towards the station which contained a number of broken wagons. I did not enter, but the place was quite untenanted, apparently. I therefore came back and worked up the roads behind but parallel to the Crise. Found a dead horse and nothing else. Then determined to climb the hill on which Berzy stood, and which, while still receiving attention, was moderately quiet compared to what it had been in the morning. I came back to it and approached it from the road leading from Noyant – a very steep road – and entered the village. It was still being shelled, and the streets were piled high with masonry which I had to clamber over. I searched the front edge of it, and found a post of two or three Frenchmen at the North East corner. They told me that some French and Scots were behind in the Village, but where they did not know. They did not know who was in front, or on their flanks. So therefore there was a thousand yards gap between Pat Fraser and this post and some 600 or more yards between Pat Fraser and the nearest post to the South of him!

I began to search the village, and found a French Artillery post in the centre of it, and in it a big crowd of French, and our own Argyll wounded. I then came upon a sort of cave, and found in it a number of unwounded and wounded Argylls. At the Western corner of the village was a big crowd of our dead – caught obviously by shell fire.

I then went downhill at the bend of the ridge and found little Sandy Miller and his platoon, all properly placed at the bottom of the ridge, but less a number of casualties. He had managed to keep his men together better than the others, but he had never received operation orders! When caught by the shelling he had gone forward with his men, and although he was in a rotten hole, by this judicious action he had succeeded in keeping down the number of his casualties. Of his immediate situation and surroundings he knew absolutely nothing, except that he himself had been over a certain amount of ground. His men had seen Langridge and me cross round in front of them, but had not told him. Of the remainder of his Coy (B) and of his O.C. Coy he knew nothing, and so, of course he could only stay where he was.

I came back up again to report and found A Coy in their new position, minus a good many casualties. A Coy had received their orders alright. On the way back to Bn HQ to report we came across several more casualties – one or two of them runners, poor devils.

Battalion HQ were relieved to get my news. Neither Battalion HQ nor Brigade HQ nor Divisional HQ had the foggiest idea about what had happened.

Lieutenant MacKay had joined the 8th Argylls after several years with the 11th Argylls, when it had been reduced to a cadre, and had been awarded the Military Cross (MC) the previous October. He was to be awarded a Bar to the MC for his efforts that day. At last with usable information, General Reed planned a new artillery barrage, but then discovered that the French could not co-operate, so a further attack was suspended. Both of the flanking battalions had suffered severely during that morning; 7/8th KOSB, on the right, had lost almost half of its officers and men – thirty-six killed and 287 wounded or missing – and the Argylls had suffered a similar loss. Although the 8th Argylls had managed to maintain some contact with the French 69th Division on its left, the weakened 7/8th KOSB on the divisional right had found their flank in the air, and were given a reinforcement of a company of the 10th Scottish Rifles. Later that day General Reed sent them a further makeshift reinforcement of the personnel of 46 Trench Mortar Battery, formed into a small infantry company.

The net result of the first day's action was some progress in the centre, but heavy losses on both flanks. At 6.00pm the Germans launched a strong counter-attack from Chivry Farm, supported by a fairly heavy artillery barrage. This was repelled by artillery and machine-gun fire and the forward units began to consolidate, in some cases by pulling back to occupy better cover. That night the American artillery pulled out. From then on Lieutenant Colonel Ingham, the divisional CRA (Commander Royal Artillery), had just the thirty-six 75mm guns of the 253rd French Artillery Regiment to support the forty-eight 18-pounder guns and 4.5-inch howitzers of his two RFA brigades. However, before leaving, the American ambulance service, which was part of the 1,000-strong 1st Division Sanitary Train, also earned the gratitude of the Scots. It used its four companies of motorized ambulances to remove from the battlefield and treat over 400 Scottish wounded who would otherwise have lain untended for another day until the Scottish field ambulance medics could arrive.

24, 25, 26 and 27 July 1918. Holding the line opposite Buzancy.
Although there were no more attacks made for the next two days, 24 and 25 July, the Scots continued to consolidate their positions, while

suffering heavy German shelling. On the 24th, 44 Brigade moved forward to relieve 46 Brigade. On the 26th the division received orders to extend its front southwards (to the right) by taking over part of the front held by the 91st Regiment of the French 87th Division. The subsequent relief was carried out during the night of the 27th in a much smoother way than on the 23rd, and brought 44 Brigade into the line directly opposite Buzancy. Just prior to this relief, Lieutenant Colonel Turner, the young Commanding Officer of the 13th Royal Scots was killed by shellfire in his headquarters' bunker, a location clearly known to the Germans who had vacated it days earlier. On the morning of the 27th, the French 87th Division finally captured the village of Villemontoire. General Reed was then ordered to maintain the momentum of the advance by capturing the heavily-defended stone village of Buzancy and the high ground east of it, on the following day.

Sunday 28 July 1918. 44 Brigade attacks Buzancy, supported by 45 Brigade.
The picturesque village of Buzancy stands, with its château, on a high ridge commanding the key road from Soissons to Château Thierry. The main attack was to be carried out by the comparatively fresh 44 (Highland) Brigade, reinforced by 10th Scottish Rifles from 46 Brigade, a section of 91 Field Company Royal Engineers, 45 Light Trench Mortar Battery, and a French flame-thrower section. The French had captured stocks of these terrifying weapons from the Germans, and begun, with delight, to turn them on the enemy. To support the assault, five companies of the French 91st Regiment were to attack from Villemontoire and take the area south of Buzancy, clear the woods south-west of Buzancy and capture a feature called the 'Grenade Work'. At the same time 45 Brigade was to advance on the left and take up positions in the woods south of Chivry Farm. Interestingly, Zero hour was scheduled for 12.30pm. This timing was a key part of the plan developed by the staff of XX Corps to achieve surprise and allow for observation by French aircraft. Efforts had been made to subject the enemy to barrages at irregular times, which were then not followed up by an attack, and which it was hoped had conditioned them not to expect an attack to follow the next barrage. Furthermore, it was hoped that the 12.30pm barrage would catch the Germans at their mid-day meal.

Precisely at two minutes before Zero hour, an extremely fierce artillery barrage fell on the enemy positions. A Company of the Seaforth, with the Stokes mortar team, led the attack on the château of Buzancy. It was followed by the Seaforth's C Company, together with a section of engineers and the half section of the flame-throwers and B Company of the Black Watch, which was to capture and clear the village of Buzancy and then meet up with the 91st Regiment. Behind them came D Company of the Seaforth, who were to keep on the right of the Gordons and take the final objective on the high ground east of the village. The 5th Gordons were to take the ground running north-east from Buzancy to the Bois l'Évêque.

At first the attack seemed to have gone well, as British troops were seen advancing on the plain south-east of Buzancy. In fact A Company of the Seaforth had quickly moved forward behind the barrage and taken the château within twelve minutes. However, the Germans soon recovered from their surprise, and the clearing of the village by C Company of the Seaforth and B Company of the Black Watch encountered considerable resistance from isolated strongpoints. This opposition was dealt with by the flame-thrower section setting fire to one house, the engineers blowing up another and Lieutenant Badenoch of the Black Watch gathering a few men and clearing a machine-gun post from a third house. While there was fierce fighting going on throughout the village, 100 Germans were found sheltering in a cellar of a building, which was rushed, and they were taken prisoner. Shortly after 1.00pm, Captain Murray, commanding D Company of the Seaforth, reported he was consolidating on the high ground east of Buzancy and had captured a German strongpoint. The 5th Gordons also reported that, having bombed some machine-gun posts, they had by 1.30pm reached their objectives and were consolidating, although still troubled by heavy machine-gun fire from parts of Buzancy and Noyant.

However, soon after 2.00pm the French artillery observers on the right flank reported that the Germans were counter-attacking from the east, and French air observers reported that German troops were seen in Buzancy. The message was written on the back of a photo of a very charming French lady, and the pilot's message said that he had lost his notebook and requested return of the photo of his 'girlfriend'. Later a second observation message arrived written on the back of a photo of an even more charming lady, the pilot again requesting the return of his 'girlfriend's photo'. The account of the battle, reported from divisional headquarters, illustrates all too clearly the difficulty of controlling such a complex engagement from a relatively remote headquarters even though it had moved up to a battle headquarters just north of Glaux Farm, or indeed of ever knowing what had actually gone on when relying primarily on messages brought by runners. By the time divisional headquarters could react to the overwhelming power of the German counter-attacks it was too late, and the troops gallantly holding Buzancy were in danger of being cut off.

The Germans had appreciated only too well that the key to holding the Buzancy plateau, and the area up to the River Crise, was Buzancy itself, and put major efforts into counter-attacking and pushing fresh machine-gun teams back into Buzancy via the sunken road which led into the village from the south. These troops were probably from the 5th and 50th Reserve Divisions, which had been despatched hastily to the area by Ludendorff. A feature of German tactics was also to keep large numbers of men hidden in cellars and caves, where they were safe from artillery fire but could then emerge to man static defences or attack the enemy from the rear. They had moreover strongly resisted the attempt by the French 91st Regiment to advance from Villemontoire, as a result of which they were still able to counter-attack from the east.

The attempt by 15th Division to arrange a fresh artillery barrage on the 'Grenade Work' and woods south of Buzancy, and a new attack by the 91st Regiment, was too late. The Seaforth, Black Watch and Gordons of 44 Brigade were forced to return to their start lines. Twelve men of the Seaforth, under a company sergeant major, went forward to give covering fire to the retirement. A German machine gun, which had got to within fifteen yards of the hole in the château wall that was the only exit point, was bombed by the Seaforth using German grenades. Nevertheless, as the Scottish troops pulled back they were subjected to fire from a number of German machine guns pressing forward, and they suffered further heavy casualties.

By 6.00pm it was all over; 44 and 45 Brigades had achieved their objectives taking Buzancy and the plateau east of it, and inflicted severe losses on the enemy. In addition six officers and over 200 soldiers had been taken prisoner. The support units, particularly the engineers and the machine gunners, had proved their value in the attack and done everything they could to support the infantry. Unfortunately, due to the failure to seal off the village from the east, the Germans had been able to mount a vigorous counter-attack and retake the village, and the Scots were therefore driven right back to their start lines.

Monday 29 July to Wednesday 31 July 1918. 15th Division exchanges positions with the French 87th Division to face Taux.

That evening, just as 15th (Scottish) Division was shaking itself out after the bitter experience of being forced to withdraw from Buzancy, it received orders to begin changing places with parts of the French 87th and 12th Divisions on its right. A part of this movement had to be carried out the same night, which was not easy to arrange. Nevertheless, by the next night, the 29th, the relief was completed. However, as a further offensive was expected very soon, it was decided to leave the divisional artillery in place, so that the 15th Division's artillery would support the 87th Division, and vice versa.

The new planned operation was for the French 12th Division, from the south, and 15th Scottish, from the north, to encircle the Bois d'Hartennes on either side of the forest, with the aim of securing the main Soissons road, thereby cutting the major German supply route to the south of the Aisne salient. It was planned to make this two-pronged assault dependent on the success of an attack farther south by French forces on the same morning.

The new positions occupied by the 15th and 12th Divisions were not especially favourable. There was little cover in the approaches to the start line, and in any case the whole of the divisional front was overlooked by the three hillocks, nicknamed the 'three breasts', in a long ridge, which provided very good observation for the Germans. Not only that, but two deep and narrow re-entrants gave the Germans a covered approach to their positions.

Thursday 1 August 1918. 46 Brigade attacks Taux.

The XX Corps' plan was for the divisional attack to swing right to encircle the Bois d'Hartennes, which was almost a rerun of the same attack which 34th Division had been ordered to undertake so precipitously and disastrously on 23 July. In fact the German XVII Corps of Lieutenant General Günther von Etzel, with four divisions, had been brought up on 20 July to reinforce the units in this area, and the Germans were determined to hang on to their salient at Tigny, and thereby protect their possession of the road, now the D1, which ran through Hartennes.

General Reed had ordered 46 Brigade to attack on the right with the task of securing the two wooded hills, or 'mamelons', as far as Taux. Once secured, 44 Brigade was then to move through its positions and capture the final objective, namely the northern end of the Bois d'Hartennes, where it would link up with the French division coming from the south; 45 Brigade was positioned on its left with the task of protecting the flank of 46 Brigade by securing the Soissons road.

In command of 46 Brigade was the 35-year-old Brigadier General Victor Fortune DSO, who later commanded 51st (Highland Division) in France in 1940. After arrival in France, the 51st (Highland) Division was substantially reinforced, to move hundreds of miles away from the BEF to fight in Lorraine. As a result, it was not involved in the epic evacuation of the BEF from Dunkirk. Instead it was located hundreds of miles away in Lorraine, fighting under French command, to defend the French frontier and the forts of the Maginot Line. The formidable Maginot Line was still intact when it was ordered to move west, to defend the line of the River Somme alongside General de Gaulle and his 4th Armoured Division at Abbeville. Finally, as part of the French IX Corps, it fought against General Rommel's 7th Panzer Division in Normandy. An attempted evacuation by the Royal Navy failed, and two-thirds of the 51st Division was forced to surrender on 12 June 1940 at St Valery-en-Caux. The 51st (Highland) Division was soon reconstituted from survivors and merger with its sister division, 9th (Highland), and later had the satisfaction of defeating Rommel's forces in North Africa and eventually liberating le Havre, St Valery and Veules les Roses in Normandy. General Fortune, while a prisoner, also served as the Senior British Officer (SBO) of all the British PoWs in Europe (apparently some 200,000 men). He suffered a stroke in 1944 and was offered the opportunity to be repatriated, but chose to remain with his fellow prisoners until final liberation in April 1945.

The major initial problem for 46 Brigade was the lack of cover in the area up to the start line, so it was ordered to undertake the very risky tactic of moving the infantry of 9th Royal Scots and 7/8th KOSB forward at night and making them lie down in the standing corn until the signal for the attack was given. There was to be no preliminary bombardment, but the advance was to be covered by an artillery and machine-gun barrage. This was the same type of cornfield which had given so little protection to 102 Brigade of 34th Division on 23 July, and, of course, the success of the infantry assault was directly dependent on the effectiveness of the artillery barrage.

As ordered, the two battalions crept forward during the night and by 4.45am were lying immobile in the cornfield. They expected to launch their attack about two hours later at 7.00am. However, although the southern French attack, by XXX Corps, including 34th Division, described on page 236, achieved its objectives, the XX Corps' signal to advance was not given until 8.25am on 1 August, which meant the Scottish assault could not commence until 9.00am. As a result of this delay, the Scottish infantry were required to lie perfectly still on the ground while under enemy observation for almost five hours. Sadly, as soon as the two lead battalions stood up in the cornfield, in the bright sunlight, they were swiftly cut down by heavy artillery and machine-gun fire. The enemy fire came from the wooded knolls and from machine guns concealed in some destroyed French tanks located in the fields ahead of them. Despite desperate heroism, the two lead battalions of 9th Royal Scots and 7/8th KOSB suffered grievous casualties and were unable to advance more than 250 yards. The field of ripe golden corn turned rapidly into a scene of carnage filled with the bodies of hundreds of killed and wounded soldiers. The follow-on battalion, 10th Scottish Rifles, and 44 Brigade, which had come up behind the two lead battalions, were halted to await orders to advance. Nevertheless, Private Richard Owenson of the Scottish Rifles came forward, under intense machine-gun and shrapnel fire, and tended the wounds of many injured men. Owenson was later awarded the DCM, the Médaille Militaire and the Croix de Guerre for this heroic action.

Fire from the wooded knolls also hit the French 12th Division, which had managed to occupy Tigny on the right but was then driven out by strong German counter-attacks. Although General Reed ordered artillery and Stokes mortar fire to be opened up on the German knoll positions with every available weapon, it did not seem to have any effect. A new more effective barrage was laid on from 3.00pm, but enemy machine-gun fire still bore down on the Scots, who were unable to make progress, and plans for a further assault on Taux was abandoned. By 4.50pm the whole line, south of the Camerons, was back at the start point.

However, the subsidiary attack by 45 Brigade on the left had enjoyed rather more success. The Cameron Highlanders had got forward to the Soissons road at about 11.00am, as did 13th Royal Scots, who then formed a defensive flank farther north along the hedge east of the road.

By this time most of the battalions of 44 and 46 Brigade had been reduced to less than 250 all ranks, and, as further German attacks were anticipated, the division decided, as a desperate measure, to send forward to each battalion that night, the 'final battle reserve' of two officers and fifty men. (It was the British custom, before every major attack, for a 'final reserve' to be created and sent to the rear, in order to have a cadre on which a new battalion could be built if the casualties from an attack proved extremely heavy.) It was later decided to relieve the two lead brigades. On the division's right, 44 Brigade came forward and relieved 46 Brigade, with 4/5th Black Watch on the left and 5th Gordons on the right. On the left, the 9th Gordons, the Pioneer Battalion, supported by a company of 8th Argylls, relieved the Camerons and consolidated their position. However, later that evening, General Reed was informed that Tenth Army would be arranging the relief of his whole division during the following two nights.

Taux was the third major attack mounted by 15th Division. It is no reflection on the bravery or dedication of the officers and men to point out that all three attacks had resulted in very heavy casualties and failure to gain all the objectives. However, the divisional narrative is short on any kind of analysis of the battle plan that day. It seems strange that 46 Brigade had been ordered forward to undertake a very risky operation with just one section of two Vickers machine guns allotted to it in direct support; 45 Brigade was given two sections. The rest of the heavy machine guns were used to reinforce the artillery barrage, which seems to have focused on the northern edge of the Bois d'Hartennes. The Scots had left their own artillery and heavy mortars in front of Buzancy, and were therefore totally reliant on the cover provided by the artillery of 87th Division. There may have been a failure to anticipate the level of German resistance, and once again a failure to ensure that a sufficiently good protective barrage fell immediately in front of the exposed infantry; there is no mention of even a smoke barrage. Certainly the 3.00pm barrage was described as more effective than the morning barrage, but it still failed to take out many of the German machine guns. As it was, 15th Division had suffered another costly setback resulting in close to 1,000 casualties. C and D Companies of 9th Royal Scots, leading the attack, had been almost wiped out, with 110 officers and men of the Royal Scots killed.

Friday 2 August 1918. Germans withdraw and 15th Division advances to River Crise.

Although it may have appeared that the division had not achieved very much for all its brave efforts, it is very clear from German accounts that their forward units had been severely weakened by the constant enemy attacks. The Germans had no alternative but to withdraw from their positions in front of the division that night, as they made a general withdrawal to a line which they hoped they could hold south of the River Vesle. Indeed their heavy counter-attack against the French in Tigny was a typical German tactic to give themselves some manoeuvre space to complete their withdrawal free of enemy interference. During the night of the 1st the Germans withdrew to an intermediate defence position, and then on the following night they withdrew to the prepared defences in the new 'Blücher' defence position on the Rivers Vesle and Aisne, blowing all the bridges around Soissons.

Accordingly at 8.30am the next day, General Steel was informed that the Germans were retiring and he could give orders for his battalions to send out strong patrols. The Scots had to maintain contact with the French on both flanks, while trying to follow up speedily the retreating enemy, who had in fact drenched the woods, caves and dugouts they had formerly occupied, with gas, and rigged explosive shells. The advance guard (F Company) of 9th Gordons reached Ambrief by 4.00pm. By the evening of the 2nd the jubilant soldiers of 44 and 45 Brigades had crossed the River Crise north of Chacrise, and were almost three miles east of the line they had occupied that morning. The division had been ordered to advance in a north-easterly direction, and the forward battalions formed a crescent from Rozières through Ecuiry and Ambrief, and on to Chacrise. After the desperate fighting of the previous days and the difficulties in front of Taux and Buzancy, an advance of three miles, despite intermittent German shelling, and torrents of rain in the evening, was intoxicating for the troops. They had no doubt that their efforts had forced the Germans out of their positions. French cavalry were out reconnoitring the ground in front of their pickets, and Soissons was entered by the French Army that evening.

Units quickly moved in to occupy many of the caves and dugouts vacated by the Germans, not realizing that the Germans had deliberately contaminated them with gas. As a result some brigade commanders and their staffs were affected very badly by the gas and were hospitalized afterwards for up to two weeks. Orders were received to continue the advance the next morning but, in view of the significantly diminished strength of the division, it was decided to relieve the division with troops of the French 17th Division that night. However, part of the 15th Machine Gun Battalion remained in position until the afternoon of the 3rd in order to provide cover for the 17th Division. In addition to providing guides for the new units coming into line, each battalion left five officers and four NCOs in the line for twenty-four hours to assist the relieving troops; this was a considerable improvement on the treatment that the division had received as it had come into the line.

Therefore, despite taking part in three generally abortive attacks, with a very heavy cost in casualties (the division suffered total casualties of 165 officers and 3,351 men, including thirty-four officers and 441 men killed), the 15th (Scottish) was able to end its tour in Champagne on a very positive note. Moreover, the division had established a close rapport with both the French XX Corps and 17th Division. General Gassoins, the commander of 17th Division, was so impressed with the sacrifice of the Scots that he ordered his engineers to erect a special memorial to the 15th Division. This rough stone memorial, a unique tribute from a French division to a British division, was originally placed where the body of the furthest Scottish soldier was found at Buzancy. It now stands within the dignified and peaceful British military cemetery which contains many of the dead of the 15th Division and lies, appropriately, close beside the château in Buzancy. Scottish veterans maintained a warm connection with 17th Division for many years after the war.

The division concentrated at Vierzy over the next two days. In cases where promised transport did not arrive, the soldiers marched to their bivouac areas before being bussed to Liancourt, where they entrained for Arras. By 8 August the division was back in the British zone and fully located around the Houvin Houvignol area, once again as part of First Army.

During August significant reinforcements arrived and some 129 officers and 2,939 other ranks joined to bring it up to strength. Tragically, the division had lost three battalion commanding officers in the brief campaign in the Champagne. Lieutenant Colonel J. A. Turner DSO MC of the 13th Royal Scots was, at the age of only 27, a young and outstanding commanding officer. He was killed by shellfire on his headquarters on 26 July. Lieutenant Colonel G. A. Smith DSO, a volunteer officer commanding the 5th Gordons, was killed on the day of the attack on Buzancy. Lieutenant Colonel H. H. Kennedy, who was a regular officer commanding the 8th Seaforth Highlanders, was also killed by shellfire on 29 July. Lieutenant Colonel Turner is buried in the Vauxbuin French Military Cemetery, just to the west of Soissons. Here, many of the dead of the 15th and 34th Divisions lie in the middle section of the cemetery, sharing the same ground as the thousands of French and German soldiers buried around them.

In January 1919, 45 Brigade was sent to Brussels to participate in a Victory Parade before the King of the Belgians. The weather was appalling and the parade took place in a snowstorm. However, as the men of 45 Brigade marched past the saluting dais in their distinctive tartan kilts and trews, there were cries of 'les Ecossais.' Some senior French officers standing near the King then shouted out, 'The Highlanders, le division de Buzancy.'

Historical Postscript: Some twenty-six years later, both the 15th and 51st Divisions were given the honour, by Field Marshal Montgomery, of leading the British amphibious crossing of the Rhine on 23 March 1945, which led swiftly to the occupation of north Germany and the liberation of Denmark. A few days earlier, taking advantage of the foothold gained at the Ludendorff railway bridge at Remagen, the American 1st Infantry Division, serving in First United States Army under General Courtney Hodges, also crossed the Rhine into central Germany.

The New 34th Division joins XXX Corps in Tenth Army

The history of the 34th Division was symbolic of the national hopes which had driven the British war effort. It had been raised with great enthusiasm in June 1915 as one of Kitchener's New Army divisions composed of 'Pals' battalions drawn mainly from the North-East of England and Scotland, and arrived in France in January 1916. Like the green American divisions, which arrived in France two years later, each of the thirty divisions had twelve infantry battalions, each of about 1,000 men. The men had been workers in mines, mills and factories before volunteering to join with their friends to serve in the same battalions and undergo their basic training. Uniquely these soldiers, recruited from the crowded industrial cities of northern England, came with strong bonds of friendship already firmly established.

As these new soldiers waited for their first battle on the morning of 1 July 1916 they brimmed with confidence. The German trenches opposite had been bombarded for a week by the British artillery firing 1.7 million shells and long saps had been dug under some of the trenches. However, the British just did not possess enough guns for counter-battery fire and less than one third of the artillery was medium or heavy guns and two-thirds of the shells contained just shrapnel, which could not possibly destroy the deep German bunkers or fields of barbed wire. Although huge mines were exploded under the German trenches, the Germans were alerted and the resulting craters became obstacles for the heavily-laden troops to cross. Much of the barbed wire was not destroyed, and the overburdened British infantry stumbled forward into the deadly fire of hundreds of German machine guns and support artillery.

Therefore, despite the long preparations, the first morning of the Battle of the Somme turned into a bloody disaster for the British. Along twenty-two miles of front, thirteen British and eight French divisions had launched their attack. It was anticipated that the infantry of 158 British battalions, roughly 158,000 men, would be able to penetrate the German defence lines and end the stalemate of trench warfare. However, total casualties on that first dreadful day were so great that they became a byword for disaster for a century afterwards: 19,240 men were killed out of total casualties of 57,470.

This tragedy had a wider effect than just for Britain, as the British Army included formations from its Empire and Dominions. The fate of just one unit, the sole battalion of the Newfoundland Regiment, was an extreme example (the Royal prefix was awarded in 1917). The volunteer Newfoundland battalion had been raised quickly and sailed to Britain in October 1914. It served with the 29th Division which, as part of IX Corps, landed at Gallipoli in April 1915. On 1 July 1916 it attacked at Beaumont-Hamel and suffered some 90 per cent casualties within minutes of leaving its assembly trench. Over 500 Newfoundlanders were killed and only sixty-eight men returned unwounded from the 801 who attacked that morning. The battalion was rebuilt and continued in 29th Division, distinguishing itself at Arras and in the later battles of Ypres in 1917 and at Bailleul in April 1918. However, the heavy losses suffered on 1 July affected the viability of Newfoundland as a separate Dominion, and in 1949 it confederated with Canada.

The Battle of the Somme continued for almost five months and eventually involved over fifty British and forty-eight French divisions, resulting in 420,000 British and 220,000 French casualties for an advance of just six miles. There is considerable uncertainty about actual German casualties, but these were estimated at being at least 400,000. This undoubtedly led to manpower shortages in the German Army which, within ten days, was obliged to halt its bloody offensive at Verdun, to the relief of the French Army. General Falkenhayn, the German commander, was eventually dismissed and replaced by Hindenburg and Ludendorff, and this led to the German decision to adopt a defensive posture as they pulled back to their fortified lines known as the Hindenburg Line in February 1917.

The baptism of fire in the Battle of the Somme cost the 34th Division dearly. Its two brigades of Northumberland Fusiliers, the Tyneside Scottish and Tyneside Irish, were cut to pieces in the attack on la Boisselle. Two-thirds of the men became casualties and the brigades had to be transferred to another division while waiting to receive reinforcements. They did not return until 22 August. The destruction of so many fine battalions of volunteers is commemorated by the divisional memorial of a female statue of victory which stands on the high ground at la Boisselle. The division then endured two more years of murderous trench warfare, including participation in the successful battles of the Scarpe in April 1917. In February 1918, some of its original Pals battalions were disbanded, as the division reduced to three battalions per brigade.

In March 1918 the division was back for a heavy pounding on the Somme at St Quentin as it found itself attempting to withstand the centre of the Operation MICHAEL offensive by three German armies, which carved a huge fifty-mile dent in the British front. It was then moved north to recuperate in the quiet Lys valley in Flanders, where it arrived just in time to meet the Operation GEORGETTE attacks on 9 April. The British lost some five miles of territory, but the division fought well, including repelling the first attack on the Kemmel Ridge and garnered much praise for its efforts before it was pulled out of the line to rest. As a result there was enormous surprise, to put it mildly, when on 21 April 1918, the GOC, Major General Nicholson, was informed by the army commander that 34th Division was to be reduced to cadre.

The 34th Division had fallen victim to Lloyd George's surreptitious campaign against Haig. Although Lloyd George did not dare to sack Haig, he disagreed with Haig's policy of seeking to concentrate on defeating the Germans in France. Accordingly he replaced Haig's ally, the CIGS (Chief of the Imperial General Staff, or the professional head of the British Army) General Robertson, with the more compliant General Henry Wilson and starved Haig's army in France of reinforcements. This lack of replacements was not just an administrative inconvenience for Haig and his staff, but thereby threatened to destroy an extremely important element of the morale which kept the sorely-tried men fighting, namely their regimental *esprit de corps*. By February 1918 the Army was forced to reduce every brigade from four to three battalions. The combat losses and shortage of reinforcements eventually forced Haig to disband a total of 145 battalions and, in April 1918, after the two draining German attacks, three divisions were disbanded.

In a swift and sad process, this fine division, with all its accumulated experience and capability, was reduced to cadre. For two weeks the division continued digging emergency defence lines and standing to as the Germans unsuccessfully made last gasp attempts to break through at Villers-Bretonneux and Mont des Cats. Then, by the middle of May, six of the nine infantry battalions were reduced to cadres of ten officers and forty-five other ranks, and the remaining men were dispersed to other units. However, three of the infantry battalions,

9th Northumberland Fusiliers, 11th Suffolk Regiment, and 1st East Lancashire Regiment were not actually reduced but transferred together to the 61st Division, where they became 183 Brigade. By their transfer they replaced three Scottish battalions, which were then moved to 15th (Scottish) Division, and thereby also joined the battle in Champagne. Its two field artillery brigades, three Royal Engineer field companies and machine-gun battalion were not reduced to cadre but posted to other divisions.

The divisional and three brigade headquarters, namely 101, 102 and 103 Brigades, and the remaining six battalion cadres were then used as training cadres for a succession of American and British divisions. A British brigade headquarters was attached to each American brigade and a battalion cadre to each American regiment, with a company cadre attached to each American battalion. Spare units were used to assist and support the training. Training courses were put together with the American officers, to pass on the benefit of the British experience, and a Light Trench Mortar School was established.

The scaled-down headquarters of 34th Division provided an extremely valuable contribution to the training of the new American divisions, which were arriving in increasing numbers in France, but entirely without battle experience. Altogether, a total of forty-two complete combat divisions were mobilized by the Americans, and twenty-nine of those divisions actually reached the front before the war ended. Apart from the first six American divisions, which were rushed to France and then into combat with, usually, only limited training, most divisions followed a deliberate programme of training and battlefield exposure. After six months' basic training the conscripts were supposed to be gradually exposed to frontline conditions in France although General Pershing was wary of them becoming too defence-minded. The 34th was directly involved in the training of three American divisions, 28th, 78th and 80th Divisions.

The value of this transfer of dearly-bought experience was soon tested. The 28th (Pennsylvania) National Guard Division, also called the Keystone Division, was first into action at the Marne briefly in early July, and then played a key role in the Second Battle of the Marne. When the Germans attacked on 15 July, most of 28th Division was deployed several miles back in a reserve position. However, parts of its 109th Infantry Regiment were positioned forward, under command of the French 125th Division, manning trenches overlooking the River Marne, to the east of the American 3rd Division. During a fierce engagement with the German 36th Division, its L and M, Companies became surrounded, and were almost wiped out to a man. The remainder of 28th Division then held the perimeter of the Marne salient for three days, thereby preventing the Germans from expanding their salient southward, and its steady defence earned it the nickname 'Men of Iron' from General Pershing.

The 28th Division supported the 3rd Division in its crossing of the Marne, and then took part in the hard-fought liberation of Sergy on the River Ourcq. It continued advancing northwards and, at the end of the main phase of the Second Battle of the Marne, remained on the Vesle and spent almost a month, from 18 August to 7 September, in bitter fighting with the Germans around Fismes. During its defence of Fismes two companies, G and H of 112th Regiment, were captured by overwhelming German counter-attack forces at Fismette. The 28th Division then moved to the Argonne front, where it was fated to endure more severe combat conditions. Altogether, 28th Division suffered more than 14,000 casualties during its five months in combat, thereby justifying its other nickname, the 'Bucket of Blood' Division.

The 78th and the 80th Divisions were also given British equipment and battle training, including trench experience. Haig wanted to use them to support his own offensives, but on 12 August Pershing asked for the return of these formations which he required for the attacks he was planning. Haig was deeply disappointed. He had already lost to the French the first five divisions which had trained in his sector, 4th, 28th, 35th, 77th and 82nd. Therefore he had hoped to retain the new divisions, but was forced to agree to their move in late August. Eventually he was allowed to train and keep just the 27th and 30th, which formed the American II Corps. The 78th (Lightning) Division took part in the St Mihiel offensive in September, and then joined the American Argonne offensive in October, enduring heavy fighting until relieved by the 42nd (Rainbow) Division on 4 November.

The 80th (Blue Ridge) Division went into the British line near Arras on 18 July and some units participated in the Second Battle of the Somme during August, when it was with the 38th (Welsh) Division. Apart from its 315th Machine Gun Battalion, it was in reserve for the St Mihiel attack. It was then deployed three times for each phase of the Argonne offensive, during which it took each of its objectives, thereby suffering some 6,000 casualties.

The training of the American divisions continued until 27 June when, again to its great amazement, the 34th Division was ordered to reconstruct itself with fresh units. However, its cadre battalions were not replenished with reserves but went on being disbanded or being used for the training of British troops until the Armistice and eventual demobilization. As each battalion normally recruited from a small local town or region, the demobilization of the battalion cadre was a significant event for the communities from which it was drawn.

As a final tribute, each of these cadres of splendid volunteer battalions was presented with its King's Colour, the battalion's ceremonial flag, which was taken home to England by a small party of officers and men. The Colour was then laid up with great ceremony in the local church or cathedral of the area from where the battalion had originally been recruited.

The 10th Battalion of the Lincolnshire Regiment provides a fine example of this proud but sad process. The 10th was one of the hundreds of Pals' battalions raised in 1914 to fill Kitchener's New Army. It was formed from enthusiastic volunteers who had grown up together in the fishing town of Grimsby and was famously known as the 'Grimsby Chums'. It served in the original 101 Brigade alongside two battalions of the 'Edinburgh City Pals' (15th and 16th Battalions of the Royal Scots). The men of these Pals' battalions were all closely bound together. For example, one company of the 16th Battalion was made up of the entire first team, other players, staff and supporters of the Heart of Midlothian Football Club.

After initial training the 10th Lincolns crossed to France in January 1916. However, the battalion was almost destroyed as a military organization in its first action, the attack on la Boiselle on 1 July 1916 during the Battle of the Somme. Despite a week-long artillery bombardment, the battalion was cut to pieces by German machine guns as it advanced. Some 500 men were killed and wounded and only two officers and about 100 men came back unwounded. The battalion was reformed in time to attack at Vimy Ridge and Roeux in April 1917. It advanced successfully, but suffered as it held its positions for many days and, once again, some 450 men became casualties. It was again reformed and took part in the wet and cold attacks at Passchendaele in the autumn of 1917. On 21 March 1918 it was attacked by the first great German assault at Bullecourt on the Somme. It was then moved north to Armentières just in time to be attacked once more on 9 April. The battalion suffered more casualties as it was driven back for ten days, but was not broken. However, given the shortage of manpower, it was decided that it would no longer be rebuilt, and that it should be disbanded. Therefore, on 10 June 1918, a sad Colour Party of 'Chums' returned to lay up its Colour in the St James' Church in Grimsby where there is a memorial to the 810 soldiers who were killed.

By the end of June the new complement of infantry and pioneer battalions had arrived at 34th Division. During the first week of July, its artillery, engineer and machine-gun support units returned. All of the ten replacement battalions were new to France and 34th Division, but these were not newly-trained recruits. The battalions were in fact mainly composed of veteran 'old sweats', being mainly territorial soldiers who had been serving in India, Egypt and Palestine since the beginning of the war. They were now being released back for service in France, while Empire troops, mainly from India, took over their task of fighting the Turks in Egypt and Palestine. The three infantry brigades were then organized as follows:

101 Brigade
   2/4th Battalion Queen's Royal Regiment
   4th Battalion Royal Sussex Regiment
   2nd Battalion Loyal North Lancashire Regiment

102 Brigade
   4th Battalion Cheshire Regiment
   7th Battalion Cheshire Regiment
   1st Battalion Herefordshire Regiment

103 Brigade
   5th Battalion King's Own Scottish Borderers
   8th Battalion Cameronians (Scottish Rifles)
   5th Battalion Argyll and Sutherland Highlanders

Pioneers
   2/4th Battalion Somerset Light Infantry

As before the reorganization, the 152nd (Nottingham) and the 160th (Wearside) Brigades of the Royal Field Artillery, with X.34 and Y.34 Batteries of 6-inch medium mortars, together with the 34th Divisional Machine Gun Battalion and the three light trench mortar batteries provided the divisional fire support. Engineering support came from 207, 208, and 209 Field Companies, and medical support was provided by 102nd, 103rd and 104th Field Ambulances. The division continued to be supplied with its food, ammunition and equipment by its 34th Divisional Train of the Army Service Corps.

The new division had barely two weeks for training and organization before, with just a few hours' notice, it was entrained on 16 July for an unknown destination. This turned out to be the area of Senlis, north-east of Paris, from where the division marched farther east to the Vivieres Soucy area, where, on 20 July, it came under command of General Penet's XXX Corps, part of General Mangin's Tenth Army. On the night of the 21st it completed a tiring approach march from Puiseux through the thick Forest de Retz, where the British 4 Guards Brigade had fought a costly rearguard action against the Germans on 1 September 1914, to Villers-Hélon, the birthplace of Alexandre Dumas. This lay only a short distance from the German front lines, which had just been driven back to defensive positions in the stone-built farms and villages lying close to the road running south from Soissons to Château-Thierry.

As related earlier, General Mangin's Tenth Army had surprised the Germans with its great counter-attack on 18 July against the flank of their salient, and had already driven the Germans back more than seven miles (twelve kilometres). Allied divisions, including 34th Division, were now being committed at a rapid rate in order to exploit this success and prevent the Germans from consolidating their defence. The 34th was therefore ordered to relieve the French 38th Division during the night of the 22nd and to commence an attack early on the morning of the 23rd against the twin villages of Hartennes-et-Taux. Unfortunately, the Allies had been terribly short of additional troops to exploit their initial success, and the Germans had already been given far too much time to bring up reserves and prepare their defences.

The 38th 'Moroccan' Division had stormed forward between the 1st and 2nd American Divisions, from the Forest of Retz at 4.35am on the 18th and, within forty-five minutes, had taken the small hamlet of Longpont, where today can be seen the magnificent remains of a Cistercian abbey. They then advanced a further two and a half miles (four kilometres) and seized Mont Rambœf. The following day they advanced again and took the hamlet of Parcy. In Parcy today there is a somewhat neglected monument to the RICM (*Regiment d'infanterie coloniale du Maroc*), marking the farthest point of its advance on 19 July 1918. There are also monuments to the 38th Division on the

Chemin des Dames, commemorating their key and bloody role in the victories of October 1917 when the Germans were pushed off the ridge.

Tuesday 23 July 1918. The 34th Division opens its attack against Hartennes-et-Taux.
The urgency and necessity for this attack was well understood, but this did not diminish the difficulties faced by the division. Ironically, the 34th was in very much the same condition as the American divisions it had just finished training in that it was virtually a newly-constituted division, with troops new to France and fighting Germans. Added to this local inexperience was the fact that it had spent three exhausting days getting into position, and was required to relieve 'foreign' troops at night and then assault an enemy whose positions were not known as there had been no opportunity for reconnaissance. Moreover the French 38th Division was more 'foreign' than most. It was a favourite colonial division of General Mangin, and included the famous RICM, colonial *Tirailleurs*, as well as a battalion of the Foreign Legion and the Russian Brigade. Serving directly under French command, 34th Division was supported well by the abundant French artillery, but it found communication with the French was a problem, and its own artillery had not been able to get all of its guns forward, and certainly had had no opportunity to register its guns. In any case, the British found the French maps provided were unfamiliar and lacking the detail they were used to.

The lack of preparation was to be felt even more keenly because the newly-arriving Allied troops did not know that already by midday on the 18th, the day of Mangin's opening attack, the experienced staff officers at the Crown Prince's Headquarters had reacted swiftly to the surprise attack. Although six of the frontline divisions had collapsed or been destroyed, they had ordered reserve divisions to move swiftly to the threatened area and instructed Seventh Army to prepare two back lines, strongly fortified with machine guns, on which the hard-pressed German divisions could retire. The first line ran north-south along the line of the road from Soissons through Hartennes to Château-Thierry, and the second was about three to five miles farther east. The Germans were expert in constructing interlinked defensive works and, although the British were being pressed to make a rapid assault, the Germans had already been given more than enough time to construct a virtually impenetrable defence line.

French military philosophy emphasized the importance of the 'cult of the offensive' (*offensive à l'outrance*) to the exclusion of almost all other tactics. It was based on the belief that the enemy could not be defeated just by presenting a strong defence; he needed to be surprised and overcome by the ferocity of the attack, before he could regain his balance. However, the British had already learnt that this tactic was extremely costly in soldiers' lives and the only way to be certain of defeating the dogged German infantry occupying strong defensive positions was by a carefully prepared supporting artillery plan. Artillery fire can be a clinically accurate weapon but unless properly directed it can also be a very blunt weapon. For success, it was an absolutely essential prerequisite for the infantry to establish close collaboration with its supporting artillery, which in this case was very difficult. A further disadvantage was, that being under direct French command, it was not easy to point out that the British had been given no time to view the ground while the enemy had been given ample time to prepare and reinforce his defences. Additionally, only half the British artillery had actually got into position, and even they had no time to register. General Mangin was not a man to brook such feeble reasons for delaying one of his all-out attacks and the divisional history records in typical British understatement that 'the whole proceeding was rather unsatisfactory'.

Despite these very great difficulties, the relief of 38th Division was accomplished in the dark. The two lead brigades, 102 and 101, relieved the 4th Zouaves-Tirailleurs on the left the 8th Tunisian Tirailleurs on the right. They then took up their positions in preparation for the attack which was to commence, behind a strong barrage, at 7.50am on the 23rd; 103 Brigade was detached and sent to Blanzy to act as corps reserve, while General Nicholson retained the 5th KOSB and the pioneers as his divisional reserve. XXX Corps' plan was to launch a powerful three-divisional assault by the French 25th and 58th Divisions on either side of 34th Division. The plan depended on a successful move forward by the French XX Corps on its left, which was to advance across the Soissons-Château-Thierry road and capture Tigny-Villemontoire and Taux, and then turn the enemy flank around the woods north of Hartennes.

Precisely at 7.50am, 102 Brigade, with 7th Cheshires and 1st Herefords leading, advanced through high standing corn, following closely behind the barrage. The high corn made control difficult, but gave no protection from the heavy German machine-gun fire. Nevertheless, the two battalions advanced some 1,200 yards until brought to a halt by the intensity of enfilade fire from the Bois de Reugny and Tigny, which had apparently not been captured. The surviving infantry then dug in.

On the right of the division 101 Brigade was five minutes late in starting behind the barrage, because messages and signals had not got through to its forward battalions, and consequently they suffered appallingly from the German machine guns. On its far right the leading wave of the 2nd Loyals was practically wiped out within the first fifty yards, and their attack was halted. On the brigade's left flank two companies of the Queen's got across the Coutremain-Tigny road, exterminating a number of German machine gun posts, but were then counter-attacked and driven back. Each battalion had been supported by a half company (eight Vickers machine guns) of the 34th Machine Gun Battalion. Due to the lack of progress, the machine guns had not been able to move forward, but took up positions covering the front, where they could at least hold up any counter-attack. The brigade then occupied part of the GMP Line, the original trench line guarding Paris, which had been dug on the orders of the military government of Paris, which ran through their area.

The French divisional attacks on the outer flanks of XXX Corps also made no progress. It later became clear that the three divisions of XX Corps had also been unable to get forward; the losses sustained by the 15th (Scottish) Division in its attack on the Berzy-Buzancy ridge are described earlier on page 212. The only progress to report that day was the 1,200-yard advance by the two battalions of 102 Brigade, which had suffered casualties of some 420 men as the price of their success. On the whole, the 'green' 34th Division had done very well, in its first attack, to make some progress against the vicious network of German machine guns. However, it had attacked precipitately, without reconnaissance and without proper artillery preparation in order to conform to the battle plans of French Tenth Army, which had the prime aim of maintaining the pressure on the Germans. As a result, 34th Division had suffered almost 1,300 casualties for small gain.

The Tenth Army plan for this major attack required that the advance of XXX Corps was to be conditional on the success of XX Corps in actually crossing the Soissons road. Infuriatingly, General Penet had *assumed* that XX Corps had been or would soon be successful, and had given his order for the advance based on that assumption. In fact this major attack by six Allied divisions failed not just because the troops had insufficient time to prepare their attacks, but also because it met a resolute German defence which had been given the luxury of almost four days to solidify its positions.

It was all too obvious that the Germans, after the shock of being pushed back from their advanced positions on 18 July, were putting every possible effort into maintaining a firm defence along the back line covering the Soissons road, which they knew to be an absolutely vital supply artery. Meanwhile their leaders debated what to do with the huge Aisne salient, which they had gained so unexpectedly at the end of May. Ludendorff would have preferred to concentrate on breaking the British in Flanders and recognized the high cost and risk of garrisoning the vulnerable Aisne salient. However, occupation of the salient had been far easier than anticipated and had brought the Germans within striking distance of Paris, and it was difficult to surrender such a sweet prize without a struggle.

Nevertheless, the containment of the GNEISENAU (Matz) offensive in June and the dismal failure of the final FRIEDENSTURM offensive around Reims on 15 July, demonstrated all too clearly that the French military capability had recovered rapidly. The Germans themselves were now weakened and suffering from the heavy French counter-attacks, which threatened to encircle part of von Boehn's Seventh Army. Moreover, time was needed to retrieve the divisions which had expended so much blood crossing the Marne. Even after their withdrawal, the Germans were determined to sell possession of the whole Aisne salient as dearly as possible to the Allies. Retention of the Soissons road was the key to holding on to the salient, and already on 19 July the 19th (Royal Saxon) Ersatz Division had been ordered to make a nineteen-mile (thirty kilometres) forced march from Verdun to position itself by the 20th as the counter-attack division just south of Hartennes. On the 21st the 19th Ersatz Division relieved the German 51st Reserve Division which had been decimated by earlier French attacks. It then remained on the line until the 31st, when it was finally withdrawn, having suffered very heavy attrition.

Wednesday 24 to Saturday 27 July 1918. 34th Division occupies defensive positions in front of Tigny

Having had its poorly-prepared attack halted so bloodily, 34th Division took up defensive positions in its trenches west of the Soissons road where it remained confronting the enemy, largely the German 9th Division, in Tigny and Hartennes, until it was relieved on the night of the 27th. By then, the French 12th Division had finally taken Villemontoire, but the Germans stubbornly retained the small Tigny salient. Tenth Army, although unable to obtain any additional reinforcements, had ordered a new attack by XXX and XI Corps to reach the high ground north of Grand Rozoy, close by the village of Severnay.

The new XXX Corps' attack plan ambitiously required 34th Division to execute a right hook turning movement about five miles (eight kilometres) farther south of its current position. This was part of a two-divisional hooking attack to be executed on Sunday the 30th by the French 25th Division, with the 34th Division on its right. For 34th Division this required two extremely difficult night manoeuvres. Firstly, its forward troops had to be relieved by the inward extension of the two flanking French divisions on the night of the 27th. It then had to withdraw westwards with its guns and take up a hide position in the woods before daybreak. It was then planned to move the division forward on the 30th, to cross the Soissons road and attack the high ground on the Grand Rozoy Ridge. In the meantime, the French XI Corps, on the right, had managed to make significant progress by taking the Butte de Chalmont on the 27th, while the American I Corps, comprising the French 167th and American 26th Divisions, had taken Trugny and was approaching Fère-en-Tardenois. The bottom of the salient was being rolled up and the Allies could detect that there were growing indications that the Germans were preparing to pull back. Therefore, on the 28th, it was decided to bring the Grand Rozoy Ridge attack forward one day to the 29th.

As planned, the withdrawal during the night of the 27th put the British troops in the Bois de Bœuf and the Bois de Nadon by early morning on the 28th. However, bringing forward the attack date meant that 34th Division only had part of one night to make its ten-mile approach march through the woods to a new jumping-off point just south of the Bois de la Bayette. Fortunately they were aided by the provision of knowledgeable guides from the French 5th Division which was holding that part of the line. Some units were shelled as they moved through the woods, particularly the Royal Sussex and the 5th KOSB, who thus only got to the jumping-off point just before Zero hour at 4.10am on 29 July. While this complex manoeuvre was clever and designed to fool the enemy, it left very little time for effective reconnaissance, or to get the artillery properly into position. Only one gun per battery of the field artillery did manage to get into position early enough to register, but the four supporting French artillery regiments were unable to register.

Monday 29 July 1918. 101 and 103 Brigades attack Beugneux-Grand Rozoy.

Although the approach march had been rushed and disrupted by enemy shellfire, the attack still started on time at 4.10am behind a heavy rolling barrage, including gas, which thickened the morning fog. For this advance 102 Brigade was in divisional reserve, less 4th Cheshires in corps reserve, at the western end of the Bois de la Bayette, together with half of the Machine Gun Battalion, 2/4th Somerset Light Infantry and the three engineer field companies. The comparatively fresh 103 Brigade took post on the right with the 8th Scottish Rifles on its far right and the 5th KOSB on their left. Advancing on the division's left was 101 Brigade, with its 2/4th Queen's on its right, alongside 5th KOSB, and 4th Royal Sussex taking the far left flank next to the French 25th Division, and with the 2nd Loyals in support.

The initial part of the assault went according to plan, although to add inconvenience, the German artillery, probably 47th Ersatz Field Artillery Regiment, fired a blind barrage which fell about 200 yards ahead of the start line. The Green Line, which more or less coincided with the GMP, and was about one mile ahead, was taken without difficulty and the battalions re-organized on it, before commencing to advance again at 6.00am. It was later appreciated that they had spent too long reorganizing on the Green Line, thus allowing the Germans time to recover. By 7.00am the Beugneux-Grand Rozoy road had been cleared of enemy and the British came up against the ridge of high ground in and beyond Beugneux. This was considered crucial to the German defence of the area and was stuffed with numerous stubborn German machine-gun teams, who occupied Beugneux, the wood behind and Hill 158.

The 8th Scottish Rifles, despite heavy losses, pushed on as far as the foot of Hill 158. The 5th KOSB passed round the north-west of Beugneux and climbed well up the slopes of Hill 189 where they were surprised to meet elements of A and C Companies of 2nd Loyals, led by Captain Atkinson. The 2nd Loyal North Lancs was supposed to provide support to the Royal Sussex on the left of the division but had become detached during their passage of the woods and had therefore fortuitously decided to seize the crest of Hill 189 at 7.40am. By 10.20am the French 25th Division had occupied Grand Rozoy on the left, but it became apparent that the divisional front consisted of widely dispersed parties of troops spread over the slopes of Hill 189, or held up in front of Beugneux. The 5th Argylls, reserve battalion of 103 Brigade, were sent forward to try to turn Hill 158 and Beugneux from the south, but were halted by severe enemy machine-gun fire.

The reserve 102 Brigade was then ordered forward at 2.30pm with the pioneers of the 2/4th Somersets and a company of machine guns to attack Beugneux from the west, but did not arrive before a heavy German counter-attack drove the British back and the French out of Grand Rozoy. As the left-hand enemy division, 19th Ersatz Division, had been reduced to less than 1,000 effectives and had lost touch with the similarly weakened German 40th Infantry Division on its left, the counter-attack was mounted by two fresh regiments from the Guards Ersatz Division. Due to this very strong counter-attack, the British fell back and began reforming in the GMP line, which they had first reached before 6.00 that morning. Effectively all three brigades were forward, but many units were disorganized. The brigades then shook themselves out, and during the night patrols were pushed forward, and an outpost line established along the Beugneux-Grand Rozoy road.

At 6.00am on the 30th the French re-occupied Grand Rozoy and the rest of the day passed peacefully. It was planned to recommence the attack the following day, but this attack was then postponed until 1 August.

Thursday 1 August 1918. Second attack against Beugneux-Grand Rozoy.
The attack on 1 August commenced with a heavy bombardment of the enemy positions from 4.00 to 4.45am which then changed into a rolling barrage. The carefully-planned heavy Allied gunfire was an important element in the eventual success of the attack, for by this stage 34th Division had suffered some 2,800 casualties and had been reduced to less than 350 effectives per battalion. The 5th Argylls, for example, had just 260 men and only six officers, including the battalion commander, Lieutenant Colonel Barlow DSO, who was to be killed later that day during another attack on Hill 158, available for the attack. The 2nd Loyal North Lancs were commanded by their senior officer, Captain Atkinson, their own battalion commander, Lieutenant Colonel Jourdain DSO, having been killed during the attack on the morning of the 29th. Just to emphasize that shells and machine-gun bullets were no respecters of rank, Lieutenant Colonel Dooner, the chief staff officer

of the division (GSO 1) was also killed on the 31st as he returned from organizing the following day's attack. Together with many other casualties from the division, including five lieutenant colonels, he lies buried in the Raperie British Military Cemetery near Villemontoire.

The Allied artillery barrage was exceptionally strong and well-registered for the attack on 1 August and proved the value of taking time to prepare properly for an attack against a dug-in enemy. The divisional front was covered by 108 field guns and thirty-two howitzers, including twelve heavy French 155mm howitzers, with effectively one gun for every fifteen yards of front. Ammunition stocks had been built up and the guns were therefore able to bombard the enemy positions for forty-five minutes from 4.00am, before switching to a creeping barrage to provide cover for the advance. This was a double barrage of high explosive (HE) nearest to the advancing infantry and timed shrapnel beyond the HE. Smoke shells were also included to add to the cover of the morning fog.

This carefully prepared barrage soon proved its worth in cowing the enemy and helping the infantry forward as 103 Brigade attacked on the right with two battalions up. Because it was so understrength, 5th Argylls had deployed three companies forward for its mission to take Hill 158. The 5th KOSB, who advanced outside the Argylls, on the divisional right flank, had to leave the divisional area and swing through the aviation grounds to make a flanking attack on Hill 158 from the south before moving on to dig in around Point 189. Both the two leading battalions had a company of Vickers heavy machine guns and two companies of the Scottish Rifles in close support. At their second attempt 5th Argylls took Hill 158. The importance of this hill to the Germans was soon clear, for, on its summit, the Argylls captured an enemy battalion commander, his adjutant and two other officers, together with forty soldiers and ten machine guns. However, this bloody attack cost the battalion all but one of its remaining officers, as well as twenty men killed, and it had to borrow two junior subalterns from 5th KOSB for the consolidation phase beyond the objective. There it was joined by the 1st Herefords from 102 Brigade, whose task was to secure the high ground around Point 194. However, the Herefords were unable to make progress before they dug in between the 5th KOSB and 5th Argylls.

On the left of the division 101 Brigade attacked with 2/4th Queen's on the left, 4th Royal Sussex on the right and with the 2nd Loyals, again, in reserve. Each battalion had three companies forward to clear the woods in front of the Grand Rozoy-Beugneux road. The attack through the woods with fixed bayonets, and utilizing one section of 101 Brigade Light Trench Mortar Battery to silence numerous enemy machine guns, was a textbook operation and entirely successful. Fifty enemy soldiers were killed, and almost another fifty were pursued and captured, together with twelve machine guns. By 6.00am, 101 Brigade reported that it was on its Brown Line objective and in touch with 103 Brigade on its right. However, in this position the troops were enfiladed by fire from Hill 203, which, although outside the division's left boundary, was promptly cleared by D Company of 2nd Loyals.

The original plan had been for 102 Brigade, in divisional support, to provide two battalions to follow through the lead brigades as soon as they reached their objectives. It was then, rather ambitiously, to occupy and hold the high ground above the farms at Mont Jour and Bucy le Bras, about 1,000 to 1,500 yards ahead, thereby covering the advance of the two flanking French divisions. But, as already described, the right-hand battalion, 1st Herefords, had been held up in its advance. However, the left-hand battalion, 4th Cheshires, came forward to reinforce D Company of the Loyals on Hill 203, and then attacked le Mont Jour. The Cheshires' attack was successful, but their commanding officer, Lieutenant Colonel Swindells, was killed in the assault, and they suffered additional casualties when a German ammunition dump exploded. However, by 11.00am the remnants of 4th Cheshires could hand over le Mont Jour to the French 127th Division and then withdraw into dead ground.

The line remained stationary for the rest of the day while the battalions consolidated and rotated fresh troops forward. The field artillery had already brought two of its batteries forward as soon as they completed firing their barrage. Gradually all the artillery batteries were brought forward some 4,000 yards and got ready for action again. In the early evening it became clear that enemy troops in the valleys east of Hill 199, particularly in the village of Arcy, were able to fire on the French 68th Division in Servenay, causing them many casualties. Accordingly a new assault was mounted at 7.00pm, under a creeping barrage, which pushed the line forward some 300 to 400 yards in front of 34th Division and part of 68th Division on the right.

The German 19th Ersatz Division had become so severely depleted in the fighting that it had been totally withdrawn on the 31st when it was relieved by the Guard Ersatz Division. However, its artillery brigade remained to support closely the defence of Hill 203 and le Mont Jour against the British attack mounted on 1 August. It had strict orders not to retreat and suffered accordingly as some of its batteries were overrun and stocks of stored ammunition exploded. The remainder were withdrawn that night.

Friday 2 August 1918. Allied advance to the Crise River and withdrawal of the 34th Division.
The successful occupation of Beugneux and the high ground beyond was the last action by 34th Division in the Aisne area. Early the next morning the French 25th Division came through their positions to follow up the enemy who had already begun slipping away in the fog during the night of the 1st. By the evening of the 2nd the Germans had pulled back three more miles to the line of the River Crise and the French had begun to re-occupy the devastated city of Soissons. The men of 34th Division were disappointed not to be involved in the pursuit of an enemy they felt they had beaten but, given their reduction in strength to just 250 effectives per battalion, their withdrawal was necessary. It became clear later, from captured German orders, that the loss of the important ridge north of Grand Rozoy and Beugneux finally induced the Germans to retreat all the way back to the River Vesle. The capture of the key part of this ridge by the British 34th Division, fighting alongside the French 25th, 68th and 127th Divisions, of XXX Corps, was decisive for this withdrawal. It provided a clear example of the success of the combined Allied effort, which also included the attacks on their right by the two new American corps towards the heart of the Tardenois.

On 4 August the men of 34th Division began to move back by bus and on foot to the entraining area, and then travelled by uncomfortable train to Bergues where they had entrained some three weeks earlier. However, there were nowhere near as many of them as had started the journey. The division had suffered grievously, with casualties of 153 officers and 3,617 other ranks, of whom 472 were killed. Significantly, of the thirty officers killed, five were lieutenant colonels. Most of the dead initially were buried close to where they fell, and were reburied later in the Raperie Military Cemetery, near Villemontoire.

The 34th Division, like the 15th (Scottish), had served loyally under direct French corps command and had acquitted itself well in its three major attacks. In a remarkably short time, it had also earned the respect and gratitude of the French. Its first hurried attack towards Hartennes, without the benefit of reconnaissance or proper artillery support, had been an expensive failure and decimated its four assault battalions. If the lesson was needed, it demonstrated the value of preparation over momentum in a static battle against a resolute enemy. The two later attacks against Grand Rozoy and Beugneux had been better prepared and the infantry assault tactics, supported by generous artillery fire, demonstrated how proficient the British could be in the deliberate attack. The message of congratulations from General Mangin to both divisions is recorded in full below (p. 270). His admonition for the country to be proud of its sons was sadly unfulfilled. Few in England and Scotland were ever aware of the importance of these actions in a faraway place, and they were in any case soon overshadowed by the British Army's exciting successes in August and September, which pushed the Germans back to the Hindenburg Line and beyond. Some time later General Mangin also wrote a personal letter to the British ambassador in Paris, in which he stated, 'I ... had the honour of commanding the Fifteenth (Scottish) and 34th (British) Divisions during the decisive battles fought in July 1918. These Divisions contributed largely to the Allies Victory.'

Today, the participation of British units in the Second Battle of the Marne is largely forgotten by local people. The terrain over which 34th Division fought is part of the French National Memorial to the Second Battle of the Marne. The Butte de Chalmont Monument features the haunting sculptures of Paul Landowski, which symbolize both this turning-point battle and the great sacrifices made by all the French people over four long years to drive the German invaders from their soil.

Within weeks 34th Division was back in Flanders with X Corps of British Second Army. It then took part in all the main actions of the series of battles that drove the German army back to the French borders and are known as the 'Final Advance in Flanders'. This began with the Fourth Battle of Ypres on 28 September. The division's last action was under command of II Corps, in the Battle of Tieghem. Following the Armistice, many men were demobilized to return to their industrial jobs in the north of England, but the division went on to occupy Cologne in January 1919. During its war service, 34th Division had suffered a total of some 41,183 casualties.

The British contribution to Victory in the Champagne and its impact on eventual Allied Victory

The Second Battle of the Marne began with the surprise French counter-attack on the morning of 18 July which so astounded the unprepared Germans holding the western flank of its Seventh Army. The issue was then decided, not just by the initial attack spearheaded by the French XX Corps with its two large American divisions, but by constant pressure from the Allies in the following days. Barely two weeks later, by 2 August, the Germans had been forced to abandon Soissons and most of the Aisne salient, and had staged a full-blooded retreat to the Vesle river. The Allies, including eight American divisions had pursued them from the Marne to the Vesle, and continued to press them out of the bridgeheads which they attempted to hold on the Vesle. Indeed, although most fighting had petered out by 7 August, the date usually considered to mark the end of the battle, the remaining two American divisions holding the south bank of the Vesle, the 28th and 4th, continued to wage a bitter battle against the Germans.

Eventually, on 12 August, the 4th Division was relieved by a new 'green' 77th Division which earned its spurs in bitter fighting until relieved by the 8th Italian Division on 16 September. The 77th Division then moved smartly to the Argonne where it was involved in further bloody fighting, including the famous incident of its 'lost battalion'. Mangin's follow-up attack north of Soissons on 18 August, known as the Oise-Aisne offensive, also included the American 32nd Division, which advanced and took the key village of Juvigny on 30 August in extremely tough fighting. This forced the Germans to pull back even closer to the wider Aisne river and finally both banks of the Vesle, from Bazoches to Fismes, were once again in Allied hands.

There is no doubt that the Second Battle of the Marne was first and foremost a tremendous French victory. The French, driven by the leadership and vision of Foch, had provided the overall command structure and most of the manpower and supporting heavy artillery. Despite the German threat to Paris, Foch had ensured that these critical resources were secretly gathered in the thick woods around Villers-Cotterêts. Then, having withstood the greatest of all the German attacks for three days, the French counter-attacked with four of their armies and committed twenty-three of their divisions. Ultimately, this cost them casualties of some 95,000 officers and men. However, the Second Battle of the Marne, like the Battle of the Aisne just six weeks earlier, also saw the substantial involvement of many Allied divisions fighting under French command, and particularly the first really large-scale commitment of American troops.

This was the first opportunity to demonstrate the full strength of the new ally. Over 300,000 American soldiers gathered in the Marne area with nine of their hefty square divisions, together with support troops. The Americans played a major and decisive role as they first helped to halt the German attacks around Château-Thierry, then spearheaded the counter-attack, which put the Germans to flight. In all they suffered at least 30,000 casualties – Pershing later wrote that the casualty figure was 50,000 – as they continued attacking the retreating Germans. Originally Foch had agreed that the first American army should be formed in the Marne area and should command the pursuit of the Germans. However, as the battle progressed, Foch and Pétain soon recognized that it was not going to be possible to entrap the Germans, who retreated far too skilfully. Therefore, having set the German armies in motion, they were content to leave much of their pursuit to the River Vesle to just a few of the French and American divisions. This left the French Army free to continue preparations for attacks in other areas, which they hoped might yield far more strategic results.

It also suited General Pershing to leave some of his divisions to pursue and wear down the Germans as his focus moved farther east. He had already agreed with Foch that he would undertake a major operation by capturing the large St Mihiel salient, near Verdun. In fact this plan developed into the source of a considerable dispute with Foch, who had little confidence in the senior American generals and really just wanted the Americans to continue bolstering offensives by the French armies and not to undertake operations of their own. Pershing persisted with his plan for independent command and refused to be cowed by Foch's demands. Although preparations for the St Mihiel offensive were well advanced, Pershing eventually agreed to keep this as just an interim operation with limited objectives in order to mollify Foch, and to quickly switch to a new major joint offensive in the Argonne.

As a result, the pursuit of the Germans through the Tardenois was left largely to the Americans organized into two new corps. I Corps, under Liggett and III Corps, which, under Bullard, took over from the French XXXVIII Corps on 4 August. The Tardenois operation permitted these two new corps headquarters to develop their command and organizational skills over an extended piece of terrain, against a retreating but stubborn enemy. Such command experience was vital if Pershing was to achieve his ambition of fielding a fully-fledged independent United States army. The new army needed to take its place alongside the headquarters of Allied forces, which had already had four years to hone their skills. It was therefore critical to Pershing's desire for independent command that he had sufficient trained and experienced corps headquarters in order to manage the deployment of his growing number of battle-experienced divisions.

Corps commanders like Hunter Liggett, later commander of First Army after Pershing, Robert Lee Bullard, commander of Second Army, and Charles Summerall, commander of V Corps, had all advanced quickly from commanding brigades at the beginning of 1918. Undoubtedly they acquired experience as their responsibilities expanded. However, given the need to organize the complex military operations of three or four divisions, around 100,000 men, rigorous training was absolutely necessary for the hundreds of staff officers who assisted them. Pershing himself employed 600 staff officers and 2,000 soldiers at his First Army Headquarters.

Valuable staff skills had been taught at the Army Staff College at Fort Leavenworth prior to the war, but only to a few key officers. They were the privileged few who had learnt how to analyse tactical situations and produce the necessary comprehensive orders for movement, logistics and fire support. Accordingly, the AEF Staff College at Langres was established to provide comprehensive staff training in France for the huge numbers of staff officers suddenly required. However, this theory needed to be supplemented by hard experience, which could only really be gained on the battlefield. This real experience was absolutely vital for the expanding American Army, not only for planning operations, but to avoid obvious mistakes, such as bringing heavy artillery up a road incapable of bearing the weight of its guns, and ensuring rapid fire and logistical support through the chaos which inevitably accompanied a major advance.

The Second Battle of the Marne involved huge numbers of French and American troops. Therefore the commitment of the British with just four divisions, representing less than 10 per cent of the assault troops, may appear only a token effort. Indeed many accounts of the Second Battle of the Marne totally fail to register the British participation. However, the British contingent of almost 60,000 troops suffered over 13,000 casualties in little more than ten days of bloody combat, and the eleven British cemeteries found in the Champagne region bear witness to the active involvement and sacrifice of the British in this and the earlier Champagne battles.

Initially Field Marshal Haig had been extremely reluctant to send more of his precious reserves to the French front. His own intelligence services had provided him with ample evidence of German preparations for further heavy attacks on the vulnerable northern front, where the narrow coastal strip between the frontline trenches and the British army's supply ports, was, temptingly, barely a few miles wide. Moreover, he had already experienced the almost total loss of the five divisions which he had sent to recuperate on the Aisne front in May. Therefore he had little confidence that the French would make the best use of his soldiers. Indeed, he received direct instructions from London to recall the four divisions of XXII Corps before they were used. However, as the German preparations for FRIEDENSTURM became increasingly obvious and threatening, Allied unity demanded that he should offer some reserves. Equally there was no gainsaying that, despite some initial French reluctance, the British defence in Picardy and Flanders had benefited enormously from the arrival of French reserves which had helped them to survive the first two German offensives. Under the new Allied Supreme Commander, Foch, the Allies had agreed the principle that providing switchable reserves would serve to nullify the German advantage of centralized control over all their troops' resources, and make them all much stronger.

Certainly, although they represented only a small increment, these four British divisions provided additional resources at a crucial time when there were only limited numbers of French divisions available to be used for attacks to drive the Germans back from the salient they had occupied. In each area where they fought the British divisions delivered a significant impetus to the attack when overwhelming numbers of Allied troops were simply not available. Moreover, they proved to be an extremely useful and flexible asset as they quickly adapted their tactics to the new fighting conditions in the Champagne region. As a result, their capture of key German defensive positions with relatively small numbers of troops was vital in convincing the German commanders to pull back to more easily defended locations.

At first the Germans had benefited from the additional divisions and artillery which they had originally brought to the Champagne area to support their own mighty offensive. However, a major transfer of these supplementary heavy artillery units to Flanders to join the long-planned HAGEN operation had already commenced on 16 July. The Germans were then forced to halt these transfers after the French counter-attack on 18 July, and bolster their defence with reserves hastily brought from other fronts. As the Germans themselves admitted, although they were not actually outnumbered, their troops became worn-down and exhausted by the succession of defensive battles that were forced on them. It was later estimated by French Intelligence that some seventy-five German divisions fought on the Marne compared to forty-five French divisions.

Although the Allies were recovering rapidly from the German attacks they were still under pressure, and it is important to bear in mind that the Second Battle of the Marne was a victory achieved on an Allied manpower shoestring. The commanders of the attacking French armies were repeatedly reminded that no further reinforcements were available to support them, and thus the French were especially reliant on the Americans, Italians and British, who crucially provided almost half the troops for this decisive victory.

Eventual French success on the Marne produced a narrow but stunning victory, which had an instant impact in dislocating key elements of Ludendorff's meticulous plans. In preparation for his long-planned HAGEN attack, Ludendorff had carefully accumulated substantial reserves in the Bavarian Crown Prince Rupprecht's Group of Armies, the Fourth and Sixth, which was arrayed against the British in Picardy and Flanders. By the beginning of May 1918, thirty-two reserve divisions had been gathered, but eighteen of them had to be used when the attacks around the Reims area were expanded in June and July. Despite the disappointing failure of FRIEDENSTURM, Ludendorff remained committed to undertaking the HAGEN operation in late July, and had begun shifting Colonel Bruchmüller's 'battering train' of heavy artillery to Flanders. Then came the astonishing news of Mangin's devastating attack on 18 July. This unexpected and threatening display of French military strength totally disrupted his plans. The German defensive forces were caught off balance and vital reserves had to be despatched immediately to defend the critical Soissons area. The seizure of the strategic initiative by the French affected immediately not only his Marne operations, but also Ludendorff's Flanders plan. Even while continuing with his HAGEN preparations, Ludendorff had also ambitiously planned to maintain pressure with fresh attacks against Reims and Épernay. However, the new French attacks represented such a threat to the divisions trapped in the south of the Marne salient that he had no option but to use all available reserves for purely defensive operations to reinforce the shoulders of the vulnerable salient at Soissons and Reims.

As serious students of the art of war, every German commander dreamed of inflicting a Cannae-type encirclement defeat on the enemy. Perversely this made them over-sensitive to the possibility that such a crushing defeat might be inflicted on their Seventh Army, as actually happened to the German Sixth Army at Stalingrad almost twenty-five years later, and again almost two years later to the German armies at Falaise in Normandy. Therefore the Germans were particularly sensitive to the need to reinforce the vulnerable flanks at the neck of their Marne salient, to prevent the marooning of the bulk of Seventh Army trapped south of the River Marne. In the following days, as the pressure from the French, American and British divisions continued, more reserves had to be despatched and, by 20 July, Ludendorff had no option but to announce the indefinite postponement of his HAGEN attack. Perversely, it was Ludendorff himself, who, by his over-ambition in the Reims area, caused the dispersion of his carefully-hoarded reserves.

Ludendorff's decision became known to the British from prisoner reports within days. It instantly lifted the threat to the British Second and Fifth Armies entrenched around the Lys valley and, as a result, Haig could confidently exploit this reprieve to consider implementing a number of his own long-planned attacks. Freed from the threat of a surprise attack, the five rebuilt British armies were able to prepare their own crushing attacks on the vulnerable German troops occupying the opposing trenches. These troops were clearly vulnerable, as most were occupying lines of temporary trenches and shell-holes in advanced positions with poor logistic support, instead of sitting securely behind the formidable fortifications of the Hindenburg Line.

Perhaps even more importantly, the sacrificial contribution of the nine British divisions was an important element in reinforcing the mutual regard and confidence between the French and British commanders, who usually fought separately and were therefore often suspicious of each other's conduct and motives. Particularly the rapid destruction in May of the five divisions on the Chemin des Dames, and the dogged way in which the British maintained a fighting defence as they retreated through the Ardre valley, with the final stand on the Montagne de Bligny, earned the respect of many French commanders. This was summed up in the rather florid tribute which General Maistre, commanding the *Groupes d'armées du Nord* (*GAN*), sent to General Hamilton-Gordon, commanding IX Corps, recording the thanks of the French for the magnificent defence put up by the British:

> With a tenacity, permit me to say, truly British, you have untiringly reorganised fresh units from the remnants of divisions decimated by the enemy tide. Again and again you have thrown them into the fight, and ultimately they have enabled us to establish a barrier against which the hostile waves have beaten and shattered themselves. This, none of the French who witnessed it will ever forget.

Other senior French army commanders, such as Berthelot and Mangin, also expressed their high regard for the four British divisions which had helped them to drive back the Germans from their Marne salient. General Fayolle, who commanded the army group that included Mangin's Tenth Army, was sufficiently moved to write a special letter to Haig, in which he expressed his appreciation for the services of the 15th and 34th Divisions and included this tribute: 'Both of them by their dash, their courage, and their devotion, have excited the admiration of the French troops in whose midst they fought.'

Regretfully, the brave sacrifices of these men went largely unreported at home, and never generated the same attention and admiration in Britain. The British official historian sadly observed, 'Their share [that of the 15th, 34th, 51st, and 62nd Divisions] ... in the first victorious Allied offensive has been fully and gracefully acknowledged in France, but almost entirely overlooked by their fellow-countrymen'. Not unnaturally, the valiant achievements in the faraway Champagne region were not well reported. Moreover, they were very quickly overshadowed by the success of the great British victory on 8 August and the many successful attacks which quickly followed during the final 'Hundred Days' as the British advanced almost 100 miles against the Germans in little more than three months. In this astonishing feat of arms, and at a cost of some 326,000 casualties, the main British armies, including the four Champagne divisions, retook all the territory lost in the German spring attacks. They then crossed the formidable Hindenburg Defensive Line, captured 189,000 prisoners and re-entered Belgium where the war had begun more than four years earlier.

The Second Battle of the Marne marked an epochal turning point in the course of the long struggle of attrition between the Allies and the Germans. The Germans had made impressive territorial gains during their spring offensives. The first, MICHAEL, and third, BLÜCHER-YORCK, had achieved complete surprise, and resulted in huge salients being driven into the Allied fronts, which seemed to demonstrate the superiority of the German organization, tactics and capabilities against both the British and French armies. However, although the Allies were strategically and tactically surprised, they were not broken, and the surprise effect lessened with each offensive. The second offensive, GEORGETTE, in the Lys valley, also surprised the British initially, but they were able to recover relatively quickly and, although they lost some ground, they were able to block the German attacks before they could break through to the coast. Impressively, the French Army was also able to recover quickly from the heavy losses suffered in losing the Aisne salient and was very effective in blocking both the fourth and fifth offensives towards Compiègne and around Reims. Thus the stage was set for the great Marne counter-attack battle.

Furthermore, as the French and British were to demonstrate so convincingly in their shock attacks on 18 July and 8 August, the combination of surprise and carefully-planned destructive artillery bombardments could work equally well for either side. The attack of the British Fourth Army at Amiens was so surprising, to the Germans, and so successful that it came to be seen as the turning-point battle for the British. It destroyed five German divisions and resulted in close to 40,000 German casualties, including 15,000 prisoners on the first day. In its power and shock it was almost exactly a mirror image of what the German had achieved with their 27 May attack on the Chemin des Dames.

Equally, it was notable that, while these carefully stage-managed assaults could easily overwhelm frontline positions, such attacks usually only made their greatest impact on the first day of the battle. It still remained far harder to maintain momentum across shell-scarred land and to achieve significant breakthroughs against quickly-assembled blocking reserves. Thus the Allied policy of limited offensives repeated across the whole front was far more successful than Ludendorff's independent hammer blows, which were allowed to expand following the line of least resistance, thereby exhausting the attacking troops and allowing time for the Allies to recover. Eventually, the series of controlled British advances actually breached the defences of the Hindenburg Line at the end of September and the situation was reached where the whole pace of Allied advances could be accelerated.

The Second Battle of the Marne resulted in a clear victory for the Allies and the issue was not in any doubt as the Aisne salient was recovered. Official casualty figures were not released by the Germans, but it was calculated that they could not have lost fewer men than they did in the successful Chemin des Dames operation, in which they admitted total casualties of 130,370. It was estimated that the Germans had suffered some 168,000 casualties, including 29,367 prisoners, as well as losing some 793 guns and 3,723 machine guns. Certainly, for the Germans it was a clear defeat as, due to the lack of reinforcements, ten divisions had to be broken up afterwards. It provided a bitter lesson for the Germans as they surrendered almost all of the territory which they had gained in their three costly offensives, BLÜCHER-YORCK (Aisne), GNEISENAU (Matz) and FRIEDENSTURM (Reims), against the French Army. Within ten days the entire military situation had been reversed. The Germans were pushed back to the Vesle river, the threat to Reims was lifted, and the important rail centre at Soissons was liberated on 2 August.

Although this great victory damaged the Germans severely, it was not as cheap for the Allies as it could have been. It has to be asserted that this was mainly because the French generals insisted on attacking to maintain forward momentum when the pre-requisites for quick success were not necessarily in place. By attacking when there was no time for reconnaissance or for the preparation of accurate supporting artillery fire plans Allied units were thrown against well-located German machine-gun nests with only their raw courage to support them, which, as at Belleau Wood, proved a very costly tactic.

Time and time again, Allied units reported being unable to get forward because of enfilade fire from their flanks, which had not been dealt with by their artillery. Moreover, the habit, ingrained from trench warfare, of forming extended lines to advance in unfamiliar country made the Allied infantry easy targets for the German machine guns, which often survived untouched by ineffective artillery barrages. For example, on the morning of 23 July, 34th Division attempted to implement the attack plan of the French 38th Division, which itself had hardly made any progress since its tremendous advance on 18 and 19 July, over ground it had never seen and its two leading brigades suffered severely. The French commanders assumed that the withdrawal from south of the Marne meant that the Germans were withdrawing everywhere, and wanted to catch the Germans off balance. In point of fact, the Germans were far too proficient to be caught off balance for very long. By the 19th they were desperately strengthening their defences, particularly in the two critical areas south-west of Soissons and Reims. As a result, neither the 34th nor the flanking French divisions could make any real progress and the small advance achieved by the 34th cost it almost 1,300 casualties. This was a very significant loss for a single small division to suffer on one morning, even in the context of total losses for the whole battle of some 95,000 casualties for the French, some 13,000 for the British and at least 30,000 for the Americans.

Only in retrospect can we truly see how dreadful and unnecessary was this sacrifice of veteran British soldiers, many of whom had first volunteered for service in 1914. It was mirrored on the first day of battle on the Ardre, when XXII Corps sent five brigades of British infantry advancing against an unknown enemy in the manner of 1916. That assault, without reconnaissance and proper artillery liaison, resulted in the five brigades being cut to pieces, causing the British almost 3,000 casualties within the first few hours. The inevitable resulting shortage of infantry manpower forced the two divisional commanders to be more economical, and to plan better. Consequently, some of the most significant British successes were then achieved with comparatively small numbers of troops. For example, just two days later, a few hundred soldiers of the 5th Duke of Wellingtons resolutely threaded their way through the Bois de Petit Champ and captured forty-one enemy machine guns from the determined German defenders.

The stealth tactics used by both the 5th Duke of Wellingtons and 8th West Yorkshires in their clearing operations in the Bois de Petit Champ illustrated the growth in experience and improvements in training of the infantry, which had transformed the British Army since its bloody sacrifices in 1916. While each British division of 1918 had barely half the manpower of a pre-war division this had been more than compensated for by the huge increase in its firepower. The ready availability of close-support weapons, such as the Stokes mortar, and the abundance of Vickers and Lewis machine guns had transformed its

The British contribution to Victory in the Champagne and its impact 251

attack capabilities. From just twenty-four machine guns in 1914, each British infantry division had, by 1918, acquired almost 400 machine guns, and forty light, medium and heavy mortars. Moreover, despite suffering heavy casualties, the officers and men had become battle-experienced veterans with some four years of hard fighting under their belts.

It is also no surprise that the artillery arm had grown as a proportion of the British Army and, by 1918, numbered over half a million men. In 1914 the BEF had taken just 410 artillery pieces to France, but by 1918 it possessed over 6,000 guns of all types. As the difficulty of reducing the formidable German fortifications had become obvious, the British had deliberately built and expanded their capability from virtually no heavy artillery in 1914 to hundreds of batteries equipped with heavy 60-pounder guns, as well as 6-inch, 9.2-inch and 15-inch siege howitzers. By late 1918 the British Army alone had as many guns as the whole German Army but it also had the advantage of being supported by a home industry which provided abundant supplies of ammunition (in late 1918 industry delivered over 9,000,000 shells per month) and transformed the attack potential. For example, during the September 1918 Canal du Nord operation, the British artillery fired some 3.5 million shells in a week. They had also developed advanced sound-locating and rangefinding capabilities, so that scores of medium and heavy batteries could be used effectively for the vital counter-battery work and to ensure the destruction of enemy strongpoints. What is more, as the artillery generally took fewer casualties than the infantry, the divisional field artillery batteries were manned by increasingly experienced officers and detachments, who were proficient in providing close support to the infantry with their forty-eight 18-pounder guns and 4.5-inch howitzers

Added to those British capabilities, but really outside the scope of this book, was the support provided by the largest air force in the world, comprising both fighters and bombers, and the largest force of battle tanks. This extensive capability was all on show at Amiens on 8 August, when the British opened their attack with 1,386 field guns and 684 heavy howitzers. Incredibly, with no preliminary bombardment, these 2,000 guns aimed to hit at least 504 of the 530 German guns at Zero hour. The surprise attack by seven assault divisions included Canadian, Australian, British and American infantry. It was supported by 580 tanks and over 800 aircraft. The impact of the accurate artillery bombardment was heightened by the presence of the tanks, which spearheaded the assault and, with their mobile fire, rapidly dealt with machine-gun nests. The presence of so many tanks had an enormous and instantaneous impact on the morale of the German defenders, who had virtually none.

While the Germans had also benefited from a huge increase in their artillery firepower, many of these guns were usually too heavy to be used except in a defensive role. Moreover, as General von Kuhl commented, it was often just as expensive in casualties to remain on the defensive as it was to attack. However, following their loss of the strategic initiative, the Germans had little option but to re-adopt a defensive posture. While each German division was proficient at using its 300 machine guns to stitch together a formidable network of death this no longer enabled them to halt the avalanche of Allied attacks, particularly when supported by tanks. The German Army repeatedly demonstrated its competent ability to execute skilful fighting retreats and avoid routs, but this left its soldiers moving in only one direction. Moreover, having retrained to become a skilful attack force, German morale suffered badly after the dramatic failure of their final 'Peace Offensive' on 15 July. German soldiers stolidly reverted to occupying successive temporary defensive positions while waiting to be hammered senseless by artillery barrages, which preceded attacks by aggressive bayonet-wielding, grenade-throwing infantry.

At first Ludendorff found it impossible to believe that his great vision of successive attacks had failed to break the Allies. He knew the German Army had suffered heavy losses, but he also believed that the Allies had suffered commensurately, and he was convinced that he could hold most of the Aisne salient and still threaten Reims, which he considered to be on the verge of surrender. Therefore he pushed in reserves with which the Germans stubbornly sought to establish an impenetrable defence line, based on holding the line of the River Ourcq through Espilly to Marfaux.

However, the courageous assault by British and New Zealand troops on 23 July finally took the nodal village of Marfaux, and the Germans had to pull back to a new line, which ran through the Montagne de Bligny. A supposed counter-attack by German First Army on the 25th was hardly felt by the British, and a further gallant British attack on the 28th captured the key vantage point of the Montagne de Bligny. Simultaneously, the capture by the 42nd (Rainbow) Division of Sergy, just ten miles to the west, forced the Germans, despite numerous counter-attacks, to pull back to a new line running from Chacrise to

Tramery, and then to the Vesle river. Therefore, despite committing reserves, Ludendorff was reluctantly forced, in barely two weeks, to allow his troops to vacate, initially, their small salient south of the Marne and then, finally, the whole of the huge Aisne salient south of the Vesle river.

This retreat was not completely to the disadvantage of the Germans. They had actually improved their defensive situation by exchanging territory with poor communications and vulnerable borders, which required thirty-three divisions for its defence, for a formidable position on high ground fronted by the rivers Vesle and Aisne, which could be manned by just twenty divisions. With some justification, the Germans congratulated themselves on their defensive capabilities. As their spokesman, General Baron von Ardenne, wrote in August 1918:

> On July 15th our attempted surprise failed, and, despite his losses, the enemy's numerical superiority had increased. Then the German command, swift as lightning and without the least hesitation, knew how to find the transition to the now necessary, although momentary, defensive.

However this optimistic German assessment deliberately chose to ignore the fact that their enemies had also been able to reduce the forces needed to cordon the much-reduced salient and, moreover, could utilize the released troops to attack at some other weak point as they exploited their possession of the strategic initiative. In fact, the series of rapid Allied hammer-blows which followed kept the Germans perpetually on the defensive and retreating until only the final Armistice saved them from being driven back into Germany. The Allies quickly demonstrated that the loss of the Aisne salient was just the first of a succession of German losses. Within weeks, other large salients were lost, underlining the vulnerability of the German forces, as the huge Somme, Lys, Matz and St Mihiel salients fell to the Allies. Each loss exacted a heavy price from the Germans, not only in territory, guns, stores, casualties and prisoners, but even more crucially in morale and reputation.

The failure of FRIEDENSTURM and their subsequent defeat in the Second Battle of the Marne damaged German credibility with its own allies, Austro-Hungary, Bulgaria, and Turkey, who, losing faith in ultimate German victory, began to expedite preparations for separate peace treaties with the Allies. No matter how well-organized, victories are not gained by efficient evacuations, and many of their best attacking soldiers, who had been promised a war-ending victory, also began to lose heart and the belief in ultimate victory, which had made their sacrifice worthwhile.

The Second Battle of the Marne also presented the Allies with an opportunity to achieve something they had unsuccessfully sought, many times, during the long years of war. Suddenly they had the prospect of breaking out from the stalemate of trench warfare and returning to a war of movement. With their spring offensives, the Germans had vacated their prepared defences in a desperate bid to attack and take territory from the Allies in the hope of forcing them to accept a negotiated peace. However, once in the open, the Germans were themselves vulnerable to defeat in the field. General Mangin later characterized this aspect of the Second Battle of the Marne:

> This constituted a regular classic battle of manoeuvre. The battle opened with the driving back of the enemy line ten kilometres in the first two days under the shock of a sudden attack. Then he brought up reserves and rallied. After that the objective was clear and definite. It was the eastern end of the long ledge that runs unbroken save by the Saviere Valley from west of Villers-Cotterêts Forest to the region of Grand Rozoy and Arcy. That was the key position of the struggle, as it dominated the north-western plateau toward Soissons, which was the bastion of the enemy's resistance. Once we were masters of that on August 2nd, the enemy's retreat was inevitable. He knew it, too, and the battle was won.

Crushingly for the Germans, defeat in the Second Battle of the Marne, after five significant victories, as the German High Command represented their attacks to their own people, marked the demise of all the German hopes for a battlefield victory momentous enough to force the Allies to the negotiating table. Conversely, although the Allied advances were to be slower and much more deliberate than the original German advances had been, the Allies were confirmed in their belief in ultimate victory although most thought this would not come until 1919. Already, by 24 July, well before the Battle of the Marne was over, Foch was able to convene a meeting of the army commanders – Pétain, Haig and Pershing – to discuss future co-ordinated operations. The first fruit of this new policy was the enormously successful Franco-British attack at Amiens and Montdidier on 8 August, which Ludendorff described as the 'Black Day' for the German army. Some 15,000 prisoners were taken as five German divisions collapsed and Rawlinson's British Fourth Army advanced seven miles (eleven kilometres) on the first day. By the 27th the Allies had advanced more than twenty-five miles and collected 50,000 prisoners and 500 guns. Not only was 8 August a signal victory, but it launched the sequence of Allied victories called the 'Hundred Days' which concluded the war and brought final victory to the Allies.

As this first advance ran out of steam, the British then switched their attacks farther north. Just two weeks later, on 21 August, the British Third Army began a series of attacks which recaptured the Lys salient, including Bapaume, Péronne and Albert. This forced the Germans to vacate the last section of the Amiens salient and pull back to the Hindenburg Line. Even before that, on 18 August, Mangin had launched another offensive on the flank of the Germans holding the Vesle river against the Americans, and forced them to retreat to new defensive positions in front of the Aisne river.

Then, in the following month, as the British 62nd Division once again liberated Havrincourt on 12 September, the Americans firmly demonstrated their capabilities as an organized army. The new First US Army combined the tanks of 304 US Tank Brigade, three American and a French corps to recover the St Mihiel salient. The Germans may have already decided that the heavily fortified salient could not be retained, but they had held it since 1914, and its loss cost them many casualties, including 15,000 prisoners and 257 guns. Moreover, it demonstrated that the Allies now had the capability to pick off any part of the German front at will. By the end of September, the British were breaking through the Hindenburg Line and the Americans were attacking in the Argonne.

By the severity of his attacks against them, Ludendorff had forced the British and the French to co-operate in a way which had been unthinkable in the previous three years of fighting. Even Pershing, although desperate to establish an independent unified command of the American troops, had offered his unqualified assistance to Foch during the spring crisis on 28 March. Following that crisis there began a rapid ramp-up of American initiatives. The first independent attack on Cantigny, at the end of May, was launched with just one regiment of the 1st Division. Within a week, in early June, three American divisions were moved swiftly to help defend Château-Thierry. Then nine American divisions played crucial roles in the Second Battle of the Marne during July and August as they drove the Germans back some twenty-five miles (forty kilometres).

During September General Pershing demonstrated the flexibility of his new American army by launching two major attacks on different parts of the German line. Even while he still had divisions fighting on the River Vesle, Pershing launched another nine American divisions in a bold bid to capture the German salient at St Mihiel. This was accomplished in just three days, but, even before this operation was completed, he had already begun switching his forces to the western side of Verdun. Finally, on 26 September, he committed thirty divisions to the costly and difficult Argonne offensive while, at the same time, providing two additional American corps to aid the Allied attacks in Flanders and Picardy. The offensive through the torturous difficult terrain of the Argonne Forest may not have achieved a great deal in itself – the area lacked strategic cities and it only brought the Americans to Sedan just before the Armistice – but it consumed many German divisions, bleeding them of reserves and preventing them from being switched to other vulnerable fronts.

Initially, Allied military co-operation had been signified by the joint headquarters established at Versailles, but this headquarters had no strategic role and acted purely as a talking shop. Only at the Doullens Conference in March 1918, during the crisis caused by the first German attack, was Foch charged with the co-ordination of the Allied armies. What then became crucial was the willingness of the different national armies to follow the lead of Foch and demonstrate their readiness to make mutual sacrifices.

Nowhere was this multinational effort better illustrated than in the Second Battle of the Marne. Nine American divisions attacked alongside twenty-three French assault divisions, two Italian and four British divisions. Two of the British divisions served directly under French corps commanders and were heavily involved in key actions. The 15th (Scottish) Division relieved 1st American Division and attacked Berzy, supported by a combined American, French and British artillery bombardment. Scottish soldiers recovered the American dead while its own wounded were collected and cared for by the American ambulance service. Eventually it was relieved by French divisions. The 34th Division relieved a French colonial division, which included Tunisian, Moroccan and French colonials, and then attacked three times flanked by French divisions. In the east, XXII Corps advanced through two Italian divisions alongside French colonial troops and

Algerians. Its two divisions were from Scotland and North England, but its corps cavalry comprised squadrons from Australia and New Zealand, and its famous storming of Marfaux was spearheaded by its New Zealand Cyclist Battalion.

The Second Battle of the Marne also signalled the first really significant impact of the growing presence of American troops. The American 2nd and 3rd Divisions had already played a significant role in halting the German advance around Château-Thierry. From the initial action of the 7th Machine Gun Battalion on 31 May to the final capture of Belleau Wood on 25 June, the Americans had displayed an enthusiasm, courage and tenacity which heartened the Allies and discouraged the Germans. Then, as no less than nine of the large American divisions were committed to various stages of the battle, it became clear that the huge German gamble had failed. The attacking power added by the 1st and 2nd Divisions, as well as parts of the 4th Division, at the beginning of the battle on 18 July was crucial to Mangin's initial success, which came as such a shock to the Germans. The 2nd Division had only been alerted at the last moment and needed to march in double time to join the attack. Other American divisions then played a key role in maintaining the pressure by the advances of the French Sixth Army across the Marne and up to Fère-en-Tardenois. This was fighting in woods and open country far removed from trench warfare, and was particularly costly against the concealed German machine guns. Finally the Americans continued to mop up the enemy positions, as the Marne pocket was squeezed up to the new German defence line on the River Vesle.

The ability to adapt formation battle tactics quickly was also an important factor in eventual Allied success. The initial Allied tactics, employed by French, American and British troops, exhibited praiseworthy bravery, but also a lack of preparation for the difficult fighting conditions in Champagne. The abortive attacks on the first day of action by almost all the newly-arrived British units were driven by an anxiety to get to grips with a retreating German foe. As a result, the troops were put into battle quickly, usually without time for reconnaissance and proper artillery preparation. Accordingly, the first day of action produced a high percentage of the total casualties incurred in the whole battle. Advancing steadily in extended line against an unknown enemy, as also the American marines famously did at Bouresches, only really made sense when closely following a rolling artillery barrage, which had to be effective enough to eliminate most opposition, particularly from concealed enemy machine guns.

In the absence of this assistance, or where the barrage was poorly located, infantry units needed to develop tactics such as those which meshed close-up mortar and engineer explosive and flamethrower support with small groups of infantry, as the Seaforth Highlanders of the 15th Scottish did in Buzancy on 28 July. Similarly, on the same day, the 8th West Yorkshires of 62nd Division used small section rushes to overcome enemy machine-gun nests during its incredible assault on the Montagne de Bligny. The skilled intermeshing of support weapons and infantry was illustrated again by the 2/4th Queen's and 4th Royal Sussex of 34th Division on the morning of 1 August. Advancing as platoons and companies, they launched bombs from their light trench mortars to supplement their Lewis guns, rifles and fixed bayonets as they cleared the Forest of Grand Rozoy in just two hours. The difficulty of operating in close country, against such a formidable well-ensconced enemy, is borne out by the fact that, in this wood alone, the soldiers of 34th Division killed or captured some 100 enemy soldiers manning twelve machine guns.

The Germans were determined to hold open the neck of the Aisne pocket while they gradually pulled back the troops trapped in the bottom of it and reinforced their flank defences accordingly. Without fixed defences to fall back on, they fought a brave and determined defensive battle centred on the interlocking fire from numerous well-hidden heavy machine guns as each division deployed its 300 assorted machine guns (see page 152) and 100 mortars. Their stonewall defence was supported by artillery fire and frequent infantry counter-attacks. Usually the Germans wired in their defensive posts so that they were very difficult to approach and attack and many accounts describe German machine gunners being found chained to their guns. The 51st (Highland) Division spent days threading through the overgrowth of the Bois de Courton which, like most French forests, had not been tended for four years as it engaged four German divisions. It reported that it was extremely difficult to get supporting artillery, machine guns and mortars forward in the overgrown woods it was forced to negotiate. Nevertheless, during its initial attacks on 20 July, it captured more than 368 Germans, about thirty machine guns, and eight trench mortars. This included the notable capture of a German battalion headquarters consisting of two officers and fifty soldiers from just one wired-in post in the Bois de Courton. Of course, many additional uncounted

Germans were left dead and wounded. On the following day, its 154 Brigade took forward a single Stokes trench mortar to fire forty rounds at a number of troublesome machine-gun nests, just one of which was subsequently found occupied by twelve dead German soldiers.

In summary it can be claimed that General Ludendorff finally failed in his strategic aims because he became mesmerized by the acquisition of territory rather than by concentrating on his strategic objectives. He had hoped, particularly by his Aisne offensives, to draw reserves away from the Flanders front where he still planned to achieve a significant breakthrough to the Channel coast and a signal defeat of the British army. What he actually achieved by switching his main attacks to the Aisne and Marne areas of the French front was a major diversion of effort from north to south and a weakening of his own reserve strength by three increasingly unsuccessful major attacks. By the time he focused on capturing the key city of Reims it was too late. Even if these attacks had been more successful, they would hardly have helped him to break through in Flanders where the British had been given three whole months of comparative peace to rebuild their forces to the point where, by 8 August, they could begin launching their own series of well-prepared and well-rehearsed assaults.

The Germans were also misled by their own miscalculation of the weakness of the Allies. Particularly telling was the fact that, while Ludendorff's three great attacks on the French army caused heavy French losses, and attracted some Allied reserves, it still left the French Army, bolstered by its Allies, predominantly the swelling American contingent, strong enough to counter-attack on the following day, 18 July, and wipe out most of his territorial gains within two weeks.

A major flaw in Ludendorff's strategy was his reliance on the shock and awe of his battering-train of thousands of heavy guns, mortars and aircraft, which required significant time to move from front to front in secrecy, and thus only allowed him to make sequential attacks. Moreover, maintaining secrecy to enhance surprise meant that thousands of German artillery pieces were forced to remain silent and ineffective for weeks on end. Furthermore, centralizing much of his heavy artillery – close to two-thirds were brought together for each major attack – also reduced the number of guns he had available for counter-battery work when the Allies began attacks across the whole Western Front. Crucially, Ludendorff lost the strategic initiative to an enemy who could attack virtually simultaneously on many fronts. It was an enemy who grew stronger with every battle as he captured guns and prisoners while the German Army, which had already suffered close to a million casualties in the period from March to the end of July, grew perceptibly weaker.

The German introduction of new assault tactics was at first successful but then the Allies learned how to withstand them and subsequently to counter with their own innovative tactics, including flexible defence in depth, and weapons such as their tanks and aircraft as well as counter-battery and barrage artillery. This capability was exemplified by the small-scale Hamel attack on 4 July, which acted as the blueprint for the enormously successful Franco-British attack at Amiens on 8 August. But much worse was to follow in August and September as Mangin created another 'Black Day' with his attack north of Soissons, the Americans reduced the St Mihiel salient, and the British forced a major German withdrawal by their victory at Arras. During September the Bulgarian and Turkish armies were defeated and Austria began suing for peace as its huge empire and army began to disintegrate.

Finally, a second co-ordinated succession of attacks by the Allies along the Western Front began with the French and American attacks in the Argonne on 26 September. On the 27th the British First and Third Armies attacked across the Canal du Nord towards Cambrai. The following day, Plumer's Second Army together with the Belgians and French broke out of the Ypres salient. Then, on 29 September, as the Kaiser met with his War Council of commanders and politicians at Spa to decide future policy, the British demonstrated their ability to use creative tactics. On that day the British 46th Division smashed through the defences of the St Quentin Canal at Bellenglise. Its infantry stormed across this formidable water obstacle wearing thousands of lifejackets borrowed from Channel steamers. The Germans had considered the canal an unassailable part of the Hindenburg Line, and accordingly many hundreds of Germans were trapped in the Bellenglise Tunnel. Bellenglise was just one of a series of co-ordinated attacks by the five British armies, which forever destroyed the efficacy of the Hindenburg Line on which the Germans had lavished so much effort for two years and which, they assumed, made their fortifications impregnable. In his account of that action in *Breaking the Hindenburg Line*, Major Priestley quoted an article by the famous German historian Professor Hans Delbrück in *The Times* of 11 December 1918, where Delbrück linked the rapid deterioration in German fortunes with Allied victory on the Marne:

The turn in our fortunes began with the collapse of our attack on Reims and the successful advance of the French north of the Marne. According to certain observations which had been communicated to me, Ludendorff had then already become very uncertain at heart. Nevertheless he and Herr von Hintze during the next nine weeks did nothing to ease our position politically – until on September 29th Ludendorff collapsed and completed our defeat by the offer of an armistice. [p.79]

When Foch called the Allied commanders together on 24 July he was already quite convinced that the successful attacks on the Marne salient had handed him the strategic initiative. He envisaged that, although the war could not be won by a single knock-out victory, it could be won by a succession of hammer blows even if this took a whole year. On the other side Ludendorff was prepared to admit that his immediate expectations had been dashed, but it took weeks for him to admit finally that he had actually lost the strategic initiative.

Ludendorff had repeatedly promised the Kaiser and the German people a great victory, which would enhance the size and importance of Germany. By the middle of 1918 he could still convince himself that Germany was on the verge of success. Following the Treaty of Brest-Litovsk, Germany had already made enormous territorial acquisitions in the east, mostly at the expense of Russia. He was equally determined that Germany should also have compensation for the losses in men and treasure that it had suffered in the west. At the beginning of July Ludendorff had used his powerful position, and prospect of a great victory on the Marne, to force the dismissal of the Foreign Minister, Richard von Kühlmann. This was precisely because Kühlmann had attempted to put out peace feelers to the Allies which offered the possibility of a special arrangement over Belgium. Ludendorff was adamant that no peace could be concluded that did not leave Belgium, Luxemburg, and even Holland, in German hands, as well as Alsace-Lorraine and part of occupied France. Even after the failure of FRIEDENSTURM he still had hopes of rescuing some semblance of success against the Allies through another advance west of Reims although, as we have seen, these attacks actually came to nothing.

Ludendorff had needed time to absorb the bitter draught of transition from the optimism generated by the prospect of war-winning success in the 'Peace Offensive' of 15 July to the pessimism resulting from a solid Allied victory in the Second Battle of the Marne, just two weeks later. He had drawn so much power and responsibility into his own hands that, when this plan did not succeed, he bore all the responsibility, although he was not loathe to blame others. Such was the pressure on him which followed the failure of FRIEDENSTURM that he frequently lost his self-control. Indeed, twice on 19 July, when Hindenburg sensibly suggested that the only remedy was an attack against the flank of the French counter-attack, he lost his temper with Hindenburg and contradicted him publicly. This behaviour was out of character with their normal relationship and Hindenburg had to remind Ludendorff who was chief. However, this unusual behaviour shows how Ludendorff still clung to his dream and resented any action which would have required a major diversion of precious resources from his pet plan, the HAGEN operation. Barely had Ludendorff recovered from the humiliation of the Second Marne than the British launched their great attack at Amiens which not only resulted in the capture of 50,000 prisoners, but revealed clearly the vulnerable state of German morale.

Still Ludendorff refused to accept that he had squandered the great opportunity which victory in the East had handed him in 1917. By switching the focus of his attacks from front to front he had kept the Allies under pressure, and achieved unprecedented successes with his first three attacks. However, it had required time to marshal his infantry and artillery for each attack, and his enemies had been given that time to learn and recover. In particular, the British Army had been given three months to rebuild its forces from thirty-five to sixty full strength divisions, and it was determined to demonstrate its new-found vigour. Ludendorff particularly failed to appreciate that the attempt to exploit the Marne success by the GNEISENAU operation against Compiègne was a key failure. GNEISENAU failed despite the devastating Bruchmüller barrage, because it was unable to make a deep penetration of the revived French Army and fatally delayed the final FRIEDENSTURM attack.

Further Allied successes in August and early September were just the precursor to the military crisis caused by the overwhelming Allied attacks in late September. Ludendorff bore the full weight of the responsibility for the prosecution of the war, and he had repeatedly promised victory. However, the cascade of misfortune that followed the failure of FRIEDENSTURM was so overwhelming and rapid that the German Army was suddenly faced with defeat in the field as its reserves were committed and lost on every front. Finally news arrived of the defeat of Bulgaria, and Ludendorff fell into a foaming fit of frustration on the afternoon of 28 September. Only at that time did he recognize that the strategic initiative had been irretrievably lost and thus the Germans faced the inevitability of rapid defeat unless they could create a breathing space to rebuild their forces. That evening he met Hindenburg and they agreed that there was no alternative but to seek an Armistice. On the following day, Sunday 29 September, at the Imperial Council of War, a chastened Ludendorff stated that an immediate armistice was necessary. Indeed, he demanded, quite unrealistically, that it be concluded within twenty-four hours. Then Admiral von Hintze, the new Foreign Minister, used the threat of civil unrest to suggest an appeal to President Wilson in accordance with his Fourteen Points, and the formation of a democratic government for Germany, which led inevitably, within weeks, to the abdication of the Kaiser.

Ludendorff continued to delude himself with totally unrealistic expectations. He sought a pause in operations by the Allies which would allow the German Army to rebuild itself prior to resuming combat operations. He seemed to have very little understanding of the political and diplomatic difficulties of the actions he proposed, or the impossibility of the Allies agreeing to his concept. The unpalatable situation was that his five great attacks had irretrievably weakened the German Army and, unless the Allies stopped attacking, the Army was doomed. On the evening of 18 July, when Ludendorff had offered his resignation to the Kaiser, it was rejected. However, when he tendered it again on 26 October the Kaiser had no hesitation in accepting it, and a bitter and disappointed Ludendorff ended up fleeing to Denmark in heavy disguise.

In September 1914 the First Battle of the Marne destroyed all the German hopes of a swift decisive victory over the French. At that time the Germans vastly outnumbered the unprepared Allies, particularly the British, who had joined the war in France with just five divisions. Even though by mid-1918 the Germans were able to field almost 200 divisions in France they were more than matched by the Allies. The British were able to field some sixty divisions alongside the 110 divisions of the French. These were joined by the Americans who, by September, already had twenty fresh divisions in the field and were planning to have forty of their double-sized divisions trained and ready to fight in

France by early 1919. The multi-national success of the Second Battle of the Marne in July 1918 convincingly demonstrated the renewed strength, ability and determination of the Allies, and confirmed their willingness to co-operate for victory.

Tributes to the British Units which fought in the Champagne Battles of 1918

Citations of British Units in the Daily Orders of the French Army for the award of the Croix de Guerre

2nd Battalion the Devonshire Regiment
On 27 May 1918, North of the Aisne, at a time when the British trenches were being subjected to fierce attacks, the 2nd Battalion Devonshire Regiment repelled successive enemy assaults with gallantry and determination and maintained an unbroken front till a late hour.

Inspired by the sangfroid of their gallant Commander, Lieutenant Colonel R. H. Anderson-Morshead DSO, in the face of an intense bombardment, the few survivors of the battalion, though isolated and without hope of assistance, held on to their trenches North of the River and fought to the last with an unhesitating obedience to orders. The staunchness of this battalion permitted the defences South of the Aisne to be organized and their occupation by reinforcements to be completed.

Thus the whole battalion – Colonel, 28 officers and 552 non-commissioned officers and men – responded with one accord and offered their lives in ungrudging sacrifice to the sacred cause of the Allies.

(signed) Berthelot,
General Commanding Fifth Army

5 (Gibraltar) Battery RFA
5 Battery RFA, on 27 May 1918, North of the Aisne.

The 5 Battery, RFA, was subjected from 1a.m. until 6a.m. to a violent bombardment with heavy guns and gas shells and the battery during all these hours continued to carry out without slackening its power, its barrage and counter-preparation with such guns as were not destroyed.

Throughout the night, Captain John Hayman Massey, commanding the battery, continually visited the emplacements and telephone dug-outs, cheering the men and encouraging them to live up to the past tradition of the Royal Regiment and the good old 8th Division.

Shortly after 6.30a.m., the enemy having opened a barrage fire on the main line delivered a flanking attack with his infantry on the positions occupied by the battery, Captain Massey with a Lewis gun and the surviving detachments with rifles at once counter-attacked, supported by Lieutenant Large, then severely wounded, who also had a Lewis gun. 2nd Lieutenant Button, after having destroyed all maps, records and papers, also threw himself into the fight. Unfortunately, this gallant band was overwhelmed by vastly superior numbers. Only three gunners who were unarmed and were ordered to retire, and one with a rifle who fought his way through, survive.

The heroic resistance of this battery had a great influence upon the issue of the battle. Its gallant conduct deserves to be mentioned as an example and does great honour to the 8th British Infantry Division.

(signed) Berthelot,
General Commanding Fifth Army

The award of the French medal to a Territorial battalion of the KSLI was deemed a signal honour. General Berthelot himself came to Shrewsbury on 3 June 1922 to pin the *Croix de Guerre avec Palme* to the Regimental Colour of the battalion. It was said that he had witnessed the assault by the KSLI against the German positions.

Field Marshal Haig was so impressed by the action of the KSLI that he issued the following Special Order of the Day containing an account of the action to be read out in front of every British unit, and ordered that the *Croix de Guerre avec Palme* be displayed on the Regimental Colour:

The 1/4th Battalion of the King's Shropshire Light Infantry, which had been held in reserve, was called upon to counter-attack an important position from which their comrades had just been ejected. With magnificent dash this battalion rushed the hill on which the enemy had established themselves, inflicting heavy losses on them and, in the course of hand-to-hand fighting, captured one officer and 28 other ranks. Thanks to this gallant and spirited recapture of the key to the whole defensive position, the line was completely restored. The dash, energy and intrepidity with which, on this memorable occasion, the 1/4th battalion of the King's Shropshire Light Infantry carried all before it was largely responsible for the retrieval of a situation which had temporarily become critical.

'Bligny' was conferred as a unique battle honour on the 4th KSLI and Bligny Day was celebrated as a 'Regimental Day' on the Sunday nearest to 6 June. It continues to be commemorated and honoured in this way down to the present day within the Rifles, the successor regiment to both the KSLI and the Devonshire Regiment, and the red and green striped ribbon of the Croix de Guerre is worn on both arms of the uniform of all of its seven battalions.

56 Infantry Brigade of 19th Division
The Croix de Guerre with Silver Star was also awarded to the entire 56 Brigade consisting of the 9th Cheshires, 8th North Staffords and 4th KSLI, for its defence of the Montagne de Bligny on 5 and 6 June 1918.

8th Battalion the West Yorkshire Regiment

Fifth Army Staff
HQ, 10 December 1918

Extract from General Order No. 430

The General Officer Commanding the Vth Army mentions in his Army Orders:

8th Battalion the West Yorkshire Regiment

A most distinguished battalion. Under the energetic command of Lieutenant Colonel Norman Ayrton England it took a brilliant part in the fighting between the 20th and 30th July which resulted in the capture of the valley of the Ardre. On the 23rd July 1918, after forcing a way through the thick undergrowth of the Bois de Petit Champs, it carried an important position in the face of sustained fire of enemy machine guns. On the 28th July, 1918, it captured the Montagne de Bligny with magnificent dash though this hill was strongly defended by superior enemy forces, and held it in spite of heavy losses and the determined efforts of the enemy to recapture it.

(GHQ Decision No. 22389 dated 16th October 1918).
GUILLAUMAT
General Officer Commanding the Vth Army

6th Battalion Black Watch (The Royal Highland Regiment)
The general officer commanding the Fifth (French) Army hereby mentions in orders the 6th Battalion Royal Highlanders. This battalion d'elite, under the command of Lieutenant Colonel Francis Rowland Tarleton, has given splendid proof of its dash and fury in the course of several hard-fought battles between the 20th and 30th July 1918. After seven days of furious fighting, in spite of exhaustion and heavy losses caused by intense enemy machine-gun fire, it successfully stormed a wood splendidly fortified and stubbornly defended by the enemy

GUILLAUMAT
General Officer Commanding
Fifth (French) Army

During the First World War, the Croix de Guerre was awarded to a further five British units:

- 9th Bn Tank Corps (later 9th Bn Royal Tank Regiment) – Croix de Guerre with bronze palm – for Souvillers/ Moreuil, 23 July 1918.
- 12th Bn Cheshire Regiment – Croix de Guerre with bronze palm – for Dorian (Salonika), 18 September 1918.
- 7th Bn South Wales Borderers – Croix de Guerre with bronze palm – for Dorian (Salonika), 18 September 1918.
- 12th Bn Argyll & Sutherland Highlanders – Croix de Guerre with bronze palm – for Dorian (Salonika), 19 September 1918.
- 24th Field Ambulance, RAMC – Croix de Guerre with silver gilt star – for St Amand, 22-25 October 1918.

Tributes to British Units after the Second Battle of the Marne.

General Berthelot's tribute to the British Divisions of XXII Corps:
Order of the day No. 63 of the Fifth French Army (translation)

Now that the XXII British Corps has orders to leave the Fifth (French) Army, the Army Commander expresses to all the thanks and admiration which the great deeds that it has just accomplished deserve.

The very day of its arrival, feeling in honour bound to take part in the victorious counter-attack which had just stopped the enemy's furious onslaught on the Marne and had begun to hurl him back in disorder to the north, the XXII Corps, by forced marches and with minimum opportunity for reconnaissance, threw itself with ardour into the battle.

By constant efforts, by harrying and driving back the enemy for ten successive days, it made itself master of the valley of the Ardre, which it has so freely watered with its blood. Thanks to the heroic courage and the proverbial tenacity of the British, the combined efforts of the brave Army Corps have not been in vain.

Twenty-one officers and 1300 other ranks taken prisoners; 140 machine-guns and 40 guns captured from the enemy, four of whose divisions have been successively broken and repulsed; the upper valley of the Ardre with its commanding heights to the north and south reconquered; such is the record of the British share on the operations of the Fifth Army.

Highlanders under the orders of General Carter-Campbell, commanding the 51st Division; Yorkshire lads under the orders of General Braithwaite, commanding the 62nd Division; Australian and New Zealand mounted troops; all officers and men of the XXII Army Corps so ably commanded by Sir A. Godley, you have added a glorious page to your history.

Marfaux, Chaumuzy, Montagne de Bligny – all these famous names will be written in letters of gold in the annals of your regiments. Your French comrades will always remember with emotion your splendid gallantry and your perfect fellowship in the fight.

BERTHELOT,
30 July 1918   Le General Commandant la Vme Armée

General Mangin's tribute to the 15th and 34th Divisions

Ordre General No. 343
(Translation)

Officers, Non-Commissioned Officers, and Men of the 15th and 34th British Divisions – You entered the battle at its fiercest moment. The enemy, already once vanquished, again brought up against us his best divisions, considerably outnumbering our own.

You continued to advance step by step, in spite of his desperate resistance, and you held the ground won in spite of his violent counter-attacks. Then during the whole day of the 1st August, side by side with your French comrades, you stormed the ridge dominating the whole country between the Aisne and the Ourcq, which the defenders had received orders to hold at all cost.

Having failed in his attempt to retake the ridge with his last reserves, the enemy had to beat a retreat, pursued and harassed for twelve kilometres.

All of you, English and Scottish, young soldiers and veterans of Flanders and Palestine, you have shown the magnificent qualities of your race: courage and imperturbable tenacity. You have won the admiration of your companions in arms. Your country will be proud of you, for to your Chiefs and to you is due a large share in the victory we have gained over the barbarous enemies of the free.

I am happy to have fought at your head, and I thank you.

Mangin

Tribute of General Gassoins, Commanding 17th Division, to the 15th Scottish Division

After relieving your Division in the pursuit on the Vesle, I established my headquarters at Buzancy. I found there the traces still fresh of the exploits of your Scottish soldiers, and the officers of my staff were able to see clearly what hard fighting you had to gain possession of the village, and, above all, the park.

Wishing to leave on the spot some lasting tribute to the bravery of your soldiers, I entrusted one of my officers, Lieutenant Réné Puaux, the task of erecting there with the materials at hand, a small monument, emblematic of the homage and admiration of my Division for yours.

This monument has on it a medallion, on which are inscribed thistles and roses, and beneath the words:

> HERE THE NOBLE THISTLE OF SCOTLAND WILL FLOURISH
> FOR EVER AMONG THE ROSES OF FRANCE.

Address by General Mangin to the American Army

Official Address by General Charles Mangin to the soldiers of the American Army, on 7 August 1918
Officers, Non-commissioned Officers, and Soldiers of the American Army:

Shoulder to shoulder with your French comrades, you threw yourselves into the counter-offensive begun on July 18th. You ran to it as if going to a feast. Your magnificent dash upset and surprised the enemy, and your indomitable tenacity stopped counter-attacks by his fresh divisions. You have shown yourselves to be worthy sons of your great country and have gained the admiration of your brothers in arms.

Ninety-one cannon, 7,200 prisoners, immense booty, and ten kilometres of reconquered territory are your share of the trophies of this victory. Besides this, you have acquired a feeling of your superiority over the barbarian enemy against whom the children of liberty are fighting. To attack him is to vanquish him.

American comrades, I am grateful to you for the blood you generously spilled on the soil of my country. I am proud of having commanded you during such splendid days and to have fought with you for the deliverance of the world.

British Units which fought in the Champagne Battles

IX Corps

8th Division

23 Brigade
2nd Bn Devonshire Regt
2nd Bn West Yorkshire Regt
2nd Bn Middlesex Regt

24 Brigade
1st Bn Worcestershire Regt
1st Bn Sherwood Foresters
2nd Bn Northamptonshire Regt

25 Brigade
2nd Bn Royal Berkshire Regt
2nd Bn Rifle Brigade
2nd Bn East Lancashire Regt

Pioneers
22nd Bn Durham Light Infantry

8th Machine Gun Bn, Machine Gun Corps (MGC)

Royal Field Artillery
33rd and 45th Brigades RFA
X8 and Y8 Medium Mortar Batteries RFA
8th Divisional Ammunition Column

Royal Engineers
2, 15, 490 Field Companies RE

8 Divisional Signals Company RE

24, 25, 26 Field Ambulances RAMC

8th Divisional Train, Army Service Corps (ASC)

21st Division

62 Brigade
1st Bn Lincolnshire Regt
2nd Bn Lincolnshire Regt
12/13th Bn Northumberland Fusiliers

64 Brigade
1st Bn East Yorkshire Regt
9th Bn the King's Own Yorkshire Light Infantry
15th Bn the Durham Light Infantry

110 Brigade (Leicestershire Tigers Brigade)
6th Bn Leicestershire Regt
7th Bn Leicestershire Regt
8th Bn Leicestershire Regt

Pioneers
14th Bn Northumberland Fusiliers

21st Machine Gun Bn, MGC

Royal Field Artillery
XCIVth and XCVth Brigades, RFA
X21 and Y21 Medium Mortar Batteries RFA
21st Divisional Ammunition Column

Royal Engineers
97, 98, 126 Field Companies, RE
21 Divisional Signals Company RE

63, 64, 65, Field Ambulances RAMC

21st Divisional Train ASC

25th Division

7 Brigade
1st Bn Wiltshire Regt
4th Bn South Staffordshire Regt
10th Bn Cheshire Regt

74 Brigade
3rd Bn Worcestershire Regt
11th Bn Lancashire Fusiliers
9th Bn Loyal North Lancashire Regt

75 Brigade
11th Bn Cheshire Regt
8th Bn Border Regt
2nd Bn South Lancashire Regt
(*6th Bn Cheshire Regt joined the brigade on 28 May 1918)

Pioneers
6th Bn South Wales Borderers

25th Machine Gun Bn MGC

Royal Field Artillery
110th and 112th Brigades RFA
X25 and Y25 Medium Mortar Batteries RFA
25th Divisional Ammunition Column

Royal Engineers
105, 106, 130 Field Companies RE
25 Divisional Signals Company RE

75, 76, 77 Field Ambulances RAMC

25th Divisional Train ASC

50th (Northumbrian) Division

149 Brigade
4th Bn Northumberland Fusiliers

5th Bn Northumberland Fusiliers
6th Bn Northumberland Fusiliers

150 Brigade
4th Bn East Yorkshire Regt
4th Bn Green Howards
5th Bn Green Howards

151 Brigade
5th Bn Durham Light Infantry
6th Bn Durham Light Infantry
8th Bn Durham Light Infantry

Pioneers
7th Bn Durham Light Infantry

50th Machine Gun Bn MGC

Royal Field Artillery
250th and 251st Brigades RFA
X50 and Y50 Medium Mortar Batteries RFA
50th Divisional Ammunition Column

Royal Engineers
7, 446, 447 Field Companies RE
50 Divisional Signals Company RE

75, 76, 77 Field Ambulances RAMC

50th Divisional Train ASC

19th Division
(The 19th Division was originally stationed as a reserve formation away from IX Corps, but was brought up on 29 May to support IX Corps. 19th Division left the line on 19 June 1918.)

56 Brigade
9th Bn Cheshire Regt
4th Bn King's Shropshire Light Infantry
8th Bn North Staffordshire Regt

57 Brigade
　10th Bn Royal Warwickshire Regt
　8th Bn Gloucestershire Regt
　10th Bn Worcestershire Regt

58 Brigade
　2nd Bn Wiltshire Regt
　9th Bn Royal Welsh Fusiliers
　9th Bn Welsh Regt

Pioneers:
　5th Bn South Wales Borderers

19th Machine Gun Bn MGC

Royal Field Artillery
　LXXXVIIth and LXXXVIIIth Brigades, RFA
　X19 and Y19 Medium Mortar Batteries RFA
　19th Divisional Ammunition Column

Royal Engineers
　81, 82, 94 Field Companies RE
　19 Divisional Signals Company RE

　57, 58, 59 Field Ambulances RAMC

　19th Divisional Train ASC

XXII Corps

15th (Scottish) Division

44 Brigade
　4/5th Bn Black Watch (Royal Highlanders)
　8th Bn Seaforth Highlanders
　5th Bn Gordon Highlanders

45 Brigade
　13th Bn Royal Scots Regt (The Lothian Regiment)
　6th Bn Queen's Own Cameron Highlanders

8th Bn Argyll and Sutherland Highlanders

46 Brigade
9th Bn Royal Scots (The Lothian Regiment)
7/8th Bn King's Own Scottish Borderers
10th Bn The Cameronians (Scottish Rifles)

Pioneers:
9th Bn Gordon Highlanders

15th Machine Gun Bn MGC

Royal Field Artillery
LXXth and LXXIst Brigades, RFA
X15 and Y15 Medium Mortar Batteries RFA
15th Divisional Ammunition Column

Royal Engineers
73, 74 and 91 Field Companies RE
15 Divisional Signals Company RE

45, 46, 47 Field Ambulances RAMC

15th Divisional Train ASC

34th Division

101 Brigade
2/4th Bn Queen's Royal Regt
4th Bn Royal Sussex Regt
2nd Bn Loyal North Lancashire Regt

102 Brigade
4th Bn Cheshire Regt
7th Bn Cheshire Regt
1st Bn Herefordshire Regt

103 Brigade
5th Bn King's Own Scottish Borderers
8th Bn The Cameronians (Scottish Rifles)

5th Bn Argyll and Sutherland Highlanders

Pioneers
2/4th Bn Somerset Light Infantry

34th Machine Gun Bn MGC

Royal Field Artillery
152nd (Nottingham) and 160th (Wearside) Brigades RFA
X34 and Y34 Medium Mortar Batteries RFA
34th Divisional Ammunition Column

Royal Engineers
207, 208, 209 Field Companies RE
34 Divisional Signals Company RE

102, 103, 104 Field Ambulances RAMC

34th Divisional Train ASC

51st (Highland) Division

152 Brigade
5th Bn Seaforth Highlanders
6th Bn Seaforth Highlanders
6th Bn Gordon Highlanders

153 Brigade
6th Bn Black Watch Regt (Royal Highlanders)
7th Bn Black Watch Regt (Royal Highlanders)
7th Bn Gordon Highlanders

154 Brigade
4th Bn Seaforth Highlanders
4th Bn Gordon Highlanders
7th Bn Argyll and Sutherland Highlanders

Pioneers:
1/8th Bn Royal Scots (The Lothian Regiment)

51st Machine Gun Bn MGC

Royal Field Artillery
255th and 256th Brigades RFA
X51 and Y51 Medium Mortar Batteries RFA
51st Divisional Ammunition Column

Royal Engineers
400, 401, 404 Field Companies RE
51 Divisional Signals Company RE

2nd, 3rd, 2/1st Highland Field Ambulances RAMC

51st Divisional Train ASC

The 62nd (2nd West Riding) Division

185 Brigade
1/5th Bn Devonshire Regt
2/5th Bn West Yorkshire Regt (Leeds Rifles)
1/8th Bn West Yorkshire Regt (Leeds Rifles)

186 Brigade
2/4th Bn Duke of Wellington's Regt
5th Bn Duke of Wellington's Regt
2/4th Bn Hampshire Regt

187 Brigade
2/4th Bn King's Own Yorkshire Light Infantry
5th Bn King's Own Yorkshire Light Infantry
2/4th (Hallamshire) Bn Yorkshire & Lancashire Regt

Pioneers:
9th Bn Durham Light Infantry

62nd Machine Gun Bn MGC

Royal Field Artillery
310th and 312th Brigades RFA.
X62 and Y62 Medium Mortar Batteries RFA

62nd Divisional Ammunition Column

Royal Engineers
457, 460, 461 Field Companies RE
62 Divisional Signals Company RE

2/1st, 2/2nd, and 2/3rd West Riding Field Ambulances RAMC

62nd Divisional Train ASC

Total Casualties of the Nine British Divisions in the Champagne Campaigns

The Battle of the Aisne (27 May to 19 June 1918)

IX Corps	Officers	Other Ranks
Corps Troops	26	448
8th Division	366	7,496
19th Division	151	3,460
21st Division	202	4,624
25th Division	201	4,137
50th Division	352	7,240
	1,298	27,405

The Battle of the Tardenois (July 20 to August 4 1918)

XXII Corps	Officers	Other Ranks
Corps Troops	5	104
15th (Scottish) Division	165	3,351
34th Division	153	3,617
51st (Highland) Division	115	2,950
62nd (2nd West Riding) Division	118	3,865
	556	13,887

IX Corps suffered particularly heavy losses in its corps and divisional artillery units, which were located too far forward. XXII Corps had no corps artillery units under command, but did have an Australian cavalry regiment with Australian and New Zealand mounted squadrons and the 22nd New Zealand Cyclist Battalion.

Altogether these two major battles, one defensive and the other offensive, cost the British a very heavy toll of some 43,000 casualties. Of these, close to 6,000 were killed. The losses of the 8th and 50th Divisions were particularly heavy as their units were almost completely destroyed in their Chemin des Dames positions by the Bruchmüller artillery onslaughts on 27 May. Many of the bodies of those killed were never identified and a separate memorial to some 4,000 officers and men, whose last resting-place was unidentified, was erected in the centre of Soissons after the war. This poignant memorial remains an evocative reminder of the sacrifice by so many. The white Portland Stone memorial is carefully maintained by the CWGC and the Municipality of Soissons.

American Cemeteries and Memorials in the Champagne

A visit to the Marne area offers the opportunity to visit the magnificent American Memorial above Château-Thierry, and the two American military cemeteries near Belleau, on the edge of the wood taken by the US Marines of the 2nd Division, and at Fère-en-Tardenois. Taking the Champagne route from Fère-en-Tardenois to Épernay, also makes it possible to see the memorial fountain at Chamery erected in memory of Lieutenant Quentin Roosevelt, who was killed on 14 July 1918.

American Memorials at Château-Thierry.
Within the town of Château-Thierry itself, just on the banks of the Marne, is a large stone memorial to the American 3rd Division, which defended Château-Thierry in the Aisne offensive and during the Second Battle of the Marne. The Memorial is located close to the Post Office and main bridge in the town centre. Also in the centre of the town is the Protestant Church built in 1924 with funds raised by American Methodists. The church has a glass wall commemorating some of the American generals, and the long history of Franco-American friendship.

Towering above Château-Thierry on Hill 204, just off the N3, is the triumphant memorial commemorating the nine US divisions that fought in the Second Battle of the Marne. The Memorial is a huge double colonnade of stone, which towers high above the town, and is an outstandingly impressive marker on the western skyline. It was inaugurated by General Pershing in 1937 and is visible from most parts of Château-Thierry.

Aisne-Marne American Cemetery, Belleau.
Not far from the memorial on Hill 204, is the beautifully maintained Aisne-Marne American Military Cemetery at Belleau, which is located close to the village of Bouresches. On its 42.5 acre site are buried 2,289 bodies, 251 of whom are unknowns. It has a staffed visitors' centre, which provides information about the Memorial and the events of 1918,

when the 2nd, 3rd, 26th and 28th Divisions defended this area against the German Aisne and Marne offensives. The cemetery and its chapel, which was erected on the site of the 2nd Division's trenches, adjoins the 200-acre Belleau Wood, which was renamed the 'Wood of the Marine Brigade'. Located in the wood is the original stone tower fought over so many times, as well as remnants of the trenches that were dug. In the centre of the wood is the Marine Memorial and flagpole, with a display of preserved guns and mortars used by the American, French and German forces nearby. Standing near to the cemetery entrance is also a rebuilt church, which commemorates the 2,700 soldiers from the 26th Division who were killed in the war.

Oise-Aisne American Military Cemetery near Fère-en-Tardenois
At least 30,000 American soldiers became casualties driving the Germans from the Marne salient in the Second Battle of the Marne, which began with the attack by the 1st and 2nd Divisions alongside French divisions on 18 July 1918. Of these some 6,000 were killed and are commemorated by the much larger American cemetery located at Nesles near Fère-en-Tardenois. A burial ground was originally established on this site by the 42nd (Rainbow) Division, and it contains the grave of Sergeant Joyce Kilmer, the war poet from the 165th Regiment. The cemetery now contains some 6,012 graves, 597 of which are unidentified. The graves are laid out in four rectangular plots around a central mall, which leads to the imposing memorial arches and chapel. A further 241 soldiers are commemorated on the Walls of the Missing. The visitors' centre and superintendent's office, is located on the opposite side of the road, and provides an important source of further information about the important events which took place here in 1918.

British Cemeteries and Memorials in the Champagne

The Soissons Memorial to the Unidentified Dead of the Nine Divisions
The 3,987 officers and men from the nine British divisions who gave their lives in the two major battles in this area and have no known graves are commemorated on this large but sad Portland Stone memorial. The memorial stands right in the centre of Soissons, close to the cathedral on the side of the square on the Rue Charpentier. The tablets of the memorial record the fact that the nine divisions fought in the area from May to August 1918, and lists the names of those soldiers, who have no known graves, by regiment.

Buzancy British Military Cemetery
This small well-kept cemetery lies in a quiet sunlit corner of Buzancy, near the château. It contains the graves of 225 known and ninety-six unknown soldiers, mostly from the 15th (Scottish) Division. It also contains the unique memorial to the heroism of the 15th Division that was commissioned by General Gassoins, the commander of the French 17th Division. The Scots had taken the village on 28 July, but lost it to a heavy German counter-attack, and when Gassoins' own division took the village some days later, he was so impressed by the heroism of the Scots that he ordered that a memorial should be erected. Accordingly, a rough stone memorial was quickly built and erected by his engineers containing the following rough inscription, 'Ici fleurie a toujours le glorieux chardon d'Ecosse parmi les roses de France'. ('Here will flourish forever the noble thistle of Scotland among the roses of France.') It is inscribed with the date of 28 July 1918 and is marked as a tribute from the 17th French Division to the 15th (Scottish) Division. The stone was originally placed where the furthest body of a Scottish soldier was found, but now sits within the cemetery, as a unique tribute from French soldiers to the Scottish soldiers who died helping to free their country. There are many fine memorials in France, but this is surely a unique tribute to a British division.

Chaumuzy British Military Cemetery

This small neat cemetery stands on the RD980 road, opposite Chaumuzy, a little west of the Montagne de Bligny. It contains about 400 graves of men mainly from the 19th and 51st (Highland) Divisions.

Courmas British Military Cemetery

This peaceful enclosed cemetery sits at the end of a track, just outside the village of Courmas. It holds 207 graves, half of which are unidentified. Most of the dead are from the 62nd Division, which attacked the Château de Commétreuil on 20 and 21 July 1918.

Jonchery-sur-Vesle British Military Cemetery

In the village of Jonchery, just beside the River Vesle, lies this quiet and remote well-kept cemetery. It contains some 377 graves, mostly of men from IX Corps, who were killed during the German Aisne offensive of 27 May 1918.

La Ville-aux-Bois British Military Cemetery

This lonely and somewhat ugly cemetery, with bunkers still embedded in its boundary wall, lies beside the busy D1044 Reims to Laon road. It contains some 564 graves of men mostly from IX Corps, including many of the 2nd Devons, who fell nearby in their famous last stand at the Bois des Buttes.

Marfaux British Military Cemetery

This neat cemetery lies on a low hillside beside the road running from Pourcy to Marfaux. It contains some 1,129 graves, including fifteen New Zealanders. Most of the casualties came from the 51st and 62nd Divisions, including the 19-year-old Sergeant Meikle VC of the 4th Battalion Seaforth Highlanders. Sergeant Meikle was killed on the first day of the battle, attacking German machine-gun nests in the Bois de Courton. There is also a special memorial to ten of the New Zealand cyclists, who died taking Marfaux from the Germans and have no known graves.

Raperie British Military Cemetery

Located just outside Villemontoire, this remote cemetery contains just over 600 graves, mainly of men who served in the 34th Division, including five lieutenant colonels. In addition, it commemorates the 110 officers and men of 9th Battalion Royal Scots, from 15th (Scottish)

Division, who died on 1 August 1918. They were cut down by enemy machine-gun fire as they stood up in an open cornfield during the abortive attack on Taux.

Sissonne British Military Cemetery
This small cemetery lies in the middle of what was a major German army camp for most of the war. It lies next to a huge German military cemetery and contains some 291 graves, presumably of men who died from their wounds after becoming PoWs.

Vailly British Military Cemetery
Just south of the western end of the Chemin des Dames at Vailly-sur-Aisne, next to the large French military cemetery, is this well-kept cemetery containing the graves of some 650 men. Many of these were killed in the opening battles of the war in 1914, including Brigadier General Neil Findlay CB and Captain Theodore Wright VC of the Royal Engineers, who was awarded the Victoria Cross for attempting to blow up a bridge during the Retreat from Mons. He was killed in Vailly during the first British advance in September 1914. A minority of graves are of men from the 1918 battles.

Vauxbuin French Military Cemetery
South-west of Soissons is the large French military cemetery on the busy N2 to Paris. In its centre is a section of some 281 British graves, including many from the 15th (Scottish) and 34th Divisions. There is also a very large German cemetery adjacent.

Vendresse British Military Cemetery
This is a sunny well-kept cemetery about halfway down the hill from Cerny, near the centre of the Chemin des Dames. It contains some 700 graves, of which about half are unidentified. Almost 200 graves are of the British soldiers who were killed in the first attempts to assault the German positions on the Chemin des Dames in September and October 1914. The majority, however, are men of the 8th Division, killed in the German offensive of 27 May 1918, including Brigadier General Hussey commanding 25 Brigade. It also contains a small stone memorial erected in October 1915 by the French 57th Infantry Regiment as a tribute to their British comrades, which was originally placed in the Verneuill Château Military Cemetery.

Memorial to the Loyal North Lancashire Regiment on the Chemin des Dames

In the middle of Cerny village on the Chemins des Dames stands a classical style column bearing the insignia of the 1st Battalion, Loyal North Lancashire Regiment. The memorial was erected in honour of the 'Lancashire lads' who fought at Cerny in September 1914. Half the officers and men were killed or wounded in this, their first, action. The memorial, paid for by public subscription, was inaugurated in 1923.

Memorials in la Ville-aux-Bois to the 2nd Devons and 5 (Gibraltar) Battery

Close to Pontavert, and opposite the church in la Ville-aux-Bois are memorials to the 2nd Battalion Devons, which was wiped out nearby at the Bois des Buttes, and to 5 (Gibraltar) Battery RFA, which was also overwhelmed on 27 May 1918.

19th Division Memorial on the Montagne de Bligny

Standing close to a track running from the Italian military cemetery at Bligny is a simple cruciform memorial to the 19th Division, which sits almost completely hidden among the trees on the top of the Montagne de Bligny. It commemorates the infantry battalions and support units of the 19th Division who occupied this area in June 1918. It is not really obvious that this simple memorial commemorates the remarkable feat of arms on 6 June 1918 when several hundred men of 56 Brigade, led by Lieutenant Bright of the King's Shropshire Light Infantry, stormed up the hill and took the trenches on the summit from its German defenders, and finally halted the German advance.

The Germans re-occupied the Montagne de Bligny during their final offensive on 15 July. However, it was retaken by the 8th Battalion West Yorkshire Regiment on 28 July 1918, when the 62nd West Riding Division drove the Germans from this area.

The Italian Military Cemetery at Chaumuzy

This evocative and picturesque cemetery sits astride the D980 on the Montagne de Bligny. Its arch proclaims that 5,000 Italians died for France. The Italian Corps actually suffered some 4,375 killed, of whom some 3,040 are buried in graves, with another 400 bodies in an ossuary. There is another Italian military cemetery at Soupir which commemorates the 593 Italians who were killed in the attack there on 1 October 1918.

French Memorials to the Second Battle of the Marne

Sadly Champagne was the scene of intense fighting throughout the whole war and has far too many French military cemeteries and memorials to list them all in this book. The area south of the Chemin des Dames is rich in museums and memorials which attempt to relate some of the history of the great sacrifices endured by the French during more than four years of fighting. If time can be found they are well worth a visit. Briefly the following can be mentioned:

Fort de Condé near Mailly just east of Soissons. Following the defeat by Prussia in 1870, this well-preserved fort was built by General Séré de Rivières in 1883 to defend France's new frontier. It was fought over a number of times and occupied by the Germans after their successful advance on 27 May 1918. Although it quickly became redundant due to the advances in gunnery and shell technology, it is an impressive well-preserved example of military fortress architecture with multi-language displays inside.

The Great War Interpretation Centre at Suippes attempts to provide a realistic impression of the terrors and trials of a soldier's life during the First World War.

The Dragons Cave (La Caverne du Dragon) Chemin des Dames
This well organized museum is located at the eastern end of the Chemin des Dames. It is housed in a large modern building above an old stone quarry, which was transformed by the Germans in 1915 into barrack and hospital accommodation. It provides conducted tours of the underground passages and conveys a vivid impression of the conditions endured by ordinary soldiers in the First World War.

The Fort de Pompelle stands on the RD944 road from Reims to Châlons. This key fort was attacked many times and totally devastated by German artillery but never surrendered. Indeed, even today, it still looks like a battle-torn wreck, but parts of the interior have been restored and house an impressive collection of memorabilia and displays. Its ruined structure is redolent of the violent struggles of 1918.

The French National Memorial to the Second Battle of the Marne at Butte de Chalmont, Grand Rozoy. This official memorial overlooks the valley near where the British 34th Division and the French 17th Division fought on 1 August 1918. It commemorates the sacrifice and suffering of the people of France. Set into the hillside are the evocative statues *les Fantômes* (the Ghosts) created by the famous sculptor Paul Ladowski. France is represented by the single female figure bearing a shield at the bottom of the hill. At the top of the hill are eight figures representing different soldiers as well as death, and in between are the four rising flat stages which symbolize the four long years of struggle during the war.

The French National Memorial to the Second Battle of the Marne at Dormans
A rather more religious monument was created on the southern bank of the Marne in the grounds of Dormans castle. It is a very ornate church-like memorial containing the remains of almost 4,000 soldiers. It has a chapel and gift shop and provides impressive views of the Marne Valley from its terraces.

The French National Cemetery at Ambleny (Bois Roger)
About one mile west of Soissons on the northern side of the N31 is the sadly impressive cemetery of Ambleny, containing more than 10,000 graves. This beautifully kept cemetery remains an evocative memorial to the many French and colonial soldiers killed in this area, particularly during the fighting at Confrécourt and during the Second Battle of the Marne.

The front line ran through the woods in this area for a number of years and extensive caves and remnants of the fighting can still be visited by contacting the Tourist Office in Vic-sur-Aisne.

The Museum and Memorial to the Signing of the Armistice at the Rethondes Site near Compiègne. Farther west along the N31 is the site of the historic November 1918 Armistice signing, which was preserved for posterity after the First World War. In June 1940 Hitler ordered that the signing of the Armistice with France should take place in exactly the same railway carriage as that used by Marshal Foch for the surrender of German forces in November 1918. Afterwards the carriage was removed to Germany and later destroyed. The restored museum at Rethondes has a huge collection of First World War memorabilia and has been reconstituted on the original rail tracks and using an identical *wagon lits* carriage, which has been remodelled to look exactly like Foch's original personal train. The museum is open daily as a poignant reminder of the futility of Hitler's war.

Wolf's Lair 2. The Fuhrer Headquarters at Margival and Laffaux just north of Soissons. (*Wolfsschlucht* 2) Following the abortive Anglo-Canadian landing at Dieppe in August 1942, Hitler ordered that a new secret headquarters should be built in the steep valleys lying just north of Soissons. Hitler planned to use this huge headquarters to command his projected invasion of Britain, to be undertaken as soon as he had dealt with the Russians. Over the following eighteen months, 22,000 workers constructed some 860 structures on the huge nine-kilometre-square site, including some 400 fortified battle and command bunkers. Hitler actually only visited the site just once, when he summoned Field Marshals Rommel and von Rundstedt to a meeting on 17 June 1944 to discuss how to deal with the Allied Normandy landings. This is the only surviving example of Hitler's wartime headquarters and although, over the years, large parts of this site have been vandalized, it remains an evocative reminder of the power of the Third Reich. The buildings are now in the care of an enthusiastic local preservation society which seeks to protect this site and provide regular tours of Hitler's personal bunker and of some of the restored battle bunkers. Visits can be arranged via www.asw2.new.fr.

During the First World War one end of the Hindenburg Line ended at Laffaux and was the scene of much fighting. Hitler was familiar with this area personally, having served there and been presented with his Iron Cross First Class at Soissons in 1918. There is a restaurant and bunker on the side of the N2 at Laffaux where the remnants of a monument to the *Crapouillots* (mortarmen) still stands.

Fort de Malmaison, Chemin des Dames, near Soissons
Just two miles away, en route to the Chemin des Dames, is the rather mysterious ruin of the fortress of Malmaison. It is another of the forts designed by General Séré de Rivières and was completed in 1882 to

guard the western end of the Chemin des Dames. However, after the invention of more powerful explosives in 1884, the French army tested their effect on this fort and decided that the new explosives were so powerful that they had made all such masonry forts redundant. It was therefore abandoned, but occupied by the advancing Germans in 1914. It was retaken a number of times during the war but remains a rather dangerous ruin, closed to the public. Nearby is a very large German Military Cemetery.

Bibliography

History of the Great War, Military Operations, France & Belgium 1918. Brigadier-General J E Edmonds, CB, CBE, CMG. Macmillan & Co. Ltd, London. 1922

The American Heritage History of World War 1. American Heritage Publishing Co. Inc. 1964

The Military History of World War I, Vol 7, 1918 The German Offensives. Colonel TN Dupuy & Julia Crick. Franklin Watts Inc., New York. 1967

The Papers of George Catlett Marshall. Larry I. Bland and Sharon Ritenour Stevens. The John Hopkins University Press, Baltimore and London. 1996

George C. Marshall Interviews and Reminiscences for Forrest C. Pogue. Larry I. Bland Editor. George C. Marshall Foundation, Lexington Virginia. 1996

George C. Marshall. Education of a General 1880-1939. Forrest C. Pogue. The Viking Press Inc., New York. 1963

Life of an Irish Soldier. General Alexander Godley. John Murray, London. 1939

British Fighting Methods in the Great War. Paddy Griffith. Frank Cass, London. 1991

Battle Tactics of the Western Front (The British Army's Art of Attack 1916-18). Paddy Griffith. Yale University Press, New Haven and London. 1994

Command and Control on the Western Front. Don Todman and Gary Sheffield. Spellmount Ltd., Staplehurst, Kent. 2004 (Including: *British Corps Command on the Western Front 1914-18.* By Andy Simpson)

A History of the Great War 1914-1918. C.R. F. M. Cruttwell. The Clarendon Press, Oxford. 1936

The German Offensives of 1918. Martin Kitchen. Tempus Publishing, Charleston SC 29401. 2001

The Warlords Hindenburg and Ludendorff. John Lee. Weidenfeld & Nicholson, London. 2005

Handbook of Artillery: including mobile, anti-aircraft and trench materiel. United States Army Ordnance Department. Government Printing Office, Washington. May 1920

From Private to Field-Marshal. Field-Marshal Sir William Robertson GCB, GCMG, KCVO, DSO. Constable & Company Ltd, London. 1921
To Win a War. John Terraine. Sidgewick & Jackson, London. 1978
Love and the Loveless. Henry Williamson. Macdonald & Co. Ltd, London. 1958
Forgotten Victory. Gary Sheffield. Headline Book Publishing, London. 2001
The British Campaign in France and Flanders Vol. VI: July–November 1918. Arthur Conan Doyle. Hodder and Stoughton, London. 1919
"Monty" The making of a General 1887-1942. Nigel Hamilton. Hamish Hamilton, London. 1981
Memoirs of an Infantry Officer. Siegfried Sassoon, Faber & Faber, London. 1931
The First World War. Hew Strachan. Simon & Schuster UK Ltd. 2003
History of the First World War. Basil Liddell Hart. Cassell & Co., London. 1970
The German Offensives of 1918. The Last Desperate Gamble. Ian Passingham. Pen & Sword Military Campaign Chronicles. 2008
The War to End All Wars by Edward M Coffman, Oxford University Press, Inc, New York Copyright 1968 page 246 also The University Press of Kentucky in 1998
See How They Ran. William Moore. Leo Cooper, London. 1970.
The Kaiser's Battle. Martin Middlebrook. Penguin Books Ltd, London. 1978
Crisis 1918. Joseph Gies. W. W. Norton & Company Inc. New York. 1974
The Defeat of Imperial Germany 1917-1918. Rod Paschall. Alonquin Books of Chapel Hill. North Carolina. 1989.
The Paris Gun. Lieutenant Colonel Henry W. Miller. George Harrap & Co. Ltd, London. 1930
The Great War Generals on the Western Front 1914-1918. Robin Neillands. Robinson Publishing. 1999
1918. Barrie Pitt. W. W. Norton & Company Inc. New York. 1962
The Marne. Blond, Georges.. translated by H. Eaton Hart. Macdonald. London. 1965
Operation Victory. Major-General Sir Francis De Guingand. Hodder and Stoughton Ltd London. 1947
Meine Tâtigkeit im Weltkrieg 1914-1918. General Friedrich von Lossberg. Berlin. 1939.

British Regimental and Divisional Histories:
The Eighth Division in War 1914-1918. Lieutenant Colonel J. H. Boraston CB OBE, Captain Cyril E. O. Box. The Medici Society Ltd., London. 1926
The history of the 19th Division 1914-1918. Everard Wyrell. Edward Arnold & Co. London.
The 15th (Scottish) Division 1914-1919. Lieut.-Colonel J. Stewart and John Buchan. William Blackwood & Sons, Edinburgh. 1926
The 25th Division in France and Flanders. Lieut-Col. M. Kincaid-Smith. Harrison & Sons, London. 1918
The Thirty Fourth Division 1915-1919. Lieutenant Colonel J. Shakespear CMG, CIE, DSO. H F & G Witherby, London. 1921
The History of the 50th Division 1914-19. Everard Wyrall. Lund Humphries & Co. Ltd. The Country Press, Bradford and London. 1939
History of the 51st (Highland) Division 1914-1918. Major F. W. Bewsher. William Blackwood & Sons, Edinburgh. 1921
History of the 62nd W.R. Division 1914-19 Vol II. Everard Wyrall. The Bodley Head, London. 1926
"The Bloody Eleventh" History of the Devonshire Regiment Vol III 1914-1969 WJP Aggett. The Devon and Dorset Regiment, Exeter. 1995
The Astonishing Infantry. The history of the Royal Welch Fusiliers 1689-2006. Michael Glover. 2006
The Devonshire Regiment 1914-1918. C. T. Atkinson. Eland Brothers, 236 High Street, Exeter. 1926
The Royal Hampshire Regiment Vol. 2 1914-1918 C. T. Atkinson. Robert Maclehose & Co. Ltd. The University Press, Glasgow. 1952
The West Yorkshire Regiment in the War 1914-1918, Vol II 1917-1918. Everard Wyrall, The Bodley Head, London. 1926
Regimental History of New Zealand Cyclist Corps in the Great War 1914-1918. By Officers. Printed and bound by Anthony Rowe Limited, Eastbourne.

German Regimental Histories:
Troilo, Hans von, Das 5 Westphalische Regiment No. 53 in Weltkrieg 1914-1919
Schoning, Arthur, Unser Regiment in Weltkriege. Kriegegeschicte des 3 Thuringische Infanterie Regiment Nr. 71
Rudorff, Frannz von, Das Fusilier Regiment General Ludendorff No. 39
Richter, Alfred. Das 2 Thuringische Infanterie Regiment Nr. 32
Das Konigliche Sachsische 13 Infanterie Regiment Nr. 178

Neumann, Gerhard. Das Infanterie Regiment Nr. 343 in Weltkriege 1914/1918
Schmidt, Georg. 2 KurHessisches Infanterie Regiment Nr. 82
Rudolf Binding "A Fatalist at War" 1927

Index

Abbeville, 216
Aillette River, 59
Aisne River and Salient, 2, 17, 22, 26–7, 34, 58–70, 80, 118, 168, 204, 215, 219, 233, 239, 242, 249, 253, 255, 258–9
Aisne-Marne American Military Cemetery, 22
Albert, 255
Albricci, Gen, 148
Alexander, Gen, 121
Algiers Conference, May 1943, 123
Allen, Gen Terry, 114
Alsace-Lorraine, 261
Ambleny, 22
American Army:
  AEF HQ Chaumont, 122
  Army Staff College, Leavenworth, 243
  AEF Staff College, Langres, 243
  Armies:
    Fifteenth Army Group (1944), 121
    First, 92, 118, 122, 243, 255
    First (1944), 120–1
    Second, 243
    Third (1944), 121
    Fifth (1944), 121
    Seventh (1943), 120
    Ninth (1944), 120
  Corps:
    I, 109, 113, 116–18, 234, 243
    II, 42, 105, 226
    II (1942), 119
    III, 96, 109, 117, 243
    IV, 118
    V, 113, 118
  Divisions:
    1st, 4–5, 18, 20, 47, 87, 89, 91–4, 96, 108–109, 112–13, 115, 206, 256–7
    1st Infantry Division (1945), 114, 221
    2nd, 2, 4, 20–1, 81, 89, 105, 108, 115, 206, 257
    2nd Armoured Division (1941), 119
    3rd, 2, 20–1, 77, 81, 102, 105, 106–109, 117, 142, 225–6
    4th, 19, 108
    4th Infantry Division (1944), 113–14
    5th, 91, 103, 120
    26th, 12, 88–9, 109–11, 116, 234
    27th, 42, 105, 132, 226
    28th (Keystone), 19, 107–109, 117–18, 143, 225–6, 241
    29th (NG) Infantry Division (1944), 114
    30th, 42, 105, 132, 226
    33rd, 93–6, 120
    32nd (NG), 108–109, 117, 241
    35th, 19, 119, 226
    40th (Sunshine), 88
    41st Infantry Division (1943), 112
    42nd (Rainbow), 12, 25, 88–9, 108–12, 116–17, 252
    77th (Liberty), 19, 108, 117–18, 226, 241
    78th (Lightning), 225–6
    80th (Blue Ridge), 225–6
    82nd, 19, 226
    83rd, 105
    90th, 113
  Units:
    1st Field Artillery Brigade, 207
    1st Sanitary Train, 211
    7th Infantry Regiment, 21
    7th Machine Gun Battalion, 102–103

10th Field Artillery Regiment, 108
38th Infantry Regiment, (Rock of the Marne), 107–108, 142
102nd Regiment, 110
301st Heavy Tank Battalion, 105
American Legion, 113
Amiens, 14, 16, 56, 117, 197, 254
Amiens, Battle of (8 August 1918), 33, 226, 247–8, 254–5, 259, 262
Anderson-Morshead, Lt Col, 63–4, 70
ANZAC, 16, 40
Ardenne, Gen Baron von, 253
Ardre River, 4, 59, 71, 76–7, 131, 143, 151, 162–3, 167, 172, 175–6, 186
Moulin de l'Ardre, 126
Ardre Valley, 2, 5, 7, 21, 78–80, 126, 128, 147, 150, 154, 157, 170, 183, 185, 199, 247, 250
Argonne, 88, 91, 96–7, 105, 111–12, 120–1, 171, 226, 241, 243, 255–6, 260
Armentières, 227
Aronde Valley, 22
Arras, 10, 14, 56, 59, 198
Arras, Battle of, 134
Atkinson, Capt, 236
Aubilly Ridge, 76–7, 188
Australian Army:
    Australian Corps, 42, 52, 93, 202
    II ANXAC Corps, 48, 127–8
    Australian 4th Division, 93
    Australian 5th Division, 42, 132
    13 Australian Brigade, 56
    14 Australian Brigade, 56
Austro-Hungary, 253, 260
Axford, L Cpl Thomas, VC, 95

Badenoch, Lt, 213
Bapaume, 132, 198, 255
Barlow, Lt Col, 236
Battle Reserve, 56, 217
Bazoches, 70, 117, 241
Beaumont Hamel, 134, 223
Bedell Smith, Gen, 116

Belgium, 123, 145, 169, 248, 261
Belleau Wood, 2, 21–2, 106, 249, 257
Bellenglise, 42, 131, 268
Below, Gen von, 13
Berdoulat, Gen, 205
Berry au Bac, 57, 68
Berthier, Marshal, 37
Bertholet, Gen, 6, 126, 131, 139, 147, 163–4, 175, 180, 196–7, 201, 247
Berzy-le-Sec, 5, 116, 205, 208–10, 232, 256
Beugneux, 6, 235–7, 239–40
Bickmore, Lt Col David DSO, 155
Binding, Capt Rudolf, 26
Bligny, Montagne de, 2, 5, 76–80, 125, 129, 143–4, 170, 180, 186–95, 199–200, 247, 252
Bligny Village, 76–8, 121, 143, 188–90
Bliss, Gen, 9
Blücher, Marshal, 72
Boehn, Gen von, 22, 26, 142
Boer War (1899–1902), 35, 37, 130
Bois d'Aulney, 73, 77, 172, 175–6, 182, 184, 186
Bois de Boef, 234
Bois de Bruyeres, 28–9, 129
Bois de Buttes, 63–5
Bois de Chatelet, 28–9
Bois de Courton, 5, 125–6, 144, 150–5, 157, 165–6, 169, 171, 175–6, 184, 198, 258
Bois de Dix Hommes, 183, 187, 190
Bois de la Bayette, 234–5
Bois de Petit Champ, 157, 159–60, 165–7, 170, 172, 174, 177–8, 180, 182–3, 191, 250
Bois de Rouvroy, 180, 183
Bois d'Eclisses, 78–9, 143, 187, 189, 195
Bois d'Hyermont, 180, 183, 187
Bouffignereux, 68–9
Bouilly, 160–1, 163, 168, 170
Bouleuse, 73–5
Bouresches, 2, 23, 106, 111, 257
Bradley, Gen Omar, 114, 120–1, 123

Braithwaite, Gen Sir Walter, 40, 42, 130–1, 162
Brest-Litovsk, Treaty of, 261
Bright, Lt, 79
British Army:
  British Army and Occupation of the Rhine (1919), 130, 199
  British Expeditionary Force (BEF), 35–6, 42, 65, 251
  Training and Battle Schools, 38
  Armies:
    First, 14, 127, 198, 220
    Second, 43, 45, 49, 52, 105, 127, 240, 280
    Third, 10, 13–14, 52, 200, 225, 255
    Fourth, 93, 96, 105, 131, 197, 248
    Fifth, 10, 13, 49, 51–2
    Fifth Army renamed Fourth Army, 13
    Eighth (1943), 120
  Corps:
    Organisation, 42–3
    1 Army Corps, 37
    II, 36, 240
    III, 96
    VII, 45
    VIII, 40
    IX, 2, 4, 6, 19, 39, 42, 45, 48–3, 54–82, 86, 131–2
    X, 48, 240
    XVI, 105
    XXII, 4, 6, 31, 125–49, 172, 202, 244, 250, 256
    XXIII, 128
  Divisions:
    2nd, 200
    8th, 15–16, 54, 56–7, 61–2, 65–6, 68, 73–4
    15th (Scottish), 5, 14, 115, 127, 202–21, 225, 239–40, 247, 256, 258
    18th, 96
    19th, 2, 54–5, 72–4, 76–7, 79–81, 96, 143–4, 194
    21st, 54–5, 68, 70, 73–4, 81
    25th, 54–5, 57, 64, 68, 73, 78, 81
    33rd, 44
    34th (Tyneside), 5–6, 115, 127, 216, 220, 222–40, 247, 249–50, 256
    35th, 45
    38th (Welsh), 226
    45th (2nd Wessex), 133
    46th (North Midland), 42, 131–2, 260
    49th (1st West Riding), 131
    50th (Northumberland), 54–7, 61, 66–8, 73, 80–1
    51st (Highland), 4, 127, 131, 134–5, 151–201, 221, 247, 258
    52nd (Lowland), 202–203
    55th (West Lancashire), 15, 99, 134
    61st, 225
    62nd (2nd West Riding), 4, 42, 127, 131–3, 150–201, 247
  Brigades:
    4th Guards Bde, 229
    7 Bde, 69, 73–5
    21 Independent Bde, 74
    23 Bde, 63, 70, 73
    24 Bde, 62
    25 Bde, 62
    44 Bde, 203, 212, 214–15, 217–19
    45 Bde, 204, 207, 212, 214, 217–19, 221
    46 Bde, 204, 207, 212, 215–18
    56 Bde, 74–5, 77–8
    57 Bde, 72, 75, 77
    58 Bde, 72–3, 75
    74 Bde, 66, 69, 71, 73–6
    75 Bde, 69, 71, 73–4
    104 Inf Bde, 45
    112 Inf Bde, 44
    149 Bde, 66
    150 Bde, 67
    151 Bde, 67
    152 Bde, 151, 155, 165–6, 172, 185, 189

153 Bde, 151, 154–5, 165–6, 172, 175, 185
154 Bde, 151, 154–6, 166, 172, 175–6, 182
183 Bde, 225
185 Bde, 129, 133, 157, 159, 162–3, 167, 190, 193
186 Bde, 133, 161, 167, 172, 177, 179, 189, 194, 196
187 Bde, 133, 157–8, 160–1, 167, 185, 188, 194
Tyneside Scottish Bde, Northumberland Fusiliers, 223
Tyneside Irish Bde, Northumberland Fusiliers, 223

Units:
5th Bn Argyll and Sutherland Highlanders, 236–7
7th Bn Argyll and Sutherland Highlanders, 137, 156, 175–6, 182, 184, 195
8th Bn Argyll and Sutherland Highlanders, 207–208, 211
4/5th Bn Black Watch, 6, 213–14, 218
6th Bn Black Watch, 151, 154, 172, 190, 194–5, 199
7th Bn Black Watch, 151, 171–2
8th Bn Cameronians (Scottish Rifles), 235, 237
10th Bn Cameronians (Scottish Rifles), 207–208, 211–12, 217
4th Bn Cheshire Regt, 235
7th Bn Cheshire Regt, 231
9th Bn Cheshire Regt, 78–9
2nd Bn Devonshire Regt, 63–4, 70
5th Bn Devonshire Regt, 133, 158–9, 163, 174, 191–2, 194, 199
2/4th Bn Duke of Wellington's Regt, 162
5th Bn Duke of Wellington's Regt, 162, 172–4, 200, 250
5th Bn Durham Light Infantry, 66–7
6th Bn Durham Light Infantry, 66–7
7th Bn Durham Light Infantry, 66–7
9th Bn Durham Light Infantry, 133, 167, 177, 179
1st Bn East Lancs Regt, 225
Gloucestershire Regt, 99
8th Bn Gloucestershire Regt, 78
4th Bn Gordon Highlanders, 155, 190, 195
5th Bn Gordon Highlanders, 214, 218
6th Bn Gordon Highlanders, 165–6, 175
7th Bn Gordon Highlanders, 151, 170, 190
9th Bn Gordon Highlanders, 6, 219
2/4th Bn Hampshire Regt, 132, 158, 177–8,
1st Bn Herefordshire Regt, 231, 237–8
5th Bn King's Own Scottish Borderers (KOSB), 234–5, 237
7/8th Bn King's Own Scottish Borderers (KOSB), 207–208, 211–12, 217
2/4th Bn King's Own Yorkshire Light Infantry (KOYLI), 161
5th Bn King's Own Yorkshire Light Infantry (KOYLI), 160
4th Bn King's Shropshire Light Infantry (KSLI), 79, 193
2nd Bn Loyal North Lancashire Regt, 232, 235–8
10th Bn Lincolnshire Regt, 227–8
1st Bn Northamptonshire Regt, 62

Index   303

4th Bn Northumberland Fusiliers, 66
5th Bn Northumberland Fusiliers, 66
6th Bn Northumberland Fusiliers, 66
9th Bn Northumberland Fusiliers, 225
8th Bn North Staffordshire Regt, 78
6th Bn Queen's Own Cameron Highlanders, 207, 209, 217
1st Bn Queen's Royal (West Surrey) Regt, 45
2/4th Bn Queen's Royal (West Surrey) Regt, 232, 235, 237, 258
8th Bn Royal Scots, 176
9th Bn Royal Scots, 207, 216–18
13th Bn Royal Scots, 207, 212, 217
15th Bn Royal Scots, 227
16th Bn Royal Scots, 227
4th Bn Royal Sussex Regt, 234–5, 237, 258
1st Bn Royal Warwickshire Fusiliers, 44
9th Bn Royal Welch Fusiliers, 78
4th Bn Seaforth Highlanders, 151, 154–5
5th Bn Seaforth Highlanders, 175, 182, 184
6th Bn Seaforth Highlanders, 155, 165, 175, 182
8th Bn Seaforth Highlanders, 212–14
Somerset Light Infantry, 130
2/4th Bn Somerset Light Infantry, 236
5th Bn South Wales Borderers, 76
11th Bn Suffolk Regt, 225
9th Bn Welch Regt, 78
2/5th Bn West Yorkshire Regt, 158, 163, 167, 191, 193, 195

8th Bn West Yorkshire Regt, 5–6, 129, 158–9, 163, 174, 181, 191–4, 199, 250, 258
2nd Bn Wiltshire Regt, 73
10th Bn Worcestershire Regt, 78
2/4th (Hallamshire) Bn Yorkshire & Lancashire Regt, 160–1, 167
XXII Corps Mounted Regt, 187–8, 196
Australian Light Horse Regt, 187–8
New Zealand Otago Mounted Regt, 187–8, 192
New Zealand Corps Cyclist Battalion, 5, 128–9, 172, 178–0, 196
41 Bde RGA, 57, 68
70 Bde RFA, 204
71 Bde RFA, 204
77 Bde RGA, 57, 68
110 Bde RFA, 68
112 Bde RFA, 69
152 Bde RFA, 228
160 Bde RFA, 228
250 Bde RFA, 67
251 Bde RFA, 67
255 Bde RFA, 156, 189
256 Bde RFA, 156
310 Bde RFA, 195
312 Bde RFA, 191, 195
5th (Gibraltar) Bty, 45 Bde RFA, 65
IX Corps Cyclist Bn, 72
15th MG Bn, 219
34th MG Bn, 232
91 Field Coy, RE, 212
Broodseinde, 50, 127
Bruchmüller, Col George, 12–13, 15, 17, 22, 24–6, 28, 61, 107–108, 138, 141, 245, 261
Brussels, 221
Buckle, Lt Col, 62–5
Buckle, Maj Gen, 63
Bulgaria, 253, 260, 263
Bulge, Battle of the, 121
Bullard, Maj Gen Robert Lee, 90–1, 243

Burma, 130
Burnett, Brig Gen, 172, 179
Butte de Chalmont, 234, 240
Butte de l'Edmond, 66,
Buzancy, 5, 116, 207, 211–15, 218–19, 232, 258
Byng, Gen Julian, 13, 39–40

Cadorno, 8
Californie Plateau, 57, 67
Cambrai, Battle of, 11, 134, 140
Campbell King, Lt Col, 90
Canada:
 Canadian Corps, 39, 41, 198, 202
 4th Canadian Division, 138
 Confederation with Newfoundland, 223
Canal du Nord, 201
Canterbury, 127
Cantigny, 18, 47
 Battle of, 91, 95–6, 255
Caporetto, 8, 11, 143
Carter-Campbell, Gen, 162
Chalons, 3, 24, 31–2, 54, 72, 83, 139, 184, 196
Chambrecy, 72, 76–7, 125, 181, 188–9, 194, 198
Champagne region, 1–2, 5, 40, 54, 81, 85, 99, 111, 129, 135, 138, 168, 170, 179, 199, 220, 240, 244–8, 257
Champlat, 143
Chandon, Comte de, 139
Chantereine, 77
Château de Commétreuil, 160, 163, 165–6, 170, 180–1
Château-Thierry, 2–6, 20, 29, 32, 81, 102–103, 105, 109, 111, 115–16, 142, 147, 206, 212, 229–30, 255, 257
Chaudardes, 66–7
Chaumont, 91
Chaumuzy, 72, 79, 144, 150, 155, 158, 188–90, 191, 195
Chaumuzy British Military Cemetery, 80

Chemin des Dames, 2, 17, 41, 44, 57–60, 86, 110, 169–70, 230, 247–9
Chipilly Spur, 96
Clark, Gen Mark, 121–2
Clarke, 2nd Lt, 64
Clemenceau, 47, 141
Clermont-sur-Oise, 104, 204
Coemy, 72, 74
Coeuvres, 205
Colenso, 203
Colville-sur-Mer American Military Cemetery, 114
Cologne, 240
Compiègne, 22–3, 248, 261
Concevreux, 68–9
Courmas, 151, 157, 160–1, 170
Craonne, 58
Crépy, 27
Crise River, 6, 207–208, 214, 219, 239
Croix de Guerre, 6, 65, 79, 194, 198, 217
Cuitron, 157, 159, 177–8, 182–3, 195

Dalziel, Pte Henry, VC, 95
DAN (*Detachement d'Armée de Nord*), 53
De Ravel, Lt, 177–9
Debeney, Gen, 93
Degoutte, Gen, 116, 147
Delbrück, Prof Hans, 260
Denmark, 221
Der Marwitz, Gen von, 13
Derbyshire, Lt, 79
Dickman, Gen, 113
Donovan, Gen William, 110
Dooner, Lt Col, 236–7
Dora Stellung, 182
Dormans, 3, 29, 68, 74, 106
Doullens, 132, 139
Duchêne, Gen Denis, 17–18, 57–8, 61, 67, 73
Dumas, Alexander, 229
Dunkirk, 216

Ecueil Farm, 195

Edinburgh City Pals, 227
Edwards, Gen Clarence, 110–11
Einem, Gen Karl von, 24, 142
Eisenhower, Gen Dwight, 114, 119–20, 123–4
El Alamein, Battle of (1942), 88
Ely, Gen Hanson, 47, 91, 121
Épehy, 201
Épernay, 3, 27, 31, 79, 126, 132, 136–8, 144, 154, 184, 246
Epieds, 116
Escaut, 105
Espilly, 154–5, 167, 169–70, 176, 182, 185–6, 252
Etzel, Lt Gen Gunther von, 215
Evans, Lt Col, DSO, 178, 180

Falkenhayn, Gen, 223
Faverolles, 71–2, 75
Fayolle, Gen, 247
Fère en Tardenois, 28, 65, 116, 140, 234, 257
First Battle of the Marne, 7, 10, 263
Fismes, 70, 117–18, 151, 164, 226, 241
  see also Valley of Death
Flanders, 1, 6, 15–19, 56, 60, 72, 85, 105, 126, 134, 156, 224, 233, 240, 244–5, 256, 259
Flesquières, 134, 139
Foch, Gen Ferdinand, 3–4, 16, 22, 32, 34, 36, 52–3, 81, 83–7, 104, 126, 130, 141, 147, 156, 164, 197–8, 205, 241–2, 244, 254–6, 261
Forest de Retz, 229
Fortune, Brig Gen Victor DSO, 216
Fox Connor, Gen, 91
Franco-Prussian War (1870–1), 24, 30, 46, 59, 83, 140, 169
French Army:
  Armies:
    First, 197
    Third, 23, 202
    Fourth, 24, 54
    Fifth, 5, 73, 86, 126, 139, 147, 164
    Sixth, 5, 17, 57, 86, 105, 116, 145, 147, 257
    Ninth, 83, 86
    Tenth, 86–7, 115, 117, 147–8, 205, 222, 229, 232, 234
  Corps:
    II Colonial, 57, 118
    V, 76
    XI, 7, 86, 234
    XVII, 96
    XVIII, 107
    XX, 5, 83, 205, 212, 215, 217, 220, 231–2
    XXI, 71
    XXX, 6, 216, 222, 229, 232, 234, 239
  Divisions:
    2nd Colonial, 148, 168
    5th, 234
    9th, 148
    10th Colonial, 77
    12th, 215, 217, 231, 234
    13th, 74, 76
    14th, 126, 182, 188, 196
    17th, 219–20
    22nd, 61–2
    25th, 234–5, 239
    28th, 75–8
    38th, 115, 229–1, 256
    39th, 107
    40th, 76–8, 112
    45th, 57, 68, 74
    47th (Chasseur), 89
    58th, 231
    68th, 238–9
    69th, 208
    74th, 72
    77th, 171, 180, 190, 194
    87th, 5, 212, 215, 218
    120th, 125, 158
    125th, 107–108, 225
    127th, 238–9
    154th, 74, 76

Units:
  RICM Regiment, 115, 206, 229–30
  Russian Brigade, 230
  Foreign Legion, 230
  4th Zouaves-Tirailleurs, 231
  8th Tunisian Tirailleurs, 231
  35th Regiment, 182
  44th Regiment,
  56th *Chasseurs-a-Pied*, 171
  60th Chasseurs-a-Pied, 171
  86th Regiment, 160
  91st Regiment, 212, 214
  161st Regiment, 78
  253rd Artillery Regiment, 211
  408th Regiment, 125
Frapelle Salient, 103, 120
French, Gen Sir John, 36–7, 65

Gallipoli, 39–42, 127, 130, 203, 223
Gamelin, Gen, 148
GAN (*Groupes d'armées du Nord*), 247
Gassoins, Gen, 220
Gater, Brig Gen, 74
George V, King, 35, 203
German Army:
  German High Command, OHL (*Oberste Heeresleitung*), 9, 32, 186, 193
  Organisation, 152–4, 168–71
  Armies:
    First (1914), 19, 27, 36, 145, 252
    First (1918), 24, 30, 33, 61, 68, 132, 142
    Second, 13, 34
    Third, 24, 30, 33, 132, 142
    Fourth, 15, 33, 60
    Sixth, 15, 60
    Ninth, 26, 32–3
    Seventh, 22, 26–8, 30, 32–3, 60, 106, 125–6, 142, 146, 185, 230
    Seventeenth, 13
    Eighteenth, 13–14, 22, 33
  Corps:
    Borne's, 3, 27, 31, 61
    Conta's (IV Reserve Corps), 20, 27, 61, 71, 81
    Etzel's (XVII Corps), 215
    Francois, 26
    Kathen's, 27
    Schmettow's, 3, 27, 30–1, 61, 170
    Schoeller's, 26
    Staab's, 26
    Watter's, 26
    Winckler's, 26, 81
    Wichura's, 27
  Divisions:
    5th Guards, 61
    5th, 214
    9th, 233
    10th, 20, 29, 102, 106–107
    11th Bavarian, 115
    13th, 94
    22nd Hessian, 151, 154, 167–70, 182
    27th, 96
    36th, 29, 107, 142–3, 226
    40th, 236
    50th, 61, 151, 160–1, 168, 170–1
    52nd, 61
    86th, 61, 68, 73, 75, 168, 170
    88th, 61
    103rd Saxe-Meiningen, 61, 151, 156, 168–70, 174, 182
    123rd Royal Saxon, 126, 151, 157, 168, 170, 174
    213th, 61
    232nd, 61, 75, 170
    240th, 168, 171, 180–1
    7th Reserve, 61, 68, 73–5
    8th Bavarian Reserve, 170
    33rd Reserve, 61
    50th Reserve, 214, 233
    82nd Reserve, 47
    Guards Ersatz, 236, 238
    19th Ersatz, 233, 236, 238
    7th Panzer (1940), 216
  Units:
    6th Regiment, 29

32nd Regiment, 169
39th Fusilier Regiment, 160–1, 165, 170, 180–1
47th Ersatz Regiment, 235
53rd, 169–70, 173–4, 181
71st Regiment, 156
82nd Regiment, 169
83rd Regiment, 154
116th Regiment, 156
158th Regiment, 170, 174
167th Regiment, 167
178th Regiment, 157, 170, 182
470th Regiment, 180–1
471st Regiment, 180–1
German Spring Offensives of 1918:
  Offensives, 3, 8–34
  Michael, 10, 14, 55, 202, 227, 248
  Georgette, 15–16, 57, 60, 126, 248
  Blücher-Yorck, 16, 23, 27, 60, 72, 77, 168–9, 194, 248
  Gneisenau, 18, 22–3, 249, 262
  Friedensturm, 3, 24, 27, 29, 32, 106, 140, 170, 204, 244, 249, 253, 261–2
Germigny, 79
Gernicourt, 62, 68
Gibbons, Floyd, 21
Gibraltar, 130
Gibson, Lt Col, 66
Glennes, 67, 69
Godley, Lt Gen Sir Alexander, 4, 127–9, 149, 162, 164, 180, 196–7
Gorringe, Maj Gen Sir George, 82
Gough, Gen Herbert, 10, 13, 49
Gouraud, Gen Henri, 24–6, 31, 132, 142
Grand Rozoy, 234–6, 238–40, 254, 258
Graves, Lt, 79
Gressaire Wood, 96
Griffin, Brig Gen, 74
Grimsby Chums, 227
Grimsby, St James's Church, 228
Grogan, Brig Gen, VC, 63–4, 70, 73–4
Gwynn, Brig Gen, 165

Hagen Operation, 3, 16, 18–19, 24, 32, 60, 146, 148, 156, 170, 181, 245, 262
Haig, Field Marshal, 18, 49, 51–3, 79, 82, 84, 130, 197, 224, 226, 244, 254
Halliwell, L-Cpl, 69
Hamel, 41, 93, 95, 260
Hamilton, Gen Sir Ian, 40, 42, 131
Hamilton-Gordon, Gen Alexander, 40, 76, 247
Hampden, Brig Gen Viscount, 129
Harper, Maj Gen, 134
Hartennes, 5, 215–18, 229–33, 239
Hartington, Lady, 129
Hautvillers Château, 177
Havrincourt, 131, 139–40, 200–201, 255
Heart of Midlothian Football Club, 227
Heath, Brig Gen, 74
Heneker, Maj Gen, 68
Hentsch, Col, 145
Hesse, 169
Hill 158, 235, 237
Hill 189, 235–7
Hindenburg, Field Marshal Paul von, 10, 32–3, 146, 185, 223, 262
Hindenburg Line, 14, 32, 34, 42, 96, 131, 198, 200, 223, 240, 246, 249, 255, 260
Hintze, Adml von, 141, 261
Hitler, Adolf, 30
Hodges, Gen Courtney, 120–1, 221
Holbrook, Col, 207
Holbrooke, Lt, 190
Holland, 261
House, Lt, 184
Humbert, Gen, 23
Hundred Days, 247, 255
Hussey, Brig Gen, 62, 70
Hutier, Gen von, 11, 13, 22

India, 228
Ingham, Lt Col, 211
Italian Army:
  Armies:
    Tenth Army, 105

Corps:
II, 3–4, 30, 125, 132, 143–4, 148, 170
Divisions:
3rd, 144
8th, 80, 147, 241
Units:
52nd Regiment, 125

Japan, 122
Jaulgonne, 17, 76–7, 117
Joffre, Gen, 83
Jonchery-sur-Vesle British Military Cemetery, 64–5, 71
Jourdain, Lt Col, 236
Juvigny, 117
Juvincourt, 57

Kasserine Pass, 119
Keaton, 'Buster', 88
Kemmel Ridge, 224
Kennedy, Lt Col, 220
Kitchener, Field Marshal Lord, 54, 203, 222
Kluck, Gen von, 19, 36, 145
Korea, 122–3
Kuhl, Gen von, 252
Kühlmann, Richard von, 261

La Boiselle, 223, 227
Landowski, Paul, 240
Langridge, Cpl, 208–10
Laon Corner, 18, 27
La-Ville-aux-Bois, 64–6
Le Cateau, Battle of, 36, 44
Le Harve, 216
Lhéry, 73–75
Liggett, Gen Hunter, 111, 243
Lloyd George, David, 10, 16, 82, 84, 224
Longpont, 115, 147, 229
Lossberg, Gen Friedrich von, 33, 185
Louis XV, 58
Lucy-le-Bocage, 20

Ludendorff, Gen Erich, 2–3, 9–10, 12–16, 19–20, 23, 27, 30–3, 56, 60, 71, 85–6, 141, 146, 156, 181, 184–5, 197, 214, 223, 233, 245–6, 254–5, 259, 261–2
Luxembourg, 261
Lys Valley, 15–16, 40, 52–3, 55–6, 60, 80, 126, 137, 224, 246, 253, 255

MacArthur, Gen Douglas, MOH, 90, 109–10, 113
MacKenzie, Brig Gen, 45
Macedonia, 169
Mailly-le-Camp, 139
Maistre, Gen, 247
Malmaison, Fort de, 59–60
Mangin, Gen Charles, 4, 21–3, 31, 59, 81, 87, 116–17, 140, 145–8, 175, 205, 230, 241, 245, 247, 254–5, 260
Marfaux, 129, 144, 150–1, 154–5, 157–60, 162–4, 167, 169–74, 177–8, 180, 182–4, 191, 199–200, 252, 257
Marne Defence Operation, 24
Marne River, 2–4, 17–19, 22, 27–8, 30–3, 46, 55, 71–2, 76–7, 83, 86, 97, 105–107, 115–18, 130, 138, 143–4, 146, 156, 197, 225, 233, 241–6, 248, 250, 253, 257, 259, 261
Marne Pocket (Marne Elbow), 151
Mars Operation, 13
Marseille, 133
Marshall, Gen George Caitlin, 47, 87–91, 104, 123–4
Martin, Brig Gen, 67, 70
Massey, Capt, 65
Matz River, 126, 253
MEBUS (*Mannschafts Eisenbeton Understände*) bunkers, 11
Meikle, Sgt John, VC, 155
Menin Road, 50
Messines Ridge, 39–40, 48–9
Meteren, 44
Metz, 81, 96
Meuse River, 96, 121

Micheler, Gen, 73
Missy, 205
Mitchell, Col Billy, 122
Moltke, Gen von, 72, 145
Monash, Gen, 41, 93, 115
Mont Ramboef, 229
Mont des Cats, 224
Mont Jour, 238
Mont Kemmel, 15–16, 40, 52, 55
Montgomery, Bishop, 50,
Montgomery, Field Marshal Bernard, 43–5, 49–52, 54, 82, 88, 90, 120, 123–4, 221
Montigny, 71
Montdidier, 34, 47, 117, 254
Moore, 2nd Lt, 160
Mount Matajurer, 143
Mudra, Gen Bruno von, 24, 142
Muller, Capt, 193
Murray, Capt, 213

Nanteuil, 176
Napoleon, Emperor, 37
Nardi Farm, 187, 193
Neufchâteau, 110
Neuve Chappelle, 52
New Zealand, 127, 130
　New Zealand Division, 49, 51, 127–8, 198, 200
　NZEF, 128
Newfoundland Regiment (later Royal), 223
Nicholson, Maj Gen, 224, 231
Nivelle, Gen, 40, 59, 83
Normandy Invasion, 123

Omaha Beach (1944), 114
Oran, 113–14
Owenson, Pte Richard, DCM, 217

Palestine, 132–3, 228
Paradis Farm, 154–5, 165, 167, 169–70, 185–6
Parcy, 229

Paris, 2–3, 15, 18, 28, 53, 72, 81, 115, 138, 145, 232–3
Paris Gun, 18, 27–8, 142
Passchendaele, 8, 39, 51, 127
Patton, Gen George, 113, 118–20
Pellé, Gen, 76
Penet, Gen, 229, 232
Pershing, Gen John, 84, 89, 92, 95, 104–105, 111, 113, 116, 118, 226, 242, 254–6
Pétain, Gen Philippe, 18–19, 41, 58, 60, 81, 83–5, 87, 164, 254
Picardy, 1, 6, 10, 14, 22, 34, 56, 60, 93, 96
Plivot, 157
Plumer, Gen, 39, 43, 45, 47–51, 105, 127, 260
Ploisy, 206
Poelcappelle, 127
Polygon Wood, 50, 127
Pompelle, Fort de la, 144
Pontavert, 63–4
Pope, Capt, 77
Pope, Cpl Thomas, MOH, 95
Portuguese Corps, 52, 55
Pourcy, 74, 125–6, 156–7, 170, 183, 199
Priestley, Maj, 260
Prouilly, 71
Puerto Rico, 113

Quetta Staff College, 132

Raperie, British Military Cemetery, 237, 239
Rawlinson, Gen, 13, 93, 197, 201
Reed, Maj Gen, VC, 40, 203, 205, 213, 215, 217
Rees, Brig Gen, 67, 70
Reims, 2–4, 19–20, 23–7, 30–2, 58–9, 73, 80, 85, 106, 116, 126, 130, 140–1, 144–5, 154, 161, 184, 193, 204, 246, 249–2, 259, 261
Reims Operation, 24
Remagen, 221
Retreat from Mons, 36, 44

Retz, Forest of, 115
Rhine, 121
Riddell, Brig Gen, 66, 70
Riga, 11
Robertson, Field Marshal, 224
Rommel, Gen Erwin, 118, 123, 143, 216
Roosevelt, Lt Col, Archie, 112
Roosevelt, Pres Franklin (FDR), 113, 122
Roosevelt, Maj Kermit, MC, 111
Roosevelt, Lt Quentin, 111–12, 114
Roosevelt, Pres Teddy (TR), MOH, 111, 115
Roosevelt, Brig Gen, Teddy Jr, MOH, 90, 112–14, 206
Rossigny, 74
Royal Air Force:
  82 Squadron, 177
Rozières, 207, 219
Rozoy, 6
Ruhr, 121
Rupprecht, Crown Prince of Bavaria, 3, 245

Sambre, 201
Sandilands, Brig Gen, 45
Sarcy, 75, 192
Savigny, 64, 71, 73
Scarpe, Battle of the, 224
Scherpenberg, 16
Second Battle of the Marne, 4, 6–7, 108–109, 117, 225, 241–2, 244, 248–9, 253–6, 264
Sedan, 112–3
Seicheprey, 91, 110
Selle River, 105, 201
Séré de Rivières, Gen, 59
Sergy, 252
Severnay, 238
Sibert, Maj Gen, 89
Sicily, 113–14
Simpson, Gen William, 120
Slapton Sands, 114
Smith-Dorrien, Gen Sir Horace, 36

Soissons, 1, 6, 17–19, 21, 26, 29, 32, 57, 59, 70–1, 112, 117, 146–7, 205, 212, 215, 220, 230, 233, 239, 241, 249–50, 260
Somme, Battle of, 39, 130, 137, 168, 197, 222–3, 227
Somme River, 10, 14, 22, 34, 56, 60, 93, 96
Smith, Col Hamilton, 206
Smith, Lt Col G.A. DSO, 220
Summerall, Gen Charles, 113, 207, 243
St Denis Farm, 126
St Euphraise, 165, 170
St Imoges, 132, 136, 157
St Mihiel Salient, 34, 85, 91–4, 118, 120–1, 186, 226, 242, 253, 255, 260
St Quentin, 10, 13, 42, 117, 131, 260
St Valery-en-Caux, 216
Stopford, Gen Sir Frederick, 40, 42, 203
Sucrerie, la, 206–207, 209
Surmelin valley, 107
Suvla Bay, 40, 203
Swindells, Lt Col, 238

Tardenois, 6, 18, 74, 130, 163, 166, 186, 195, 198, 239, 243
Taux, 215, 218–19
Teilhard de Chardin, Pierre, 116
Thuringia, 169
Tieghem, Battle of, 240
Tigny, 215, 217, 231–3
Tournai, 31
Treslon, 73
Trugny, 116, 234
Truman, Pres Harry, 119, 122
Tunisia, 113
Turkey, 253, 260
Turner, Lt Col, 212, 220

Ukraine, 8–9
Utah Beach (1944), 114

Vailly, 18
Valley of Death, 117
Varennes, 142

Vaux, 21
Ventelay, 64, 69
Verdun, 8, 10, 107, 120, 169–70, 242, 256
Versailles, 9
Vesle River, 7, 17, 68, 70–1, 117, 147, 150, 171, 197, 226, 241, 253, 255–6
Veules les Roses, 216
Ville-en-Tardenois, 75–7, 189
Villeblain, 6
Villemontoire, 212, 214, 231, 237
Villers-Bretonneux, 13, 15–16, 93, 95, 224
Villers-Cotterêts, 4, 24, 87, 242, 254
Vimy Ridge, 39, 41, 134, 171, 227
Vittorio-Veneto, Battle of (Oct 1918), 105
Vladivostok, 105
VMI, 89
Vollenhoven, Capt, 115
Vosges Mountains, 120

Waterloo, Battle of, 37
Wilhelm II, Kaiser, 32, 35, 141, 146, 260, 263
Wilhelm, German Crown Prince, 230
Wilson, Field Marshal Henry, 131, 224
Wilson, Pres, 263
Woolridge, Capt Jesse, 107

Ypres, Battles of, 9, 40, 49, 53, 105